P9-AQC-157

Chains of Opportunity

System Models of Mobility in Organizations

Chains of Opportunity

System Models of Mobility in Organizations

Harrison C. White

Harvard University Press, Cambridge, Massachusetts
1970

© 1970 by the President and Fellows of Harvard College
All rights reserved
Distributed in Great Britain by Oxford University Press, London
Library of Congress Catalog Card Number 78–105374
SBN 674–10674–1
Printed in the United States of America

to Cynthia

Preface

"Social science deals with problems of biography, of history, and of their intersections within social structures" (C. Wright Mills, *The Sociological Imagination*, 1967). Illuminating one such intersection—constraints on men's opportunities to move within large organizations—is the goal of this work. The theme is how interactions among local events cumulate into massive structural constraints.

Several audiences are addressed.

Social theorists may find imbedded in the technical analyses new insights into general concepts: duality, matching, discreteness, contingency, stratification, mobility, equilibrium, and flows across system boundaries.

I especially hope that this work will help to link sociology to institutional economics on the one side (Chapter 8) and to operations research and management science on the other (Chapters 7 and 9). Statisticians can find fresh problems in estimation and testing in the early chapters.

Much is known about national patterns of mobility, but their relation to movements in particular organizations and systems needs to be explored. Chapters 1 and 9 are a beginning. Chapter 10 criticizes the usual focus on simple aggregation of careers. Demography must be extended to deal with dualities between men and positions.

Analysts of bureaucracies will find career patterns linked to mobility in a new way. New uses for personnel registers, aided by the sampling schemes in Appendix B and the other apparatus of analysis, may occur to historians. Chapters 6 and 12 should be of particular interest to institutional historians and, I hope, to clergy and ecclesiastical administrators.

Implicit in the whole work is a view of how to build and use mathematical models in social science. A single concept, opportunity chains, stimulated and directed the research. But analyses of concrete data shaped the models from the first months, and the data is discussed in enough detail so that colleagues and students can try their own hands. To exploit ideas and data fully, alternative mathematical formulations are used—compare Chapters 2, 7, 9, and 11. And the depth to which one can explore particular topics using models, often with simplified assumptions about empirical context, is illustrated repeatedly (see especially Sections 2.7, 7.6, and 10.4). At all times I tried to use the simplest mathematics which could express the ideas. Some knowledge of linear algebra, probability, and calculus is assumed. Students will, I hope, gain in maturity in working through this material, maturity not so much in mathematical knowledge as in how to approach and handle analyses of social systems. Estimates as a rule are reported with more places than are necessary, to ease the path of those who wish to do some reanalyses. The original data can be recovered completely from information in Appendix C.

Judged by my initial goals, the book does not move far into the study of sociological network theory. I had hoped to use vacancy chains as a probe into the topology of social structure. Much simpler categorical models proved sufficient, to my discomfiture. Only in Chapter 12, plus certain sections of 1, 8, 11, and 13, does the original design show through. Sprinkled throughout these parts are suggestions for a next stage, a look at the networks of relations which must underly the categorical models.

Acknowledgments

The work reported here has been supported under Grants G23760, GS-243, and GS-448 of the National Science Foundation, for which the author is grateful.

In early days at the University of Chicago, Morris F. Friedell was more a colleague than a research assistant: the imprint of his contribution is particularly clear in Chapter 12. Later at Harvard University while I was wrestling with conundrums of network structures another collaborator, Michael H. Schwartz, appeared in the guise of research assistant to help move the project toward the stratified models of Chapter 2. During both those periods Joel H. Levine made a different kind of contribution, posing the continuing challenge of a wholly different approach to the analysis of mobility.

I am particularly grateful to the succession of students who coded difficult material with care and patience: E. Michael Murphy, Don C. Fowles, Paul R. Levitt, Ruth M. Adler, and others. Many substantive or mathematical contributions were made by these four as well as by members of a research seminar given annually, especially by Dr. Richard P. Boyle, Joel E. Cohen, Alan M. Zaslavsky, Phillip F. Bonacich, Mark S. Granovetter, Michael Useem, Michael S. Novey, and David L. Ragozin. Ideas contributed by Scott A. Boorman are cited in several notes. The substance of Section 6.3 is a contribution by Michael E. Adler, who influenced the whole chapter. Francois P. Lorrain helped clarify Chapter 7. The contributions of Mr. Levitt, mathematical and psychedelic, are too varied to be cited specifically. Mrs. Adler fought brave battles with redundancy and syntax but brought much harmony in other ways, in collaboration with Carol B. Hoffman, always an invaluable secretary and lately an expert typist. Ilse H. Fersing typed the bulk of the manuscript, several times, with intelligence, precision, and speed.

At this point, with colleagues not yet mentioned, the author is forced to abandon his self-image as a lone researcher. Colleagues may not wish to be associated with this rather odd book, but I must at least thank O. Dudley Duncan, George C. Homans, and James A. Davis for their encouragement and help. Help in generous

Acknowledgments

measure came also from I. Richard Savage, disguised as harsh criticism of earlier drafts, which has led to some improvement. To H. M. Blalock, C. Frederick Mosteller, Mason Haire, John T. Dunlop, and Robert W. McGinnis I am grateful for the opportunity to speak at conferences or seminars they have arranged. On such occasions early mimeographed drafts of some parts of this work have been circulated.

The Venerable Herbert L. Johnson furnished insight into the structure and working of the Episcopal church and helped in other ways with the study of mobility among its ministers. I am indebted to him. I thank Peter Crossland for illuminating the workings of a Methodist conference. Very limited aspects of ministers' roles are treated here, and even then only within a limited technical framework: an inadvertent byproduct is a secular flavor which is not true to my own perceptions of the concerns and styles of ministers.

Several librarians, especially Charles Woodbury of the Andover-Harvard Theological Library and Miss Elisabeth Hodges of the Episcopal Theological School Library, were extraordinarily patient with prolonged drains on their stacks. Ellen Farrow, of the Harvard University Press, improved the manuscript through editing as perceptive as it was meticulous.

In many ways my greatest debt is an impersonal one, to the previous work, much of it cited and criticized in Chapters 8 and 9, which makes possible an attempt at a further step.

Quoted material in Section 8.2 is abridged from pp. 211, 212, 227, 239, 240, 242, 244, 245, 246, 267 in *The Structure of Labor Markets* by Lloyd G. Reynolds (Harper & Row, 1951). It is reprinted by permission of the publishers.

Quoted material in Section 8.3, and Figure 8.1 there, is abridged from pp. 74, 82, 92, 93, 94, 101 in "The Concept of Job Vacancies in a Dynamic Theory of the Labor Market" by Charles Holt and Martin David, in *The Measurement and Interpretation of Job Vacancies* (National Bureau of Economic Research, 1966). It is reprinted by permission of the publishers.

H.C.W.

Cambridge, Massachusetts
March 1970

Contents

Contents

Contents

Chapter 1
Logic of Opportunity

Conflicts among individuals over opportunities are central to many theories in social science. Less often noted is the regenerative nature of much opportunity. When one man buys a new car another man can acquire the first man's trade-in and, in turn, pass on his old car, and so on. The origins, nature, and implications of such chains of moves is the subject of this book. The main focus is mobility among jobs in large systems, although other contexts such as housing markets will be discussed in Chapter 13.

Many jobs are social entities as stable and independent as men. This fact about social systems requires a new view of the nature of mobility. Marriage provides a convenient paradigm. A job no more than a woman can safely be considered a passive, pliant partner in initial choice of a union or in decision to terminate a union. A society in which frequent divorce and remarriage is institutionalized would have a pattern of mobility parallel in form to that in a system of stable jobs. The duality between men and jobs is the distinctive feature of such mobility, and it helps explain why mobility has been so hard to analyze systematically.

"Job" is often used loosely to refer to a general occupational status; it then becomes a mere description of class membership, usually by some major skill criterion, as in the "job of welder." Many men, mainly at lower levels of prestige, hold jobs which have little further structure; their position is specified by simultaneous categorization by function, say laborer, and employing organization. The minimal requirement for a job to be a stable and independent entity is that it have a recognized individual identity, if not an explicit title. Such a job will normally have a stable number of occupants, and if it does it is called a fixed job.

Mobility among fixed jobs is highly constrained; movements must dovetail in order to maintain the fixed numbers of occupants. Mobility is enmeshed in a network of contingencies. When an incumbent leaves the job, one speaks of the creation of a "vacancy" and then the filling of the vacancy when a replacement enters the job. A tenure is the concept parallel to marriage. Each tenure is preceded by a vacancy and followed by another vacancy, but these two are too far apart in time to be part of the same pattern of contingencies. Instead, tenures just ending must alternate with tenures just beginning.

The discussion thus far could be applied to many kinds of positions —offices in voluntary organizations, committee memberships, perhaps even certain role-types in face-to-face groups and property ownership of some kinds. In Western societies, jobs are very distinctive types of positions. Occupations are defined with respect to an economic system which is a relatively separable and paramount aspect of the social system. Essentially all men try to have jobs during the full period of adulthood, and the cost of men is such that redundant jobs are eliminated. There are two crucial points: (1) jobs are so defined that a man has but one at a given time (or if there are more, one is usually primary in terms of effort and identification); (2) men are so defined that a job tends to have a minimal and fixed number of incumbents. Mobility by a well-defined population of eligible men among a system of fixed jobs independently demarcated is the general theme of the present work.

1.1 Strategy

The strategy is to deal primarily with the overall structure of events in a mobility process rather than with the individual's motives. There is some long-range order in mobility, as influences pass along complex networks of interrelations. A given event is usually caused in some sense by events remote from both it and the participants. These indirect structural effects are the target. Official records of the organizations studied are the source of data.

The causal sequence of moves cannot be analyzed without examining mobility into and out of specific individual jobs. A descriptive study may observe and trace moves only when they cross the boundaries of large strata or categories, measuring the corresponding rates and correlating changes in them with other variables. Such an approach, however, ignores all moves within strata and is unable to trace sequential dependencies. Few studies, even traditional economic studies of mobility in labor markets, reach the level of the individual jobs; even then, the moves are studied as isolated events and not in connected sequences.[1]

Sociologists since World War II have put a great deal of effort into the study of a particular kind of social mobility; namely, mobility between occupational strata in successive generations. As O. D. Duncan[2] has shown recently in an incisive critique, such studies do not really deal directly with successive generations. In mobility studies generations are a myth, a construct with only the vaguest connection with replacement of observable cohorts of men in actual jobs. Such studies in fact deal with change in status of one population of men over a long period of time, say from the year of entering the labor market to the present. This study is such a different kind of process from the study of mobility from one job to the next that a different term would reduce confusion. Section 10.8 will argue that only in some very indirect, aggregate sense can such studies deal with cause and effect.

It is hard to measure movement directly in any science. It is usually inferred from a change in state between successive times. Most studies of mobility, including this one, have to work with such inferences, instead of with reliable reports for entire populations of moves as such. The spacing of successive observations in time becomes a crucial choice because moves within the spacing are missed. This is the central problem in the major monograph on mathematical sociology by James S. Coleman,[3] and he suggests that one should try to find the underlying structure of instantaneous rates which could generate the more complex structure of rates actually observed with discrete spacing. This problem is of little importance in the present study. The tenures of men in fixed jobs are long enough to find all moves, including those which actually take place between successive observation times, by a combination of observation and detailed logical inference. Since individual tenures are examined, moves confined within a large stratum are included—moves which are omitted in the usual mobility study even when they do not fall between observation times.

When a mobility investigation attempts to fit individual moves into larger sequences the focus is usually the career.[4] The career, though important as a concept, tends to obscure causal analysis. Men have long work-lives as measured on a time scale appropriate to social structures. Most organizations have shorter lives than men. Even when a bureaucracy continues as a whole over long periods its constituent departments are not likely to remain unchanged for even a decade. Some men may shape their own careers and some organizations may try to do the job for them; but at best, the shaping is vague

3

and unreliable. Not only do causes precede effects, but also efficient causes are those close in time to their effects.

1.2 Concomitants of Mobility

An understanding of mobility should help clarify basic conceptual difficulties in theories of social structure. Current theories of social structure have an abstract, ideological quality. Actors in roles abound, but concrete persons and positions seem to belong to another, divorced, level of discourse. Balanced structures of roles are filled by actors subject to the abstract harmonies of generalized value orientations. The harmonies are so strong that most of the conceptual problems of a system of men in positions defined relative to one another disappear; at most a few actors with a few very general attributes suffice logically to people the system.[5]

Sociology seems to have had less trouble in dealing with people. Demography is a well-established field, as are methods for the study of attitudes. Both censuses and sample surveys of persons have elaborate methodologies. But the study of persons is not effectively joined to the analysis of social structure. Positions in social structure, as are physical attributes, are treated as if they were solely a matter of class membership. Ingenious forms of contextual analysis give some structural depth to survey analysis—the attitudes or other attributes of persons are shown to depend on the composition of the collectivities to which they belong.[6] Simultaneous cross-classification of persons on many attributes increases the "dimensionality" of the social "space" in which they are required to dwell; all kinds of social "distances" and measures of association can thus be created and analyzed.[7]

The view of social reality implicit in these approaches seems incomplete. Individual identity is always in the end defined by position in an interlocking structure. A fixed job cannot be defined merely by a title or set of skills however specific. It must be referred to a set of counterpart jobs with which it has regular, prescribed relations; each of them is defined similarly so that a fixed job is defined relative to a whole structure of cumulated, interlocking relations. Names of men have an almost magical power in Western societies; the implicit assumption is that the name defines the man. The effective definition of a man, however, rests primarily on locating him by his position in a network of regular, prescribed relations among persons, often

4

largely in terms of kinship. Consider how an imposter is exposed. The interlocking structures defining fixed jobs and those defining men cannot be kept entirely apart. Fixed jobs are a later social invention than are independent persons, but there is some duality.[8] The tendency is for fixed jobs to exist in systems with well-defined populations of eligible men. Churches and their priesthoods are surely the oldest example, and they are the main empirical basis for the work reported here. The "persona" of a priest can only be defined relative to his church—and is relatively independent of his membership in networks of kin and nonchurch friends—and a priestly office must be defined with respect to the sacerdotal validity of the men who can fill it.[9]

Mobility, including recruitment and retirement as special cases, is a process wherein the interconnection of persons and positions in social structure should be especially evident. S. F. Nadel[10] in his brilliant analysis of the meaning of social structure suggests that mobility is one of the three processes whose study can give reality to the concept of social structure. Mobility studies usually have more concrete motives, but there are surprisingly few explicit statements of their purpose and value. Sorokin's book[11] is a landmark in the area, both in summarizing previous scattered work and in stimulating subsequent large-scale surveys. He emphasizes the study of mobility essentially for its intrinsic interest, and draws analogies between mobility in society and the circulation of vital fluids in living organisms. Sorokin's actual analysis emphasizes a geometrical view of movements among locations in social space, with horizontal geographical dimensions and vertical prestige dimensions.

Mobility may have impact on an individual's feelings and perceptions and in turn the latter presumably affect his chances and choices in mobility. Large sample surveys of mobility are necessary to establish the actual numbers of moves as well as to permit assessment of their consequences and antecedents in attitudes. Duncan has argued, in the paper cited above, that there is no convincing evidence of the impact of moving, as such, on individuals. He therefore suggests that changes in attitudes and behavior may be accounted for as a simple additive mixture of habits in the initial and in the terminal statuses, with no role left to the experience of moving itself. However, perhaps the main impact of mobility experiences on the individual may evade current techniques of measurement. Almost invariably the latter are formulated in terms of categories, usually gross strata in prestige or classes of similar jobs. The implicit assumption is that gross changes in status constitute the major share of the impact of mobility experience on the individual. This may not make sense in terms of the frame of reference of most persons. Introspection will suggest that great amounts of thought and emotion are devoted to changes in status which seem minuscule in terms of overall social structure. Large jumps in standing or type of job may be rare. They may have the all-or-nothing quality suggested by Duncan: once in a new stratum, a man may rapidly adapt to it, with some retention of old habits, and may thereafter think in a framework conditioned almost exclusively by the microscopic changes of job and pay normal there. The overall impact of the small successive changes and the amount of conscious thought and planning devoted to them may well be the bulk of the total effects of mobility. Only study of individual job changes within systems of related jobs and eligible men can deal with this impact.

More important to the study of social structure may be the changes in sociometric patterns caused by mobility. A set of positions is little more than an ideological program until filled by persons; persons in turn have social identities largely defined by their simultaneous position in several networks and structures of positions filled by other persons. To study mobility is to get at the nature of these structures and interrelations, especially the closeness of coupling of different institutional areas and the extent of the empirical duality between man and position.

Mobility necessarily suggests questions about attractiveness of jobs for men and appropriateness of men for jobs. It is plausible that study of mobility in terms of gross categories may identify the coupling of most importance in overall social structure. It is hard to see how attractiveness of jobs for men can be separated from mobility in terms of individual jobs. Men mainly think in terms of moves to particular jobs. The circulation of elites is the classic mobility topic related to appropriateness of man to job (attractiveness of elite jobs to any man being taken for granted). The impact of mobility on men's emotions is being assessed in some sense, but the main interest runs the other way and is more social than psychological. If "ability" is needed in positions of great authority, and ability is either distributed randomly or at least is not easy to inculcate deliberately, then for the system to function effectively there must be mobility of men from all strata to the elite.[12] Studies of the whole pattern of moves among individual jobs in a system are more relevant than they may seem at first sight. Whether a man moves to a higher stratum by achievement or ascription, he rarely moves directly into a specific position of high authority; rather, he enters a system of particular high-level jobs where movement thereafter is subject to the same kind of logic and constraint as in wider systems of jobs. In many societies and organizations, recruitment to elite strata cannot be completely open and visible.[13] The man marked for highest success must appear to be part of the same system of mobility as others. Thus he must to some extent be implicated in the dynamics of the larger system, and often he may slip out of the implicit elite route and some other man step in.

1.3 Delays between Mobility Events in a System of Fixed Jobs

Two types of decisions are being made in the mobility process; one on the termination and the other on the formation of incumbencies of men in fixed jobs. At least two sides are involved in each type of decision, the job controllers and the man who leaves (is to enter) the job. In the entry to a job, the choice of man is as important as the timing, whereas timing is the substance of the choice to terminate. An analysis is to be made of the interconnections of moves in a large system of fixed jobs and eligible men. Detailed inquiry into the putative motives and perceptions of all parties to each change is impractical and possibly misleading. Instead, primary reliance is placed on the observed sequences of events and the lengths of delays as clues to the causal structure of the mobility process. These sequences and lengths can, in general, form extremely complex patterns which reflect the multiplicity and complexity of the constituent decisions and their interlocking. My main practical goal is to show how in some kinds of systems the number of independent events is reduced and the pattern of mobility brought within the reach of rather simple models.

Consider a set of fixed jobs and a set of men qualified to fill them who normally hold posts. The two taken together are the system in which mobility is to be examined. Changes of men by jobs and jobs by men must be intercalated together in the mobility process. Time intervals between successive events are an obvious criterion of classification. Natural labels are shown in the following chart:

1. Logic of Opportunity

	Successive incumbencies	
Type of interval	Men in a job	Jobs for a man
Delay	Vacancy	Limbo
Anticipation	Split	Merge

Positive delay times are by far the most common, and they alone will be considered in this chapter. Doubling up of men in jobs and of jobs on a man does occur and will be dealt with in Chapter 3.

Four major types of system operation are differentiated by examining the lengths of delays:

1. *Tight* systems—limbos are shorter than vacancies; men move with little or no interval from one incumbency to the next whereas some time is required to fill vacancies.
2. *Loose* systems—vacancies are shorter than limbos; vacancies are usually filled at once whereas men spend some time floating in a limbo status between successive jobs.
3. *Coordinated* systems—vacancies and limbos are both negligible in length.
4. *Matchmaking* systems—limbos and vacancies are (on the average) comparable and substantial in length (*note:* some part of the defined system of jobs if examined separately might fall within this type although the whole system is tight or loose).

When delays are not negligible it follows that at any given instant either some appreciable fraction of the population of fixed jobs must be temporarily vacant or many men are unsettled. Such frictional effects must be common in even the most rigid social structures. The volume, accuracy, and timing of the information needed to keep assignments of men to jobs completely matched would alone stagger any control system. Yet much can be done through legal fictions to obscure the mismatches. Appointments can be predated and departures postdated. Reported delays are a useful but fallible guide.

Tight systems are those that are tight in men but have jobs to spare. There is a prima facie case for incumbents being in a favorable bargaining position and jobs in an unfavorable one. The converse applies to loose systems. The close timing in coordinated systems may be explained by some kind of central planning and control, but it may also reflect a convention as to the announcement of changes.

The full duality between jobs and men possible in mobility is most likely to be manifest in matchmaking systems, where, as in marriage, both sides are usually circulating freely before matches are made. In matchmaking systems it seems likely that complex interdependencies between different sets of bargains arise during sequences of offers and moves. Carried to the limit of long vacancies and limbos, the matchmaking case will differ in basic structure from the others. Men will no longer be moving *from* one job *to* another, nor will jobs be moving *from* one man *to* another. The explanation of mobility would be broken into disjunct parts: first, the movement of a man and his job from status in a tenure to generalized status in a pool of free agents and, second, movement of jobs and men from the pool to create tenures.

Only during tenure in a job does a man draw pay, which he uses in all other aspects of his life; thus he tries to maintain an unbroken occupational tenure. Partly for this reason a man without a job is usually in a weaker bargaining position. Job controllers often reason that he is not as prudent a man as a candidate who is incumbent in a job. A fixed job, however, can remain effective for short periods even without an incumbent; the services rendered usually are not so clear-cut that cessation has immediate effects. The controllers of the job often need time for the sheer mechanics of search. If they neither control other jobs to which an incumbent may move nor have the effective option of dismissing an incumbent, the controllers will have little advance notice of vacancies. In any case, vacancies can be to the advantage of the job controllers: their authority is more effective during the vacancy, for example in redefining the nature of the jobs.

These arguments are neither proposed for social positions in general nor for jobs in general but rather for systems of fixed jobs, which normally are jobs of substantial status. By these arguments both very short limbos and appreciable vacancies, that is a tight system, will be the norm. A critical question is: When is a vacancy substantial but still not too long to be a normal part of the mobility pattern? An obvious rule of thumb is that it should not be comparable in length to an average tenure. Beyond that, boundaries must be established for each concrete system. The temporary vacancy normal in the given mobility process must be differentiated from the chronic empty state in a job. The latter often signals an eventual abolition of the job. Similarly, chronic unemployment must be divided from temporary limbo.

9

1.4 Chains of Moves among 1–1 Jobs

For simplicity, consider a system in which at most one person enters and one person leaves each fixed job in the period under consideration. The simplest way to guarantee this is to consider only the job which is defined as being for a single incumbent. Call it a 1–1 (one-to-one) job. Then, the replacement of one person by another in a job can be uniquely identified in the mobility process. Only 1–1 jobs will be considered here. Section 7.8 will show how to extend the models to apply to any system of fixed jobs.

Bumper chains

Suppose the system is a loose one; that is, there is a surplus of men, vacancies are filled almost instantly, men spend some time in limbo between one incumbency and the next. Look at a man F, in such an interim limbo. He will, after some months, move into a new incumbency. The previous incumbent, E, will at that point enter limbo; a few months later, E can be expected to enter another job, leading to still another man, C, departing to temporary limbo and so on.

The chain traced from F must end somehow. C may retire or otherwise leave the system or he may move into a new job or one that had been empty until C's arrival so that no one leaves on his arrival. The chain also must have begun somewhere. Suppose that F had been pushed out of his former job by the arrival of the incumbent, L. L began the chain, considered as events within the defined system of jobs and men, if he were a new recruit. The chain could also have been begun by the abolition of a job that L had heretofore held so that no entry by some antecedent man, A, need be assumed. Figure 1.1 is a diagrammatic representation of the chain.

Examine the time structure of the chain in this loose system. Vacancies are of negligible duration, so the time span of the chain consists of a series of periods spent in temporary limbo by men, each starting at the end of the preceding period. The earliest event is the arrival of the man, L, from outside or from a job that had been abolished. If, in some sense, one event causes the chain, it should be the arrival of L, given the accepted ideas about the direction in which cause flows in time and if the possibility of prior understandings between men in the chain is neglected. F is unlikely to have left his job for limbo voluntarily. The job controllers are able to choose among a variety of candidates at a time of their own choice.

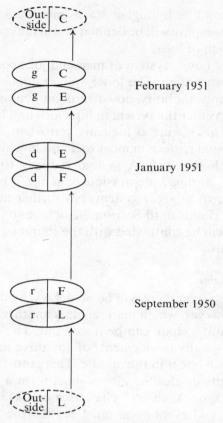

Figure 1.1 Bumper Chain. The chain begins at the bottom and ends at the top because all delays in filling vacant jobs are assumed to be zero. Tenures are represented by ovals with the man in the right half and the job in the left. Delays—the length of time in limbo for each man—are represented by arrows of varying lengths. The direction of each arrow is from an earlier to a later time. (The same conventions will be used in Figures 1.2 and 1.3.)

There are prestige differentials in jobs and men, and these affect the dynamics of mobility. A bump of one man by another seems plausible when the bumper is of much higher status than the bumpee and than the normal level of men expected in the particular type of job. A bump is also plausible, and often seen in unionized factories, when one man has a prescriptive right to move to another job if his current tenure is terminated. Such prescriptive rights are often determined by seniority in a well-defined system of jobs and men. Given an average of promotion to higher status jobs over time, prescriptive bumping also would be by higher status men bumping into lower status jobs. The bumping will be defined and arranged by controllers of the whole system of jobs.

It is hard to see how a system of men and jobs could persistently function as a loose system. The loose system implies bump chains. Bump chains imply mobility downward on seniority or prestige grounds, and men enter the system in high jobs and leave the system from low jobs. This picture is logically consistent, but it does not conform to the usual pattern in most societies in which social standing increases with seniority. A system is likely to be loose only temporarily, say, during a depression or if the job is in a special auxiliary relation to a larger system. No further attention will be given to bumper chains until Section 7.2, where some properties of bumper models will be contrasted with the characteristics of models for vacancy chains.

Simultaneous chains

In a coordinated system there will be no delays, by definition. If the jobs are fixed, however, which man replaces another man in a given job can be seen and a chain can be traced out. The order of moves can be inferred logically to an extent: of any three moves in a chain it can be said which one is in the middle. There must either be a pair of boundary events or else the moves must form a loop, that is, a circle, as in the "musical chairs" chain (see below) with no one left out. If there are end events one must be like the beginning of a vacancy chain—death of man or birth of job—and the other must be like the beginning of a bump chain—abolition of a job or recruitment of a man. It cannot be said which boundary event is the cause (the earliest) and which the effect. The presumption is that some central authority arranged the whole chain, since the problem of coordinating the negotiations of all incumbents and job controllers to arrive at a simultaneous chain would be a formidable one to be solved by local initiative.

Musical chairs: chains of matchmaking

The matchmaking system is completely different from the co-ordinated system. Consider a job, d, from which a man, E, leaves; and a job, r, left by a man, F, who will eventually replace E in job d. The departure of F may well precede the departure of E, or it can coincide or follow. Both the vacancy period in a job and the period a man spends in limbo between incumbencies are substantial and of the same size on the average. It is therefore implausible to speak of a flow of causation. The successive departure and entry events in a chain zig forward and then backward in time. Figure 1.2 illustrates such a chain; the game of musical chairs is a natural analogy.[14] When the music starts everyone gets up and circulates; all "men" are in limbo and all "jobs" vacant. Everyone scrambles when the music stops, no central person directs the flow. Some men are left over, as in the marriage market.

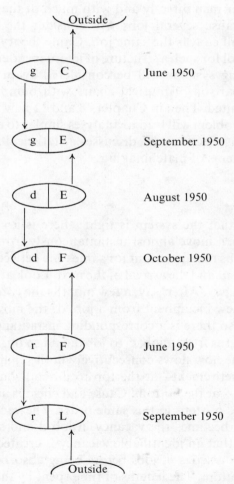

Figure 1.2   Time Structure of Events and Delays in a Musical Chairs Chain.

Mobility in the matchmaking system is intrinsically a complex process. The acts of entry and departure are independent and must normally be treated separately. Yet the same kind of status considerations can enter as in the other systems; for example, a man's attractiveness may be defined in large part by the kind of job he has held. In each act it is possible that both the job controllers and the man have some bargaining power. The important point is that the numbers of jobs vacant and the numbers of men in limbo are comparable. Mobility negotiations are carried on between two sides with roughly equal numbers. Each man's chances will interact with those of several other men directly and with much of the group in limbo indirectly, because several jobs will consider the same man and several men will canvas the same job. Game theory would seem an appropriate tool for such a structure of interdependent bargaining.[15]

Matchmaking systems will be considered again in Section 7.2, where a comparison of musical chairs with bumper and vacancy chains is presented. Then in Chapters 8 and 11 new formulations of the mobility problem will lead to analyses similar to those for matchmaking systems. Section 11.5 discusses a statistical assessment procedure for systems of matchmaking.

Vacancy chains

Suppose now that the system is tight: there is a slight surplus of vacant jobs, men move almost instantaneously from the old to the new job, but jobs remain vacant for some time between the departure of one incumbent and the arrival of the next. Look at a job, g, in such an interim vacancy. After, say, a few months the controllers of job g will recruit a new incumbent from a job, d; the move of the man is instantaneous so there is a corresponding instantaneous transfer of the vacancy status from a job, c, to job d, and so on. Figure 1.3 illustrates this: time now flows consecutively in the chain from a beginning—here a retirement—at the top to an end—in recruitment of man L to job r—at the bottom. Cause and effect is assumed to operate in the series of steps in this same order. The vacancy created by C's retirement becomes the vacancy in job d and so on. It is convenient to say that an identifiable vacancy is created at the top and moves through a series of jobs before being absorbed by the "outside" at the bottom. The lengths of time spent by the vacancy in the various jobs differ.

Mobility takes place as if a vacancy jumped from job to job in a system of jobs that were usually filled. The creation of a vacancy, whose subsequent movements define a chain, can be either the disappearance of a man or the appearance of a new job. The disappearance of a vacancy, which ends the chain, can be either recruitment of a man from outside or the abolition of a job. The time structure

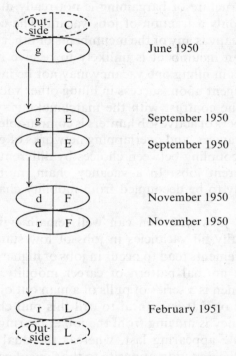

Figure 1.3   Vacancy Chain. All delays between successive jobs for men are zero, and the tenures occur in pairs in which the upper one is just beginning and the lower one just ending. L's entry from and C's departure to the "outside" end and begin the chain.

of the chain is simple. The earliest event is the creation of a vacancy. The periods men spend in limbo are negligible, so the chain length in time is the sum of the successive vacancies, each beginning when the previous one ends.

It is plausible that the incumbent in a job effectively controls his time of departure, and this is coincident with his entry to a new job previously vacant. It follows that he will move because of a positive

15

attraction to the vacant job offered him; that is, he is likely to move to a job of higher standing. There will be no clear preponderance in bargaining power either on his side or that of the controllers of the vacant job; they want to fill the vacancy and he wishes to move to a more attractive job. The previous incumbent in the vacant job is likely to have little say about the replacement who comes in some months later.

Again, the structure of bargaining is not really dual. At a given time there are only a fraction of jobs vacant. The controllers of a vacant job can canvas any of the incumbents of other jobs; there are so many that an incumbent is unlikely to receive more than one inquiry. Success in filling one vacancy may not be interlinked with, and thus contingent upon, success in filling other vacancies (but see Chapter 11). The contrast with the matchmaking system is great. There the numbers of active job hunters is comparable to the number of available vacancies, and overlapping networks of preferences will lead to strong coupling between choices by different men and also choice by different jobs. In a vacancy chain, mobility into one vacancy is likely to be decoupled from mobility chances for other vacancies.

A system of jobs and men can well remain tight indefinitely. Recruits normally fill vacancies in jobs of low standing, whereas deaths and retirements tend to occur in jobs of higher standing, conforming to the normal pattern of career mobility. The chain of movements of men is a series of pulls of a man out of one job into a more attractive one. It is natural to call this pull chain a vacancy chain; the vacancy is moving from the job appearing earliest in the chain to the one appearing last, whereas the dual series of men change jobs in the direction opposite to the flow of cause and effect. The beginning event—creation of a vacancy as through death of an incumbent—causes the chain; it generates the opportunity to move seized by the new incumbent, whose departure in turn generates a new opportunity, and so on.

It is an idealization to say mobility is moves by vacancies. If it is just the vacancy that moves, some degrees of freedom have been lost somewhere. Specifically, the decision to leave a job is considered not an independent one but rather an integral part of the decision to move into a specific vacant job. Various detailed interpretations of who decides what are logically consistent with the vacancy chain. One concept is that controllers of a vacant job have the initiative on hiring, a candidate is in a passive position and says "yes or no," and the controllers of his job have little say about his departure.

The vacancy chain is an abstraction, a theoretical construct. The models to be proposed to explain the vacancy chains add further layers of abstraction and idealization.[16] Nevertheless, the remarkable feature of opportunity chains models in general and vacancy chain models in particular is that they are able to show the interrelations of a wide range of social phenomena at both structure and process levels. Chapters 2 through 6 will be devoted to developing and testing models for vacancy chains.

The coupling and decoupling of events in mobility is the central issue. It has arisen at three different levels of aggregation. In the perspective of the whole system of jobs and men, mobility acts are seen as necessarily coupled together in a set of sequences, in some kind of chains of mobility acts. Yet, in the usual operation of mobility processes in a system of fixed jobs, the various chains are decoupled from one another, each running its course independently. At the level of individual acts, leaving one job and entering the next are treated as a coupled, integral unit in vacancy chains; in bump chains, it is the arrival of one individual in a job and the departure of his predecessor that are coupled as an integral unit. The middle level, of coupling between different moves in the same vacancy chain, is treated as problematic, to be assessed for each observed system in terms of the models of Chapter 2.

1.5 Vacancy Chains and Organizations

A system of fixed jobs and eligible men will not normally coincide with a formal organization. System boundaries should be chosen so that transactions with the environment—the outside—have a once-and-for-all quality; that is, a recruit to the system normally can be expected to remain for periods of the same order as careers. System boundaries should also be chosen such that all parts of the system have some interconnection through mobility with one another.

In a given organization there often are several broad categories of men whose careers intersect little if at all—say blue collar versus white collar versus administrative-professional. The lower categories may move to and from wholly different kinds of organizations, since the nature of their work may have little connection with what is special about a particular organization. It is men and jobs of the upper category, administrative and professional, whose mobility can best be cast in chains of movements in a system of fixed jobs. Even here mobility is not usually confined within a particular organization but rather within an institutional system of organizations.[17]

There are four broad types of connection between vacancy chains and organizational structure. *Degree of centralization* is a major concern of organization theory. So far there is not even an accepted measure or criterion for centralization.[18] The structure and length of vacancy chains could be material for such a measure. The single most important question about a mobility chain is whether it has a beginning point and an end point. If it does not, the chain is really a loop, a closed cycle of events. The alternation of time flow in successive limbos and vacancies in the cycle must be such as to make closure possible. It is hard to see how this could often happen without centralized planning and coordination. If the number of loops is not consistently negligible, then the percentage of mobility which occurs in loops could in itself be a measure of centralization.

Recruitment is recognized as a central problem in all organizations. Usually it is thought of as a special, separate process, the continuing renewal of a pool of newly eligible men. In the perspective of vacancy models, recruitment is not a separate process (except when vacancy chains are loops) but an integral aspect of the whole process of reassignment and mobility within the organization. A recruit comes in to fill a vacancy that has been generated as a byproduct of reassignments within the organization and transfers between the several organizations in the system. Conversely, retirements have more causal impact on the dynamics of matching men to jobs in an organization than is usually noticed. Even if personnel is controlled in a highly centralized way, the planners will be constrained by the sequential logic of vacancy chains. The planning of careers, either by the individual or the company, will not be a realistic endeavor except as it is keyed to the vacancy chains which are the operational constraint on mobility. The same remarks will apply in a dual sense to jobs. Each act for creation or expulsion of either a man or a job from the system will tend to create a chain of effects, possibly for jobs and men remote from the initial act.

Merger and fission are fairly common occurrences in most types of organizations.[19] It is often difficult to know how real and effective an announced fusion or split-off is. Turnover of personnel—percentage of movers who cross new or former boundaries—can say a lot about the extent of integration of different segments of an organization. In themselves, such percentages are an incomplete representation of causes of mobility. The rate of crossing between two organizations recently split may be low, but these movers may all be in vacancy chains that reach across the boundary so that all the moves in one are contingent upon boundary events in the other organization. New jobs and retirements may appear mainly in one organization, so that the pattern and amount of mobility in the other organization is dependent on policies of the former.

Prestige and authority differentials are the most difficult aspect of organization structure to measure and assess.[20] Salary scales are common[21] and so are elaborate tables of organization;[22] each, however, may be violated so often in concrete cases as to be meaningless except as a convenient ideology and language for discussion. Attitudes can be surveyed and opinions of the insiders probed. It is never clear that either guides concrete individual acts, nor is it obvious that either will get at the overall interconnections of acts in a system. There is no reason to think that any individuals perceive, much less control, the chains of events in large organizations and systems. Undoubtedly there are lawful, subtle connections between what happens and what is perceived, but it is too much to hope that these connections are a perfect match.

The main question is how the overall structure of prestige and authority affects and is affected by the patterns of mobility.[23] Individuals surely do respond to opportunities for what is viewed as promotion. Individuals do try to shape careers. However, when all the individual acts and perceptions are pieced together, what is the overall result? Does the degree of inequality in the distribution of prestige among jobs control the amount of mobility? Perhaps, but it is not clear that the correlation is positive. A very steep gradient of prestige may inhibit mobility. A vacancy implies the departure of an incumbent, and an incumbent faced with a steep step to the next job may not be able or inclined to move at all. Sharp differentials in a prestige structure could imply short vacancy chains and low mobility. As always, the question is only meaningful in terms of a comparison with another possible state of affairs. Consider the extreme case of equality in jobs. Mobility could well be very high. A job is always a complex entity with many attributes and many interconnections with other jobs. Even if jobs are equal in some kind of generalized status, they will always differ in an enormous number of ways. Just because there is no difference in prestige, men may be more ready to respond to other kinds of differences or to move in sheer restlessness. It is conceivable that the main effect of prestige differentials is to reduce mobility when the structure is viewed as a whole. The natural restlessness of most men may be controlled by training them to respond only to differences in a limited kind of social assessment known as prestige. Vacancy chains might be longest in an egalitarian system.

This book has three distinct parts. Part I, beginning with Chapter 2 and ending with Chapter 6, develops and applies a class of stratified probability models of vacancy chains for data spread over fifty years in three systems of men and jobs. Part II, Chapters 7, 8, and 9, compares these models, somewhat extended and refined, with two other major families of mobility models. Part III, Chapters 10 through 12, probes the foundations of the vacancy chain models.

Chapter 2 is a terse and technical account of how to analyze and predict vacancy chains, in which contrasts are drawn with more familiar models. Chapter 3, to which many readers may wish to turn first, defines the system studied and shows how to code vacancy chains from published data. After the models are applied to data in Chapters 4 through 6, Chapter 7 develops a new, aggregative view of mobility systems.

Part I
Moves by Vacancies
in Organizations

Chapter 2
Markov Models of Vacancy Chains

Some familiar and practical mathematical framework is needed to begin analyzing vacancy chains. Probability ideas are natural since the influences at work in any vacancy move are too numerous and subtle to permit exact determination. In the systems studied, men and jobs do not fit into any regular lattices of relations and are too numerous to be handled as disparate individuals; thus some grouping of similar individuals is essential. A special type of Markov model is built up in the first three sections of this chapter and is interpreted in the remaining sections.

2.1 Moves in a Chain

Consider a large population of distinct jobs, which are partitioned into a few strata, labeled from 1 to s. Each job can have but one incumbent, and a man holds exactly one job at a time. The system studied is the population of jobs together with their incumbents.

A vacancy enters the system by occupying some job. From any job it can move to any other job or back outside the system; label the outside 0. Consider the next move of a vacancy now in some job in stratum i. Let q_{ik} be the probability that this move is into stratum k, for $k = 1, 2, \ldots, s$, or to the outside, for $k = 0$. A vacancy must leave its present job within some fixed maximum span of time. Hence

$$\sum_{k=0}^{s} q_{ik} = 1 \tag{2.1}$$

for any initial stratum, $i = 1, \ldots, s$.

Arrange the termination probabilities q_{i0} in a column vector, designated as $\mathbf{p}$. Arrange the transition probabilities between strata in a square matrix called Q such that q_{ik} lies in the ith row and the kth column of Q. Let $\mathbf{l}$ represent a column vector with s components, each unity. By equation (2.1),

$$Q\mathbf{l} + \mathbf{p} = \mathbf{l} \tag{2.2}$$

23

2. Markov Models of Vacancy Chains

In all applications of the models, each of the termination probabilities is greater than zero.

A vacancy chain is the sequence of moves made by a vacancy subsequent to its arrival in the system. The length of the chain is the number of moves, including the terminal move to the outside. Let the length be called j, since it equals the number of jobs which the vacancy has occupied while in the system.

Consider the special case where there is but one stratum, $s = 1$, all jobs being lumped together. The matrix Q reduces to a single number, q_{11}, and the vector $\mathbf{p}$ similarly reduces to q_{10}. It is convenient to relabel the former q and the latter p. Moves of a vacancy correspond to Bernoulli trials where failure terminates the sequence; so the model with one stratum is called the binomial model.[1]

Let P_j be the probability on the binomial model that a vacancy chain is of length j. However many times a vacancy has moved from one job to another within the system, the probability that the next move is terminal remains p. Hence

$$P_j = q^{j-1}p \qquad (2.3)$$

where j is any positive integer. These probabilities form a geometric series whose sum is unity whatever the value of the probability p. The mean length, λ, is

$$\lambda = \sum jP_j = \frac{1}{p} \qquad (2.4)$$

In the general case, to each stratum in which the vacancy can arrive there corresponds a distinct probability distribution. For each chain length let these probabilities be gathered in a column vector $\mathbf{P}_j$. In the matrix Q raised to the power $j - 1$ the entry in the ith row and the kth column is the sum of the probabilities of the various sequences of $j - 1$ moves that begin in stratum i and end in stratum k, each such probability being simply a product of the appropriate transition probabilities. The product of the ith row of Q^{j-1} and the column vector $\mathbf{p}$ is the probability that a chain begun in stratum i will end in exactly j moves. That is,

$$\mathbf{P}_j = Q^{j-1}\mathbf{p} \qquad (2.5)$$

an exact parallel to (2.3) for the binomial model. It can be shown that each distribution is normalized,

$$\sum \mathbf{P}_j = \mathbf{1} \qquad (2.6)$$

and, if mean lengths are arranged in a vector λ according to stratum of arrival for the vacancy,

$$\lambda \equiv \sum j\mathbf{P}_j = (I - Q)^{-1}\mathbf{1} \tag{2.7}$$

where I is the identity matrix. This equation reduces in the binomial case to equation (2.4). In the matrix $(I - Q)^{-1}$ the entry in the ith row and k^{th} column is the expected number of times a vacancy which had arrived in stratum i will appear in stratum k.

2.2 Cohorts of Vacancies

All vacancies in the system are assumed to move independently of one another and in conformity with the same probability model. Only conditional probabilities have been used because in the data exact timing, unlike sequential order of moves in a chain, cannot be specified. The two successive years between which a sequence of moves took place are known, and usually this sequence is the entire vacancy chain. To simplify the models, arrivals of vacancies are treated as successive yearly cohorts, each of which has left the system before the next cohort arrives. In Section 7.7, arrivals will be described by one stochastic process in continuous time, and another will model the spacing of moves.

Represent by $F(t)$ the number of vacancies arriving in the cohort for year t, with the row vector $\mathbf{F}(t)$ giving the breakdown by stratum. Let $\mathbf{f}(t)$ be the proportions of arrivals in the various strata, $f_i = F_i/F$. The transition probabilities q_{ik} are required to be constant within a year, during all the moves in the chains for one cohort. If appropriate strata are used, these parameters should be constant over very long periods so no time dependence will be indicated.

The overall length distribution of chains predicted for a cohort is easily computed from (2.5) as

$$\mathbf{f}(t)\mathbf{P}_j$$

Let the overall mean length predicted be designated by adjoining parentheses to j; from (2.7)

$$j(t) \equiv \mathbf{f}(t)\lambda = \mathbf{f}(t)(I - Q)^{-1}\mathbf{1} \tag{2.8}$$

In the binomial model, $\mathbf{f}(t)$ becomes just unity and the overall mean length $j(t)$ is identical with the λ of (2.4).

The total number of moves ever made from stratum i by a cohort of vacancies is important in computing mobility. Let $M_i(t)$ stand for the prediction of this number; the vector $\mathbf{M}(t)$, the array for all strata; and $M(t)$, the total number predicted. All moves take place within a year, the maximum lifetime of the chains. Every vacancy makes at least a first move so $\mathbf{F}(t)$ is also a count of first moves by stratum. Those vacancies with first move to another stratum are counted in $\mathbf{F}(t)Q$ by stratum of destination which necessarily is initial stratum for the second move. Thus the predicted counts are

$$\mathbf{M}(t) = \sum_{h=0}^{\infty} \mathbf{F}(t)Q^h \qquad (2.9)$$

where by convention Q^0 is the identity matrix. The summation yields

$$\mathbf{M}(t) = \mathbf{F}(t)(I - Q)^{-1} \qquad (2.10)$$

The inverse matrix $(I - Q)^{-1}$ serves as a multiplier which transforms arrivals into total moves.

Moves were counted in (2.7) for a single vacancy and according to the stratum in which the chain itself began. The total predicted number of moves from all strata $M(t)$ should and does equal the product of the observed number of chains times the overall average length of the predicted chain; that is,

$$F(t)j(t) = \mathbf{F}(t)(I - Q)^{-1}\mathbf{1} = \mathbf{M}(t)\mathbf{1} = M(t) \qquad (2.11)$$

This relation is particularly simple in the binomial case:

$$M(t) = F(t)/p \qquad (2.12)$$

Turnover, the distribution of individuals initially in one stratum according to stratum occupied at a later time, is the focus in many probabilistic models of mobility. Prediction of vacancy turnover would be pointless since the times of moves within a year cannot be specified from the data; no simple relation exists between turnover of vacancies and turnover of men. In a later section, formulas for the latter are derived. Section 2.3 turns to mobility of men and flows of men and jobs across the boundaries of the system.

2.3 Men and Jobs

The system, by definition, contains only men who are in jobs. A man who leaves his job without immediately entering another thereby leaves the system and in so doing, creates a vacancy said to have just arrived in the system. Newly created jobs are vacant when they enter the system and thus define another flow of vacancy creations. The overall numbers of vacancies in a cohort, $F(t)$, are the sums of these two contributions in every stratum. To avoid proliferation of arbitrary subscripts, let the two flows of vacancies be designated $F_{man}(t)$ and $F_{job}(t)$ respectively.

A job in the system may be vacant, but by hypothesis this vacancy will move on within a matter of months. The parameter q_{ik} is the probability a vacant job in stratum i will be filled by a man from some job in stratum k, $k = 1, \cdots, s$. The number of vacancies in the system at a given time is assumed to be small compared to the total number of men. The vacant job may also be filled by a new recruit— a man from outside the system who leaves no vacancy behind him. The residual possibility is the other way for the vacancy to "leave" the system, as the vacant job is abolished. The termination probability q_{io} subsumes both ways. The subscripts "man" and "job" can be attached to p to indicate the separate and stable probabilities of termination in each way for each stratum.

Mobility rates are fractions of men who move in a standard interval. Counts of vacancy moves are counts of moves by men in the opposite direction. In the systems studied, men move at most once a year and so, at most, once on a given cohort of vacancies. Let $N_i(t)$ be the number of men in jobs in stratum i at the end of year t, with $N(t)$ the corresponding total. The number of men expected to move into jobs ("in-mobility") in stratum i during year t is a fraction, $M_i^{in}(t)$, of the number of moves out of stratum i by vacancies, $M_i(t)$, predicted by (2.10). Since each of the $M_i(t)$ moves by vacancies has a chance $(q_{io})_{job}$ of being a terminating move by a vacant job out of the system, the relation is

$$M_i^{in}(t) = M_i(t)[1 - (q_{io})_{job}] \qquad (2.13)$$

The in-mobility rate predicted, $\mu_i^{in}(t)$, is:

$$\mu_i^{in}(t) = M_i^{in}(t)/N_i(t) \qquad (2.14)$$

the fraction of men in jobs in stratum i at the end of year t who arrived there during the year. In the binomial model the equations reduce to

$$M^{in}(t) = M(t)(1 - p_{job}) \qquad (2.15)$$

$$\mu^{in}(t) = M^{in}(t)/N(t) \qquad (2.16)$$

2. Markov Models of Vacancy Chains

In Chapter 7, the total number of men in each stratum and total number of jobs, is predicted over time from the exogenous flows of new vacancies into the system, using a deterministic form of the model in continuous time. Errors in such predictions cumulate from year to year; therefore in predicting mobility in a given year the total number of men have been taken as observables. Calculation of "out-mobility" for men requires counts of vacancy moves according to stratum of destination. In the binomial model the equations are obvious:

$$M^{out}(t) = M(t) - F_{job}(t) \qquad (2.17)$$

$$\mu^{out}(t) = M^{out}(t)/N(t - 1) \qquad (2.18)$$

2.4 Interpretation

A 1–1 (one-to-one) matching of men to occupied jobs is stipulated, therefore each vacancy is a distinguishable individual whose successive moves from job to job can be traced uniquely in a vacancy chain. (This stipulation will be relaxed somewhat in Section 7.8.) The exact timing of a move is not considered (until Section 7.7). Jobs are grouped into strata such that the probabilities of various destinations on the next move are the same whatever job the vacancy occupies within a given stratum.

A probability is assigned to all the jobs within a stratum taken together as one possible destination of the next move from a given stratum. A vacant job thus has a fixed probability of calling a replacement from each stratum of incumbents, but these probabilities need not be proportional to the numbers of incumbents or to the numbers of jobs; nor do these models assume that each incumbent in a destination stratum has the same chance of receiving the call.

The models can be described as imbedded Markov chains of first order with absorbing states[2]—"imbedded" because timing of moves is not specified and "Markov chains" because a distinct probability is assigned each possible transition between states for vacancies, which here are strata of jobs. "Absorbing states" is specified because vacancies may leave the system through either influx of men or departure of jobs, a fixed probability being assigned to each possibility for the next move of a vacancy in a given stratum. Jobs may leave the system only when vacant just as men may enter the system only when called to fill vacant jobs. "Of first order" is used because the destination probabilities for the next move of a vacancy in a given stratum are assumed not to depend on what strata it has been in previously. Higher order Markov chains could readily be defined if this assumption proved untenable. One special case of great importance will be treated in Chapter 10. The move of a vacancy might be affected by some personal attribute of the previous incumbent in that job, and there also might be separate transition probabilities to the destination stratum for various types of incumbents there. This special case can be called a $1\frac{1}{2}$ order Markov chain, a term reflecting the compound character of a vacancy.

All vacancies move independently of one another. Interaction across competitions among various sets of candidates for vacant jobs and competitions among sets of jobs for candidates at a given time is not considered until Chapter 11. The Markov chain models for vacancies subsume the sequential interaction among moves by men between jobs but, at a given time, cover interactions only between candidacies for a single vacant job. As long as some jobs are occupied in each stratum there is no inconsistency in assuming vacancies move independently according to fixed transition probabilities.

Time appears explicitly only in the label for each annual cohort of vacancies. The probabilities of staying in the same state—the diagonal entries in the matrix of transition probabilities—are not measures of inertia as in the usual Markov chain. They are, instead, conditional probabilities that the next move will be to another job in the same stratum. It is this definition which permits all moves of vacancies to be counted from the stratified model even though moves are defined by individual jobs. Limitations of the available data suggested the definition of conditional transition probabilities, which definition can perhaps be replaced by transition probabilities defined for fixed intervals;[3] then moves within strata would have to be counted by a separate calculation.

Lifetimes of vacancies within the system are restricted. An upper limit is set to the stay of a vacancy in a given job after which the job is assumed to be abandoned—ejected from the system because of failure in the search for a new incumbent. All moves in a chain are assumed to take place within a year, whether because their number is limited or because they are closely spaced in time.

Since vacancies appear in successive annual cohorts, each of which is gone before the next arrives, equilibrium is reached within each year in turn. Therefore the models are reversible within each year, as are Markov chains for closed systems in equilibrium. For example, the same overall distribution of chain lengths is predicted if each chain is assumed to run in the opposite direction. The cause, the exogenous driving force behind mobility is the input of new vacancies.

Creations of jobs and deaths of men add together, and each is free to vary arbitrarily from year to year in total size and in distribution among strata. (In Sections 7.3 and 7.5, the effects of correlation between retirements and total number of men in the system are analyzed.) Growth and decline of men and of jobs in the various strata depend on the balance between these inputs and the predictions from the chain model of terminations by recruitment and by the abolishing of jobs. However, mobility predictions require more than data on net flows, they depend on the number of vacancy creations at one end and estimates for termination probabilities at the other end of chains. Estimation and prediction procedures for these models are developed in the next sections.

Four basic ideas can be distinguished in the maze of particular postulates for these stratified probability models: (1) "deaths" of men and "births" of jobs add together in initiating chains of moves; (2) constraints implicit in matching men to jobs give vacancies rather than men the initiative in moves; (3) deaths of jobs and recruitment of new men are the two parallel ways for disturbances—the vacancies causing mobility—to leave the system; (4) vacancies but not men move independently of one another. Without this last assumption the probability models would not be justified. All four ideas are rejected in the family of probability models which uses Markov chains for moves by men (Chapter 9) and in the family where unemployed men and vacant jobs are matched (Chapter 8).

2.5 *Estimates and Tests*

For each system studied, strata must be chosen and transition probabilities estimated. In each period, exogenous variables—the flows of vacancy creations—are to be recorded and also numbers of men and jobs since, until Chapter 7, these are treated as initial conditions each year. Suitable dependent variables for prediction must be chosen, observations recorded, and the appropriate tests specified. Not only the stochastic variability inherent in the model is to be allowed for but also sampling variability, since each system studied is too large for exhaustive inventories to be feasible.

Appendix B details the three-stage sampling scheme used for the three systems selected and precisely specified in Chapter 3 and Appendix A. From a random sample of men in a year, estimates for the populations of filled jobs can be derived. The second stage is finding moves of men by tracing the sample back or forward one year. The third stage is tracing a complete vacancy chain through each vacancy move. Estimates are obtained both for the analytic systems of men and jobs used in the vacancy models and for some residual categories of men and jobs in the concrete organizations studied. (Appendix C gives details on these residual categories and also on loops of vacancy moves, which are inconsistent with the vacancy chain models. Appendix C reports and assesses dependent and independent variables in terms of the binomial model, with all jobs in a system lumped in a single stratum.)

The sampling scheme is complicated. The models are complicated. The operational specifications of constructs and variables are complicated. All three are interrelated and together influence the choice of test variables for prediction. All vary slightly from one to another of the three organizations studied. Sampling fluctuations affect both the parameter estimates and the independent variables used in prediction, as well as the observations of the variables predicted. Stochastic variability of predictions must be allowed for in tests. This is not a situation in which the formal theory of statistical inference is easy to apply rigorously, and it will not be used.[4] Sampling variability will be assessed by comparing observed means, on several variables, in independent samples from the same period. Predictions and observations will be juxtaposed in tables, and the reader will be invited to agree with the author's intuitive assessment of the fit (enough detail is supplied to allow the reader to apply some conventional tests of statistical significance).

Homogeneity among jobs within a stratum and divergence between strata should be sought on some job attribute bound to be related to mobility. The model's validity and usefulness can then be assessed in several ways; from the stability of estimated transition probabilities among those strata; from the plausibility of the relative sizes of transition probabilities; and from the closeness of fit between prediction and observation of dependent variables. Chapters 4 and 5 follow this general pattern. Once it seems certain that some stratified model is sure to be valid, the logic can be reversed. Stability, coherence, and closeness of fit for the given sets of data can be used to choose among different possible assignments of jobs to strata. This approach is emphasized more in Chapter 6. Hierarchical attributes, such as size of job, predominate; but some models using regional divisions are tested.

The total number of moves by vacancies from stratum i to stratum k are observed in the sample from one cohort to be $a_{ik}(t)$ and the number of terminal moves to be $a_{i0}(t)$. The observed number of vacancy creations in the sample in stratum k can be denoted $a_{0k}(t)$; the entry $a_{00}(t)$ is identically zero. The sum of all moves from stratum i, including terminal moves, is denoted by $a_{i.}(t)$. It is natural to estimate the transition probability q_{ik} by the observed fraction of moves from i which go to k. Let $\hat{q}_{ik}$ stand for the value of q_{ik} estimated from a sample:

$$\hat{q}_{ik} = \frac{a_{ik}(t)}{a_{i.}(t)} \tag{2.19a}$$

The distribution of vacancy creations among strata in the cohort for year t can be estimated in the same way:

$$\hat{f}_k(t) = \frac{a_{0k}(t)}{a_0.(t)} \tag{2.19b}$$

where $\hat{f}_k$ denotes an estimate from a sample.

The sample of moves in (2.19b) will be all moves in some complete chains in the cohort for year t.[5] Each chain and move has a sampling weight which corrects for differential exposure to the three-stage sampling process. The a_{ij} will be decimal numbers rather than integers, that is, sums of weights rather than pure counts. Since the moves form complete chains, each move out of a stratum, including terminations, must be matched by a move into that stratum, including creations. Let the column sum be $a_{.k}(t)$:

$$\sum_{i=0}^{s} a_{ik}(t) = a_{.k}(t) \tag{2.20}$$

then

$$a_{k.}(t) = a_{.k}(t), \quad k = 0, 1, 2, \ldots, s \tag{2.21}$$

The choice of dependent variables to be predicted by a stratified model is important. The data available does not permit examination of the exact numerical delays in filling vacant jobs. Comparison of these delays with the periods men spend in limbo between successive jobs was the main validation suggested in Chapter 1 for the concept of the vacancy chain. The various postulates in a stratified model will not be tested separately, instead the model as a whole is considered.

Turnover of men among strata across long periods is the main test used for Markov chain models of *men's* moves (discussed in Chapter 9). Deviations from predictions can supply evidence of the need for higher order Markov chains. Since fixed time intervals are not used in predicting moves by a cohort of vacancies, turnover of vacancies would have to be calculated across a fixed number of moves in sequence. Although an adequate test of the model, prediction of vacancy turnover is not in itself useful. A vacancy lives only a year or so and there is little intrinsic interest in its history.

Complete vacancy chains were the focus of interest in Chapter 1, and the basic samples of moves constitute complete chains. The number of moves in a chain, that is, its length, is a chain's most distinctive attribute; it is a measure of career length for that individual vacancy. From lengths, overall mobility can be computed easily, and prediction of the distribution of lengths tests the probability model. The prediction depends on the numerical values of the parameters as well as on the general postulates. The same sample of chains can yield both the observed length distribution and, after decomposition into constituent moves, the transition probability estimates of (2.19). The latter cannot be deduced from the lengths of the chains from which the moves came, and the test remains a genuine one.

In the vacancy models predictions of chain length distributions replace turnover predictions as the main test; that is, the distribution of vacancies across strata after a fixed number of moves is replaced by the distribution of the number of moves required to reach a particular state, the outside, which all vacancies reach eventually. Equation (2.5) is the prediction formula for length distribution by beginning stratum of the chains. Equations (2.19) and (2.20) are the formulas for estimating transition probabilities. Timing of events within the cohort's year enter none of these equations.

Predictions of the overall length distribution using different definitions of strata can be compared directly with each other and with the observed distribution for the cohort as a whole. If a *given* stratified model is run backward from the observed endings of chains, the overall distribution of chain lengths predicted is unchanged. Equation (2.19) is replaced by its transpose, with column sums as the denominator, and the counts of creations $\mathbf{F}$ are replaced by counts of terminations. A bump chain model yields the same length distribution as the vacancy chain model estimated from the same cohort and the same strata. (The dualities between bump chains and vacancy chains are discussed further in Chapter 10.)

The predicted total number of moves from stratum i by a cohort of vacancies cannot be deduced from the predicted length distributions of chains. Mean chain lengths as well as numbers of moves are derived from the multiplier, the inverse matrix $(I - Q)^{-1}$. However, mean chain lengths are seen from (2.7) to be row sums whereas numbers of moves, from (2.10), are weighted column sums. The only agreement necessary between them is in overall total number of moves, shown in (2.11). Prediction of the vector of total moves by stratum, $\mathbf{M}(t)$, yields a test of the model that is different from those based on length distributions; the vector $\mathbf{M}(t)$ must be calculated in order to predict mobility rates for men from (2.14) and (2.16).

Whereas distributions of chain lengths depend essentially on the probabilistic treatment of moves by individual vacancies, predictions of total moves by stratum require only the tracing of aggregate flows among strata by a cohort. Chapter 7 develops that view, in which transition probabilities are converted into the proportions in which a total flow is split into determinate subflows to various destinations. This view is particularly convenient when long-term development of the total sizes of the system in men and jobs by stratum is the focus of interest.

Time is used at two different levels in the vacancy models. Each cohort is labeled by the year in which its vacancies trace out their lifetimes. The duration of that "year," when measured in units of the average spacing between vacancy moves, must in principle be limitless. In practice the proportion of chains predicted to have lengths greater than, say, 20 is negligible. Each stratum, no matter how small or large in number of jobs, can be expected to have both a substantial termination probability and a substantial transition probability to at least some other stratum. The number of strata is kept small and the number of jobs in each is kept large, first to minimize interaction in the model between moves by different vacancies and second to avoid sampling fluctuations which might lead to an estimate of zero for a termination probability for some cohort. If the models are to be of much practical value, transition probabilities must remain the same through many cohorts.

2.6 Turnover: Models for Men versus Models for Vacancies

Before embarking on elaborate estimation and testing, it is important to see how predictions from vacancy models would differ from those based on more familiar models. Turnover of men among jobs is analyzed, and comparison is made with simple models for moves by men. As will become clear in Chapter 9, predictions of turnover serve as the main test for the latter models. The concern in this book is with qualitative differences in predictions made by each kind of model.

In this section annual turnover in various years is the focus. Section 2.7 takes up turnover across long periods. Stochastic variability in the predictions for a cohort was not emphasized in earlier sections nor will it be here. The model for men's moves will be treated as a deterministic one.

The number of men who will move from each stratum to each other stratum over a year is a major interest in studies of mobility. The simplest assumption, and the one used most frequently in prediction, is that the proportions of men from a given stratum who move to various other strata per year remain fixed over a long period. Changes in the numbers of moves per year from the given stratum to others simply reflect changes in the total number of men in the stratum at the beginning of each year. The latter changes can be computed from the difference between the number of men who left a stratum and the numbers who entered from other strata, plus the new recruits over the preceding year. Call this model the constant turnover model.[6] The vacancy chain model predicts the pattern of turnover on a quite different basis. In order to compare them the constant turnover model must be specified in detail.

Let $N_r(u)$ be the total number of men observed in stratum r at the beginning of year $u + 1$. Let t_{rc} designate the fraction of all men in stratum r who move to stratum c during the year; t_{rc} is the same in all years. Let s again be the number of strata. The "immobility" rate, t_{rr}, has a special residual status; it is the fraction of men who did not leave stratum r. Some men in stratum r will leave the system in one way or another; the moves can be counted as ones to a special category, the outside, designated as 0. Their number will affect t_{rr}

but not the other turnover rates. It is not necessary, but it simplifies notation, to assume a fixed fraction, t_{r0}, of the men in stratum r who leave the system each year. Then

$$t_{rr} + t_{r0} = 1 - \sum_{\substack{c=1 \\ c \neq r}}^{s} t_{rc} \qquad (2.22)$$

New recruits from outside the system do not affect the predicted number of men who move from one stratum to another in the year.

Let the predicted number of men changing from stratum r to stratum c in the year $u + 1$ be called $b_{rc}(u)$. Then

$$b_{rc}(u) = N_r(u)t_{rc} \qquad (2.23)$$

where r and c range through $1, 2, \ldots, s$. The observed number of men who move from stratum r to stratum c during the year is also the observed number of vacancies which move from c to r. The counts of vacancy moves to and from the outside may include creations and terminations of jobs so that there is no necessary relation between these counts and the counts reflected in the rates t_{r0} and t_{rr}.

Usually the transition rates cannot be specified numerically on theoretical grounds but must be estimated from an earlier year; call the earlier year $u' + 1$ and let the observed counts of moves be indicated by $\hat{b}$; then

$$t_{rc} = \hat{b}_{rc}(u')/N_r(u') \qquad (2.24)$$

The prediction becomes

$$b_{rc}(u) = \frac{N_r(u)}{N_r(u')} \hat{b}_{rc}(u') \qquad (2.25)$$

The number of moves of men from r to c predicted is just the number of moves in the year used for estimation, times the ratio of the number of men in stratum r at the beginnings of the two years. Nothing could be simpler than this proportional extrapolation, but it is a very rigid type of prediction that could hardly hold over a very long time.

A more flexible prediction comes from the vacancy chain model. In parallel to the constant turnover model, the transition rates, or more precisely the transition probabilities q_{rc} that correspond to rates, will be assumed constant. These rates do not apply to the total population of men in various strata but, instead, to the appearances of vacancies. The number of vacancies created in each stratum at the beginning of a year, $F_r(u + 1)$, are not predicted but observed, just as the total numbers of men in a stratum at the year's beginning, $N_r(u)$, are taken as data for the constant turnover model. These creations are obviously much more subject to fluctuation from year to year—as, for instance, different cohorts of men approach retirement or as job expansion campaigns get underway—than are the total numbers of men in the various strata. Nonetheless there is no necessary connection between the sizes of F_r and of N_r. This is the first major difference between the constant turnover and the vacancy chain models; predictions in one model are based on observed counts almost independent of those on which the predictions of the other are based for the given year.

All moves in a year are treated as a single wave of events in the constant turnover model. In the vacancy model, each creation sets off a chain of successive moves of the vacancy; the observed totals for a given year thus combine many waves of moves in the year by the vacancies created at the beginning of that year. This multiplier effect is summed up by (2.10), which counts in a vector, $\mathbf{M}(u)$, the total expected number of moves made from each stratum by vacancies as a result of the initial creations of vacancies counted in the vector $\mathbf{F}(u)$.

The prediction from the vacancy model parallel to (2.23) is

$$b_{rc}(u) = M_c(u)q_{cr}, \quad c \neq r \tag{2.26}$$

Since predictions are made in terms of vacancy moves, rows and columns are transposed on the right, and the equation does not predict the number of men who remain in a stratum, $b_{rr}(u)$. As in the constant turnover model, it is assumed that no man can move more than once in a year. From applying (2.26) to the earlier year $u' + 1$, q_{cr} can be estimated:

$$\hat{q}_{cr} = \hat{b}_{rc}(u')/\hat{M}_c(u') \tag{2.27}$$

Equation (2.27) parallels (2.24) and is the same as (2.19) when the sample assumed there becomes the whole population. The relation between turnover in two years, parallel to (2.25) for the constant turnover model, becomes

$$b_{rc}(u) = \frac{M_c(u)}{\hat{M}_c(u')} \hat{b}_{rc}(u') \tag{2.28}$$

2. Markov Models of Vacancy Chains

A second difference between the constant turnover model and the vacancy chain model leads to a simple way to test them. In (2.25) the predicted number of moves in year u by men from stratum r to stratum c will be unchanged from the number in year u' if the total number of men in stratum r is unchanged, and it will change in proportion to the change in this total. In (2.28) it is column sums that determine the ratio of moves in the later year to moves in the earlier; that is, the number of men who move from stratum r to stratum c vary in proportion to a count performed for the *destination* stratum c. The reason for the difference is obvious intuitively: in the vacancy chain model it is vacancies that have the initiative.

In the constant turnover model, the numbers of men in a row of the turnover table will always maintain the same proportions, the proportions among the t_{rc} for the given row r. In the vacancy chain model, if the transition probabilities are constant, it is the numbers of men in a column of the turnover table that maintain the same proportions to one another. Without any estimation of parameters or use of equations, an observed series of turnover tables can be tested to see whether proportions are fixed in each row or in each column. This comparison is simple: a direct test of whether moves in the system studied are most profitably seen as moves by vacancies or moves by men.

The parallel between (2.28) and (2.25) is only partial. In (2.25) the predictions for a given stratum are based on the observed count of men in that stratum only at the beginning of the year. In (2.28) the predictions for a given stratum r depend on the predicted total number of vacancy appearances in every stratum, $M_c(u)$. Each of the latter depend on all the components of $\mathbf{F}(t)$, the vector of observed creations of vacancies, as can be seen from (2.10).

The third major difference between the two models is now clear. In a vacancy model observed counts for all strata (the $\mathbf{F}$ components) are needed to predict turnover figures from or to a single stratum: in the fixed turnover model the moves out from a given stratum to others can be predicted from observations solely on that stratum. The fourth main difference also follows from the use of (2.10) in (2.28). Only one of the parameters of the fixed turnover model, one of the turnover rates t_{rc}, affects the value of a particular b_{rc}. In the vacancy models there is one transition probability, q_{cr}, which plays the same role in fixing a particular b_{rc}; the whole set of transition probabilities also enters the determination of each b_{rc}, through the multiplier $(I - Q)^{-1}$. The fifth difference between the models is in the treatment of moves within a stratum. Such moves are ignored, indeed undefined, in the constant turnover model. The number of men in each diagonal cell, b_{rr}, is the total number who have remained within the stratum. The corresponding rate, t_{rr}, is not really a transition rate but an immobility rate.

The central fact about the constant turnover model is that it says nothing about individual jobs. Thus no interrelations, no contingencies among individual moves, can be traced. One move is not seen as generating a train of later moves. There is no mechanism to insure that sufficient jobs exist to accommodate the movers. The distribution of men among strata at the end of the year, the column totals, are determined solely by the initial numbers and the fixed rates of movement. Much the same kind of model is often used to predict changes in attitudes in a population of men, changes which, presumably, are subject to no reality constraints. The vacancy chain model not only deals with individual jobs but also assumes their needs take priority over the wishes of men in determining mobility. A man moves only to fill a vacancy. The model guarantees that a job is waiting for, indeed calling, any man who moves. New jobs and terminated jobs are kept track of on the same footing as recruitments and deaths, all being tallied together in the row and column for transactions with the outside. There is a duality between men and jobs.

2.7 Selection of Movers and Long-Term Turnover

Only half the mobility process has been treated. Annual turnover defines numbers of moves between various strata but not which particular men move. For either the constant turnover or the vacancy model, the only assumption about men required in Section 2.6 was that a man moved at most once a year.

In the logic of the vacancy model, a divorce between amount of and selection for mobility is natural. No particular probability mechanism is implied for choice of movers within a stratum of men. Retirements and death depend on age; so random selection of men within a stratum to initiate vacancy chains is not reasonable. The same men could repeatedly be called to vacancies over the years, others remaining in their initial jobs indefinitely, without affecting the prediction of turnover each year. Separate transition probabilities could be defined for different categories of incumbents in the stratum to which a vacancy moves (this will be done in Chapter 10), but moves of men from different categories interact because of common exposure to the same flow of vacancies.

It is possible, although not as plausible, to maintain the same divorce within a model for moves by men at constant rates. The price paid is the determinism required. If *who* moves must be left unspecified, it cannot be argued that each man in a stratum is exposed to certain fixed transition probabilities; it can only be asserted that fixed fractions of the population in a stratum will move to various destinations. Also, men's states must be specified by job strata and not by personal attributes when defining turnover rates. The compromise was made in Section 2.6 so that a model of constant turnover of men could be contrasted with the vacancy chain model solely on grounds of the numerical magnitudes of movement predicted in various years.

Long-term turnover, the cross-classification of men by stratum now and stratum a number of years later, cannot be predicted until the choice of movers each year is specified. Unless men who move into a stratum are indistinguishable from men long in the stratum in their subsequent movements, it is very difficult to compute net turnover across many years. Therefore men selected to move in either model will be assumed to be representative of the composition of the incumbents of that stratum by previous history. The fractions of men who move from a stratum in a year will be treated as selection operators, not just as numbers.

The most familiar and explicit interpretation of representative selection is random choice, which requires a probability model for moves by individual men. Superimposition of random selection for men on the probabilistic model for vacancy moves is too complex to be worthwhile. It would be easy to describe the constant turnover model in terms of Markov chains (as is done in Chapter 9), but the equations using selection operators are also valid for expected values in such a probability model.

Consider first the constant turnover model. A rather detailed explanation is needed to ensure clarity. Turnover parameters are estimated, as in (2.24), from data for some trial year or years (which may or may not be included in the period for which net turnover is predicted). These fixed parameters are taken as given, and the cap notation for estimation is suppressed hereafter. New recruits will enter the system each year, but they play no role in the calculation of turnover for the initial population.

Let the initial year be labeled with $u = 0$. Let the number of the initial incumbents in the system who are predicted to be in stratum c at the beginning of the next year be $R_c(1)$. From (2.23)

$$R_c(1) = \sum_{r=1}^{s} b_{rc}(0) = \sum_{r=1}^{s} N_r(0)t_{rc} \qquad (2.29)$$

Since new recruits are not included but since some men die each year, the stratum totals decline year after year. By the end of this year, $R_c(1)$ will in turn be redistributed among strata in accordance with (2.23):

$$R_g(2) = \sum_{c=1}^{s} R_c(1)t_{cg} \qquad (2.30)$$

The problem is the turnover across the two year period; that is, the composition of $R_g(2)$ in terms of the strata its members were in initially. Let t_{rc} in (2.29) be not just a numerical fraction applied to a numerical magnitude but also a selection operator. That is, the same fraction t_{rc} can be applied to each subset of the men counted by $N_r(0)$, when they are partitioned into subsets according to some arbitrary attribute. The same assumption is made for the t_{cg} in (2.30) —that is why recruits from the previous year could be omitted. By (2.29) $R_c(1)$ is partitioned into s subsets, according to the stratum its members were in initially; the fractions t_{cg} apply to each subset separately. Therefore (2.30) can be rewritten

$$R_g(2) = \sum_{c=1}^{s} [t_{cg}N_1(0)t_{1c} + t_{cg}N_2(0)t_{2c} + \cdots + t_{cg}N_s(0)t_{sc}] \qquad (2.31)$$

Each term in parentheses can be summed over c separately:

$$R_g(2) = N_1(0)\left(\sum_{c=1}^{s} t_{1c}t_{cg} \right) + N_2(0)\left(\sum_{c=1}^{s} t_{2c}t_{cg} \right)$$

$$+ \cdots + N_s(0)\left(\sum_{c=1}^{s} t_{sc}t_{cg} \right) \qquad (2.32)$$

The turnover during two years is made clear: (2.32) indicates the composition of the men in stratum g in terms of what stratum they were in two years before. To be more precise, (2.32) indicates what fraction of the men initially in a given stratum are now in stratum g. The two sides of (2.32) are numerically equal, whether selection of movers is blind or not; by simple deduction from equations (2.29) and (2.30), and (2.32), it would normally be written in more compact form:

$$R_g(2) = \sum_{r=1}^{s} N_r(0)\left(\sum_{c=1}^{s} t_{rc}t_{cg} \right) \tag{2.33}$$

It is natural to rewrite (2.33) in matrix form combining equations for separate values of g. Let $\mathbf{R}(u)$ be the row vector whose g^{th} column contains $R_g(u)$. Let the set of turnover fractions t_{rc} be written as a matrix, T, exactly parallel in form to the matrix Q of transition probabilities. The generalized form of (2.32) is

$$\mathbf{R}(2) = \mathbf{N}(0)T^2 \tag{2.34}$$

The components of each stratum sum $R_g(2)$ are not kept separate but added together in (2.34).

Turnover can best be exhibited as a two dimensional array. The turnover for the first year is given by b_{rc} of (2.23), which can be written in a matrix B with s rows and s columns. To compute each entry in a row r of B, the corresponding entry in row r of T must be multiplied by the total number of men in stratum r at the beginning of the year. To accomplish this by multiplication of matrices, the various $N_r(0)$ must be inserted along the diagonal of a matrix whose other entries are zero. Instead of combining the N_r into a vector $\mathbf{N}$, they are put together in a diagonal matrix, N_D:

$$N_D \equiv \begin{pmatrix} N_1(0) & 0 & 0 & \cdots & 0 \\ 0 & N_2(0) & 0 & \cdots & 0 \\ 0 & 0 & N_3(0) & \cdots & 0 \\ 0 & 0 & 0 & \cdots & 0 \\ \cdot & \cdot & \cdot & \cdots & \cdot \\ 0 & 0 & 0 & \cdots & N_s(0) \end{pmatrix} \tag{2.35}$$

The correct formulation of (2.23) in terms of matrices is

$$B = N_D T \tag{2.36}$$

Let $B^{(i)}$ represent turnover across i years, with the entry $b_{rg}^{(i)}$ being the number of men initially in stratum r who are in stratum g, i years later. The constituents in (2.32) can be rewritten in a series of equations:

$$b_{rg}^{(2)} = N_r(0)\left(\sum_{c=1}^{s} t_{rc}t_{cg}\right)$$ (2.37)

for $r = 1, 2, \ldots, s$. In matrix form (2.37) becomes

$$B^{(2)} = N_D T^2$$ (2.38)

parallel to (2.36). The generalization is obvious:

$$B^{(i)} = N_D T^i$$ (2.39)

where $B^{(i)}$ is understood to mean the B in (2.36). On the left side of (2.39), i is a superscript, which designates a span of years not a calendar year; on the right side, i is the power to which the matrix T is raised.

The logic of operators for representative selection already developed for the constant turnover model will also be used for the vacancy model. The transition probabilities q_{rc}, which are assumed to remain constant, are taken as given. Selection is indicated by introducing a factor, N_r/N_r, which is redundant numerically, into (2.26):

$$b_{rc}^{(1)} = N_r(0)\left(\frac{M_c(0)q_{cr}}{N_r(0)}\right) \quad \text{for } r \neq c$$ (2.40)

Here and later the superscript attached to b indicates the number of years over which turnover is computed. On the right side of (2.40), the quantity in parentheses is simply a numerical selection operator —the analogue to the t_{rc} parameter—and will be designated $v_{rc}(0)$:

$$v_{rc}(0) \equiv M_c(0)q_{cr}/N_r(0) \quad \text{for } r \neq c$$ (2.41)

(2.41) can be called a turnover coefficient. The $N_r(0)$ factor on the right side of (2.40) is not just a number, it stands for the actual men in stratum r at the beginning of the turnover period.

When $r = c$, (2.40) as does (2.26) counts the number of men in stratum r expected to move to other jobs in stratum r during the first year. This count is not relevant in the prediction of turnover by strata; instead, $b_{rr}^{(1)}$ counts the total number of men who remain within stratum r during the first year, whether they change jobs or not. (This is the meaning of b_{rr} in the constant turnover model.) The equation is

$$b_{rr}^{(1)} = N_r(0) - \sum_{\substack{c=1 \\ c \neq r}}^{r} b_{rc}^{(1)} - b_{r0}^{(1)} \tag{2.42}$$

In (2.42), $b_{r0}^{(1)}$ counts the men leaving the system from stratum r during the first year; it cannot be greater than $F_r(0)$, the observed number of creations of vacancies in stratum r during the first year. To simplify the notation, the proportion of the men in a stratum who leave the system each year is defined; it is appropriate to call this proportion t_{r0}, parallel to the constant turnover model. Define a new parameter parallel to those in (2.41):

$$v_{rr}^{(0)} = 1 - \sum_{\substack{c=1 \\ c \neq r}}^{r} v_{rc}(0) - t_{r0}(0) \tag{2.43}$$

Equation (2.40) can be rewritten in a condensed form, valid for all values of r and c:

$$b_{rc}^{(1)} = N_r(0)v_{rc}(0), \quad r, c = 1, \ldots, s \tag{2.44}$$

When $r = c$, the equation counts the men remaining in the stratum, whether they shift jobs or not. This set of equations can be rewritten as a matrix equation in the same way (2.23) was converted into (2.36):

$$B^{(1)} = N_D V(0) \tag{2.45}$$

In (2.45) $V(0)$ is the matrix of the numerical turnover coefficients $v_{rc}(0)$ in the initial year in the vacancy model, which are defined in (2.41) and (2.43); N_D is the diagonal matrix defined in (2.35).

In the next year of the turnover period, a new set of vacancies will be created. They will generate a new total number of vacancy moves from each stratum g, represented by $M_g(1)$. The expected number of men called from stratum c to stratum g is simply $M_g(1)q_{gc}$. These men are drawn from the men observed to be in stratum c at the beginning of the year, $N_c(1)$; $N_c(1)$ can be predicted from $B^{(1)}$, as can the recruitment coefficients q_{ro} and the $N_r(0)$, although it is simpler to take $N_c(1)$ as observed. The selection fraction is $M_g(1)q_{gc}/N_c(1)$, which applies to each group of men from the initial population who are in stratum c at the beginning of the second year, whatever their stratum r may have been initially. $M_g(1)q_{gc}/N_c(1)$ is exactly parallel to the fraction in (2.41), so it is natural to label it $v_{cg}(1)$:

$$v_{cg}(1) = \frac{M_g(1)q_{gc}}{N_c(1)}, \quad c \neq g \qquad (2.46)$$

For $c = g$, the definition of $v_{gg}(1)$ is exactly parallel to that in (2.43); the death rate $t_{ro}(0)$ is replaced by $t_{ro}(1)$, which need not be the same value.

$V(1)$ is defined as the matrix containing the $v_{cg}(1)$ as entries. $B^{(2)}$ is defined as the matrix containing $b_{rg}^{(2)}$; which represents and counts the men initially in stratum r who are in stratum g two years later, regardless of what stratum c they were in at the one-year mark. It follows by the same logic as in (2.38) that

$$B^{(2)} = N_D V(0)V(1) \qquad (2.47)$$

The two numerical coefficients $v_{rc}(1)$ and $v_{rc}(0)$ may be far from equal. The denominators count the total numbers of men in stratum r at the beginning of two different years. More important, $M_c(1)$ and $M_c(0)$ are calculated by (2.10) from the vacancy creations in the two successive years, which may differ radically in total number and in distribution among strata. Hence the matrices $V(0)$ and $V(1)$ are distinct. Equation (2.47) is not and should not be exactly parallel to (2.38) for the constant turnover model.

In each successive year of a turnover period of, say, i years, labeled $0, 1, \ldots, k, \ldots, i - 1$, a distinct matrix of coefficients $V(k)$ is used. Each matrix derives from the matrix of transition probabilities for vacancies, Q, which remains unchanged. It is actually the transpose of Q whose entries appear as factors in the corresponding entries of the matrix $V(k)$. Such transposition seems a simple step, but it also entails the replacement of row sums by column sums as the base numbers for computing fractions and simultaneously the replacement of counts of vacancies by counts of men. The $M_c(k)$ can be written in a diagonal matrix of numerical entries, $M_D(k)$, parallel in form to the diagonal matrix for $N_r(0)$ in (2.35). The numerical reciprocals $N_r^{-1}(k)$ can similarly be written as a diagonal matrix. In this new notation, the matrix of coefficients $V(k)$ can be computed directly from other matrices. Q^* is the transpose of Q; then

$$V(k) = N_D^{-1}(k)Q_d^* M_D(k) \qquad (2.48)$$

2. Markov Models of Vacancy Chains

The subscript d has been attached to Q^* to indicate a substitution has been made for the diagonal elements q_{rr} in order to yield the correct formulas, parallel to (2.43), for the diagonal entries in $V(k)$:

$$q_{rr}^* = \frac{1}{M_r(k)} \left[N_r(k) - \sum_{\substack{c=1 \\ c \neq r}}^{r} M_c(k)q_{cr} - N_r(k)t_{r0}(k) \right] \quad (2.49)$$

The general equation for long-term turnover is obvious:

$$B^{(i)} = N_D V(0)V(1) \ldots V(i-1) \quad (2.50)$$

or, equivalently,

$$B^{(i)} = N_D \prod_{k=0}^{i-1} V(k) \quad (2.51)$$

In (2.51) N_D is the diagonal matrix in (2.35) whose entries are the numbers of men initially in the various strata. In addition to the components of $\mathbf{F}(k)$, another set of observed counts for the year enters the calculation $V(k)$; namely, the number of men in each stratum at the beginning of the year, $N_r(k)$. These can be computed from previous predicted turnover and predicted recruitment, but the calculation would be very complex.

Equation (2.50) is to be contrasted with (2.39) for the constant turnover model. The former equation is much more complex. In comparing predictions for annual turnover from the two models it was sufficient to see whether it was numbers of men in a column or numbers in a row of the turnover table that maintained the same proportions in different years. No such simple comparison is possible for predictions of long-term turnover. The principal difference between the two models is in the observations on which prediction is based. In the constant turnover model, even the long-term predictions of turnover are based solely on counts of men by stratum in the initial year, because each man is assumed to move independently.

Equation (2.50) can be reduced to the simple structure in (2.39) if and only if each element in the matrix of coefficients $V(k)$ is a constant, that is, the same each year. Then the product of these matrices can be written as the ith power of the constant matrix, V. From (2.41) it is clear that $v_{rc}(k)$ is the same for all k if and only if $M_c(k)/N_r(k)$ is also the same. This ratio can be independent of k for all pairs of values of r and c if and only if all the N_r and all the M_c

change by the same factor each year. The M_c are determined by **F** from (2.10). The conclusion of this argument is that the matrix $V(k)$ is independent of k only if the ratio $F_r(k)/N_r(k)$ is the same in every year. Except under these very special conditions, predictions from the two models will be different.

Chapter 3
Tracing Vacancy Chains

To trace a vacancy chain one must be able to identify particular jobs with individual men and follow a series of replacements of one incumbent by another. The chain of replacements may stretch through many parts of one or more large organizations. Data on linked individual events of this sort is expensive to collect. The jobs involved will normally be in higher strata within organizations, and it is not easy to get permission to investigate such jobs even in one organization. For both these reasons it was desirable to carry out the initial case studies for self-contained organizations that routinely published detailed data on incumbencies of men in jobs. The main problem then becomes inferring chains of movement from successive static reports on assignments of men to jobs. Jobs for single incumbents, 1–1 (one-to-one) jobs, must be distinguished from other jobs and statuses for men in the organization.

3.1 Three American Churches

The movement of clergy among pastorates in national churches proved to be an ideal topic. Each national church publishes annuals in which the job of every minister is recorded; and in many churches, regional subdivisions publish journals yearly with even more detailed characteristics of individual priests and parishes. Many of these series for American churches go back well over 100 years, so longitudinal studies of trends as well as comparative studies of different churches are feasible.

All seminaries and many secular libraries contain collections of these annuals for one or several national churches. No permission is needed to study this material. To an extent unusual in social science research, the data is public. No need for concealment can arise in publishing the analyses. The specific data used will be identified explicitly (see Table C.8 and C.11). Every fact and every measure reported below can be checked by other investigators from the public records.

Clergy are special, it can be argued; they are special in many ways. They hold roles of sufficient importance in our society to motivate extensive research; and much material has been published.[1] In America, clergy, especially Protestant clergy, can also be viewed as not atypical professional men. Mobility of men in higher strata is the subject of analysis, and no particular universe of men in these strata will be really typical of the whole situation. Eventually, comparison of mobility in different universes will be the goal. At present the task is to develop and test the fruitfulness of a new method of analysis centered on a new construct, the vacancy chain.

The Protestant clergy makes as good a test case as any. Over the past century they have become increasingly professionalized in many senses; in particular higher specialized education is becoming close to a necessity (a general trend in the United States). Clergy are to a high degree committed to careers in a particular organization; so are military officers and, to a lesser extent, higher civil servants. Clergy must be "ordained" by legitimate authority and are subject to pervasive discipline by these authorities, as are other professionals in bureaucracies; for that matter, so are "free" professionals. Like middle managers, clergy move or are moved among jobs (and locations) and must often uproot and resettle their families.

The central consideration is that ministers repeatedly over the years move to new jobs. As do other professionals, ministers have special commitments to the substance of their work wherever it may lie; as do others, they change in interests and abilities and grow restless from time to time. They can have ambition. They judge themselves and are judged in part by the size and scope of the jobs they hold relative to others at particular stages of their career. Salary and fees are an important component of these judgments; but, as in other occupations, locale and more subtle considerations of status and potential enter in. Clergy are high-status American men oriented toward mobility in their occupational life.

A denomination and its clergy are clearly defined. There is relatively little transfer of clergy between particular denominations. The churches chosen for study from the long list of American denominations are the Episcopal church, the Methodist church, and the Presbyterian church of the United States. They differ from one another in size, in history, and in major structural features. They all have regional units (called dioceses, annual conferences, and presbyteries respectively) which are close to autonomous in ordinary activities. All have strong national legislative assemblies to define doctrine, structure, and procedures.[2]

The Methodist church in the twentieth century has nearly 20,000 fully ordained clergy, more than twice the number either of the other two has. It was split during the Civil War, but in 1940 the two halves along with one of the numerous smaller Methodist churches merged. Vacancy chains may provide an especially apt instrument for measuring the speed and extent of true behavioral unification under-lying the formal merger. In the nineteenth century, the practice and, in the twentieth century, the ideology was for a "traveling minister" to stay a relatively short time in one place and then transfer else-where. Partly as a result, secular authority is highly centralized in the hands of a relatively few men, bishops. However these fifty or so men do not have, sacerdotally as bishops, as distinctive or elevated a status as in the Episcopal church. Between the Methodist bishop and minister is an intermediate layer of officials with considerable authority, the district superintendents, who number from three to six in each of the one hundred or so annual conferences. The main interest of this study in the Methodist church is whether the great formal centralization of authority to appoint ministers to jobs leads to very different actual behavior, as reflected in vacancy chains, from that in the decentralized Episcopal church.

The Episcopal church has many more bishops, each attached to a particular and often small diocese. The bishops are of much more importance ideologically but with much less concrete power than in Methodism. The lay vestry of the self-supporting Episcopal parish has complete authority to choose the rector. Once installed, however, he has life tenure by the formal rules. The overriding element of the system is not so much decentralized power in the hands of laity as it is a low level of power everywhere. Both the Episcopal and Methodist churches are offshoots, in quite different ways, of the Church of England. The Episcopal church, even in the twentieth century has close ideological ties with other Anglican churches; in the data from earlier in this century and before, there is seen a fair amount of movement of clergy among the units of the loose-knit Anglican communion. The Episcopal church has had none but the most trivial fractionating tendencies, and it survived the Civil War intact. Perhaps as a result, it has a more clear-cut tradition than do the Presbyterian and Methodist churches of ideological parties within it—a small but intense Catholic movement; a larger evangelical or nonliturgical wing; and a large, central mass. The Episcopal church has the highest social status of Protestant churches in the United States and a tradition of a scholarly, well-paid clergy.[3] It does not excel in missionary zeal and generosity and maintains its size in both clergy and membership only through large-scale entrance by adult members from other religious backgrounds. The main interests of this study in the Episcopal church lie in the possible effects on mobility of a voluntaristic structure with low levels of power, ideological as opposed to organizational splits, and a great concern with status.

Split by the Civil War, the Presbyterian church has never reunified, but there is extensive interchange of clergy between the northern and southern branches. Admission and discipline of clergy, as in the Methodist church, are in the hands of the collegium of clergy of the basic regional unit. There are, however, no bishops, only officials elected for short terms from the clergy; and control of policy is in the hands of the group of clergy. Perhaps as a result, the size of the effectively independent regional unit, the presbytery, is much less than that of even the Episcopal diocese. The local congregation both appoints and can dismiss the minister. The main interest of this study in the Presbyterian church concerns the effects of decentralized lay power in appointments.

These are only thumbnail sketches of very complex historical bodies. More detail will be introduced in explaining the rules for coding vacancy chains and when interpreting the results of measurements and models. The central facts about all these churches, seen as organizations of clergy, that make them useful for study as test cases are:

1. There is a set of long-lived jobs, mainly rectorships of churches, with distinct names and fixed locations.
2. There is a clearly defined population of men eligible for the jobs—ordained clergy of the given national church.
3. Most of the jobs are 1–1 jobs, that is, a single individual fills each job.
4. Most of the clergy at a given time are in a 1–1 job.
5. Mobility among jobs is frequent.
6. Reliable, regular accounts of the assignments of men to jobs for the whole populations of men and jobs are available in published form, arranged and indexed systematically.

7. The accounts cover more than a century.
8. There is extensive data and analysis available concerning the history, ideology, and social structure of each organization. The abstract models to be developed to predict to and from the data on vacancy chains can be correlated with independent evidence of structure and changes.

Churches are much more than organizations of clergy, but this aspect of churches is a relatively separable one, that can be studied independently of the whole matrix of a church. Certain lay actors, such as the vestry, are relevant in the abstract analysis, but these roles can be considered as an aspect of the organization of clergy. It is not unusual in studying any organization to separate out in this way a layer of full-time, paid managers or professionals whose behavior has a systematic character that is, to a first approximation, independent of the behavior of the remaining actors—of the workers, or volunteers, or clients, and so on. It is unusual, but not unique, for most of the full-time, paid workers in a formal organization to be high-status professionals, such as, say, a research and development corporation or a private social work agency.

3.2 General Coding Rules

A vacancy chain links together a series of transfers, each by a man from an active incumbency to a temporarily vacant job. The date of resignation of the former incumbent and the subsequent date of acceptance of the new incumbent in a given 1–1 job, together with knowledge of a continued vacancy in the interim, establish a link. To fit individual events into chains, systematic indexes of events in terms of the job and man involved in each are needed. Such data, reliable and complete, are unlikely to be available for most large structures of jobs and systems of men.

It is much easier to find a reliable, systematic account of what man is in what job at a given time. If such accounts are available at a brief regular interval, it is natural to infer actual movements by a comparison of successive cross-sections. The interval should be brief compared to the usual length of an incumbency so that it is highly unlikely that more than one meaningful change in incumbency can take place. The interval should be long with respect to the usual length of an interim vacancy so that it is possible for all events in a whole vacancy chain to occur in the interval between two successive cross-sections of men in jobs. A year is a satisfactory interval on both counts for the three churches studied.

In every published annual, the incumbent is named opposite each job in a list of jobs in fixed order. Transfers of men between jobs are linked by reference to the alphabetical index in each annual. Suppose Jones moves from Trinity in 1919 to Resurrection in 1920. Smith, listed at Resurrection in 1919, can be located in 1920 from the index for that year and so on toward the beginning of the chain. Doe, listed at Trinity in 1920, can be traced in 1919 from that index and so on toward the end of the chain.

Some jobs within an organization are not filled by a fixed number of incumbents, and others are hardly more than a definition of a general status. Moves between such jobs and 1–1 jobs are terminal events in vacancy chains. The system of 1–1 jobs and their incumbents through which vacancy chains are traced is imbedded within the whole church to be studied, just as the church can be seen as imbedded within some larger system of men and jobs associated with religion.

Terminal events

At a given time, three classes of men are distinguished: (1) *incumbents*, who hold 1–1 jobs; (2) *floaters*, who are eligible for and can legitimately fill 1–1 jobs but who do not, at the time, hold one; and (3) *outsiders*, all other persons.

Jobs are also distinguished into three classes: (1) *filled* jobs, 1–1 jobs that have incumbents or that are temporarily vacant in the course of a chain; (2) *empty* jobs, 1–1 jobs that are not filled; and (3) *other* jobs, all other possible statuses, positions, roles, and so on, that can be conventionally assigned to men. That class is parallel to class (3) for men; by convention, the category includes jobs that have died or are yet to be created.

A *vacancy* is a period spent by a class (1) job in class (2) except the period is too short to remove the job from class (1). A *tenure* is defined jointly: a continuous period spent by one man in a single 1–1 job. The *middle of a vacancy chain* is the trace of a sequence of joinings; that is, the end of one tenure of a man joins the beginning of his next, which is joined by a vacancy in that job to the end of the tenure of the previous occupant, and so on. The *boundary events of a vacancy chain* are transition of a man or a job from or to class (1).

3. Tracing Vacancy Chains

In more abstract language, a vacancy moves out of class (1) at the end, into class (1) at the beginning, of a chain. There is a duality: a vacancy moves "out" of class (1) if either a man moves "in" or a 1–1 job moves "out," and conversely.

It is useful to refine further each class (2). Within *floaters*: *limbo* refers to unemployment or irrelevant occupation (*retired* is treated as a special category of limbo); *pool* refers to holding jobs that are not 1–1 but are accepted by men in the system as part of normal careers.

The second class of jobs, *empty*, refers to neglected jobs, while *piecemeal empty* refers to jobs whose essential functions are kept going by part-time or supervisory persons.

Appendix A is largely concerned with detailed rules for distinguishing these various classes and subclasses of men and jobs and with relating them to geographical divisions. It also describes the specific data sources used for each of the three churches.

How long is a vacancy?

No fixed numerical answer should be given to this question. A vacancy is the interim period between the departure of an incumbent from a 1–1 job and the seating of the replacement. In most organizations there will be a range of normal delays in the replacement process; and their average magnitude will reflect the normal procedures for terminating incumbencies, assessing potential replacements, and initiating incumbencies. If a vacancy endures for a period well outside the normal range for the given organization, its chain of moves is terminated.

In some organizations an attempt is made to announce and effect all job changes at a particular time on the calendar. In principle all vacancies would then be virtual—there would be no recorded delay in filling jobs. Any delay of over a day in filling a job would end that vacancy chain, since the initial standard search for a replacement in that job would have failed.

A vacancy chain is a sequence in which one event sets off, or creates the occasion for, the succeeding event. The filling of a job that has been vacant for a long time by the norms of that organization is not an event triggered in any useful sense by the departure of the previous incumbent. Often the men responsible for recruiting the replacement will change during a prolonged vacancy, and usually the job itself will shrink and change. Once the normal search activities set off by the departure of an incumbent have run their course over the "usual" period without success, the search process will die out. Some new decision, event, or persons must intervene to start the later wave of search that eventually leads to filling the empty job.

The transition of a job from the status of having an interim vacancy (class 1) to the status of being *empty* (class 2) is treated as a separate step in the vacancy chain. Conversely, any later successful search to fill a chronic vacancy (class 2) is coded as being activated by the "arrival" of an interim vacancy which moves that job into the filled class (1). Thus the initiation and the termination of a chronic vacancy are coded in parallel to the ending and the founding of a job. Therefore the length, j, of a vacancy chain counts the number of 1–1 jobs that appear in the chain.

Inference from cross-sections

The technique for tracing chains treats the events in a chain as simultaneous. When the events are actually following each other with a typical lag of a few months anomalies arise. Suppose that the death of man A in job a in July of 1919 initiated a vacancy chain. Man B filled the vacancy three months later in October 1919 and resigned from his job, b, earlier, in the same month; man C was installed in b two months later in late December, having resigned from job c in mid-December; and so on. The annual report of *who* is *where* in the organization must go to press at a definite time each year. Suppose this is in January of each year. The annual for 1919 will list A in job a (even though he died in July), B in job b, C in job c, and so on. The 1920 annual will list B in job a and C in job b. How will job c be listed? (1) It will be listed as *empty*, if D replaces C in job c only in February or later, yet this delay in filling the vacancy in c may have been less than three months. D will be listed in his old job, d, in the annual for 1920 even though he is installed in c during almost the whole of 1920. (2) It will be listed as filled, if D replaced C only a week after C's resignation, but then job d left by D will no doubt be listed as vacant.[4] The conclusion is that a listing of a job as empty in one annual may be a clerical artifact, given the usual delays in filling vacant jobs in that organization. In such a case, the coding of replacements in the vacancy chain should continue, skipping over the listing in 1920 of an empty job to the man entered in that job in the next annual (1921), then back to the job he held in 1920, then on to his replacement listed in the 1921 annual, and so on.

In this analysis it was assumed that moves out of and into jobs were always reported immediately to the editor of an annual. Suppose, instead, that there is an average delay of a month, then news of C's resignation from job c will be at hand when the 1920 annual goes to press but not of his installation in job b. Thus man C will be listed as without a job, that is in limbo, in the 1920 annual; job b will be listed as vacant, as will job c.

It is clear that (depending on the lengths of the actual interim periods, their timing relative to each other, the publication date, and the delays in reporting changes) any combination of one-year hiatuses for jobs or men can appear in successive annuals, even though the underlying events in the vacancy chain have followed one another in a quite regular sequence of only moderate delays in filling vacancies (and very short or zero delays between resignation of one man and new appointment of the next). It would be possible to construct a complex typology of the actual timings in chains of events which could lead to various possible combinations of one-year gaps for jobs or men in successive annuals. But if there were available the full lists of actual dates of all changes which would be needed to apply such a typology, there would be no need to use inference from cross-sections. The sensible strategy is to adopt simple overall coding rules which will correspond to the true timing of events, most of the time.

1. If typical delays in filling vacancies are small, say under a month, and if conversely a man is in a new job within a few days of leaving the old one, the best approximation is to count each empty entry for a job and each limbo entry for a man in an annual as a boundary event. Some of these entries will be the effect of clerical delays near the end of a calendar year and so on, however, some abnormal delays of a half-year or more will not be manifest in the annual entries. This is the rule appropriate for the Methodist church, both before and after merger of its fractional parts in 1940 (Section 12.1 discusses effects on distributions of chain lengths from recoding Methodist chains to pass through one-year vacancies, as in the Episcopal church).

2. When typical delays in filling vacancies are of the order of a

few months, the best rule is to "run" a vacancy chain through a vacancy in one annual.[5] Only when a job is vacant in two successive annuals will there be coded a transition to the empty class and, thus, a boundary event. This is the rule used for the Episcopal and Presbyterian churches. The number of one-year vacancies in each chain is tabulated, and the average value is reported for each set of chains sampled. A detailed chronological justification for tracing chains through one-year vacancies in the Episcopal church is included in Section A.4.

Pool jobs

Movement of a man between a pool job and a 1–1 job is a boundary event for the vacancy chain. A pool job has been distinguished from all other statuses for men in class (2), floaters, as being a normal and desirable part of a career in the organization. Pool jobs are jointly held by a number of men that can vary from time to time, but in other respects they are integrated into the organization. Detailed lists of which jobs are coded as *pool* are given in the coding instructions for each church in Appendix A.

The distinction between pool and limbo is important in tracing chains, as well as in differentiating types of end point. The number of years spent in a pool job, as in a 1–1 job, is not considered in the coding. If a man stays only a year in a pool job to which he's moved from a 1–1 job, it is an initiating event for a vacancy chain; but a move to limbo for one year is not necessarily coded as an initiating event. In fitting the actual spread of events in a chain to the framework of successive annual reports, registrars may assign a man to limbo in a given year as the simplest way around the anomalies discussed above. The assumption here is that a pool job cannot be treated in this cavalier way; to list a man in limbo in a year when he changes jobs is at most an omission, whereas to list him in a pool job when he is not is a positive error. In addition to this reason involving clerical procedure, there is a substantive reason for the difference in treatment of pool and limbo statuses. Even a brief period in a recognized job in an organization redefines the standing and changes the associations of a man; he moves to a new job from this status rather than from his previous job. A man who actually spends a year unemployed, however, is, throughout that time, oriented to the new 1–1 job he will try to enter on the strength of his reputation as it stood during his preceding incumbency.[6]

3. Tracing Vacancy Chains

The distinction between pool job and 1–1 job, like that between pool job and limbo proper, is hard to draw in some situations. Increasingly common in the twentieth century has been the hiring of several assistant ministers, under a variety of titles, by large churches. Where a single man is added to such a post in one year, and exactly one of the men listed there in the immediately preceding year is gone, a replacement event is assumed and the vacancy chain is continued through that event. The job is assumed to be a fixed job, and it is assimilated to the 1–1 jobs since a vacancy chain can be uniquely traced. The possibilities for movements in and out of assistantships are numerous and require complex coding decisions, which are specified in detail in Appendix A.

Another kind of difficulty arises with a job like that of chaplain of a college, where there can be at most one incumbent but where there may not be any significant pressure to keep the job filled regularly. Somewhat arbitrary coding decisions have had to be made; they vary between one era and another as the relative importance of some of these auxiliary jobs has grown. Fortunately the main measure, the length of the chain, is not often affected much by a change in coding rules for such borderline cases. Usually these cases are in low status jobs normally held by young men. If the chain were continued through an event where the present coding rules would terminate it, usually it will end at the next step, with recruitment of a newly ordained priest from a seminary.

In principle, the criterion for a 1–1 job is simple: the departure of the incumbent at once leads those in authority over the job to search for a successor to fill that specific job.

Compound jobs

Several small congregations are often served by the same minister. In the Methodist church, a pastoral charge consisting of a number of scattered congregations was the norm in the rural America of the nineteenth century and is still common. In its annuals, such charges are normally listed under a single key entry, the seat of the charge.

Compound charges of this kind are still common in the Episcopal church as well. Here each congregation normally is listed separately under its town and with its chosen saintly name. The name of the incumbent priest is listed only once, for the congregation and town that is the seat of the charge. Opposite the other congregations, reference is made in italics to *the rector* of this principal congregation (compound charges lie wholly within a diocese).

The important point is that the combination of several small congregations into a "charge" large enough to support a full-time minister is usually stable. If so, the compound pastorate is treated as a 1–1 job. Such charges are normally small even in aggregate, but they represent a substantial fraction of the total number of 1–1 jobs in most churches even today.

There are congregations that are too new or too poor to sustain a normal organizational framework and to support, even in aggregate, a resident minister. Missionaries, under various titles, minister to such congregations. Almost all missionary jobs are coded as pool, since the number in a particular area fluctuates according to resources in men and money. In addition, all missionary jobs outside the United States are coded as pool, even when they are for large, stable congregations because they are outside the normal frame of reference for filling and seeking jobs.

Compound vacancy chains

Sometimes when an incumbent leaves a compound job, it is split; and different men are the replacements in different congregations. The result is a compound vacancy chain; or, a new incumbent may merge two formerly separate charges left vacant simultaneously. The possible patterns of moves involving compound jobs are extremely numerous, and some are very complex. They occur with most frequency in the Episcopal church. In practice, fairly simple coding rules are appropriate.

The "main" vacancy chain is always traced through the replacement in the seat congregation of the charge, which is normally the largest one. Congregations that split off as a group to constitute a new charge, whether or not the incumbent of the former charge changes, are considered to form a new job, which initiates a new vacancy chain. (When subsidiary congregations are reassigned to another charge whose seat becomes the seat of the enlarged charge, no replacement event is coded, whether or not there is any change in the incumbent of the first or of the second seat; the size of the first charge is reduced and of the latter charge enlarged, that is all.) Mergers are handled in a parallel way. When a charge left vacant is merged with an existing charge without the seat moving from the latter, this is coded as an end event for the vacancy chain; that is, the defining 1–1 job has been abolished, as such, whether or not the incumbent of the receiving charge changes at the same time. In short, compound chains are broken up into a main chain plus various subsidiary chains started or ended by the creation of a new or the ending of an old charge; the ruling criterion is always events in the incumbency of the seat church of a charge.

At every step of a vacancy chain, the list of jobs is scanned to determine whether there is any change in the dependent congregations of a charge. The subsidiary chains will always be encountered in tracing the main chain and vice versa. It is a time-consuming task to locate the entry point to a chain. So, attached chains are always traced out in full and sampling weights are defined accordingly.

Individual measures

When easily available, all the following measures are noted for every item in the chain for flexibility in developing stratified models: *man*— seniority in the system, source and level of professional education, kinship to others in system; *job*—size of resources controlled, hierarchic status, geographic location, functional type; *incumbency* —salary and length of time in each one just terminated.

Two major kinds of measures of the size of pastoral charges are normally available: (1) the number of members, by various criteria; and (2) the amount of money raised, from various sources for various purposes. Data on the number of members is notoriously unreliable. The criteria may be vague and usually are interpreted in a variety of ways, even by different charges in the same church. A typical pattern is a rising number of members listed for a charge in successive years of an incumbency. Then, with a new incumbent, the number is often sharply reduced, presumably as he weeds through the records to straighten them out but, possibly, because of dissatisfaction with the newcomer. When the 1–1 job is an assistant rectorship or one not defined by a congregation, an assimilated rank must be attached —the size of a church whose rector would have roughly equal status.

There are compensating advantages to the use of the number of members. It is the only measure reported each year in the national annual for each congregation in all three of the churches. The number of ministers in each church has risen roughly parallel to the growth in numbers, so that the membership figure has roughly the same meaning in different eras. In recent years, there has been growing pressure on churches to adopt roughly equivalent criteria for defining membership (comparative data are published regularly by the National Council of Churches).[7] The number of members is a major criterion in establishing the importance and influence of a parish in its region, as well as a direct measure of the number of souls to be influenced.

Data on financial contributions from a charge are more reliable but are hard to interpret. The fraction of the money that is raised explicitly for, or sent to, supralocal units of the church varies widely from one church to another. Building fund drives and other special drives lead to sharp fluctuations in total collections. In the Episcopal church especially, income from endowments for the local church can be a significant factor, as can large annual gifts from a few wealthy members. In short, money raised cannot be used as a reliable indirect indicator of number of effective members, nor yet is it a stable indicator of the financial resources of the local unit.

The salary paid the rector is the most obvious measure to use for size of job in a study of mobility, although it is more accurate to speak of it as a measure for a particular tenure. Salary paid will be used as one measure for the Methodist church. For the Episcopal church, the data could only be gathered by referring to annual reports of each of the constituent dioceses, and they do not reveal adequate data. The cash salaries are not high on the average in any church. Perquisites that are very hard to compare and measure accurately, such as parsonage and car and telephone allowance, are a large fraction of the real income. Retirement plans and costs vary. In some cases, salaries of rector and assistants are reported as one sum. Therefore the principal measure of job size used in all three churches is number of members.

Loops

A *loop* is a closed circle of events in which a first man replaces the second in a 1–1 job, the second replaces the third, and so on until the jth replaces the first man in his 1–1 job. There are no boundary events; it is not possible to assign a time order and, thus, no causal order can be inferred for the events in the loop. With that exception, the coding rules above apply to loops. To the extent that loops exist, the hypotheses proposed for the genesis of vacancy chains and their role in mobility are wrong.

3. Tracing Vacancy Chains

3.3 *Examples of Vacancy Chains*

Figures 3.1 through 3.9 are examples of different kinds of vacancy chains. At the top of each chain is (1) initials of person who actually coded the chain of events in the annuals; (2) sampling frame used (designated from the symbols defined in Section B.2); the chain measures—(3) sample weight integer and (4) chain length, *j*.

The format for reporting a chain is a simplification of that in Figure 1.3. Men are listed on the left in the order in which they move,

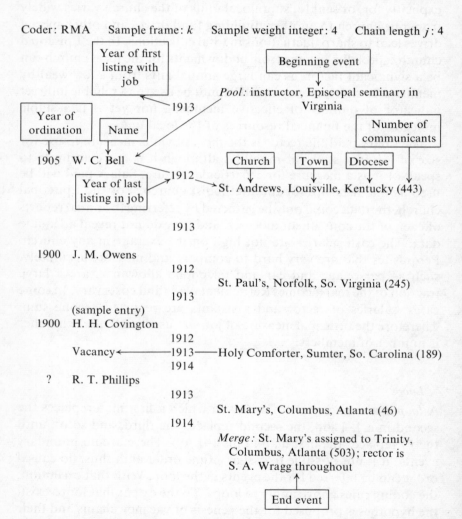

Coder: RMA   Sample frame: *k*   Sample weight integer: 4   Chain length *j* : 4

Figure 3.1   Vacancy Chain in the Episcopal Church from a National Sample Drawn in 1912–1913.

Coder: HCW Sample frame: none Sample weight integer: none *j*: 8

			Retired
		1955	
1919	A. R. McKinstry		
		1954	
			Ordinary, Delaware
		1955	
1940	J. B. Mosley ———	1954 ⟶	elected Coadjutor (Delaware) Oct. 28, 1953 and so listed in 1954 annual
		1953	
	Vacancy ⟵———	1954 ——	*Dean*, Cathedral, Wilmington, Delaware
		1955	
1943	T. M. W. Yerxa		
		1954	
			Good Shepherd, Austin, Texas (892)
		1955	
1939	S. N. Baxter		
		1954	
			Archdeacon, Western New York
		1955	
1935	H. P. Krusen		
		1954	
	Vacancy ⟵———	1955 ——	St. George, Central Falls, Rhode Island (1173)
		1956	
1939	G. E. Condit		
		1955	
			St. Matthias, Philadelphia, Penna. (361)
		1956	
1947	A. B. Narbeth		
		1955	*Grace*, *Waverly*, Central N. Y. (240) Christ, Wellsburg, Central N. Y. (66)
		1956	
?	Ronald A. Wyckoff		
		1955	
	Vacancy ⟵———	1956 ——	St. George, Chadwicks, Central N. Y. (100)
		1957	
1953	E. G. Molnar		
		1956	
			Pool: sole curate for one year at Calvary, Utica, C. N. Y. (712); no curate for two years before and three years after 1956 Annual

Figure 3.2 Chain begun by Retirement of an Episcopal Bishop.

with the man who is first to move on the top. Jobs are listed on the right in such a way that each man's name falls between the job he is just entering and the one he has just left. Each pastorate is designated by name of church, city, and official regional unit (often a state). If the job is an assistantship, it is so noted, but no notation is added if the job is as a rector (the more common case). Other jobs are listed by title and are underlined. To the left of each name is the year the man was ordained to the diaconate or to an equivalent status. The year in which he is first listed in the annual with the new job is the upper number to the right of each name. The year of the annual in

Coder: HCW   Sample frame: *D*   Sample weight integer: 2   *j*: 2

New job: not listed in 1958 or earlier annuals

1958

Mission, Acton, Mass. (76)

1959

1956   D. A. Stowe

1958

Assistant (sole)

Holy Trinity, Collingswood, N.J. (931)

Assistant (sole)

1959

1958   R. L. Conklin

1958

Ordained: S.T.B. from Pacific Divinity School in 1958

Figure 3.3   Episcopal Vacancy Chain from Massachusetts Sample Drawn in 1958–1959. The new mission which begins the chain is renamed Good Shepherd and grows to 113 communicants by the 1961 annual, when Wooton takes over as rector.

which he last was listed with the old job is the lower number to the right of each name. Opposite a job "vacancy" is listed, if the chain was traced through a one-year vacant entry there. To the right of each job, in parentheses, is the number of communicant members in the first year of the new incumbency there.

In each figure, the beginning event appears at the top and the end event at the bottom, with one exception: an exchange of jobs between two Methodist ministers, a loop without beginning or end, is diagrammed in Figure 3.8. Figures 3.1 through 3.6 report vacancy chains traced in the Episcopal church, 3.7 and 3.8 are Methodist chains, and Figure 3.9 reports a later chain in the Presbyterian church. In national samples (k and k' frames) each chain was entered through a move uncovered by comparing the job held by a minister in the index sample of the given year with the job held in a neighboring year. That move is usually in the middle of the chain and is indicated by a note in parentheses. In regional samples (the D frame of Figure 3.3 for example) all changes in jobs between neighboring years in the given diocese are traced out into complete chains. The sample weight integer counts the number of chances that chain had to enter a

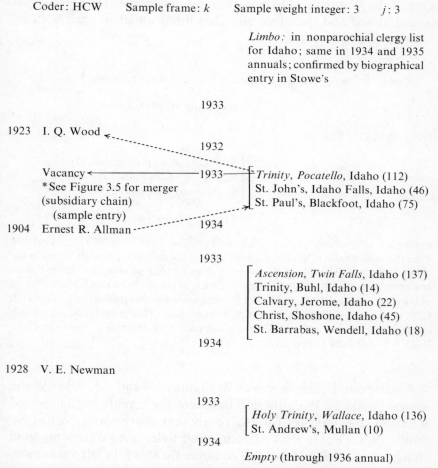

Coder: HCW   Sample frame: k Sample weight integer: 3 j: 3

Limbo: in nonparochial clergy list for Idaho; same in 1934 and 1935 annuals; confirmed by biographical entry in Stowe's

1933

1923   I. Q. Wood

1932

Vacancy   1933   *Trinity, Pocatello,* Idaho (112)
*See Figure 3.5 for merger   St. John's, Idaho Falls, Idaho (46)
(subsidiary chain)   St. Paul's, Blackfoot, Idaho (75)
(sample entry)
1904   Ernest R. Allman   1934

1933

Ascension, Twin Falls, Idaho (137)
Trinity, Buhl, Idaho (14)
Calvary, Jerome, Idaho (22)
Christ, Shoshone, Idaho (45)
St. Barrabas, Wendell, Idaho (18)

1934

1928   V. E. Newman

1933

Holy Trinity, Wallace, Idaho (136)
St. Andrew's, Mullan (10)

1934

Empty (through 1936 annual)

Figure 3.4   Main Branch of an Episcopal Vacancy Chain from a National Sample Drawn in 1933–1934. The subsidiary chain, Figure 3.5, contributes nothing to k in this case.

3. Tracing Vacancy Chains

sample drawn in that frame: to correct for sampling bias the reciprocal of that integer is used. Appendix B contains a full explanation of sampling and weighting. Table B.1 reports, in shorthand, the complete sample of Episcopal chains in which the chain in Figure 3.1 was drawn; Table B.2 shows each step in the calculation of the weighted length distribution for that sample.

No sampling frame or weight is applicable to Figure 3.2. It is one of the complete population of chains defined by the promotions of the men who are principal bishops of Episcopal dioceses in 1962. One of the jobs in that chain is a compound charge. The seat church is underlined and the other churches listed under it, each with its number of communicants.

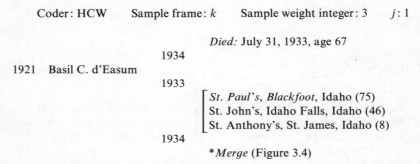

Coder: HCW   Sample frame: k Sample weight integer: 3 j: 1

Died: July 31, 1933, age 67

              1934

1921   Basil C. d'Easum

              1933

                         St. Paul's, Blackfoot, Idaho (75)
                         St. John's, Idaho Falls, Idaho (46)
                         St. Anthony's, St. James, Idaho (8)

              1934

                     *Merge (Figure 3.4)

Figure 3.5   Subsidiary Chain to chain in Figure 3.4. The k value of 3 comes entirely from the main chain; d'Easum, the only man in the subsidiary branch, is not in the clergy index in 1934 (only in the necrology) and so has no chance to enter this or any other sample tracing from year $x + 1$ back to year x. Note that d'Easum is one of the clergy ordained late, at 54. The St. James mission was reassigned to Fort Hall (150) whose rector, Stringfellow, remains throughout. That event is consistent with coding the endpoint as "merge," but it does not play any role in the main chain (Figure 3.4) or in any other chain.

A compound chain is shown in Figures 3.4 and 3.5. After Wood leaves Trinity in 1932, the job is vacant for a year. In that period d'Easum, the minister for the compound charge with seat at St. Paul's, dies. Thus in 1934 Allman is able to leave his own compound charge elsewhere in Idaho and combine the two jobs left vacant into a new compound charge.

Each chain contributes to a sense of the patterns of mobility in that national church. Figure 3.1 is an early one (although sets of chains were successfully traced in Massachusetts as far back as 1875) and illustrates the tendency at that time for the South to be relatively self-contained in the Episcopal church. The Methodist church then and the Presbyterian church still were actually fissioned into independent organizations in South and North.

Figure 3.2 largely runs through elite positions and elite men. Figures 3.3, 3.4, and 3.5 are at the other end of the spectrum, representing the struggles of new young priests and of older men in obscure work in the hinterlands during the Depression. The Canadian in Figure 3.6 is coded as ending the chain by taking over the Redeemer

Coder: PRL   Sample frame: k' Sample weight integer: 2 $j: 2$

		Retired
	1943	
1922 P. T. Edrop		
	1942	
Vacancy ⟵———	1943 ——	*Dean*, Christ Cathedral, Springfield, W. Mass. (1033)
	1944	
1931 D. J. Campbell (sample entry)		
	1943	
		Redeemer, Providence, R.I. (701)
	1944	
1930 L. D. Batchelor		
	1943	
		Transfer: received from Church of England in Canada

Figure 3.6   Episcopal Vacancy Chain from a National Sample Drawn in 1943–1944.

in the United States; but, no doubt, his departure set off a chain of moves in the Canadian Anglican church. If it were not wartime it seems unlikely that a "foreign" priest would have received such a rich job as his first appointment, although the Redeemer was probably a "high" church in ritual and ideology that would be more likely to invite someone from the rather "high" and conservative Canadian church.

As can be seen in Figure 3.7, moves in the Methodist church are much more likely to fall in chains completely contained within one

3. Tracing Vacancy Chains

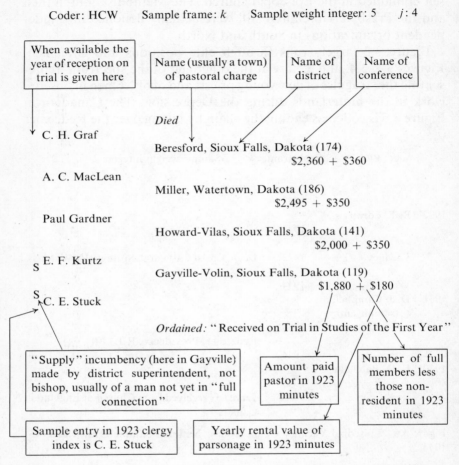

Figure 3.7 Vacancy Chain in the Methodist Church from a Fall Conferences Sample Drawn in 1922–1923. There are two groups of annual conferences, one in the spring and one in the fall; minutes are published separately. A one-year vacancy terminates any Methodist chain. Hence, year need not be specified here. The year of the first national minutes in which a new incumbency appears is always 1923 and the last year of each old incumbency is always 1922. Compound charges are hyphenated in the minutes and are done so here. The minutes do not report data separately for the constituent congregations.

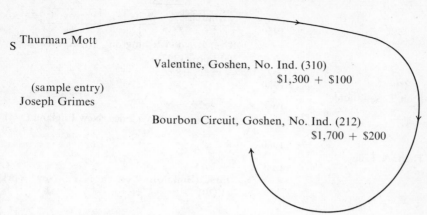

Coder: RMA   Sample frame: k Sample weight integer: 2 j: 2

S Thurman Mott

Valentine, Goshen, No. Ind. (310)
$1,300 + $100

(sample entry)
Joseph Grimes

Bourbon Circuit, Goshen, No. Ind. (212)
$1,700 + $200

Figure 3.8   Loop of Two Moves in the Methodist Church from a Spring Conferences Sample Drawn in 1922–1923.

diocesan unit. Presbyterian chains, like typical Episcopal chains, spread through many regions; the church is so decentralized in personnel practices that calls to new clergy take a long time. In consequence, there are many more listings of clergy in limbo status in the course of a chain, as illustrated in Figure 3.9.

The coding rules, like the sampling procedures defined in Appendix B, are complex. Much of the intricacy would be required in any careful study of mobility, whether or not vacancy chains were introduced. Splits of jobs, the meaning of listing jobs as vacant for a year, the distinction between pool and limbo status, these and other problems have to be resolved just to define operational measures of mobility. It is unlikely that coding rules for other organizations will be simpler than for clergys.

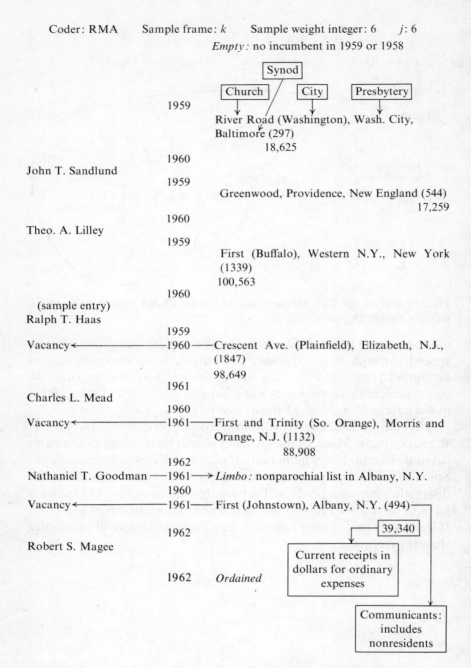

Coder: RMA   Sample frame: *k*   Sample weight integer: 6   *j*: 6

Empty: no incumbent in 1959 or 1958

Synod

Church   City   Presbytery

1959

River Road (Washington), Wash. City,
Baltimore (297)
18,625

1960

John T. Sandlund

1959

Greenwood, Providence, New England (544)
17,259

1960

Theo. A. Lilley

1959

First (Buffalo), Western N.Y., New York
(1339)
100,563

1960

(sample entry)
Ralph T. Haas

1959

Vacancy ⟵ —————— 1960 —— Crescent Ave. (Plainfield), Elizabeth, N.J.,
(1847)
98,649

1961

Charles L. Mead

1960

Vacancy ⟵ —————— 1961 —— First and Trinity (So. Orange), Morris and
Orange, N.J. (1132)
88,908

1962

Nathaniel T. Goodman ——— 1961 ⟶ *Limbo:* nonparochial list in Albany, N.Y.

1960

Vacancy ⟵ —————— 1961 —— First (Johnstown), Albany, N.Y. (494) ——

1962

Robert S. Magee

39,340

1962   *Ordained*

Current receipts in
dollars for ordinary
expenses

Communicants:
includes
nonresidents

Figure 3.9   Vacancy Chain in the Presbyterian Church from a National Sample Drawn in 1959–1960. The Baltimore synod was changed to Chesapeake in 1960. Much more often than in the Methodist church there are mergers, splits, and transfers of presbyteries and even synods.

Chapter 4
Specifying a Stratified Model

Most moves occur in chains of substantial length (see Appendix C). Given a beginning event it should be possible to explain successive moves in, and the termination of, the chain. In Chapter 2 a family of models was formulated in terms of probabilities of transitions by vacancies. Here particular models are specified for application to national samples of chains in the Episcopal church. Stability of and coherence among transition probabilities are the principal criteria in specifying models. Suitable groupings of 1–1 jobs into three strata according to size are worked out in some detail in Sections 4.3 and 4.4. Values of the transition probabilities among strata are estimated separately from samples drawn at ten-year intervals, and the model is given a preliminary test for each decade independently. The meaning of the estimated values is explored. On the assumption that these parameters are constant, more stringent tests of the fit of the model to the observed chains will be developed in Chapter 5.

4.1 Length Distributions of Chains over Five Decades

Moves are tabulated by chain length in Appendix C. Here the chains themselves are tabulated according to length. The weighting procedure is explained in Appendix B. Table 4.1 supplies the distributions found in five national Episcopal samples. The mean length of chain observed, designated as J_c, fluctuates around 2.0, dropping sharply in the Depression and perhaps rising to a new plateau in recent years.[1] Sampling variability can be assessed by comparing the means from the subsamples, k and k', of which each K sample in Table 4.1 is composed. This variability is substantial, as seen in Table 4.2, but not so large as to obscure the rank order of decades by mean length of chain.

J_c can also be estimated from just the sample entries to a set of chains; in Section B.7, formulas are developed for two different estimates of J_c on the basis of such a set of moves. These estimates are given in Table 4.2. They should agree with the J_c from weighted chains, if the weights have been computed properly. Agreement can

4. Specifying a Stratified Model

Table 4.1 Percentage Distributions of (Weighted) Chains by Length j,[a]
K Samples[b] in Five Decades in the Episcopal Church

j*	1912–1913	1922–1923	1933–1934	1943–1944	1954–1955
1	60.0	47.7	65.8	61.2	40.9
2	26.4	32.4	24.0	18.5	32.4
3	4.6	2.1	6.0	12.1	12.6
4	3.6	8.5	4.2	5.3	5.6
5	2.0	4.5		0	2.0
6	1.5	2.7		0.8	3.3
7	0	2.1		1.5	1.2
8	1.2			0.6	0.4
9	0.6				0.7
10					0.6
11					0
12					0.3

$$N_K** = 18.050 \quad N_K = 16.451 \quad N_K = 14.567 \quad N_K = 17.972 \quad N_K = 28.026^c$$
$$J_c\dagger = 1.75 \quad J_c = 2.06 \quad J_c = 1.49 \quad J_c = 1.76 \quad J_c = 2.23$$

Raw number[d] (41)   (39)   (31)   (35)   (81)

[a] Table B.2 shows the calculations required for the sample set of chains in Table B.1, which is the k sample contained in the K sample for the 1912–1913 decade here.

[b] K samples are minus the loops; that is, without chains which form complete cycles without beginning or ending events. These loops are itemized in Section C.2; if they are added to the sets above, the resulting distributions are consistent with those for moves reported in Table C.1.

[c] Three sets are included here, two from the k sample frame and one from the k' frame. As a result, the sampling ratio is 50 percent larger than in the other decades, in each of which one k and one k' set are combined.

[d] This consists of number of entries to chains drawn in the k and k' samples, minus the number of loops, plus the number of subsidiary chains from compound chains, plus any enlargements of k' and k samples in constructing the K sample (see Section B.2).

* In this and subsequent tables, j will represent length.

** In this and subsequent tables, N_K will represent total weighted number of chains.

† In this and subsequent tables, J_c will represent mean length.

only be approximate because entry and chain estimates are each subject to sampling variability. The agreement seems reasonable except that the sample entry estimates are rather consistently higher.

The weighted number of chains in a set N_K is an estimate of the number of chains attributable to the sample of clergy drawn from the index and traced to the neighbor year. Each chain has one beginning point and one end point; N_K should agree with the number of end events and with the number of beginning events found among moves by the index sample. The latter two numbers are listed at the bottom of Table 4.2. Both are lower than the corresponding N_K with one exception.

Both k and k' sample entries have been combined to yield the estimates of the preceding two paragraphs, which are compared with the weighted chain estimates for the combined K sample. But k samples are blind to deaths as sample entries, and the index samples drawn in the k' frame cannot include moves by new recruits into jobs.

Table 4.2   Other Estimates of Mean Chain Length and Number of Chains

Source	1912–1913	1922–1923	1933–1934	1943–1944	1954–1955
Subsamples of weighted chains					
			Mean chain length		
Forward trace (k')[a]	1.78	2.25	1.53	2.15	2.22
Back trace (k)	1.73	1.92	1.42	1.45	2.29
Sample entry moves alone					
			Mean chain length		
J_c (moves into jobs)[b]	1.88	2.60	1.33	2.00	2.24
J'_c (moves out of jobs)[b]	1.71	2.60	2.90	2.14	3.50
			Number of chains[c]		
Beginning events	16	13	15	14	25
Ending events	17	13	16	14	18

[a] See Appendix B. Enlarged as described in Table C.2 to correct for overlooked chains.
[b] Formulas given in Section B.7.
[c] To be compared with N_K in Table 4.1.

Hence both the number of end events and the number of entry events are underestimated when the k and k' sample entries are combined. It is to be expected that the J_c from sample entries is too high and the number of chains too low.

Two purposes have been served by comparing sample entry estimates with weighted chain estimates. First, the concept of weighting is shown not to be greatly in error, since there is rough agreement. Second, it is shown that estimates from sample entries alone, not traced out into full chains, have systematic biases. Mobility is a complex pattern that depends on both creation and death of both jobs

4. Specifying a Stratified Model

and men. No simple sampling of one kind of event for one kind of actor can yield complete measures of mobility.

4.2 Binomial Model

All jobs are lumped in a single stratum. In each decade, two estimates of the termination probability can be made. One estimate, based on all *moves*, uses equation (2.19), which reduces to (2.12). The other is the fraction of all *chains* that are of length one (see Table 4.3).

The binomial model predicts that the number of chains decreases by a fixed ratio between successive values of j [see equation (2.3)]. Inspection of the observed distribution for any decade in Table 4.1 does not confirm the prediction—each pattern of decreases is quite irregular. However, an observed pattern for a small sample cannot be expected to conform to the expected values predicted from a stochastic model.

The variation in each estimate of p from decade to decade in Table 4.3 is substantial. If there are no independent grounds for expecting the kind of variation observed, it is natural to question whether it could be due to variability in sampling alone, the population of chains being the same in each decade. It seems clear from

Table 4.3 Two Estimates of p, the Overall Termination Probability per Step of Chains

	1912– 1913	1922– 1923	1933– 1934	1943– 1944	1954– 1955	All five decades
Observed fraction[a] of all (weighted) chains that are length 1	.600	.477	.658	.612	.409	.533
Observed fraction[b] of all (weighted) moves that are terminal	.570	.485	.673	.569	.447	.524[c]

[a] Same as row for $j = 1$ in Table 4.1.

[b] Same as reciprocal of mean length J_c given in Table 4.1.

[c] From the first column of Table C.7, a related estimate can be made—the observed fraction of all moves by men into jobs that are not from other 1–1 jobs. It is $61/147 = 0.415$. These moves are the inverses to moves by vacancies that terminate chains; but no moves by men correspond to termination of chains by jobs being ended, merged, or left empty. Hence, if p is computed from sample entries for men alone, as are those in Table C.7, it will always be an underestimate.

Table 4.2 that this null hypothesis cannot be rejected with great confidence.

On this null hypothesis, the five samples can be combined to test whether the observed distribution of lengths is consistent with the predicted distribution. The estimates of p from the combined samples are given in the last column of Table 4.3. The second estimate, $p = .524$, is based on more observations and is used in equation (2.3) to make the predictions. Table 4.4 lists side by side the observed and

Table 4.4 Binomial Predictions versus Observed Length Distribution; Combined Samples from Five Decades (percent)

j	Predicted[a]	Observed
1	52.41	53.31
2	24.94	27.39
3	11.87	8.15
4	5.65	5.44
5	2.69	1.75
6	1.28	2.01
7	0.61	0.98
8	0.29	0.38
9	0.14	0.33
10	0.07	0.17
11	0.03	0
12	0.01	0.09
Total	99.99	100.00
	$\lambda = 1.908$[b]	$J_c = 1.908$
		$N_K = 95.066$[c]

[a] From equation (2.3).

[b] From equation (2.4). The reciprocal of the observed mean length J_c is used as the estimate of the termination probability p, which is the predicted fraction of chains of length 1.

[c] This is the total weighted number of chains excluding loops but including subsidiary chains and K-corrective chains.

predicted distributions from the five decades combined. They agree quite well, even allowing for the fact that they have been forced to agree on mean chain length.

The sequences of linked moves in mobility among 1–1 jobs have been called vacancy rather than replacement chains. The implication is that the filling of a vacancy is not directly coupled to the behavior and characteristics of the prior incumbent, to the job he had gone to, or to still earlier events in that sequence. The agreements between rows in Table 4.3 and between columns in Table 4.4 are some support for this view. Moves are contingent upon other moves in a chain, in that opportunities—vacant jobs—must exist before a move can be realized; beyond that, there is little dependence. This assertion is built into the binomial model (although in an extreme form) in which the only way men who move into jobs are differentiated is by whether they come from other jobs or from outside the system.

The binomial model makes a sweeping claim: a vacancy's probability of moving outside the system can be taken to be the same for all types and categories of 1–1 jobs. Table 4.4 is consistent with this claim, but it is necessary to probe further. There are some signs of systematic discrepancy between observation and prediction. In particular, observed percentages of chains of length 5 or more are greater than predicted, with one exception—the true probability of termination surely does vary by decade as, for example, for the Depression. Aside from these arguments, it is simply not believable that the biggest churches are as likely as the smallest churches to fill vacancies from men not in 1–1 jobs.

4.3 Job Strata and Types of Jobs

There are no clear-cut dividing lines in the range of job sizes found in the Episcopal church and thus no natural number of strata to use. This is true whether size is measured in number of communicants, in revenues, or in salary. Only the number of communicants will be used below, for reasons explained in Section 3.2.

In a variety of official Episcopal reports and analyses, churches with less than 100 communicants are considered small. Churches of this size usually cannot support a pastor without outside aid. Often they are in rural or declining areas. Yet a substantial fraction of total membership is included in them, even after subtracting those combined to form compound jobs of substantial size. It is reasonable to define a separate stratum of jobs for pastorates with less than 100 communicants.

Large jobs should also be differentiated from "middle-size" ones in a study of mobility. Several strata of larger churches could be distinguished, but estimation problems would be formidable. If there are s strata, there are $s(s + 1)$ transition probabilities to be estimated. With total sample size of the order of 50 in a decade (see the row for M in Table C.1) it would be hard to make estimates with any reliability using as many as four strata. Moreover, any one stratum which had only a small fraction of the jobs would yield too few observations for meaningful estimation.

In Table 4.5, sizes of 1–1 jobs are reported by decade for the

Table 4.5   Classification of Pastorates by Number of Communicants in Five Decades in the Episcopal Church

	1912–1913	1922–1923	1933–1934	1943–1944	1954–1955	Total
Total size of clergy index samples	290	267	306	315	590	
Total in 1–1 jobs in year drawn[a]	202	176	195	186	386	1145
Pastorates						
Total number of communicants						
1000 +	3	8	4	12	29	56
999–900	2	1	2	0	4	9
899–800	0	4	2	1	8	15
799–700	2	4	7	7	10	30
699–600	6	9	5	9	9	38
599–500	4	7	7	9	23	50
499–400	9	7	13	22	29	80
399–300	17	15	24	21	34	111
299–200	29	15	26	42	62	174
199–100	50	40	45	45	79	259
99–0	54	45	35	6	55	195
Subtotal	176	155	170	174	342	1017
Median size	162.5	177	213.5	281	253.5	
Assistantships						
Number of communicants per assistant						
800 +	8	3	5	2	15	33
less than 800	10	4	3	7	10	34
Other						
Bishops	4	5	12	1	6	28
All other 1–1 jobs	4	9	5	2	13	33

[a] Table C.7, for all decades combined, includes men not in 1–1 jobs. It is not exactly comparable to this table. Here, a man is counted according to his status in the year in which the index sample was drawn, which can be either year $x + 1$ (for k samples) or year x (in k' samples) in Table C.7. Also, here all three samples for 1954–1955 are included, whereas only one k sample plus the k' sample are included in Table C.7 for 1954–1955.

national index samples drawn.[2] Pastorates constitute well over 80 percent of all 1–1 jobs in every decade, and strata will be defined in terms of sizes of pastorates. Assistantships and other 1–1 jobs also must be assigned to appropriate strata. The tentative definition of the lowest stratum seems reasonable: pastorates with under 100 communicants are a substantial fraction of all pastorates, declining from somewhat above one-fifth in 1910–1920 to somewhat below one-fifth in 1954–1955. (The few churches for which communicant figures were not published are included in this stratum.) Coarser grouping of the larger pastorates was advisable for further exploration, and breaks were made at 800 and 400 communicants.

Job categories which differ sharply in total mobility rates should be in different strata, whatever model is used. Table 4.6 exhibits the percentages of the entries in Table 4.5 who move between the sample year and its neighbor. Again the category of pastorates with under 100 communicants stands out. In every decade, its mobility is at

Table 4.6   Percent Mobile,[a] by Size of 1–1 Job, in Index Samples

	1912–1913	1922–1923	1933–1934	1943–1944	1954–1955	Average length of incumbency in years[b]
Pastorates						
Total number of communicants						
800 +	0	0	0	8	5	27
799–700	5	11	3	13	8.5	12
399–300	6	7	8	10	9	12
299–200	0	20	4	14	21	7.6
199–100	18	15	4	18	16.4	6.8
99–0	17	33	20	17	27	4.1
Assistantships	28	14	12	11	20	5.2
Other						
Bishops	0	0	0	0	17	28
All other 1–1 jobs	0	0	20	0	30	8

[a] Each percentage is to be referred to the corresponding total number in Table 4.5. The product, rounded to the nearest integer, is the number of sample entries in the year drawn not in the same job in the adjacent year. (In the terms used in Appendix C, it is a mixture of in-mobility and out-mobility.)

[b] An approximate projection. The sum of total entries in Table 4.5 is divided by the sum of the numbers of mobile entries. Essentially, these figures are the reciprocals of the average mobility rates.

least that in the other categories and usually substantially higher, averaging around 25 percent. Mobility rates in the three job categories for 300 or more communicants typically run below 10 percent. In the two intermediate categories, mobility tends to run between 15 and 20 percent. Three strata of pastorates separated at 100 and at 300 communicants is a reasonable choice on these grounds.

Table 4.7   Percentages of All Moves and of Total
Entries in Various Categories of Jobs
in the Episcopal Church[a]

	Moves	All entries
Pastorates		
Total number of		
communicants		
800 +	1.9	7.0
799–400	11.0	17.3
399–300	5.8	9.7
299–200	14.8	15.2
199–100	24.5	22.6
99–0	30.3	17.0
Assistantships	8.4	5.9
Other	3.2	5.3
Total	99.9	100.0
	$(N = 155)$[b]	$(N = 1145)$

[a] Combined index samples of clergy in five decades for 1–1 jobs.
[b] In subsequent tables, N will represent base number.

The reciprocal of a constant mobility rate must equal the mean length of the corresponding incumbencies. For example, if one-fifth of the men in a set of jobs leave each year then, if the jobs are kept filled, the average time in the jobs must be five years. The mobility rates in Table 4.6 are based about half on entries and half on exits, but the argument is symmetric. In the last column in Table 4.6, average tenures in different categories are calculated from the average mobility rates over the five decades. Once again, on the basis of the same data interpreted differently, pastorates with 100 and 300 communicants seem reasonable dividing points. In addition, it seems desirable to split assistantships and allocate some half to the medium stratum (100–299) and the other half to the bottom stratum.

4. Specifying a Stratified Model

Estimates of transition probabilities for vacancies are based on the total number of moves from a stratum. Each stratum should contain a substantial fraction of all moves, given the smallness of the total number observed, if the estimated probabilities are to be reliable. As a guide for this, Table 4.7 gives the percentage of all moves that are by men in jobs of a given category, for all index samples of men combined. The three top categories must be combined if the highest stratum is to have as many as one-sixth of all moves, even though these categories contain over one-third of all entries as shown in the second column. Once again the lowest category of pastorates seems a reasonable choice for lowest stratum, since it contains nearly a third of all moves (although only one-sixth of all men) in the sample. The assistantships and other 1–1 jobs contain about the same percentage of moves, 11 percent, as of men.

It is vacancy chains that are to be studied in terms of the job strata. Mobility of individual men among the strata will be predicted from vacancy chains. Enough chains should start in each stratum to supply reliable estimates of **F**, the distribution of chains by size of initial job. Table 4.8 supplies the percentages of all (weighted) chains observed in the five decades that have initial jobs in the various categories.[3] The highest stratum must include at least the top three categories, those pastorates with more than 300 communicants, if it is to contain more than 10 percent of the initial jobs.

Vacancy chains that start in bigger jobs should tend to be longer. Big jobs, unlike small jobs, are not often filled by new recruits or left empty. The man who moves into a big job usually will have had at least a medium-sized job, which will be filled most likely by a man from a job of equal or less status, and so on. Mobility tends to be asymmetric between prestige levels and to decline the further apart the levels. Therefore, mean chain length should decrease with size of initial job, and the variation can help to suggest appropriate grouping of job categories into broad strata. The second column in Table 4.8 supplies the figures, which confirm the anticipated monotonic decline of J_c. A better cutoff point than 300 communicants in a pastorate would be 400, if the jumps in mean chain length are reliable. The 300 figure must be retained, however, to ensure reliability in estimates of **F** (see the first column in Table 4.8) and of the transition probabilities (Table 4.7). It seems reasonable to assign assistantships to the middle or to the lowest stratum of pastorates according to whether there are more or less than 800 communicants for each assistant.[4] The category of "other" 1–1 jobs has also been split between strata of pastorates in view of the mean chain length there and the percent of incumbents who are mobile (Table 4.6).[5]

It might seem desirable to replace the model using strata with a model in which transition probabilities vary continuously with the number of communicants in the pastorate of origin and also in the destination job. Firstly, the idea is impracticable. There are hardly

Table 4.8 Distribution and Mean Lengths of Vacancy Chains by Size of Initial Job, over Five Decades

	Percent of weighted chains with first job in a given category	J_c (mean length)
Pastorates		
Total number of communicants		
800 +	2.0	4.22
799–400	6.0	2.75
399–300	4.6	2.04
299–200	10.1	1.98
199–100	27.1	1.90
99–0	40.0	1.63
Assistantships		
Number of communicants per assistant		
800 +	4.1	2.02
less than 800	2.7	1.35
Other	3.5	2.52
Total	100.1	1.92
	$N = 95.139 = N_K$	$N = 182.297 = M$

enough observations to give reliable estimates of the transition probabilities among a few broad strata. If a precise relation among the probabilities for different pairs of job sizes were known, estimation for a continuous state model could be reduced to estimation of a few constants, it is true; but there is no obvious basis for such a formula. Secondly, the process model is no more likely than the chain model to be true in any final sense. Markov models of mobility do not deal directly with the actual detailed influences at work—social pressures and networks of acquaintance, information, and ideology. Markov chains are used as sophisticated accounting devices, that is, as procedures for making more accurate extrapolations, and will remain such unless some theory can be developed that explains and predicts the values observed for transition probabilities. The vacancy chain as a construct needs such an accounting framework to permit investigation of its validity and significance. Eventually, vacancy chains must be directly related to a substantive theory of mobility events, which may not be easy to express in terms of transition probabilities. Meanwhile, the simple Markov chain with few strata is the easiest model to use; since the strata are somewhat arbitrary, it provides a conservative test of vacancy chain ideas.

Stratum boundaries have been defined by absolute sizes, being set at pastorates of 100 and of 300 communicants. Strata could be defined to include fixed percentages of all pastorates. The median number of communicants has increased, as shown in Table 4.5, so that boundary sizes would have to be increased over the five decades to keep the percentage in each stratum constant. There are many objections to this strategy. Present samples are not large enough to estimate changes in boundary sizes accurately; therefore, the true percentages in each stratum would vary in spite of adjustments in boundary size. The number of moves in various strata are more important than the total number of jobs, and the sample bases for estimating the distribution of moves by size of job are even smaller. It is not obvious that transition probabilities between given jobs, which in part reflect ideas about promotion, will vary as the size distribution of occupied jobs changes. The desirability of a change from a job of one size to a job of another presumably will adapt to changes in the sizes of jobs men hold, but the process may be very slow. If the transition probabilities between fixed strata do change, it is as well to be able to see this, rather than to confuse the change by variations in stratum boundaries. Interpretation of changing transition probabilities will be ambiguous even with fixed boundaries, since particular jobs may grow or decline from one stratum to another (see Section 7.6), and the distribution of jobs among regions may change. In the end, the choice between absolute and relative stratum boundaries is somewhat arbitrary. It is a matter of taste, and objections can be raised to either strategy.

Rather intricate analyses have been needed to set strata for job sizes in the Episcopal church. Some further problems will be taken up in the next section, where official church reports on distributions of job sizes are discussed. The task has not been made appreciably more difficult because it is vacancy chains rather than simple turn-over for which models are being developed. Much of the discussion deals with the particular jobs Episcopal priests hold, but it is difficult to assign jobs in any organization to meaningful strata ordered by prestige in some form.

4.4 Official Surveys and Compound Pastorates

It is not individual churches or congregations that are examined as to size in Section 4.3; it is 1–1 jobs. The great bulk of them are pastorates, but many of these comprise several congregations. Table 4.9 reports the percentages that are compound of all sample entries in pastorates, by size categories and decades. The percentages vary substantially by size category. Large pastorates are not built

Table 4.9   Percentage of Pastorates that Comprise Two or More Congregations, by Size Category and Decade in the Episcopal Church[a]

	1912–1913	1922–1923	1933–1934	1943–1944	1954–1955	Samples combined
Total number of communicants						
800 +	20	8	12	28	10	15
799–400	19	15	16	15	11	14
399–300	35	7	25	14	20	21
299–200	21	20	42	36	16	26
199–100	34	45	42	38	30	37
99–0	28	40	51	17	31	35
Categories combined	27.8	29.0	35.3	27.6	20.5	26.7

[a] See Table 4.5 for total numbers of pastorates. Two and three are the most common numbers of congregations combined into a pastorate, but as many as fifteen have been observed in one compound pastorate (in a rural area of Alabama).

by combining several congregations: the few that are compound have the overwhelming bulk of communicants in one huge church. On the contrary, over three-quarters of all compound pastorates have less than 300 communicants altogether. In one-quarter of the cases, the individual congregations are so small, the combined size is still in the smallest stratum—under 100 communicants.

Over time the percentage of pastorates that are compound does not appear to vary much. This is surprising, since one would expect the massive urbanization of the United States in the twentieth century, through a decline in small rural churches, to have led to a marked decline in compound pastorates. Barring wholesale merger of Protestant churches, the small congregation and compound pastorate may persist indefinitely. The farm population continues to decline, but the Episcopal church at least has never ministered much to the agricultural population. Many small rural towns are disappearing, but others are converted into distant suburbs and satellites of urban areas. It is unlikely that population movements will ever stop, and they always lead to some form of fragmentation in which, in a given denomination, many communicants are scattered geographically in small clusters.

There does remain an important question about compound pastorates: is it reasonable to consider them 1–1 jobs? There are many splits and mergers in compound jobs, often at the time they figure in vacancy chains, as can be seen from the examples in Section 3.3. A small job which is simply transferred from one pastorate to another does not affect the structure of the chain; the size stratum of each pastorate is coded from the average of the communicants before and after the transfer. When a new pastorate is created by a split, or an old one ended by a merger, this is a boundary event in a vacancy chain. However, pastorates in single churches also grow and decline in size, sometimes sharply, and they can also be created and ended. Therefore, the mere existence of mergers and splits does not compromise the status of compound pastorates as 1–1 jobs. There is little evidence that in compound jobs mergers and splits are more common than are size changes, creations, and endings in single pastorates, if the comparison is made within the same size stratum.

The question just asked can be put in a more general form: is it reasonable to equate compound pastorates with simple pastorates which have the same total number of communicants? Their mobility rates can be compared by stratum, as is done in Table 4.10. They are very close.

Many official reports on distributions of clergy and jobs have been made in this era, usually published in the appendices to the triennial journal of the general convention (of the Episcopal church). The figures on communicants usually come from the national annuals and are tabulated by individual churches. They are not comparable to the tables in the previous section since, according to Table 4.9,

Table 4.10 Percent Mobile in Compound Pastorates
and in all Pastorates, by Stratum, Five Decades
Combined in the Episcopal Church

Total number of communicants	Compound pastorates	All pastorates
300 +	3	7.4
	(63)[a]	(389)
299–100	15	14.1
	(140)	(433)
99–0	22	24.1
	(69)	(195)

[a] The total on which each percentage is based is supplied in parentheses; totals can also be constructed from the earlier tables.

over a quarter of all pastorates are compound. In the late 1930s, near the middle of the five decades, the Episcopal church conducted a mail survey which achieved a respectable response rate of about 40 percent. The unit studied was called the parish, and apparently compound pastorates were treated as units (none of the official reports are very detailed or precise about methods and definitions). This distribution of parishes by number of communicants is compared in Table 4.11 with the distribution from Table 4.5 for the samples of the 1930s and 1940s combined. This is the most believable official survey found, but even here the ambiguities of interpretation are great. The surplus of small jobs in the survey as compared with the samples could result possibly because congregations were not always combined into compound parishes; it could also result because some reports from the vestries of vacant churches, which tend to be small churches, were included.

Official data on salaries may also be biased because congregations were not combined into compound pastorates. Salaries are published yearly in most diocesan journals but by individual church, not by pastorate. Even salaries for pastorates would be hard to assess because expense allowances, rectories, substantial noncontributory pension payments of 15 percent of total salary, and other hidden benefits would have to be included. Salaries vary widely among churches having the same number of communicants, but the latter are easier to combine in the compound pastorate and may be as intrinsically meaningful for mobility studies.

Table 4.11 Official Report on Size of Parishes in
the Episcopal Church Compared with Samples
of Pastorates   (percent)

Number of communicants	Parishes[a]	Pastorates[b]
800 +	9.3	6.1
799–400	19.7	23.0
399–300	11.6	13.1
299–200	17.0	19.8
199–100	24.8	26.2
99–0	17.4	11.9
Total	99.8	100.1
	(N = 2535)	(N = 344)

[a] From Appendix 34, *Journal of General Convention*, 1940. The main subject of this mail survey was lay employees. Their estimated total number was 16,700, with a turnover at least as high as for ministers. The average wage was $1,160 for the 54 percent who were full-time employees.

[b] From combined samples of 1933–1934 and 1943–1944 in Table 4.5.

Centralized control of mobility would require centralized knowledge about jobs and incumbents. Official reports from the Episcopal church, at least on the national level, seem unreliable and limited. They do not reflect knowledge sufficient even to promulgate general policies that would be realistic. Even in print there are endless discussions about putative shortages, or surpluses, of clergy. The pattern of recruitment is debated. A recent interim report by a blue-ribbon commission on theological education criticized the way most clergy become stuck in one parish; that is, clergy are often unable to move for very long periods. Most other reports criticize the high turnover rates in almost all types of pastorates.

Two conclusions are indicated. First, it is unlikely that analysis of actual mobility will turn up evidence of centralized control or of adherence to uniform policies; it is more probable that the total process will be highly decentralized and fragmented. Second, if the church should ever wish to bring more order and coherence into its recruitment and mobility patterns, a major research effort is needed. Mobility is an intricate process, and a variety of concepts and measures must be differentiated; pastorates may be compound, churches may be empty or merely temporarily vacant, and so on. An extrapolation of these conclusions can be suggested. Perhaps very few large organizations of any kind begin to have the ideas or data needed to set policy for and control the actual pattern of mobility.

4.5   Estimates of Transition Probabilities and Tests of the Stratified Model

Transition probabilities in each decade are estimated from the sample of vacancy chains for that decade. Equation (2.19) is the estimation formula. Since the moves comprise a set of complete chains, equation (2.21) must hold; it is used as a check of the accuracy of tabulation. There are three strata and therefore nine transition probabilities in the matrix Q to be estimated, plus the three termination probabilities in the vector $\mathbf{p}$.

Each set of observed chains is a sample from the total population of chains in that period. A weight, $1/K$, has been assigned each chain to allow for its differential chance to enter the sample. The count of moves between strata is not an integer count; each move of a vacancy from stratum r to stratum c contributes the weight of its chain to a_{rc}. Suppose a chain of length $j = 5$ initiated in stratum 1 consists of four moves within stratum 1 followed by a move to the outside. Suppose this chain had six chances to enter the sample, $K = 6$. Moves in this chain contribute $\frac{1}{6} + \frac{1}{6} + \frac{1}{6} + \frac{1}{6} = \frac{4}{6}$ to the a_{11}; $\frac{1}{6}$ to the a_{01}; $\frac{1}{6}$ to the a_{10}; and, of course, nothing to any other count.

The estimated transition probabilities for each decade are reported in Table 4.12. The first three columns and last three rows in each case contain the matrix Q. The termination probabilities are reported in the fourth column. In the row above each matrix is stated the fraction of the weighted number of chains that is initiated in each stratum; this fraction is $a_{0c}/a_{0.}$, in terms of the designations in equation (2.19). For each decade the weighted number of moves in each row, the $a_{r.}$ as well as the $a_{0.}$, are reported in the last column;[6] from these figures the entire set of a_{rc} can be reconstructed. Loops have been excluded, and the total weighted number of chains, $a_{0.}$, in Table 4.12 essentially agrees with that in Table 4.1, where the number is denoted N_K to emphasize the use of sampling weights. Discussion of observed variations in the transition probabilities is postponed until Section 4.6.

Three length distributions are predicted by the Markov chain

Table 4.12   Estimated[a] Transition Probabilities for and Creations of Vacancies, in Each of Five Decades

Origin stratum	Destination stratum[b]				Total number of weighted moves[c]
	Big	Medium	Small	Outside	
Outside	f_1	f_2	f_3		a_0.
Big	q_{11}	q_{12}	q_{13}	q_{10}	a_1.
Medium	q_{21}	q_{22}	q_{23}	q_{20}	a_2.
Small	q_{31}	q_{32}	q_{33}	q_{30}	a_3.
			1912–1913		
Outside	.0750	.3000	.6250		18.117
Big	.4384	.3892	.0647	.1077	3.091
Medium	.0225	.2655	.1588	.5534	12.339
Small	.0061	.1488	.1728	.6723	16.300
			1922–1923		
Outside	.1024	.1956	.7019		16.456
Big	.3344	.3862	.0802	.1992	4.814
Medium	.0720	.3885	.2682	.2713	10.793
Small	.0405	.0829	.1913	.6853	18.340
			1933–1934		
Outside	.1773	.3775	.4485		14.565
Big	.0761	.0609	.1523	.7106	3.283
Medium	0	.1479	.1738	.6783	9.015
Small	.0481	.2174	.0802	.6542	9.350
			1943–1944		
Outside	.216	.599	.185		17.971
Big	.275	.253	0	.472	6.778
Medium	.056	.217	.126	.600	18.624
Small	0	.340	.081	.579	6.184
			1954–1955		
Outside	.1612	.5157	.3231		27.981
Big	.3897	.3383	.0947	.1774	12.234
Medium	.0540	.2918	.1985	.4556	31.075
Small	.0665	.1789	.1484	.6063	19.217

[a] Estimation formulas given in equation (2.19).

[b] The "big" stratum contains pastorates with 300 or more communicants and the "small" stratum, those with less than 100 communicants. Details and justification are given in Sections 4.3 and 4.4.

[c] The figure for a_0, the number of creations observed, should agree with the weighted number of chains, N_K, in Table 4.1. The sum of the other three totals is the total number of weighted moves M in Table C.1 less the number of moves in loops, given in Section C.2. Three index samples of clergy instead of two are the basis of the 1954–1955 figures, and so the row totals are inflated.

model for each decade, as shown in equation (2.5), one for chains started in each of the three strata. The computations are straightforward and can be done easily by hand; they were, however, done on a digital computer. The corresponding observed distributions for one decade are based on samples of too few chains to be reliable. Instead, the overall observed distribution will be compared with the overall predicted distribution, in which the three components are weighted by the observed fractions of chains begun in the three strata; that is, the observed distributions reported in Table 4.1 are compared with $\mathbf{f} \cdot \mathbf{P}_j$, in the terminology of Section 2.2. The overall predicted distribution for each decade is reported in Table 4.13, which also contains the observed distribution.

The agreement between observation and prediction is encouraging. The set of chains observed in each decade is only a sample of the total population that could be traced. This source of sampling variability obviously affects the observed distribution; in addition, it affects the a_{rc} counts and hence the parameters and the predicted distribution. Quite aside from this, the predictions are made in a stochastic framework. An observed population of chains is a clue to the structure of the process that generates them; the model really describes a probabilistic process of generation, not a particular population of chains. The predicted percentages are expected values, and a second kind of sampling variability must be allowed for in comparing them to the observed distribution.

The overall predicted distribution can be compared with the distribution predicted from a binomial model, as well as with the observed distribution. There is one condition under which the overall predicted length distribution from the stratified model must agree exactly with a binomial prediction—if, in a decade, the termination probabilities q_{i0} are the same in every stratum. This condition is satisfied approximately, within a 10 percent margin, only in the data for 1933–1934. The binomial prediction, equation (2.3), is one of constant proportional decline; the stratified model for 1933–1934 predicts almost exactly a proportional decline, each percentage being one-third of the preceding percentage. The agreement between actual percentage values depends on what estimate of the termination probability is used in the binomial model. Of the two estimates shown for 1933–1934 in Table 4.3, the bottom one would yield almost the exact numbers reported in Table 4.13 for the stratified model; this is not an accident. If the q_{i0} are all the same, then the strata can be lumped

Table 4.13 Predicted (P) and Observed (O) Distributions of Lengths of Chains Started in All Strata, in Each of Five Decades[a] (percent)

j	1912–1913		1922–1923		1933–1934		1943–1944		1954–1955	
	P	O	P	O	P	O	P	O	P	O
1	59.4	60.0	55.4	47.7	67.5	65.8	56.8	61.2	45.9	40.9
2	22.4	26.4	19.6	32.4	22.0	24.0	24.5	18.5	24.0	32.4
3	9.7	4.6	10.2	2.1	7.2	6.0	10.6	12.1	13.1	12.6
4	4.4	3.6	5.9	8.5	2.4	4.2	4.6	5.3	7.3	5.6
5	2.1	2.0	3.5	4.5	0.8		2.0	0	4.1	2.0
6	1.0	1.5	2.1	2.7	0.26		0.8	0.8	2.4	3.3
7	0.5	0	1.3	2.1	0.08		0.4	1.5	1.3	1.2
8	0.24	1.2	0.8		0.02		0.16	0.6	0.8	0.4
9	0.12	0.6	0.5		0.01		0.07		0.4	0.7
10	0.06		0.27				0.03		0.25	0.6
11	0.03		0.16				0.01		0.14	0
12	0.02		0.10						0.08	0.3
13	0.01		0.06						0.05	
14			0.04						0.03	
15			0.02						0.02	
	$J_c = 1.75$	$J_c = 1.75$	$J_c = 2.06$	$J_c = 2.06$	$J_c = 1.49$	$J_c = 1.49$	$J_c = 1.76$	$J_c = 1.76$	$J_c = 2.23$	$J_c = 2.23$

[a] Observed distributions are repeated from Table 4.1. Predicted distributions are based on parameter estimates in Table 4.12. The estimates are based on the moves that form the observed chains; as a result, the predicted and observed mean lengths must agree. In the notation of Chapter 2, the prediction is $f\mathbf{P}_j$, where $\mathbf{P}_j$ is given by equation (2.5).

for purposes of calculating overall length distribution; and the estimate of the average q parameter implied is obviously based on all the moves, as are the estimates in the second row of Table 4.3.

Even in the four decades where the q_{i0} are not the same, the overall length distribution predicted from the stratified model is not far from a binomial prediction of proportional falloff. This is a frequent occurrence with Markov models. Overall predictions are not affected much when strata are divided further. To obtain a real test of the stratified model, the length distribution of chains started in a given stratum must be examined. One way to increase sample size is to combine samples from different decades. This is legitimate only if the transition probabilities remain constant.

4.6 Interpretation of Transition Probabilities

For a model to be satisfactory, the values of the parameters should make sense by themselves; that is, they should form a coherent pattern. In most decades and strata, a vacancy is more likely to make its next jump within the same stratum than to either of the other two strata; that is, a vacant job is more likely to call a replacement from the same stratum than from a stratum of larger or of smaller jobs. This effect is most clear-cut in the middle stratum. Also, exchange of replacement calls is not symmetric. A bigger job is more likely to call a replacement from a stratum of smaller jobs than a smaller job is to call a replacement from the stratum of bigger jobs. The pattern makes sense, but there are notable exceptions to it in the models for the 1930s and 1940s.

The pattern in the Q matrix cannot be divorced from that in the termination probabilities, q_{i0}. These three probabilities do differ substantially, as already noted. These differences reflect a small termination rate for vacancies in the stratum of big jobs, a medium rate for medium jobs, and a high rate for small jobs. Again, the pattern makes sense; that is, big jobs neither lie empty nor wait long for new recruits. Again, the 1930s are an exception.

Differences between strata in sheer numbers of jobs could contribute substantially to observed patterns in the q coefficients. The chances that a given vacancy will go to one stratum or another may well depend on the number of jobs in each stratum. The two higher strata defined in Section 4.3 have approximately equal numbers of jobs, but each has twice as many as the bottom stratum. Table 4.14 reports the distribution by decade as well as for all decades combined. To the extent that transition probabilities are influenced by the sheer number of incumbents available to be called, they will be smaller in the column for the stratum with a smaller number of jobs. On the basis of the estimates for combined decades in Table 4.14, this effect could be appreciable only in the third column in Table 4.12; however, the q_{i3} is often quite large, comparable to the other probabilities in its row.[7]

Table 4.14 Percentages[a] of Jobs in the Three Strata
in the Episcopal Church

Origin stratum	1912–1913	1922–1923	1933–1934	1943–1944	1954–1955	Combined
Big	23	35	39	44	39	36
Medium	45	38	42	49	44	44
Small	32	28	19	7	17	20
	($N = 202$)	($N = 176$)	($N = 195$)	($N = 186$)	($N = 386$)	($N = 1145$)

[a] Computed from Table 4.5 using the definitions of strata given in that section. Jobs without incumbents are not represented.

The three strata can differ in the numbers of moves they supply and receive whether or not they contain equal numbers of jobs. The last column in Table 4.12 states the number of moves made from each stratum by vacancies, including termination moves; this is also the number of vacancy moves received by each stratum, including creations.[8] If all five decades are combined, the bottom and the middle strata become approximately equal in total number of moves; each has about twice as many moves as the top stratum. The number of vacancies that move into each stratum in a wave should be compared with the number of men in jobs there. If the number of vacancies in a stratum is comparable to the number of men, the assumption of independent moves by different vacancies is suspect. As applied in Section 2.7, the vacancy chain model stipulates that no man moves more than once a year. In that case, the total number of vacancies to be received by a stratum during a year should be compared to the number of incumbents. It is a good approximation to equate this ratio to the out-mobility rate for men from the stratum. When the rate goes over 50 percent constant transition rates for vacancies are suspect. In none of the five decades does the out-mobility rate approach 50 percent in any stratum.[9]

The transition probabilities q_{rc} are rates per vacant job in the sending stratum r and they should not be influenced by the number of vacancies to be sent out from r (or by the total number of jobs in that stratum). The number of vacancies received by a stratum c can be seen as a dependent variable determined by products of the total numbers of vacancies sent by various strata[10] and the transition probabilities q_{rc}. To assume that the q_{rc} in a column c are affected by the total number of vacancies to be received in the stratum c is to reverse cause and effect. Taken over all decades, only the top stratum differs significantly from other strata in number of moves received. The q_{i1} in the first column of Table 4.12 is not systematically larger or smaller than the other probabilities in its row. The top stratum receives a notably smaller proportion of total moves in the first decade, but the q_{i1} is not systematically larger or smaller than the same probability in other decades.

The number of moves received by a stratum may vary faster than any other characteristic; if q_{rc} does not depend on this number, then q_{rc} may not vary at all rapidly. Apparently the transition probabilities are not affected much by the numbers of jobs in the various strata either. However, the q_{rc} are not ultimate parameters needing no further explanation; they are influenced by other factors. Obvious main candidates for influences on movement rates are *similarity* and *desirability*. There will be complex interplay between, on the one hand, the desire of job controllers for a replacement of high status and experience in similar jobs and, on the other hand, the desire of candidates for promotion to higher status but still congenial jobs. It is reasonable to expect that there should be highest rates within a stratum, higher rates of vacancy jumps to smaller jobs than to larger jobs, and low rates of calls for new recruits to fill jobs in the top stratum. It is also reasonable to expect that the resultant rates should not vary rapidly over time; they will depend on entrenched perceptions of the meaning of success on each side.

4.7 *Constant Transition Probabilities*

Sampling variability in parameter estimates may be reduced by combining samples in neighboring decades. The 1950s sample base is the largest, partly because three index samples are combined there and it is left untouched. Q and $\mathbf{p}$ estimates from the combined samples of the 1920s and 1910s are reported in Table 4.15, together with the estimates based on the samples from 1933–1934 and 1943–1944 combined.

Transition probabilities estimated from the first two decades combined seem very similar to the estimates from 1954–1955. In particular, the termination probabilities, the q_{io} that are so important in the

Table 4.15   Estimates from Combined Samples of Neighboring Decades

Origin stratum	Destination stratum				Total weighted number of moves
	Big	Medium	Small	Outside	
1912–1923					
Outside	.0880	.2503	.6616		34.573
Big	.3751	.3873	.0741	.1634	7.905
Medium	.0456	.3229	.2098	.4217	23.132
Small	.0243	.1139	.1826	.6792	34.640
1933–1943					
Outside	.1986	.4982	.3032		32.536
Big	.2099	.1904	.0497	.5499	10.061
Medium	.0375	.1947	.1418	.6260	27.639
Small	.0290	.2661	.0805	.6244	15.534
1954–1955					
Outside	.1612	.5157	.3231		27.981
Big	.3897	.3383	.0947	.1774	12.234
Medium	.0540	.2918	.1985	.4556	31.075
Small	.0665	.1789	.1484	.6063	19.217

model, are nearly the same. Contrasted with this stability in parameters is a drastic change in the pattern of creation of vacancies. Twice as large a fraction is created in the stratums of big and middle jobs in the 1950s, whereas the fraction of chains started in small jobs drops from two-thirds in the first two decades to one-third in the 1950s.

The parameters from the combined samples of the 1930s and 1940s are not the same as in the earlier or later decades. It will be argued in Sections 5.2 and 5.3 that the 1933–1934 data show effects peculiar to the height of the Depression and that the results in 1943–1944 are an outcome of extensive movement of rectors into military chaplain-cies during World War II. The vacancy chain model should still apply in each period, but there is reason to think the values of transition probabilities will be affected.

Another approach is to compare the vacancy model with two competitor models, with respect to the constancy of parameters. Inflow coefficients, estimated as $(a_{ik}/a_{.k})$ in the notation of equation (2.19), can be seen as transition probabilities in a model that requires vacancy chains to run backward.[11] This is like a model for the bump chains that were defined in Chapter 1 and are discussed further in Sections 7.2 and 10.3. Both inflow coefficients and transition prob-abilities for vacancies can remain constant only if the total number of moves in each stratum changes by the same ratio, which is obviously not the case. Table 4.16 reports inflow coefficients for the

Table 4.16   Inflow Coefficients[a] for Vacancy Moves in Three Periods in the Episcopal Church

Destination stratum	Origin stratum			
	Big	Medium	Small	Outside
	1912–1923			
Outside	.0374	.2821	.6805	
Big	.3751	.1335	.1065	.3849
Medium	.1324	.3229	.1706	.3741
Small	.0169	.1401	.1826	.6604
	1933–1943			
Outside	.1701	.5318	.2981	
Big	.2099	.1031	.0447	.6423
Medium	.0693	.1947	.1496	.5864
Small	.0322	.2522	.0805	.6351
	1954–1955			
Outside	.0776	.5060	.4164	
Big	.3897	.1372	.1044	.3688
Medium	.1332	.2918	.1106	.4644
Small	.0603	.3210	.1484	.4704

[a] Estimated as $(a_{ik}/a_{.k})$, in the notation of equation (2.19). Total moves in a row are not supplied because they equal column sums in Table 4.15, which, in turn, equal row sums [equation (2.21) for moves tabulated from completed chains]. The entries in diagonal cells here are identical with those in Table 4.15.

three combined periods used in Table 4.15 (the conclusions are not changed if estimates are made for each decade separately). The coefficient for moves within a stratum is identical with the corresponding transition probability within the stratum in Table 4.15. The other entries in Table 4.16 are not as stable over time as those in Table 4.15; attention should focus on the comparison between the top and bottom panels. In particular, the termination probabilities, which primarily determine chain length, oscillate more.

The constant turnover model was defined in Section 2.6. Estimated rates for men, t_{rc}, are laid out in Table 4.17, again from samples

Table 4.17   Turnover Coefficients for Men in Three Periods[a]
in the Episcopal Church

Origin stratum	Destination stratum		
	Big	Medium	Small
1912–1923			
Big		.01058	.00459
Medium	.01430		.03085
Small	.00505	.0396	
1933–1943			
Big		.00728	.00581
Medium	.01938		.02497
Small	.01429	.11180	
1954–1955			
Big		.01149	.00875
Medium	.02935		.02438
Small	.02105	.11216	

[a] The t_{rc} rates per year as defined in Section 2.6. Number of men in a stratum, N_r, is computed from Table 4.14. Rates to the outside are not reported and moves within a stratum are ignored in this model.

combined into three groups; these estimates also are based on the weighted moves tabulated from complete vacancy chains. Estimates of the stratum totals of men appropriate to samples of moves come from Table 4.14. Moves within strata are not counted. No rates of entry from or exit to the outside are reported since these are not comparable to the corresponding termination probabilities and numbers of creations of vacancies, which include the birth and death of jobs. (Thus immobility rates must also be suppressed.) If the Q matrix is constant, the t_{rc} rates in Table 4.17 could not be, and conversely. The turnover rates are not constant; on the contrary, there is evidence for considerable increase in the rates over the fifty years.[12]

A final basis of assessing constancy in Q and $\mathbf{p}$ comes from a return to the motivation for introducing strata in the first place; namely, dissatisfaction with the binomial model. Variation in the termination probability for the binomial model is large over the five decades. In Table 4.3, the largest estimate exceeds the smallest by more than 50 percent, whether the estimate from total moves or from chains of length 1 is examined. This large variation, though conceivably due to sampling fluctuations, reinforced the idea that one could not treat all jobs as equivalent. The Depression and war decades, it was argued earlier, should not yield the same estimates of transition probabilities among strata as the other decades; even when these two decades are excluded, the variation in termination probability for the binomial model remains large, as can be seen from Table 4.3.

The variation across decades in the termination probability from each stratum should be assessed against the variation of the overall termination probability, which is the parameter p, the sole parameter in the binomial model. The estimates of q_{i0} in Table 4.12 are shown again in Table 4.18; they are compared with the estimates of p based on counts of moves in Table 4.18. The values for q_{i0} are rounded to two places, while three digits are reported for p as a reminder that sampling variability is larger when the sample size is smaller. The binomial probability is a weighted average of the q_{i0} for that sample, but the weights are the fractions of all moves that come from various strata. These fractions can and do vary widely from year to year; therefore the q_{i0} and the p estimates are essentially independent.

The probability for a move to the outside from the bottom stratum (small jobs) is remarkably constant in Table 4.18. The total number of moves per decade from the stratum of big jobs is much the smallest and, as might be expected, the estimates in that stratum vary most. Exclusion of the Depression and war decades reduces the variability in each row of Table 4.18. In the other three decades, the binomial estimate declines from left to right whereas the stratified estimates oscillate in a manner consistent with sampling fluctuations.

An alternative estimate of the termination probability from each stratum, by decades, can be given. Lengths of vacancy chains begun

4. Specifying a Stratified Model

Table 4.18 Estimates of the Probability a Vacancy Moves Outside,
for the Stratified Model[a] and for the Binomial Model[b]

Model	1912–1913	1922–1923	1933–1934	1943–1944	1954–1955
Stratified					
Origin stratum					
Big	.11	.20	.71	.47	.18
	(3.091)[c]	(4.814)	(3.283)	(6.778)	(12.234)
Medium	.55	.27	.68	.60	.46
	(12.339)	(10.793)	(9.015)	(18.624)	(31.075)
Small	.67	.69	.65	.58	.61
	(16.300)	(18.340)	(9.350)	(6.184)	(19.217)
Binomial	.570	.485	.673	.569	.447
	(31.730)[d]	(33.947)	(21.648)	(31.568)	(62.526)

[a] Taken from Table 4.12; $\hat{q}_{io}$, rounded to two places.

[b] Taken from Table 4.3, second row; see equation (2.12) for the definition of this estimate of p.

[c] This is the denominator for the estimate, that is, the total number of moves from each stratum observed in the samples for those years.

[d] This is the total number of moves, which equals the sum of the moves from each stratum.

in a given stratum have been tabulated separately. There are too few in a decade to justify reporting a full length distribution, but the weighted number of chains of length 1 is substantial in many decades for some strata. The fraction of all chains begun in a stratum which are of length 1 is another estimate of the probability of terminating such chains at the first step. By hypothesis, the same termination probability applies at each step of a chain, in either stratified or binomial model; it should equal the probability that the next jump from that stratum by any vacancy is to the outside.

These alternative estimates are reported in Table 4.19, rounded to two figures in view of the small sample sizes. They are comparable to the estimates of the binomial probability from chain counts reported in Table 4.3. The alternative estimates in Table 4.19 agree very well with those in Table 4.18, although they are based on different counts. This agreement is of great importance in the next chapter. Tables 4.18 and 4.19 support the judgment that termination probabilities, like other transition probabilities, vary significantly by stratum and in an intelligible way; that is, the stratified model explains more about moves than does the binomial model. In Chapter 5 the stratified model will be shown to explain more about chains than the binomial model; in the main test there, however, transition probabilities in different decades are combined as if they were roughly constant.

Table 4.19 Estimates of the Probability a Chain Terminates at the First Move, for the Stratified Model[a] and for the Binomial Model[b]

Model	1912–1913	1922–1923	1933–1934	1943–1944	1954–1955
Stratified					
Origin stratum					
Big	0	0	.71	.64	.11
	(1.324)[c]	(1.686)	(2.583)	(3.879)	(4.512)
Medium	.55	0	.69	.65	.48
	(5.435)	(3.219)	(5.449)	(10.759)	(14.287)
Small	.69	.68	.61	.45	.45
	(11.290)	(11.551)	(6.533)	(3.333)	(9.039)
Binomial	.600	.477	.658	.612	.409
	(18.050)[d]	(16.456)	(14.565)	(17.971)	(28.026)

[a] The fraction of chains begun in a stratum that are length 1; in the vacancy chain model this probability equals q_{io}.

[b] Taken from the first line in Table 4.3; see equation (2.3) for this estimate of p.

[c] This number is the total weighted number of chains that begin in that stratum in that year; these numbers appear in no other table, although the sum in a row appears as a column total in Table 5.2.

[d] This number is the total number of weighted chains observed for that decade; it should be the sum of the total weighted number of chains begun in each stratum.

From the data presented in Tables 4.18 and 4.19 taken as a whole, it is not unreasonable to conclude that termination probabilities in strata are more stable over time than the overall termination probability p of the binomial model. This contributes to an overall conclusion, drawn from all approaches, that the transition probabilities Q and $\mathbf{p}$ in the stratified model tend to be stable over time, with some deviations in the war and Depression years.

Chapter 5
Tests over Five Decades

Predictions from the stratified model for the Episcopal church specified in Chapter 4 are tested here against the observed length distributions of chains by initial stratum and against observed mobility. Material is presented that prepares the ground for the later generalization (Section 7.8) of vacancy chain models beyond 1–1 jobs. Variation of chain length with type of beginning event is explained, as is the allocation of terminations of chains among the similar types of end event. The dual contributions of births and deaths of men and jobs both to beginning and to ending vacancy chains are emphasized. Ambiguities in the choice of aggregate strata to be states in the Markov chain are explored; the same data is reanalyzed in geographic terms, and the two forms of the Markov chain are compared in validity and usefulness.

5.1 Tests of the Stratified Model

A basic assumption in the vacancy chain models of Chapter 2 is decoupling between successive moves by a vacancy. In a given stratum, a vacancy behaves in the same way regardless of which step of its chain it is in. This assumption has been formulated as the independence of successive transitions in a Markov chain. The main test must be of this assumption. Comparison of the predicted with the observed distribution of the length of chains is a reasonable form for the test to take. Section 4.5 made the comparison in each decade for the stratified model, using chains from all strata, and it was satisfactory. It was, however, no more satisfactory here than it was for the simpler binomial model in which all jobs were lumped in a single stratum. A proper test of a stratified model should compare observations and predictions for separate strata.

The observed set of chains in a decade is too small for separate estimation of the whole length distribution of chains started in one stratum. However, it is possible to make useful estimates of the fraction of chains from a given stratum that is of length 1. Such estimates have already been reported in Table 4.19 for the sample in each decade. Each fraction should equal the probability that any vacancy in that stratum will move outside, if the stratified form of the Markov model of vacancy chains is correct. Probabilities for moves have also already been calculated and are presented in Table 4.18 by decades. As noted earlier, the estimates in one table agree well with those in the other; the deviation naturally tends to be larger when either or both the sample sizes in that cell are smaller. In each decade, by this crude test, the stratified model appears to fit the observations.

The main test of the model should be based on the full length distribution of chains begun in each stratum. Sections 4.6 and 4.7 have lent credence to the idea that each transition probability remains approximately constant over the five decades. The length distribution for chains started in a single stratum depends *only* on the transition probabilities, the Q and the **p** [see equation (2.5)]. Therefore it is legitimate to combine observations in all five decades. Table 5.1

Table 5.1   Transition Probabilities for Vacancies Estimated
from all Five Samples Combined

Origin stratum	Destination stratum				Total number of weighted moves
	Big	Medium	Small	Outside	
Big	.3259	.3019	.0743	.2978	30.200
Medium	.0461	.2678	.1825	.5036	81.846
Small	.0370	.1660	.1502	.6468	69.391

reports the transition probabilities estimated from the combined samples of moves in five decades. Table 5.2 reports the length distribution predicted for chains started in a given stratum; parallel to each predicted distribution is the length distribution observed in the chains of the combined samples of five decades.

The predictions conform to the observations. Vacancy chains can be treated as Markov chains among the three strata. The reality of the differences between strata as starting points cannot be doubted. Even with combined samples, sampling variability is appreciable and will lead to some deviations. The mean lengths of chain according to starting stratum are one convenient criterion of agreement. A weighted sum of the predicted mean lengths for different strata must agree with the observed mean length for all chains, but agreement

Table 5.2 Predicted (P) and Observed (O) Length Distributions of Chains by Initial Stratum, Five Decades Combined[a]   (percent)

	Big		Medium		Small	
j	P	O	P	O	P	O
1	29.8	34.4	50.4	52.4	64.7	60.5
2	29.7	25.6	26.7	27.1	19.2	28.9
3	19.2	10.7	12.0	8.9	8.4	5.4
4	10.5	11.9	5.6	5.9	4.0	3.5
5	5.4	2.9	2.7	2.3	1.9	0.9
6	2.7	7.4	1.3	2.0	0.9	0.2
7	1.4	4.2	0.6	0.4	0.4	0.5
8	0.6	1.7	0.3	0.3	0.2	0
9	0.3	0.6	0.2	0.6	0.1	0
10	0.2	0.6	0.1	0.2	0.1	0
11	0.1					0
12						0.2
		$N_k = 14.019$		$N_k = 39.294$		$N_k = 41.782$
Raw number		(48)		(93)		(86)
	$J_c = 2.54$	$J_c = 2.79$	$J_c = 1.94$	$J_c = 1.92$	$J_c = 1.67$	$J_c = 1.60$

[a] Predictions are made by equation (2.5) using the parameter estimates in Table 5.1. Loops are excluded from observed chains, which are the same chains as in Tables 4.1 and 4.4.

between predicted mean and observed mean in a stratum is not required by the estimation procedure. The divergence in mean lengths is largest where the number of chains begun in the stratum is smallest, as one would expect; even here, it is less than 10 percent. The gap between mean lengths in two neighboring strata, either observed or predicted means, is much larger than the divergence in either stratum.

All samples of chains were combined to yield Tables 5.1 and 5.2. This is a conservative procedure. The evidence in Sections 4.6 and 4.7 suggested that transition probabilities in 1933–1934 and 1943–1944 may be substantially different from those of earlier and later decades. Such differences would tend to confound the predictions of length distributions from a single set of parameters. Predictions should be even closer to observations if samples from just the first two and the last decades are used.

Table 5.3 is parallel to Table 5.2 but combines observed chains only from 1912–1913, 1922–1923, and 1954–1955. Predictions are made from transition probabilities estimated from the combined samples of the first two decades only. (These estimates were reported in the first section of Table 4.15 and will be used to predict turnover in later years in the Section 5.2.) The irregular decades have been dropped; however, the "predicted" columns are no longer based on estimates from moves in the whole set of chains reported in the "observed" columns. Again prediction and observation conform. (For the first time, the mode has moved from length 1 to 2 in the Big stratum, in predicted and observed distributions.) The mean lengths in different strata have moved further apart; at the same time, the predicted means are at least as close to their observed means as in Table 5.2.

Table 5.3   Predicted (P) and Observed (O) Length Distributions of Chains by Initial Stratum, Three Selected Decades Combined[a]   (percent)

	Big		Medium		Small	
j	P	O	P	O	P	O
1	16.3	6.7	42.2	42.6	67.9	62.1
2	27.5	31.0	28.6	32.8	17.6	29.9
3	22.7	16.6	14.2	8.1	7.1	3.5
4	14.5	18.8	7.1	7.3	3.5	2.4
5	8.5	5.3	3.7	3.9	1.8	1.1
6	4.7	12.0	2.0	2.8	1.0	0.3
7	2.6	4.3	1.0	0.6	0.5	0.6
8	1.4	2.9	0.6	0.5	0.3	0
9	0.7	1.2	0.3	1.0	0.1	0
10	0.4	1.1	0.2	0.3	0.1	0
11	0.2		0.1			0
12	0.1					0.2

	$N_k = 7.524$		$N_k = 23.086$		$N_k = 31.800$	
Raw number	(34)		(61)		(66)	
$J_c = 3.15$	$J_c = 3.68$		$J_c = 2.19$ $J_c = 2.19$		$J_c = 1.62$ $J_c = 1.60$	

[a] Observed chains are from 1912–1913, 1922–1923, and 1954–1955; these chains are reported separately by decade in Table 4.1. Predicted distribution is calculated from equation (2.5). Parameters are estimated from combined samples for first two decades only; these estimates are reported in the data for 1912–1923 in Table 4.15.

The match in Table 5.3 is not independent of the match in Table 5.2. Similarly, the predicted observations in one table are not independent of the observed distributions. Observed chains were broken down into individual moves to provide the cross-tabulation from which the model parameters were estimated. The exact degree of dependence is hard to specify.

5. Tests over Five Decades

The raw (integer) numbers of chains traced are reported in each table. The sampling weight is a unique and determinate number for a given chain and does not itself contribute to sampling variability. The weighted numbers of chains are much smaller, and the larger sampling variability that they would suggest for the observed distribution may give an impression of closer agreement of prediction to observation than is justified.[1]

(The reader may wish to calculate "significance levels" according to a suitable test based on the theory of statistical inference.[2] To fully justify such a test or, possibly, develop a new one for the rather complex situation here would be in itself a formidable problem. However, some familiar tests, in particular those based on X^2 or nonparametric procedures, have proved remarkably robust because the rather naive application has often been justified later by careful analyses. A number of such naive applications have indicated that the Tables 5.2 and 5.3 and earlier results exhibit deviations within the normal range of sampling fluctuations. There is no null hypothesis in the conventional sense. Results derived from the stratified model define the parameters of the population from which the observations are considered to be drawn. If the model is valid, the statistics computed from the observed samples should have values typical for samples from that population. The "significance level" should not be a small number such as 0.01 or 0.10 but a substantial figure such as 0.30 or 0.50; acceptance of the proposed model should not be made easy.)

A clear-cut test of a model requires a fresh set of data. To draw new samples of vacancy chains large enough to test against the predictions in Table 5.2 would be a formidable task. Instead, extensive samples were drawn for two other churches (Methodist and Presbyterian); the same stratified model that works for the Episcopal church will be shown to conform to observations on the churches in Chapter 6.

Predictions in Tables 5.2 and 5.3 are based on parameters estimated from tabulations of moves in the chains whose distribution is predicted. A clear-cut test is also possible if parameters are estimated from a fresh set of moves. Moves by men are much easier to draw than samples of complete chains (although it is surprisingly hard to code a move reliably unless the antecedent and subsequent moves are traced out), but they do not suffice because of the duality of jobs and men in vacancy chains. The estimates of all transition probabilities depend on the estimates of termination probabilities. Terminations of vacancies can occur as job endings as well as recruitments of new men. There is no way to estimate the incidence of mergers and endings of jobs from samples of moves by men. The only way to obtain coordinated estimates of both types of termination is by tracing vacancy chains.

5.2 Predictions of Amounts of Movement

Only part of the stratified model is tested in Section 5.1. Length distributions of chains by initial stratum reflect transition probabilities, and they reflect the extent to which successive moves in a chain are decoupled. The numbers of creations of vacancies and the total numbers of moves in the resulting chains do not enter. The vacancy chain model also stipulates an explicit relation between the numbers of creations and the total numbers of moves in the strata, as shown in equation (2.10),

$$\mathbf{M} = \mathbf{F}(I - Q)^{-1} \tag{2.10}$$

The vector $\mathbf{F}$ is a set of three independent variables, determined by forces not treated in the model. From $\mathbf{F}$, the vector $\mathbf{M}$ (the total number of moves in each stratum) is predicted.

The numbers of moves, $\mathbf{M}$, actually observed in a given sample of chains have been used in estimating the matrix Q of transition probabilities. The structure of (2.10) is such that when this estimate of Q is combined with the $\mathbf{F}$ from the same sample, the predicted $\mathbf{M}$ must exactly equal the observed $\mathbf{M}$.[3] However, (2.10) can be used to test the stratified model if transition probabilities are constant— predict the numbers of moves in a later sample from the $\mathbf{F}$ for that sample and the Q estimated from an earlier sample.

Transition probabilities estimated from the first decade are similar to those from the second decade, and it has been argued that they are, in fact, constant in this period. The combined estimate is shown in the top section of Table 4.15. The corresponding multiplier matrix in (2.10) is

$$(I - \hat{Q})^{-1} = \begin{Vmatrix} 1.692 & 1.039 & 0.420 \\ 0.135 & 1.627 & 0.430 \\ 0.069 & 0.258 & 1.296 \end{Vmatrix} \tag{5.1}$$

5. Tests over Five Decades

for 1912–1923. If the stratified model is valid and if the Q matrix in the 1950s is the same as in the earlier years, one can "predict" **M** for 1954–1955 from (2.10), using the observed numbers of creations **F** in that year; namely (4.512, 14.430, 9.040). The match to observation is close:

$$\mathbf{M} = (10.213, 30.485, 19.810) \tag{5.2}$$

$$\text{Observed } \mathbf{M} = (12.234, 31.075, 19.217) \tag{5.3}$$

However, this test is a redundant one. Considerable space has already been given in Section 4.7 to comparing the Q in 1954–1955 with that for the first two decades. The conclusion there was that they are the same, and the comparison above is merely a condensed repetition of an approximate equality already established.

Fresh data is needed. The estimated matrices $\hat{Q}$ for 1933–1934 and 1943–1944 are not the same as those for the first two decades (see Table 4.12). It was argued (and more evidence will be cited in Section 5.3) that special events in the church at the height of the Depression and the height of the war made it implausible that the transition probabilities were the same as in the other samples. However, by this argument, the Q matrix should be back to normal, that is, equal to that for 1912–1923, in the years 1936–1937. Hence, if the observed **F** in 1936–1937 and the multiplier matrix from equation (5.1) are inserted in equation (2.10), the prediction should match the observation. A sample has been drawn from 1936–1937 and the results are

$$\mathbf{M} = (8.272, 13.026, 10.251) \tag{5.4}$$

and

$$\text{Observed } \mathbf{M} = (6.946, 9.261, 7.582) \tag{5.5}$$

for 1936–1937.

The rank order of components by size in each vector is the same. The differences are large, but it is reasonable to attribute them to sampling variability. It is not just a percentage distribution that is being predicted but also absolute numbers. Three are observed, and they are nearly independent of one another. The creations of vacancies observed in the sample for 1936–1937 numbered

$$\mathbf{F} = (4.326, 4.449, 5.033) \tag{5.6}$$

There is even more sampling variability in **F** than in **M**, and this variability is reflected in the prediction. The total numbers of moves observed, **M**, must exceed the number of vacancies observed; there is, then, some constraint on the values of **M**, given **F**.

The vacancy chain model in its entirety can be tested from the fresh data for 1936–1937, on the assumption that the transition probability matrix Q is the same as in the first two decades. The test does not refer to lengths of chains as such. The predicted numbers of moves by vacancies from a stratum i to each possible destination are given by

$$\hat{a}_{ij} = M_i q_{ij} \tag{5.7}$$

The results for 1936–1937 are shown in Table 5.4 as the upper entry in each cell; the weighted number of vacancy moves observed in the sample set of chains for 1936–1937 are shown as the lower entry.

Table 5.4   Predicted and Observed Numbers of Vacancy Moves, by Origin and Destination, in 1936–1937[a]

Origin stratum	Destination stratum			
	Big	Medium	Small	Outside
Big	3.103[b]	3.204	0.613	1.352
	1.703[c]	2.293	0.450	2.500
Medium	0.594	4.206	2.733	5.493
	0.417	2.119	1.566	5.159
Small	0.249	1.168	1.872	6.962
	0.500	0.400	0.533	6.149

[a] The prediction is made from equation (5.7). The M_i there are from equation (5.4) and were in turn predicted by equation (2.10) from (a) the observed **F** for 1936–1937, equation (5.6); and (b) the Q estimated from data for 1912–1923, equation (5.1). The transition probability in equation (5.7) is also taken from the Q for 1912–1923, which is displayed in the first panel of Table 4.15.
[b] The upper entry in each cell is the predicted number of moves.
[c] The lower entry in each cell is the observed number of moves in 1936–1937.

Certain constraints are built into the predictions. Given the observed **F** and three columns of predicted numbers, the fourth column can be deduced; only nine of the twelve predicted entries are independent. It is not unreasonable to attribute the deviations between predicted and observed numbers to sampling fluctuations.

To assess a model properly, a reasonable alternative model should be defined. The kind of predictions made in Table 5.4 were called turnover predictions in Section 2.6, and there the "constant turnover" model was defined as the competitor model. There is one crucial difficulty in comparing fits of the two models to given data. The vacancy chain model distinguishes creations, which are independent variables that can vary arbitrarily, from other moves and bases predictions on knowledge of **F** in that year. The constant turnover model makes no such distinction and bases its predictions on the observed total number of men in each stratum at the beginning of the year. These total numbers do not change much, whereas the numbers of creations may vary widely from year to year. Therefore it would be unfair to the constant turnover model to directly contrast the accuracy of its predictions of numbers of moves with those of the vacancy model.

A simple test of the two models that avoids the incomparability in information required was suggested in Section 2.6. It applies only if the transition parameters are thought to be constant. If the vacancy chain model is valid, the relative sizes of entries in a row should be the same in turnover tables for vacancies in different years. If the constant turnover model is right, off-diagonal elements in a row should be the same in turnover tables for men in different years. Rows for vacancies correspond to columns in a table for men; the predictions for the two models, then, are quite different.

The fractions of moves from a stratum to various destinations are sufficient for this test since only relative sizes are involved. Table 4.17 reports turnover rates for moves by *men* in three periods. The underlying data are moves in vacancy chains. Table 4.15 reports transition probabilities for moves by *vacancies* in the same three periods. It has been argued that transition fractions should be the same in the first as in the last period.

The simple test of the two models can be performed by comparing the constancy of ratios of coefficients in one and in the other. There are only two coefficients in each row of Table 4.17 because of the restrictions in the data. Hence only one ratio of coefficients per row can be computed in each year, and only the corresponding ratios for Table 4.15 are relevant to the test. A simple procedure is to divide the ratio in the earlier by the ratio in the later era, in each row, for each model, and contrast the resulting ratios of ratios in the two models. The figures are shown in Table 5.5. The ratio of ratios is not unity in any stratum for either model. The three for the vacancy chain model, taken as a set, are closer to unity than those for the constant turnover model.

Table 5.5 Ratio between Different Years of Ratios of Coefficients
for the Constant Turnover Model and Corresponding Figures
for the Vacancy Chain Model

Origin stratum	Ratios of coefficients	
	Constant turnover[a]	Vacancies[b]
1912–1923		
Big	2.305[c]	5.23[d]
Medium	0.464	0.217
Small	0.128	0.213
1954–1955		
Big	1.313	3.57
Medium	1.204	0.272
Small	0.188	0.372
Ratios of ratios		
Big	1.76	1.46
Medium	0.39	0.80
Small	0.68	0.57

[a] From Table 4.17: "origin" is for moves by men.
[b] From Table 4.15: "origin" is for moves by vacancies.
[c] The leftmost coefficient in a row in Table 4.17 is the numerator of the ratio.
[d] The leftmost coefficient in a row in Table 4.15 is the numerator of the ratio.

5.3 Types of Beginnings and Endings for Chains

Vacancies are created when either men disappear or jobs appear. Retirements and new jobs were counted together in the numbers of vacancy creations in various strata, the F_i upon which predictions are based. These two types of creation may lead to chains differing in various ways. *Pool* jobs and *limbo* positions are on the border of the structure of 1–1 jobs. Moves to and from these positions define terminal events and thus help determine the number of chains. According to the stratified model, the careers and lengths of chains are affected only by the number of beginnings in each stratum, not by their type; this assumption should be justified. The composition of end events by type also must be known if the meaning of the overall termination probability from a stratum is to be understood.

Table 5.6 reports, for each decade, the allocation of beginnings and also of endings of chains, among four types of event. Included in the type labeled "death" are retirement, deposition, and transfer out (to another national church). Pool and limbus statuses have been defined in detail in Chapter 3 and Appendix A. The type of beginning labeled "new job" includes the splitting of compound pastorates and the move of a man to fill a job long empty. The four types of ending event are obvious converses.[4] Approximately one-half of all chains in a decade begin with a new or split job or with the filling of an empty job. There is also some evidence in Table 5.6 that moves to pool jobs are increasingly important as beginning events. Death (including retirement) is a surprisingly unimportant source of vacancy chains; but recruitment is the primary source of end events for chains. Each of the other three types of end events contributes a substantial share.

Table 5.6   Percentages of Weighted Chains with
Various Types of Boundary Event

Boundary event	1912–1913	1922–1923	1933–1934	1943–1944	1954–1955
Beginning event					
New job	44	54	52	7	43
Pool	16	5	2	34	24
Limbo	29	30	10	22	6
Death	10	11	36	38	27
Ending event					
Job end	28	40	23	41	18
Pool	22	10	10	21	25
Limbo	20	7	27	17	9
Recruitment	29	43	39	21	48
	$N_K = 18.117$	$N_K = 16.455$	$N_K = 14.565$	$N_K = 17.980$	$N_K = 27.981$

A type need not contribute as many beginning events as end events. Beginnings of chains in new jobs are substantially more numerous, especially in the 1950s, than endings in abandoned jobs. Conversely, recruitment is much more important as a chain terminal than is death and retirement. Neither of these inequalities directly implies a net change in the *total* stock of jobs or of men in the Episcopal church. (For instance, men could often take a pool job or move to a limbo status as a preliminary to retirement and only the former shifts, not the latter, would be beginnings of vacancy chains.) The sampling ratio in each decade is 21, and the estimated total number of vacancy chains in a year in the Episcopal church is about 400. The observed yearly increments of men and jobs which are in 1–1 incumbencies are consistent with the increments estimated from the difference in percentage of end events and beginning events of these two types. On an average, moves to and from pool jobs contribute as many beginning as end events. The same is true for limbo, and these equalities will be important when a generalization of the model beyond 1–1 jobs is developed in Section 7.8.

Table 5.7, where average chain lengths by type of beginning event are reported, illustrates the main issue. Chain length varies sharply

Table 5.7   Mean Length of Chain, J_c, According to Type of Beginning Event[a]

Beginning event	1912–1913	1922–1923	1933–1934	1943–1944	1954–1955
New job	1.24	1.56	1.37	2.8	1.80
Pool	2.30	4	4	1.35	2.08
Limbo	1.82	1.83	2.4	1.5	2.2
Death	2.9	4.2	1.27	2.08	3.33

[a] In each decade, the percent of all weighted chains for which each mean is calculated is found in Table 5.6.

by type of event. Chains started by death and retirement tend to be longest, those started by pool or limbo next longest, and those begun with new jobs tend to be shortest. These regularities are even clearer if mean lengths based on very small samples are ignored. If these regularities reflect a direct causal relation, the stratified model is an inappropriate one. If type of beginning event, as such, determines the length of the chain there must be long-range, historical dependencies among moves in a chain.

If the stratified model is to be useful it must account for Table 5.7. The obvious possibility is that the type of beginning event is closely associated with the particular stratum in which it occurs, that is, with the stratum of the job "hit" by the creation. If a type of beginning is associated more with big jobs, say, it should generate longer chains. The facts are recorded in Table 5.8, where all eleven samples from the five decades are combined. Chains with one type of beginning point are distributed in a row according to the stratum of the initial job. The total weighted number of chains of a type is given in the

Table 5.8   Percentages of Chains Begun in Various Strata, by Four Types
of Beginning Event, Five Decades Combined

| Beginning event | Initial stratum | | | Total weighted number of chains |
	Big	Medium	Small	
New job	2.2	29.5	68.3	37.948
Pool	12.5	66.0	21.5	17.816
Limbo	14.2	42.2	43.6	16.240
Death	37.5	41.1	21.4	23.085

last column; their relative sizes agree with the averages in the data
on beginning events in Table 5.6.

In Table 5.8 there is a strong association between the type of
beginning event and the initial stratum of a chain, and it is the kind
of association that explains the variation of length of chain with type
of beginning shown in Table 5.7. The average lengths of chains by
initial stratum are given in the columns marked (observed) in Table
5.2; J_c is 2.79 for the top stratum; 1.92 for the medium stratum; and
1.60 for the bottom stratum. Chains begun by death have the highest
proportion of initial jobs in the top stratum, as shown in Table 5.8;
they also have the highest average length over the five decades, as
can be seen from Table 5.7. The bottom stratum has the shortest
chains, and it is much more often the initial stratum among new job
chains than for other beginning events (Table 5.8); it is just the new
job chains that are shortest on the average (Table 5.7). The average
length of chain with one type of beginning can be "predicted" by
combining the overall mean lengths of chain by initial stratum
(Table 5.2) according to the percentages in the corresponding row
of Table 5.8. These projected figures are

new job   1.72
pool   1.96
limbo   1.90
death   2.18

They are very close to the observed lengths in Table 5.7, averaged
over the five decades.

It is reasonable to conclude that average chain length is associated
with the type of beginning event only because of its association with
the size of the initial job in the chain. The size of the initial job is

the main variable that determines mean chain length according to the stratified model. Clearly, it is size of initial job that influences type of beginning event, rather than the converse. It is hardly surprising that very few new jobs are big jobs—only 2 percent, in fact, even though more than one-third of all jobs are big jobs (Table 4.7). Almost by definition, most new pastorates and split pastorates will be small jobs. However, the percentages of deaths and retirements that leave from big and medium jobs are about the same as the percentages of these in the population of jobs (Table 4.7), as one would expect. It also seems reasonable that few men leave big jobs to go to flexible positions of a pool type, although it is not clear why two-thirds of all departures to pool positions are from medium sized jobs.

At the end of the vacancy chain, the flow of causation is to the outside of the structure of 1–1 jobs. According to the vacancy chain model, controllers of jobs with vacancies choose the new incumbents; in particular, it is their choice whether to reach outside and, if so, whether to a new recruit, to a chaplain or missionary in a pool position, or for a merger or abandonment of the vacant job. The percentage distribution of terminal moves of vacancies among types of ending events is desired, for each stratum of the terminal job; these distributions are shown in Table 5.9. In Table 5.8, the job strata defined columns not rows; in both Table 5.8 and 5.9 the rows

Table 5.9   Percentages of Chains with Four Types of Ending Events, by Stratum of the Job, Five Decades Combined

Stratum of last job	Ending event				Total weighted number of chains
	Recruitment	Pool	Limbo	Job end	
Big	15	42	27	16	8.995[a]
Medium	36.9	23.4	17.0	22.6	41.216
Small	33.1	10	19.6	37.4	44.879

[a] Row sums are the q_{io} termination probabilities times the row sums in Table 5.1.

designate categories for the earlier part of the event. It would not make sense, in the vacancy chain model, to give a distribution of types of beginning events for a stratum in Table 5.8, as is done in Table 5.9. Jobs do not create vacancies; vacancies happen to jobs.

113

Big jobs rarely resort to mergers, dissolution, or continued emptiness to settle a vacancy. Small jobs do so more than one-third of those times where the vacancy is filled from outside the structure of 1–1 jobs. Big jobs are rarely filled by recruitment of new men from outside the Episcopal church; it follows, therefore, that the bulk of the few replacements they do draw who are not in 1–1 jobs are in pool and limbo statuses. The column of total moves in Table 5.9 shows that the great majority of vacancies not filled from 1–1 jobs are in medium and small jobs. The extents to which these two strata of jobs fill vacancies from the four types of ending events are much the same, except that small jobs are less able to call replacements from pool jobs.

The real issue concerning terminations is whether it is possible that the total termination probability, q_{io}, is a meaningful entity that can be constant over long periods. It does combine four dissimilar types of ending events. The average pattern of distribution among these four types has been seen to be plausible, however. Another question is whether the absolute amount of recruitment, in particular, can fluctuate proportional to the total number of vacancies to be filled. There is a long lead time in seminary training, and most candidates are probably rather stable in their commitment to the ministry. However, according to canon law, a seminarian cannot be ordained until there is a job for him. The reality is that while ordinations can be and are delayed in various ways, flexible jobs are often made up for aspirant surplus in a given year. Such jobs will neither be stable nor 1–1, and they do not enter into the calculations in Table 5.9. It is entirely possible that recruitment to 1–1 jobs is completely flexible, that is, it is a fixed proportion of the total vacancies to be filled.

It is easier to believe that an overall termination probability for vacancies, q_{io}, is constant if each of its four components, separately, is constant. Sample sizes are small when Table 5.9 is subdivided by decades. Combinations of neighboring decades, as in Table 4.15, will be made and pool and limbo types will be grouped. Change in numbers of terminations relative to the total number of moves by vacancies can reveal any variation in relative sizes between types of ending and also the absolute constancy of the four components of q_{io}. Hence a partition of each termination probability is reported in Table 5.10, rather than just the percentage distribution as reported in Table 5.9.

The main point made in Table 5.10 is: when a total termination

Table 5.10 Partition of Termination Probabilities for Vacancies by Type of Ending Event, for Three Groups of Decades

Termination probability	Recruitment	Pool and limbo	Job end	Total[a]	Total weighted number of moves[a]
		1912–1923			
q_{10}	0	.1211	.0421	.1634	7.905
q_{20}	.0835	.2414	.0967	.4217	23.132
q_{30}	.1841	.2319	.2632	.6792	34.640
		1933–1944			
q_{10}	.0745	.3760	.0994	.5499	10.061
q_{20}	.2198	.1690	.2373	.6260	27.639
q_{30}	.1878	.2274	.2092	.6244	15.534
		1954–1955			
q_{10}	.0476	.1206	.0091	.1774	12.234
q_{20}	.2327	.2058	.0172	.4556	31.075
q_{30}	.2898	.0867	.2298	.6063	19.217

[a] The same entries will be found in corresponding positions in the last two columns in Table 4.15.

probability, q_{i0}, is the same in two or more periods, it usually is not a result of cancelling changes in its components. Many of the individual components of the termination probability tend to remain constant. The sizes of components in a stratum relative to one another do fluctuate; they do not remain at the overall average percentages shown in Table 5.9. Yet the evidence is not inconsistent with the idea that the total termination probability is a meaningful whole with a reasonable pattern among its components.

It is for 1933–1944 that the most striking irregularities appear. Components in the bottom stratum are quite similar to the corresponding ones in the other two periods, but components in the top two strata are unusually high, even though their relative sizes did not change a great deal. It is dangerous to single out observed fluctuations in this way. Selection tends to be arbitrary: Why ignore the lower value for the pool component of q_{30} in the last period? There must be independent evidence to buttress such interpretations.

In 1944, 10 percent of the clergy were in military chaplaincies (pool jobs), according to the official estimates. In the two samples drawn for 1943–1944, 20 of the 36 men in "stable" pool jobs were chaplains in the Army or the Navy. The effect of this massive growth in chaplaincies on the creation of chains is easy to show. One-fifth of the chains (counted either weighted or unweighted) observed in 1943–1944 were started by moves to military chaplaincies. The f_1 and f_2 in Table 4.12 are larger and so are the a_{01} and a_{02} in the data for 1943–1944. The important point is that men from big, and also medium, jobs for the first time moved in substantial numbers into pool jobs. Partly as a result, it became harder to fill a vacancy in a big job with an incumbent in either a big or a medium job (see the q_{11} and q_{12} values in Table 4.12 for 1943–1944). There was nowhere else to turn but to small jobs or to the outside. The distribution of job sizes among the clergy in 1–1 jobs is anomalous in 1943–1944 in the bottom stratum (Table 4.5). Only 4 percent are in pastorates of less than 100 communicants, far outside any sampling fluctuation about the overall mean of 20 percent. In a number of cases, men who had spent long periods as foreign missionaries or who were in limbo for various reasons, were called to jobs for which they would not normally have been considered. The sharp changes in the q_{ij} in 1943–1944, the rise in q_{10} and the decline in q_{11} and q_{12} seem understandable as an interconnected pattern. These changes are not to be seen as a shift in the underlying habits and structure of mobility in the church but rather as a temporary adjustment to an abnormal (war) situation. The detailed changes in the components of q_{io} in Table 5.10 fit this independent evidence.

The Depression at its height produced much the same effects in the transition probabilities as did the war, but for very different reasons. Vacancies and limbos are much more common. It is as if the whole time scale of activity were slowed. Many of the terminating "moves" by vacancies were to the empty state. Even sizeable churches did not call men to vacancies. "Curates" were appointed as rectors in effect. The most reasonable interpretation is temporary paralysis, not shifts in the normal habits and structure of mobility.

5.4 Geographical Boundary versus Job Size as Strata

Geographical contiguity provides a very different basis for aggregating jobs into states to form a Markov chain. Jobs are grouped in equivalence classes by a partition of the country into regions. As with the criterion of job size, there is no truly natural choice of boundaries: each neighbor of a given job has its own slightly different neighborhood of jobs, which in turn have neighborhoods containing still other jobs, and so on. In addition, there is little reason to assume that various regional strata fall into any natural order, whereas successive strata of job sizes can be assumed to be ordered by effective distance. In the topology of moves, the Southwest may be similar to the Northeast; both, different from the South; the Northeast but not the Southwest, similar to the Pacific area; and so on. The same samples of chains used earlier will be retabulated by regional strata to yield estimates of transition parameters. The regional model will be compared with the hierarchic model developed in earlier sections.

Dioceses in the Episcopal church have real vitality, channeling information flow and influencing vacancies to an appreciable extent; but there are far too many dioceses for them to serve as strata. The "provincial" system has remained moribund since its inception, but the grouping of dioceses into nine provinces provides a convenient definition of similarity as seen by the church. To form three regional strata, provinces were grouped together on the basis of rough similarities in churchmanship (ideology), salaries, occupancy rates for parishes and missions, and growth rate between the 1920s and the 1950s.[5]

The first step is to estimate transition probabilities among regions in the early 1920s. Table 5.11 reports such estimates for transition

Table 5.11   Estimated Transition Probabilities and Vacancy Creations with Jobs Grouped by Region, in 1922–1923[a]

Origin region	Destination region				Total number of weighted moves
	Northeast	South	West	Outside	
Outside	.303	.407	.290		16.455
Northeast	.264	.129	.159	.448	8.154
South	.019	.433	.045	.502	14.101
West	.064	.021	.426	.489	11.691

[a] The same sample of vacancy chains shown in the data for 1922–1923 in Table 4.12 are retabulated here according to the new allocation of jobs to strata.

probabilities of vacancies in samples of chains drawn from the annuals of 1922 and 1923. Table 5.11 illustrates several major differences from the model with strata based on job size (Table 4.12).

5. Tests over Five Decades

1. Termination probabilities are nearly the same for the three regions.
2. Creation of vacancies are also distributed fairly equally and are, thus, proportional to the size of the region in number of clergy.
3. The off-diagonal entries do not suggest any consistent ordering of strata by distance between them.
4. The diagonal entries, for moves within the same region, are large in every stratum. Furthermore, inspection of individual chains suggests that moves are not so much constrained within a region as such but are rather within the individual diocese; moves within a job-size stratum are as likely to cover a large as a small difference in numerical size.

The general impression is that the mobility process for vacancies does not vary from one region to another. There is certainly some segregation, especially by diocesan boundaries, and in this sense the use of geographical strata as states captures an important aspect of structure in the mobility process. One would not expect to have factored out the sources of change over time in mobility by use of geographical strata.

One key question is whether transition probabilities, especially termination probabilities, among geographical strata are stable. In Table 5.12, eight samples from the first four decades (1912 through 1944) are combined; they should be contrasted with the estimates from the three samples drawn for 1954–1955 and with the estimates already reported for 1922–1923 in Table 5.11. Changes in the transition probabilities over time, especially in the termination probabilities which largely determine chain length, seem quite striking.

Sample sizes are not large enough to support the use of many strata; the practical question is, therefore, whether regional strata are as useful as strata defined more hierarchically in terms of job size. Comparison of Tables 5.11 and 5.12 with Tables 4.12 and 4.15 suggests the greater utility of job-size strata. In both cases the parameters for the Depression and World War II years are deviant for reasons discussed in earlier sections. Overall, there appears to be more variability in parameters for regional strata over time than in parameters for job-size strata.

In the Episcopal church, as presumably in all organizations, mobility changes considerably over decades both in extent and pattern. The goal of the model is to confine this variability to the distribution of vacancy creations among strata. Creations are regarded as exogenous events not predictable within the model; transition and termination probabilities are parameters which, while not specified

Table 5.12   Transition Probabilities with Regional Strata, for 1912–1944 Samples Combined and for 1954–1955

Origin region	Destination region				Total number of weighted moves
	Northeast	South	West	Outside	
1912–1944					
Outside	.3419	.3042	.3538		67.008
Northeast	.2654	.0623	.0688	.6034	35.642
South	.0403	.3742	.0520	.5334	37.901
West	.0387	.0247	.3742	.5624	44.953
1954–1955					
Outside	.2193	.2688	.5126		27.981
Northeast	.3975	.0913	.1618	.3494	13.566
South	.0540	.4681	.0711	.4068	19.961
West	.0329	.0648	.3810	.5213	29.009

theoretically, can reasonably be expected to be stable when the structure of the organization is not changed in basic ways. When job-size strata are used, the allocation of vacancy creations among strata does change dramatically from 1912–1923 to 1954–1955 so that the rather stable transition probabilities are consistent with sharp changes in the amounts and pattern of mobility among strata. When the same samples of moves are tabulated according to the regional strata, however, the variation in vacancy creations is not as great and, correspondingly, the variation in transition probabilities appears larger.

The question remains whether moves of vacancies among geographical regions can be described by a Markov chain. As before, the main test proposed is prediction of length distributions for vacancy chains from Markov chains, with parameters estimated as in Tables 5.11 and 5.12. Prediction and observation for 1922–1923 are reported in Table 5.13 as an illustration. Included also are two predictions for the same years from the hierarchical Markov chain. In the first, parameters are estimated from the sample in that year

5. Tests over Five Decades

alone; in the second, parameters are the average estimates in Table 5.1 from combined samples of vacancy chains in all five decades. For the 1922–1923 decade the prediction from regional strata is at least as close to observation as either prediction using job-size strata.

Table 5.13   Observed Length Distribution for 1922–1923 Vacancy
Chains versus Predictions from Hierarchical
and from Regional Markov Chains

		Predicted[b] $\mathbf{fP}_j$		
j (length)	Observed[a]	Job-size strata[c]	Regional strata[c]	Job-size strata[d]
1	47.7	55.4	48.2	58.3
2	32.4	19.6	25.2	21.7
3	2.1	10.2	13.0	10.2
4	8.5	5.9	6.6	5.0
5	4.5	3.5	3.4	2.4
6	2.7	2.1	1.7	1.2
7	2.1	1.3	0.9	0.6
8		0.8	0.5	0.3
9		0.5	0.2	0.1
10		0.3	0.1	0.1
11		0.2	0.1	0.4
12		0.1		0.2

[a] Repeated from Table 4.1.

[b] Made using equation (2.5) for $\mathbf{P}_j$. In each case the distribution of vacancy creations among strata is that observed in the sample (see row for "outside" in the data for 1922–1923 in Table 4.12 for job-size strata; see row for "outside" in Table 5.11 for geographical strata).

[c] The transition and termination probabilities are estimated from the data for 1922–1923. The predictions for job-size strata are repeated from Table 4.13.

[d] In this prediction, estimates of parameters are based on all eleven samples in five decades (see Table 5.1).

A warning is sounded by Table 5.13. Pooling all samples to yield better estimates of transition parameters, on the hypothesis that they are constant over time, results in noticeable shifts in predicted percentages using the job-size strata. For higher values of j, the predictions using regional strata lie between the alternative predictions from job-size strata. Differences in estimation procedures for parameters in a given model can shift predicted overall length distributions as much as can the change from one model to another.

The main test for geographical strata is separate comparisons of predicted and observed length distributions according to stratum of origin of the vacancy chains, which Table 5.14 supplies. The Markov

Table 5.14   Predicted (P) and Observed (O) Length Distributions by Region of Origin of Chain, all Five Decades Combined   (percent)

j (length)	Northeast		South		West	
	P	O	P	O	P	O
1	53.3	53.1	49.0	53.9	54.6	53.4
2	24.7	25.2	25.5	27.6	24.5	26.7
3	11.6	7.5	12.9	8.5	11.2	10.5
4	5.5	8.7	6.4	4.7	5.2	3.1
5	2.6	2.6	3.2	1.0	2.4	1.8
6	1.2	1.1	1.5	2.1	1.1	2.4
7	0.59	0.74	0.75	0.28	0.53	1.7
8	0.28	0.70	0.36	0.70	0.25	0
9	0.13	0.38	0.17	0.57	0.12	0.36
10	0.06		0.08	0.24	0.06	0.25
11	0.03		0.04	0	0.03	
12	0.02		0.02	0.24	0.01	
	$N_k=29.119$		$N_k=35.529$		$N_k=30.506$	
Raw number	(72)		(87)		(69)	
	$J_c=1.88$	$J_c=1.95$	$J_c=2.01$	$J_c=1.89$	$J_c=1.85$	$J_c=1.92$

[a] Observed chains are those reported in Table 4.1; Predictions were made using equation (2.5) with parameter estimates from samples for all decades combined.

chain with regions as strata is acceptable in the sense that it would plausibly give rise to the distributions observed in the sample of vacancy chains. The same was true for job-size strata (Table 5.2). The fits in Tables 5.2 and 5.14 are not sufficiently different to justify giving preference to one model. Instead, the models should be contrasted according to the insight provided. In Table 5.14 the separate distributions by region of origin are very similar, and each decreases monotonically with increasing length in the same way as for a binomial model. This homogeneity results from the similarity in termination probabilities. Groupings of jobs by size, however, segregate sets of jobs that exhibit sharply different termination rates for vacancies. In Tables 5.2 and 5.3 the length distribution of chains begun in big jobs is quite unlike any binomial distribution, and even the other two distributions differ from one another in the rate of falloff with increasing length.

Partitionings of jobs by region; by size; and, no doubt, by other criteria all capture some genuine differences between sets of jobs that are relevant to mobility, that is, to vacancy moves. Only if states are defined by the intersection of several such partitions could the Markov chain be rigorously valid. If sample sizes were increased, it would be possible to justify parameter estimates for Markov chains with more refined states derived from simultaneous partitionings. Yet even total populations of moves in a given year would support neither extensive cross-classification of jobs nor numerous categories on a single dimension.

Aggregation of jobs into strata according to attributes has a still more fundamental weakness—it overlooks the network of particularist ties among jobs and men that may build up over time as particular men build career paths and acquaintance networks. One problem is a topological one of ordering the overlaps between neighborhoods in a population of tenures (see Chapter 12). Similarities of jobs and men in criteria such as size and region, obvious to the investigator, may or may not be reflected in clusterings in the tenure network. When individual vacancy moves are kept as the focus, the model of mobility will resemble a generalized random walk instead of a Markov chain. Another problem, taken up in Chapter 11, is interactions among moves by a population of vacancies, which cannot be analyzed in terms of strata.

Elaboration of strata in Markov chain models for vacancies, or introduction of higher order chains to allow for "memory," seems a less fruitful path for further analytic development than these fundamental reformulations. The first-order Markov chain models with a few gross strata remain the most useful and practicable first step toward exploring mobility and organization in a variety of contexts. Their fundamental achievement is to peel off one layer of the complex interdependencies in mobility. Vacancies are unlike men; it is at least consistent to assume that the population of vacancies in a system move as independent individuals.

Chapter 6
Models for
Three Organizations Compared

In this chapter vacancy chains in two other churches, the Methodist and Presbyterian (more and less centralized than the Episcopal church, respectively) are analyzed to explore the range of applicability of the Markov chain models. Optimum choice of strata is a major focus of attention. Three different hierarchic criteria for stratification are tested: (1) the salary of the incumbent, which reflects attributes of both man and job; (2) the current operating budget of the parish; and, of course, (3) the job size in number of members. Location of optimal cutting points between strata is investigated systematically for the job-size criterion, and the interrelation between cutting points used with the different criteria is assessed using regression techniques.

Three Methodist churches merged in 1940, but all data in this chapter is for the Methodist Episcopal church, North, before merger. In the light of the unusual behavior of (plain) Episcopal vacancy chains during the depression years of 1933–1934, the later sample of Methodist vacancy chains was drawn from their minutes for 1936 and 1937. Estimates of transition parameters for vacancies in 1936–1937 will be compared with estimates from one earlier sample, drawn for the years 1922–1923 used also for the Episcopal church.

Only the Northern embodiment of the Presbyterian church (which has yet to recombine) is treated. Estimates and observations from a recent sample of vacancy chains, for 1959–1960, are compared with those from the earlier period of 1922–1923. The sample sizes are small, and the analysis is not as elaborate as those for the Methodist and Episcopal churches.

Smaller samples of chains for Methodist and Presbyterian churches yield estimates as reliable as those for larger Episcopal samples. Indexes in both Methodist and Presbyterian annuals include names of clergy who have died, withdrawn, and so on, for one additional year (they appear in italics). Therefore, the K sample frame, in which forward (k') and back (k) trace samples are used to supplement one another, is not needed (see Section C.1). In the Episcopal church, such supplementary chains, necessarily of length 1 and weight 1, were 7 percent of the total weighted chains in the K samples; the supplementary chains were disproportionately concentrated in certain regions and job sizes. Larger samples were needed because these supplementary chains could enter only one of the two types of samples and even there had the smallest chance to appear of all chains—as reflected by the sampling weight of unity.

Recognition of the greater centralization within the Methodist church is built into the coding rules for vacancy chains. A single annual listing of a Methodist parish as vacant is sufficient to terminate the tracing of replacements, in consonance with the authority of each bishop to announce simultaneously each year all changes of ministerial assignments in one of his annual conferences. If the Markov chain model, which assumes that both the moves by a given vacancy and the different chains are independent, is to fail in any church, it should be among the Methodists. Decentralization is at least as great in the Presbyterian church as in the Episcopal, so it may be anticipated that the Markov model will work best there. (These anticipations will not be supported by the data analysis.)

6.1 Tests for the Methodist Church

All tests discussed here used Episcopal definitions of strata by job size. Differences in parish size in number of members can be expected to have similar meanings for mobility of ministers within various Protestant denominations. The first Markov chain model for the Methodist church will use the same three strata of jobs by size in members as described in Chapter 5. No substantive investigation of the meaning of the two cutting points will be made here. Some translation of terms, however, is necessary.[1]

Estimates of transition parameters for vacancies for two decades (1922–1923 and 1936–1937) separately and combined are reported in Table 6.1. The stability of these parameters over the two decades is even greater than for the Episcopal church. Comparison with Table 5.1 shows that the pattern of sizes in corresponding parameters in the two churches are similar, although termination probabilities are higher in Table 5.1. The distribution of vacancy creations (the proportions in the "Outside" row) changes substantially from the 1920s to the 1930s and differs in the earlier years from that for the Episcopal church (Table 4.12).

Table 6.1 Transition Probabilities[a] for Vacancies Estimated from Chain Samples in Two Decades for the Methodist Church

Origin stratum[b]	Destination stratum[b]				Total weighted number of moves
	Big	Medium	Small	Outside	
1922–1923					
Outside	.0869	.4915	.4216		34.199
Big	.4565	.3270	.0641	.1523	15.451
Medium	.1216	.3949	.1276	.3559	43.006
Small	.0070	.1496	.2487	.5947	27.811
1936–1937					
Outside	.2114	.4522	.3364		14.689
Big	.4619	.3307	.0288	.1786	9.957
Medium	.0813	.4415	.1039	.3733	21.110
Small	.0568	.1962	.2147	.5323	9.451
Combined samples					
Outside	.1243	.4797	.3960		48.888
Big	.4586	.3285	.0503	.1626	25.408
Medium	.1083	.4103	.1198	.3616	64.116
Small	.0196	.1614	.2400	.5789	37.262

[a] The format and estimation formulas are the same as in Table 4.12. The "outside" row gives the distribution of vacancy creations, f_i, and their total number, F.

[b] Same cutoff points for parish size, 100 and 300, as used in Chapter 5.

If predicted length distributions match the observed distributions, by stratum of origin of the chain, this three-stratum model meets the criteria of acceptability (developed in Chapter 5) as well for the Methodist data as for the Episcopal. Table 6.2 reports these distributions, with samples combined to enhance reliability. The fit is reasonable given the sample sizes (further comments are made at the end of the chapter). As in the corresponding Table 5.2, there is nothing in the estimation procedure that requires agreement between the predicted and observed distributions on any parameter, even the average length of chain.

Since these cutting points on job size appear to work well with the Methodist data, one would expect the distribution of occupied 1–1 jobs by stratum to be similar in the two churches. The last column

Table 6.2 Predicted (P)[a] and Observed (O) Length Distributions, by Stratum of Origin for the Chains, Using Combined Samples for the Methodist Church (percent)

	Origin stratum					
	Big		Medium		Small	
j (length)	P	O	P	O	P	O
1	16.3	22.8	36.2	45.5	57.9	54.7
2	22.2	17.7	23.5	17.2	20.0	24.9
3	18.9	5.0	14.5	11.3	9.0	14.0
4	13.9	13.7	9.1	10.4	4.9	1.1
5	9.5	13.7	5.8	8.8	2.9	1.4
6	6.5	6.5	3.8	2.1	1.8	1.1
7	4.3	6.5	2.5	1.3	1.1	1.3
8	2.8	0	1.6	0.5	0.76	0
9	1.9	1.7	1.1	0.5	0.50	0.7
10	1.2	1.7	0.70	0.3	0.33	0
11	0.81	0	0.46	1.2	0.22	0
12	0.53	0	0.30	0.3	0.14	0.5
13	0.35	4.6	0.19	0	0.09	0
14	0.23	0	0.13	0.6	0.06	0
15	0.15	2.9	0.09	0	0.04	0
16 +	0.39	3.1	0.17	0	0.09	0.2
	$N_K = 6.567$		$N_K = 24.153$		$N_K = 17.479$	
Raw number	(35)		(64)		(36)	
	$J_c = 3.72$	$J_c = 4.75$	$J_c = 2.79$	$J_c = 2.58$	$J_c = 2.00$	$J_c = 1.92$

[a] Predictions are made by equation (2.5) using parameter estimates in the bottom panel of Table 6.1; loops are excluded from these chains.

in Table 4.14 reports the Episcopal distribution, with the clergy index samples for all five decades combined. The corresponding distribution for the Methodist clergy is almost identical: 33 percent of the clergy in 1–1 jobs hold jobs in the top stratum, 47 percent in the middle stratum, and 20 percent in the bottom stratum. (The total sample of 316 is classified by mobility status in the first row of Table C.10.) The median sizes of occupied parishes over time are also close to the Episcopal figures, shown in Table 4.5. Substantial differences appear in only two areas: a smaller proportion of Methodist clergy are in very large parishes and a larger fraction are in the regular parochial ministry than in the Episcopal church in the corresponding period.

Different types of ending events—for example, recruitment of men and abolition of jobs—are lumped together as terminations of vacancy chains. The stability of termination probabilities by stratum observed in Table 6.1 might conceal sharp shifts among the types of events. The partition in Table 6.3, parallel to that in Table 5.10, is, on the contrary, consistent with each type of termination probability separately being constant over time, given the large sampling variability for these small probabilities.

Table 6.3 Partition of Termination Probabilities for Vacancies by Type of Ending Event for Methodist Church, by Decade[a]

Termination probability	Recruit[b]	Pool and limbo[c]	Job end[d]	Total[e]
		1922–1923		
q_{10}	.0129	.0632	.0761	.1522
q_{20}	.0968	.1271	.1319	.3559
q_{30}	.0959	.1109	.3880	.5948
		1936–1937		
q_{10}	0	.1340	.0446	.1786
q_{20}	.1224	.1190	.1318	.3733
q_{30}	.0212	.0458	.4653	.5323

[a] The format is the same as in Table 5.10.
[b] Includes ministers received into the Methodist Church from elsewhere.
[c] Includes men recalled from leave, supernumerary, withdrawn, located, and discontinued statuses.
[d] Includes jobs left empty; according to the coding rules for the Methodist Church a job is coded empty if left vacant for a single year (see Appendix A).
[e] Repeated from Table 6.1.

The most distinctive characteristic of Methodist vacancy chains is extreme localization within annual conferences (described in detail in Chapter 12). Yet the hierarchic Markov chain model, wherein geography is ignored in defining strata, works well. The model must be some kind of average of essentially separate Markov chains for individual conferences. Presumably these separate chains tend to have quite similar transition parameters, otherwise the average national parameters would be unlikely to be stable over time as the distributions of vacancy creations over strata shifted. In any case, it is clearly inappropriate to develop the kind of gross regional strata in Section 5.4.

6.2 Methodist Strata with Salaries as Criterion

A hierarchy for jobs by the salary paid to current pastor as criterion may be more closely related to mobility patterns than a hierarchy by size in number of members. Certainly the attractiveness of a job to a potential candidate may be better measured by salary differences, although the controllers of a job may assess attractiveness of the candidate more in terms of comparability in size and setting between the candidate's current job and the available job. Only explicit models of the spectrum of interrelated negotiating situations can yield predictions of the probabilities for filling vacancies according to attributes of vacant job and candidates' jobs. The ideal comparison of different ordering criteria for jobs would be with their predictive utility in such explicit models of moves, where various possible choices of scale for each criterion would be considered. Instead the salary criterion will be assessed here in terms of the coherence, stability, and predictive power of parameters in a Markov chain wherein jobs are grouped in ordered aggregate strata according to similarity in salary rather than in size. Since the practical question is whether salary is more useful as criterion than is job size, the number of strata will be fixed at three. Episcopal salary data is available only erratically from yearbooks of individual dioceses; therefore, the comparison of salary with size strata is confined to the Methodist church.

Two rationales for selecting stratum boundaries will be applied in turn. Net monetary inflation was small in the United States between 1922 and 1936, so that the meaning of given salary figures does not shift markedly over this period. One possible way to choose boundaries for salary strata is to search for values that mark off the same percentages of clergy in 1922 as in 1936. To enhance the reliability of estimates, the constraint is added that a substantial proportion of the clergy should fall in each stratum. The second rationale emphasizes the comparison between salary and size models. From a regression of salary on size over the samples of individual jobs, those values are picked that correspond to the size boundaries used in Section 6.1 and in Chapter 5.

Reporting of pay as well as size in the Methodist minutes is unusually precise. Not only the official salary but also any deficit in payment are listed for each parish. In addition, the estimated yearly rental value of the parsonage, if any, is given. The sum of these three figures is the "salary" used throughout this section. As can be seen from the illustrative vacancy chains in Section 3.3, the deficits and rental values vary widely and are often substantial compared to the official salary. Salaries of assistant ministers in a parish are not reported separately; fortunately, they were then extremely rare in the Methodist church.

Distributions of parochial clergy in 1937 and in 1923 over three salary strata chosen by eye as yielding the most stable distribution[2] are compared in the first set of data in Table 6.4. The stratum

Table 6.4   Distributions of Methodist Clergy Among Salary Strata in Two Years, for Two Choices of Stratum Boundaries   (percent)

Boundary	Salary[a] range in $ per year	1923	1937
Chosen to yield stable distribution	2,250 +	26.1	29.3
	2,249–1,250	47.1	45.0
	1,249–0	26.8	25.7
From regression of salary on job size	2,000 +	40.5	33.6
	1,999–1,400	28.8	33.6
	1,399–0	30.7	32.9
		$(N = 153)^{b}$	$(N = 140)$
	Mean salary	1,840	1,910

[a] Actual cash paid (salary less deficit) plus yearly rental value of parsonage.
[b] Men drawn in the samples (from clerical indexes in the minutes of that year) who hold parishes; see Appendix C.

boundaries at $1,250 and $2,250 per year do yield an almost stable distribution of clergy. Transition parameters estimated from all moves in the sample of vacancy chains for each year are stated in Table 6.5 for this choice of strata. Predicted and observed distributions of chain lengths are not calculated; instead, the use of salary for strata, with these cutoff points, is assessed solely by inspection of the transition parameters.

6. Three Organizations Compared

Three properties seem desirable in a matrix of transition probabilities for the Markov chain model. Most important, each parameter should be stable over time. Second, the termination probability

Table 6.5   Methodist Church: Transition Parameters for Vacancies Moving between Salary Strata[a]

Origin stratum	Destination stratum				Total weighted number of moves[b]
	2,250 +	2,249–1,250	1,249–0	Outside	
			1922–1923		
Outside	.1226	.4372	.4402		34.399
2,250 +	.5816	.3072	0	.1112	16.105
2,249–1,250	.0513	.4985	.0950	.3551	43.800
1,249–0	.0091	.0665	.3508	.5735	29.736
			1936–1937		
Outside	.1603	.2402	.5995		14.689
2,250 +	.5705	.1827	.0356	.2111	8.052
2,249–1,250	.0776	.4596	.2155	.2472	13.474
1,249–0	.0030	.1201	.3683	.5085	18.992

[a] Stratum boundaries were chosen to give the near-constant distribution of ministers shown in first panel of Table 6.4.

[b] These are taken from the same samples of vacancy chains used with size strata in Table 6.1; the overall total for a year here should be the same as in that table.

q_{i0} should vary by stratum, otherwise a binomial model would do as well. Third, variation in transition probabilities within the matrix should make sense in terms of the meaning of the strata. With hierarchic strata, the corner probabilities, q_{13} and q_{31}, should be smaller than the other off-diagonal probabilities because large jumps in salary are less probable than are intermediate jumps. Also, each probability above the diagonal, corresponding to promotions for men, should be larger than the corresponding one for demotions, below the diagonal.

The parameters in Table 6.5 are not as stable over time as those in Table 6.1 for job-size strata. Only one of the sixteen parameters shows less variation in the former than the latter table, whereas in seven cells, stability is substantially better in Table 6.1. On the second desirable property, variation in termination probability by stratum, the two tables are comparable. Table 6.5 does make more sense than

Table 6.1, however, as a hierarchical model—the pattern of off-diagonal probabilities corresponds better to a hierarchic model. Salary strata, then, with these cutoff points of $1,250 and $2,250 do not seem as cogent as do the strata by size of job, which also yield a satisfactory prediction of chain length distributions as shown in Section 6.1.

Individual salaries may be better correlated with mobility chances than membership rolls of individual churches even if the natural boundaries for strata on the two scales are equivalent. It is natural to try the model with salaries grouped in strata as comparable as possible to the strata for job size. The numbers of churches in the samples with sizes at or near the boundaries at 100 and 300 members are so small that it would be foolish to define their average salaries as the cutoff points for strata; instead, a conventional regression equation of salary on size over individual churches will be derived. The mean salaries of churches at each possible size in membership are assumed to lie on a straight line when plotted against size. Then

Table 6.6   Transition Parameters for Salary Strata[a]

Origin stratum	Destination stratum			
	2,000 +	1,999–1,400	1,399–0	Outside
	1922–1923			
Outside	.2117	.3026	.4857	
2,000 +	.6026	.1771	.0244	.1960
1,999–1,400	.0984	.3730	.1281	.4006
1,399–0	.0241	.0869	.3414	.5476
	1936–1937			
Outside	.2065	.1203	.6732	
2,000 +	.5832	.1504	.0961	.1703
1,999–1,400	.0132	.3600	.3346	.2922
1,399–0	.0517	.0676	.4068	.4738

[a] Stratum boundaries correspond to the cutoff points for size strata used in Table 6.1, as determined from a linear regression equation. The samples of vacancy chains are the same as in Tables 6.5 and 6.1.

the slope and beginning point, which together define the line, are chosen so that the sum of the squared deviations of observed mean salaries from such a line is minimized. On this hypothesized line of mean salaries, the size boundaries of 100 and 300 correspond to the salary values to be used as cutting points. Information about the relation of salary to church size at all levels of size is used to estimate the mean salary corresponding to a particular size.

The regression equation is, using combined Methodist samples,

$$\text{dollars} = 1110 + 2.89 \, (\text{number of members})$$

The correlation coefficient, which reflects the scatter among individual churches when plotted by salary and size, is $+0.725$. The cutting points for salary when rounded are \$1,400 and \$2,000.

With these salary strata, the transition probabilities estimated from the same samples of vacancy chains as before are as shown in Table 6.6. The pattern of coefficients in each year and even their sizes are close to those in Table 6.5; the judgment must be much the same. Since the correlation of sizes and salaries over individual churches is not high—only about one-half the variation in one can be accounted for statistically in terms of variation in the other—quite different sets of moves are tabulated in corresponding cells of Tables 6.1 and 6.6.

6.3 Search for Optimum Methodist Strata in Job Size

Number of members appears to be a more fruitful criterion for classifying end points of moves than does salary. It does not follow that the use of three strata or the particular cutoff points of 100 and 300 borrowed from the Episcopal model are optimal. Three desirable properties in a Markov matrix were reviewed in the Section 6.2. There they served to evaluate models with strata chosen using *ad hoc* rationales. This section develops search procedures for cutting points on size that maximize one desirable property—constancy of transition probabilities over time—given the number of strata. Then the optimum models on this criterion for various numbers of strata are compared in terms of accuracy of prediction.

Michael Adler, a Ph.D. candidate in sociology at Harvard, conceived and carried out the work reported here. His immediate concern was to replace, by objective statistical procedures, the "galaxy of intuitive and subjective criteria" used to choose strata. His broader goal was to infer organizational structure from its dynamic consequences in a systematic and objective way. (Adler emphasizes the analogy drawn in Section 9.1 between the vacancy model and the input-output model of an economy. In the latter, the transfer coefficients analogous to the q_{ij} are assumed to be determined by technology and other slowly varying contextual features. Adler argues that if the vacancy model is correct, there should be a set of true strata for which the Q matrix is invariant over time.)

Consider a series of samples of vacancy chains drawn at different times. Let each transition probability in a $\bar{Q}$ be the average of the estimates from the various samples. Calculate D^2, the sum of the squared deviations of these estimates from their average, in turn summed over all positions in the matrix. For a given number of strata, boundaries are to be chosen so as to minimize D^2. (Adler also carried through all calculations using a normalized form in which each square in D^2 is divided by the appropriate $\bar{q}_{ij}$. It seemed a less appropriate criterion because it emphasizes deviations in cells with small transition probabilities, which are less reliable, less important substantively, and require arbitrary adjustment entries when zero moves are observed in the cell. Almost all conclusions about optimum strata were the same when the normalized criterion was used.)

The number of possible partitions of a population of jobs is unmanageably large, even when the number of classes is fixed. Here, however, jobs are to be identified only by size; so the problem is reduced to choosing $s - 1$ boundary points on one dimension. Adler developed several search procedures, in the form of computer programs, that all rest on an initial arbitrary set of twenty-five equally spaced points (from size 0 to size 600 in steps of 25 with one residual category for over 600). Each sample of weighted moves was tabulated in the corresponding 25×25 grid.

The first procedure (sequential search procedure) began by collapsing each pair of adjacent intervals in turn and computing the corresponding values of D^2. Each pair of intervals in the resulting optimum set of 24 was then collapsed, and so on. Since the criterion for collapsing at a given stage takes as given all previous erasures of boundaries, it is unlikely that a set of, say, three strata reached this way is the optimum set of three strata. Instead, Adler used the set of six boundaries obtained by this procedure (see Table 6.7) as a beginning set for a second procedure.

In the second procedure, D^2 is computed for all possible ways to collapse categories in an initial matrix, here 7×7, to yield a matrix with s categories. The optimum set of boundaries for each s from 1–6 is shown in Table 6.7 for each of two different starting matrices:

one is that reached by the sequential search procedure, and the other is for an arbitrary choice of boundaries at equally spaced intervals of 100 in size. It is ironic that for three numbers of categories the

Table 6.7   Stratum Boundaries that Minimize Change in Observed Transition Probabilities Over Time, for Six Numbers of Strata, Each Using Two Different Sets of Possible Boundaries[a]

Number of strata, s	Optimum boundaries	Optimum D^2
	Possible boundaries from the sequential search procedure (450, 375, 225, 200, 150, 100)	
6	(450, 375, 225, 200, 100)	.0512[b]
5	(450, 375, 200, 100)	.0396
4	(450, 375, 200)	.0256
3	(375, 200)	.0138
2	(100)	.0040
1	no boundary	.0005
	Possible boundaries from an equally spaced grid (600, 500, 400, 300, 200, 100)	
6	(600, 400, 300, 200, 100)	.1484
5	(500, 300, 200, 100)	.0516
4	(300, 200, 100)	.0177
3	(300, 100)	.0084
2	(300)	.0029
1	no boundary	.0005

[a] Boundaries are for the Methodist church, using the samples of weighted moves for 1923 and 1936 reported in preceding tables.

[b]
$$D^2 = \sum_y \left[\sum_{i=1}^{s} \sum_{j=1}^{s} (q_{ij}^{(y)} - \bar{q}_{ij})^2 \right]$$

where y is the year, either 1922–1923 or 1936–1937, of the moves on which the estimate of the transition probability is based, and where

$$\bar{q}_{ij} = \sum_{y=1}^{N} \frac{q_{ij}^{(y)}}{N}$$

optimum value of D^2 is better when one starts from the arbitrary set of six boundaries equally spaced. In this second procedure, the optimum search for one value of s does not depend on choices for a larger value; for example, in the uppermost section the optimum boundary for $s = 2$, at 100, is not a boundary in the optimum sets of strata for $s = 3$ or 4. Since one considers every possible set of erasures of boundaries in an initial $n \times n$ matrix, the number of matrices computed in a table such as 6.7 goes up exponentially with n, specifically as 2^{n-1}.

To choose the optimum number of strata, a different approach is needed. The number of terms that can contribute to D^2 goes up as the square of s, and the average size of the individual squared differences expected by chance increases as sample size per cell decreases and, hence, as s increases. Instead of attempting to correct for these effects, Adler compared the various matrices from Table 6.7 on their power to predict mobility and to predict length distributions of chains. (There is no guarantee that for a given s and given initial matrix, the matrix in Table 6.7 chosen as having the minimum value of D^2 would also be the one to best predict mobility and lengths.)

Mobility in each year in number of vacancy moves is predicted from the observed $\mathbf{f}$ for that sample and the average $\bar{Q}$ from all years:

$$\hat{M}^{(y)} = \mathbf{F}^{(y)}(I - \bar{Q})^{-1}\mathbf{1} \tag{6.1}$$

The criterion is the square of the difference between prediction and observation [which would be zero if $\bar{Q}$ were replaced by $Q^{(y)}$ in equation (6.1)] divided by the latter and then summed over both samples. It is the overall distribution that is predicted for chain lengths [compare equation (2.8)]:

$$T_j^{(y)} = \mathbf{f}^{(y)}(\bar{Q})^{j-1}\mathbf{p} \tag{6.2}$$

where, again, the average values of transition parameters over all samples are used. The criterion here is the sum over both samples of a squared deviation of predicted from observed proportion divided by the latter, for all chain lengths j. Neither criterion for power of prediction is directly dependent on the number of strata as such.

Deviations of prediction from observation are reported in Table 6.8 for each matrix ($s < 6$) identified in Table 6.7. On both criteria for both possible sets of boundaries, the best prediction is from four strata; with one exception, the prediction with three strata is almost as good. The single best matrix judged by predictive power alone is clearly that with four strata separated by boundaries at 430, 375, and 200 members.

Overall judgment should rest also on whether transition matrices exhibit the properties desirable in a Markov chain. One reason is desire for consistency: one such property supplied the criterion by which the particular boundaries in Table 6.7 were chosen for a given number of strata. The second reason is substantive: the more stable

Table 6.8   Accuracy of Predictions, by Number of Strata[a]

	Sum of normalized squared deviations of predicted from observed	
Number of strata, s	Number of moves[b]	Proportion of vacancy chains of each length[c]
Possible boundaries from the sequential search procedure		
5	.00226	.27595
4	.00104	.20172
3	.00113	.33766
2	.00377	.27238
1	.01511	.27481
Possible boundaries from an equally spaced grid		
5	.00612	.26566
4	.00344	.25595
3	.00456	.25758
2	.00686	.28749
1	.01511	.27481

[a] With the boundaries shown in Table 6.7; these have been selected to give the least variation over time in the estimated transition probabilities.

[b]
$$\sum_y \frac{(\hat{M}^{(y)} - M^{(y)})^2}{M^{(y)}}$$

where $M^{(y)}$ is observed and $\hat{M}^{(y)}$ is the prediction from equation 6.1 for year y.

[c]
$$\sum_y \sum_j \frac{(C_j/C - T_j)^2}{C_j/C}$$

where C_j/C is the observed proportion and T_j the predicted proportion [equation (6.2)] of chains with length j in year y.

in value and coherent in pattern are the parameters in a model, the greater is its plausibility and the greater the likelihood it can be generalized. The last two reasons are methodological. Any search procedures using a fixed set of samples run greater risks of capitalizing on accidental structure in the data when only one class of decision criteria is used. Finally, the particular least-square measures used to judge deviations from optimum are rather arbitrary so that overall judgment should reflect results based on several of them.

The average matrix $\bar{Q}$ of transition probabilities using four strata is given in Table 6.9 for each of the sets of boundaries in Table 6.7.

Table 6.9 Transition Probabilities among Four Strata for Two Choices of Boundaries[a]

Origin stratum	Destination stratum				
	450 +	449–375	374–200	199–0	Outside
Boundaries I					
450 +	.3927	.1602	.2309	.0389	.1773
449–375	.1731	.1950	.3510	.1835	.0974
374–200	.0469	.0241	.3156	.3174	.2960
199–0	.0029	.0134	.1400	.3874	.4563
	300 +	299–200	199–100	99–0	Outside
Boundaries II					
300 +	.4714	.1945	.1464	.0317	.1560
299–200	.1579	.1773	.2298	.0818	.3532
199–100	.0642	.1391	.2745	.1111	.4107
99–0	.0350	.0653	.0992	.2437	.5568

[a] Average matrix $\bar{Q}$ of the two Methodist samples; the two sets of boundaries are those in Table 6.7 derived by minimizing variation in Q over time using different initial grids.

The pattern of transition probabilities seems less coherent with boundaries I than with boundaries II especially in the lower left corner of I. In each panel, termination probabilities (last column) vary widely among strata; but only in the panel for II is there a monotonic rise. Inspection of Table 6.7 shows that, with either three or four strata, boundaries chosen from the equally spaced grid boundaries II yield more stable transition probabilities than boundaries I.

Overall, the model with four strata separated at membership levels of 300, 200, and 100 seems best. However, the three-stratum model with the same cuts at 300 and 100 is almost as good in predictive power, and its transition probabilities are more stable than those in any other three-stratum model considered. These are the same three strata adopted in Section 6.1 in imitation of the Episcopal model.

No definitive choice of "optimum" strata, even on a given dimension, is possible. Quite aside from the problems created by sampling variability and the difficulty of examining all possible sets of boundaries, there is the multiplicity of plausible bases of choice. Desirable properties of transition parameters, predictive efficiency, and stability in the distribution of job-holders have all been used in this chapter; yet another basis of choice, the existence of natural breaking points in various distributions on the size dimension, played a role in Chapter 4.

If the same stratum boundaries for jobs are appropriate in different organizations of the same type, not only is the comparison of results simplified but also confidence in the validity of the models is increased. The simple split of jobs into three strata by size with cutoff points at memberships of 100 and 300 has proved to be remarkably sound in both the Methodist and Episcopal churches. It can now be applied to the Presbyterian case with confidence.

6.4 Tests for the Presbyterian Church

For the Presbyterian case, the job strata demarcated by congregations of 100 and 300 members are used. Estimates of transition probabilities from samples drawn four decades apart will be found in Table 6.10. Again, the moves tabulated are the constituent moves in the samples of vacancy chains, each given the appropriate sampling weight.[3]

The estimates of transition probabilities are not as stable over time as for the Methodist church; nor is there as wide a spread between strata in termination probabilities—the binomial model with all strata collapsed will be a good predictor of overall length distribution. Moreover, the pattern of values for a given year is not as coherent, that is, it does not fit the concepts about hierarchic strata as well. It could be argued that larger sample sizes, comparable to those in Table 6.1, are necessary to yield reliable estimates; but it is not legitimate to enlarge samples only when the initial estimates are not pleasing. Comparison with results in Chapter 5 will suggest an alternative reason for some flaws in the estimates.

Look again at Table 4.15. Estimates there for the combined

samples from 1933–1934 and 1943–1944 are deviant in sizes and pattern from those for the earlier and later years. It should not be surprising to find deviant results during the Depression or the war

Table 6.10   Transition Probabilities Estimated in Two Decades
for the Presbyterian Church[a]

Origin stratum	Destination stratum				Total weighted number of moves
	Big	Medium	Small	Outside	
1922–1923					
Outside	.0636	.4610	.4754		12.587
Big	.3445	.1867	.0918	.3770	3.626
Medium	.1225	.3538	.1818	.3419	11.512
Small	.0135	.0853	.3223	.5789	12.410
1959–1960					
Outside	.2318	.5040	.2642		20.941
Big	.3069	.2701	.0205	.4025	12.185
Medium	.1198	.3604	.0491	.4707	24.563
Small	.1119	.1914	.1767	.5200	8.489

[a] The format and estimation formulas are the same as in Table 4.12, with the same definition of strata by job size in number of communicants, using cutoff points at 100 and 300.

years, and Section 5.3 suggests specific reasons for the enhanced termination probabilities in the top two strata. In both these periods, the process of filling vacancies in higher strata is slowed. During the Depression, vestries are not eager promptly to resume paying a salary; during World War II, experienced men are drained from the system into military chaplaincies. Yet the coding rules for tracing vacancy chains are fixed; it may be that many prolonged vacancies that only reflect delays in a normal process of search are coded inappropriately as abandonments of jobs to the empty status during the Depression and the war.

Perhaps the coding rules for Presbyterian vacancy chains should not be the same as for the Episcopal chains, just as the latter perhaps should be stretched during Depression and war periods. The extreme decentralization in the Presbyterian church suggests the likelihood of many longer delays from normal search procedures for filling vacancies than is the case in the Episcopal church in normal years. In Appendix C the much higher incidence in Presbyterian chains of entries listed as vacant in one annual is remarked on.[4] Such a change in coding rules would seem to affect only termination probabilities directly and enhance transition probabilities within a row only by a constant factor. However, the eventual filling of prolonged vacancies would be coded as vacancy moves rather than as creations and so could shift estimates of transition probabilities individually.

Data on current operating expense in each tenure broken during a Presbyterian vacancy chain have been tabulated. New strata could be defined on this criterion or by choice of new boundaries on the scale of job sizes. Estimates of transition probabilities for some

Table 6.11 Predicted (P) and Observed (O) Overall Length Distributions in Two Decades for the Presbyterian Church[a] (percent)

j (length)	1922–1923		1959–1960[b]	
	P	O	P	O
1	45.7	49.3	46.8	49.8
2	24.6	19.4	24.3	23.0
3	13.3	18.7	13.1	15.5
4	7.3	2.9	7.1	4.7
5	4.0	53.	4.0	3.6
6	2.2	1.6	2.1	2.4
7	1.2	0.9	1.2	0.6
8	0.7	0	0.6	0
9	0.4	0.8	0.4	0.5
10	0.2	1.2	0.2	0
Raw number		$N_K = 12.487$ (35)		$N_K = 20.933$ (49)
	$J_c = 2.21$	$J_c = 2.17$	$J_c = 2.17$	$J_c = 2.03$

[a] The predictions made are the same as in Table 4.13. The transition probabilities used are those from moves in that year alone, shown in Table 6.10.

[b] In addition to the sample reported in Appendix C there is included here the sample drawn to increase the number of observations in Table 6.10 as explained in note 3 to this chapter.

such strata might conform better to the desired patterns. The distribution of Presbyterian jobs by number of members does have lower percentages in the bottom stratum and higher percentages above 300 than in the other two churches, suggesting a need for redefinition of strata. However, analysis has suggested that the coding rules may be inappropriate, and no choice of strata could influence that distortion.

No systematic reexamination of coding rules for the Presbyterian church has been attempted. It would be more fruitful to do so while developing rules for applying the vacancy model to still other churches or organizations. (The problem of allowable durations for vacancies arises again in a new form in Section 7.7, where the actual intervals between a vacancy's moves are treated as a stochastic variable, with a mean rate that may depend on the stratum.) Throughout these first six chapters, only the sequential order of a vacancy's moves is considered, so that prolonged duration of a vacancy has no effect on estimated transition probabilities except when it entails coding as a transition to the empty state.

Since the estimated transition probabilities are not constant, predictions of chain lengths will be based on the parameters for that year. Only overall distributions are reported in Table 6.11 because there are too few chains to justify separate tabulations for chain lengths by stratum of origin. The fit is good, but for these overall length distributions the binomial model would do as well.

6.5   Three Churches Compared

A simple Markov chain model works about as well for the Methodist church as it did for the Episcopal church, with the same definitions of three strata by job size. Some rethinking about centralization is, however, needed. There is no question that a Methodist bishop had formal authority to reassign jobs each year to all men within one of his annual conferences; as will be shown in Chapter 12, most of the Methodist vacancy chains remain within a given diocese. In Chapter 3 the main question posed about, and the reason for, choosing the Methodist church was the effects of centralized authority on mobility. The answer seems to be that the effects are slight.

There are two deviations between the Methodist data and the Markov chain predictions that may be significant. As reported in Appendix C, there are more loops—vacancy chains without end points—in the Methodist church than in either of the two other churches. Only 3 percent of the moves were in loops of length three or more, however; only these are real evidence for centralized planning. The other deviation is a pronounced "bulge" in the observed length distribution of chains begun in big jobs. Six percent of them are of length 15 or more while Table 6.2 shows only $\frac{1}{2}$ percent of chains predicted to be that long by the Markov chain model; the average length observed is 4.75 while that predicted is 3.72. It can be argued that a central authority is able and may choose to fit some moves into longer chains than would be expected by chance, given the rates of termination. The sample size is, however, too small in that column of Table 6.2 to justify an elaborate explanation of this bulge.

Three explanations for a good fit between data and model in the Methodist case can be suggested. One is that the bishop's authority is only formal. The church is supported by voluntary contributions and the bishop is constrained to defer to the wishes of lay officials in each parish, as well as to his own district superintendents. If he offends a large number of clergy by his appointments, they may try to transfer under another bishop, discourage new candidates, and so on. The result would be, in effect, a decentralized decision-making system like that in the Episcopal church.

The two other explanations reach much the same result from different starting points. Suppose that the authority of the bishop is great. He is, nonetheless, subject to objective constraints. Clergy age and die, and Methodists leave rural areas to go to new suburbs independently of a bishop's wishes. He could hardly refuse arbitrarily to place qualified new ministers, and it is the body of ministers in the conference who decide on qualifications. If a bishop placed a poorly educated minister from a small country parish, one of the many trained sketchily through the conference's own course of study, in a wealthy suburban parish, the bishop must expect to see the parish decline in numbers and, incidentally, in contributions to the conference and the national church. In short, a sensible central authority may well make decisions according to a stable pattern similar to that which evolves in a decentralized system.

The third explanation is a variant of the second. In Section 4.3 the inadequacy of official analyses of job-holding and mobility in the Episcopal church were emphasized. It was suggested that the complexities of mobility and of tenures for individual men among particular jobs across a large system are so great as to be beyond the group of normal administrative machinery. The same argument can be applied to the Methodist church, where a bishop controls several conferences, many of which are very large. For sheer lack of information and concepts adequate to support planning, the bishop and his superintendents may respond case by case to local pressures with results much like those for the Episcopal church.

Even though the same kind of probability model for individual vacancy moves applies to both the Methodist and Episcopal churches, comparison of parameters is instructive. Comparison is, in fact, much easier because the same criterion—job size in number of members—and the same cutoff points for strata yield acceptable models in both cases. Other hierarchic attributes of jobs did not prove as useful, nor did different boundaries for job-size strata. In both churches, moves were concentrated geographically. Transition probabilities among regions were not stable, and samples are too small to justify refining hierarchic strata by region.

The main difference between the two models is in termination probabilities. In each stratum, this parameter is substantially smaller for the Methodist (Table 6.1, combined samples) than for the Episcopal church (Table 5.1). As a consequence, the Methodist chains begun in any stratum tend to be longer than the corresponding Episcopal chains. Moreover, the average distribution of vacancy creations among strata over the periods studied is much the same in the two churches, and overall Methodist mobility should be substantially higher simply because of the difference in termination probabilities. In addition, the incidence of vacancy creations relative to the number of clergy in 1–1 jobs is substantially higher among the Methodists (1922–1937) than among the Episcopal clergy (1912–1955).[5]

Mobility is higher among the Methodist clergy partly because of the greater incidence of chains but primarily because termination probabilities are lower. Different types of ending events—recruitment of new men, calls of ministers in limbo or missionary work to jobs, and abandonment or merger of jobs—contribute to the total termination probabilities for a stratum. The contributions of each type for the Episcopal clergy are specified in Table 5.10 and, for the Methodists, in Table 6.3. Job endings actually are a more common destination for vacancies in the Methodist than in the Episcopal church, for every stratum and for all periods compared (except in the special case of Depression and war years discussed in Section 6.4). Overall Episcopal termination rates are greater because calls to recruits and ministers in limbo exceed those for the Methodists in every stratum for almost any comparison of years.

If data for the war and Depression years for the Episcopal case is omitted, a similarity with the Methodists does appear: for the stratum of large jobs, both the total probability of termination and the contribution from each type of ending event are roughly the same in the two churches. The differences between the two churches, then, reside in the greater willingness of Methodists to leave small and medium jobs empty and the greater willingness of Episcopalians to fill vacancies in small and medium jobs with new recruits and with men not employed in 1–1 jobs. The latter cannot be simply attributed to there being a greater proportion of Episcopal priests in vague staff jobs, missionary work, and so on (compare Tables C.9 and C.12).

The data for the Presbyterian church was the least extensive because great similarity between it and the Episcopal church was anticipated. This anticipation may not prove erroneous in the end, but it is not supported by the results from present data. Although the one stratified model tried with Presbyterian data was consistent with data in each separate period, it lacked stability over time and, thus, does not seem very useful. Extensive work is still required on coding rules, on choice of strata, and on other periods.

In the long run, mobility patterns determine the size of a church in both men and various kinds of jobs. In all three churches, most of the clergy are included in the system of 1–1 jobs, and most moves fit into vacancy chains. When parameters in the vacancy models are stable and the models meet the tests, the natural next step is applying them to the analysis of system evolution. This step will be taken in Chapter 7. The probabilistic framework and attention to chain structure needed in these first chapters in order to validate the vacancy models will be de-emphasized there.

Part II
Alternate Models

Chapter 7
Vacancy Models and Systems Evolution

Stocks of men and jobs in a system are replenished and drained in the same process that describes mobility of men between jobs. For various simple assumptions about exogenous flows, the evolution of system size will be projected from vacancy models, using the parameter estimates in Chapters 5 and 6. Difference equations could be used to cumulate the changes from yearly cohorts of vacancies in the models of Chapter 2, but it is desirable to revise the models to treat change within a year in the same framework used to treat evolution over successive years. The system will be described in this chapter by variables in continuous time with arrivals and moves of vacancies occurring continuously. The emphasis is on expected behavior of aggregates.

Discussion of approaches to equilibrium is easier in the differential calculus, which also is more widely known than the difference calculus. Treatment of individual events, arrivals, departures, and moves requires a more complex framework in continuous time than in discrete time. A brief description of the appropriate probability models is given in Section 7.7. The differential equations for aggregates will approximate results for expected values from the stochastic models for individuals in that discussion.

First considered is the analogue of the binomial model in Chapter 2 with all jobs lumped in a single stratum. It is well to clarify the logic of the new approach before going into the details of matrix equations. Section 7.2 contrasts this vacancy model with several others, one corresponding to the bumper chains in Chapter 1; it amounts to a basic reassessment of the cogency of vacancy models. The model for cohorts of vacancies in Section 2.2 is not restricted to chains of moves by identifiable vacancies among 1–1 jobs. The system can be expanded to include all jobs with fixed numbers of men, as shown in Section 7.8.

7.1 Differential Equations and Predictions for the Binomial Model

The simplest possible model is developed in this discussion. It does not lead to any substantial results that were not implicit in earlier chapters, but it should clarify three important matters: the similarity between a discrete-time model and its analogue in continuous time; the meaning of equilibrium; and the danger of tautologies in making predictions about equilibrium situations with parameters estimated from equilibrium situations. New data on system sizes is introduced and compared with predictions from the model. The model is shown to be insensitive to minor variations in the rate of creation of vacancies.

The primary variable is the number of jobs that are temporarily vacant during the calling of replacements, $V(t)$. Let $N(t)$ be the number of tenures at time t, that is, the number of jobs occupied. If $J(t)$ represents the total number of jobs,

$$J(t) = N(t) + V(t) \tag{7.1}$$

This equation is a tautology: a job that is empty for years or has been merged with another job is not included in the count $J(t)$. Similarly $N(t)$ is, by definition, the number of men in the system; men in limbo or other floating states are omitted. (Both limitations will be removed in Section 7.8.)

Let $f_{\text{job}}(t)$ be the arrival rate of new jobs at time t and let $f_{\text{man}}(t)$ be the rate of departures of men, and let $f(t)$ be the total rate of creation of vacancies. According to the model, vacancies behave the same way whether created initially by new jobs or by deaths of men (see Section 5.3 for empirical confirmation). The rate at which vacancies leave the system is proportional to the stock of vacancies; let $\Pi(t)$ be the proportionality factor. The rate at which the stock of vacancies changes is simply the difference between income and outgo:

$$\frac{dV(t)}{dt} = f(t) - V(t)\Pi(t) \tag{7.2}$$

Vacancies move from job to job within the system. That internal mobility does not change the total number of vacancies and therefore does not appear in equation (7.2); since it is of major interest, the rate Π will be recast relative to that internal mobility. Let the total rate of movement per vacancy be $v(t)$, and assign the symbol $p(t)$ to the fraction that is terminal movement and the symbol $q(t)$ to the fraction that is internal movement. Parameters such as p and v are useful only if they are stable. They may well change from one era to another but not on the same microscopic time scale as do the state variables, $V(t)$ and $N(t)$. Hereafter no explicit time dependence of p and v will be indicated. Equation (7.2) becomes

$$\frac{dV(t)}{dt} = f(t) - V(t)vp \tag{7.3}$$

The total termination rate per vacancy can be split into the fraction from new recruits, vp_{man}, and the fraction from job terminations, vp_{job}. An equation can be written for the net rate of change of jobs:

$$\frac{dJ(t)}{dt} = f_{\text{job}}(t) - V(t)vp_{\text{job}} \tag{7.4}$$

and another for the results of the income and outgo of men

$$\frac{dN(t)}{dt} = V(t)vp_{\text{man}} - f_{\text{man}}(t) \tag{7.5}$$

The sum of (7.5) and (7.3) is just (7.4), in agreement with (7.1).

Each jump by a vacancy from one job to another defines an opposite move by a man who thereby initiates a new tenure. The same is true for a jump to the outside which corresponds to the entry of a new recruit to a job in the system but not to the formal move outside of a vacancy from a job thereupon ended. Therefore, the rate of creation of new tenures is $V(t)v(q + p_{\text{man}})$. (Observe that the rate of new job formation contributes to this only at one remove, as an increment to the number of vacancies.) Define the ratio of this to the stock of tenures as the in-mobility rate, μ. Since by definition

$$q + p_{\text{man}} + p_{\text{job}} = 1 \tag{7.6}$$

the result can be written

$$\mu = V(t)v(1 - p_{\text{job}})/N(t) \tag{7.7}$$

The differential equations are simple linear ones of first order with constant coefficients.[1] They are especially easy to solve when the rates of creation, f_{job} and f_{man}, are constant. Equation (7.3) for rate of change in the number of vacancies can be solved in isolation:

$$V(t) = \frac{f}{vp} + \left[V(0) - \frac{f}{pv} \right] e^{-pvt} \tag{7.8}$$

The stock of vacancies follows an exponential decay curve from its (arbitrary) initial value $V(0)$ to its value at equilibrium, where its rate of change is zero. The value at equilibrium is

$$V_e = \frac{f}{pv} \qquad (7.9)$$

By the time $t > 3/pv$, the transient part of $V(t)$ is less than 5 percent of $V(0)$.

The number of jobs $J(t)$ can now be found from (7.4) using the known result for $V(t)$. It is not worth tracing the initial transient behavior. Once equilibrium in the number of vacancies is approached,

$$\frac{dJ(t)}{dt} = f_{job} - \frac{p_{job}}{p} f \qquad (7.10)$$

If the total parameters p and f are written as the sums of the job and man components and terms are collected, the result for the constant rate of change of the number of jobs in equilibrium is

$$\frac{dJ(t)}{dt} = \frac{f_{job}p_{man} - f_{man}p_{job}}{p} \qquad (7.11)$$

for $t \gg 1/pv$. The rate of change of men is the same, from (7.1), since the number of vacancies is constant in equilibrium. Call this rate of change r.

The system declines steadily if the flow of new jobs, weighted by the fraction of vacancy terminations due to recruits, is exceeded by the flow of men leaving, in turn weighted by the fraction of terminations which come from job abolition. Neither the total rate of vacancy movement, v, nor the fraction, q, due to internal moves affect the result. The mobility rate, μ [see (7.7)], would grow steadily since V is fixed and N decreases. After sufficient time, $N(t)$ would go to zero and then become negative according to the equations; this is meaningless in the model, and explicit restrictions must be added:

$$N(t) \geq 0, \qquad J(t) \geq 0, \qquad V(t) \geq 0 \qquad (7.12)$$

However, the model would break down before this. Unless the following numerical inequality is satisfied

$$N(t) \geq V(t)vq \qquad (7.13)$$

there are not enough incumbents to answer the calls for internal movement in a year specified by the model; unless the inequality is very pronounced, it is not reasonable to neglect interaction between calls as is done in this simple linear model. Well before the breakdown, the assumptions about f would no longer be plausible—new jobs would not keep entering a disappearing organization at the old, constant rate, nor would men continue to leave at the original rate.

The system grows steadily if the numerator from (7.11) is positive, that is, if the weighted flow of new jobs is big enough to counterbalance retirements. The mobility rate μ would decline to zero. But in the long run steady growth cannot be associated with constant f. The assumptions about the rates f_{job} and f_{man} are too simple to generate a plausible picture of behavior in the indefinite future. Men are mortal; a growing organization in the end will have a growing retirement rate. Section 7.3 improves the model by incorporating this fact.

Even this simplest model is useful for intermediate lengths of time; that is, long in comparison with $1/pv$ but short compared to the period it takes for J to change by a substantial percentage. It is essentially the binomial model for cohorts of Chapters 2 and 4. The rate $f(t)$ in (7.3) corresponds to the $F(t)$ of Chapter 2. The rate $f(t)$ is instantaneous rather than a cohort; if time is still measured in units of years, the average value of $f(t)$ over the year is identical numerically with the $F(t)$. The number of vacancies $V(t)$ is not a rate of any kind but a state variable. But when v, the total rate of movement per vacancy, is constant over a year and time is measured in years, there is a simple relation between the average, $\overline{V}$, of $V(t)$ over the year and the number of moves, M, estimated from the same data:

$$\overline{V}(t)v = M \qquad (7.14)$$

All vacancies are terminated within a year in Chapter 2, which, in terms of the continuous time model, means that p must be large compared to unity, so that equilibrium is attained. The number of vacancy moves predicted in a year is

$$M = \left(\frac{f}{pv}\right)v = \frac{f}{p} \qquad (7.15)$$

in agreement with equation (2.12). The result can, but need not, be interpreted in terms of the average number of moves made by a vacancy before extinction. Equation (7.11) shows that changes in size of the system depend more on the split of vacancy creations between new jobs and departures of men than on the total flow of creations.

Clearly M and the rate of growth, r, are observable; the relevant data is reported in Chapters 5 and 6. The predicted values of r and M do not depend on v. The other parameters and the rates f_{man} and f_{job} are the same numerically as those in the discrete-time binomial model, for which estimates have been developed in Chapters 5 and 6. No attempt will be made to estimate V. Given data restricted to successive annual records of who is in what job, V, unlike M, is not a directly observable quantity.

In equations for the quantities that have been measured, like N and the inmobility μ, V always appears in a product with v; that product equals an observable, the total number of vacancy moves per year, M. Within limits, V and v could change dramatically, one up and the other down, without affecting the predictions, as long as their product was unchanged. One expects this kind of flexibility when the differential calculus is used to develop an analogue to a model based on finite difference calculus. There is an obvious upper limit for V in substantive terms; if V becomes larger than J, the (observable) total number of jobs in the system, the model no longer makes sense. M must also be less than J if the model is to be meaningful. At the other extreme, there is nothing to restrain V from being very small and v very large (except the discrete, integer nature of V and J). A larger v means that pv is increased, and the system approaches the steady rate of growth, r, even more quickly than before.

An organization with efficient procedures and dissemination of information may well have a very large v and small V, together with normal values of the other parameters and the rates f. It is also possible that a high degree of centralization may lead to ritual reporting of all moves at fixed times so that vacancies appear to be filled with bewildering rapidity. V can thus come close to being unobservable even if exact dates for all moves are available. The model of vacancy moves can nonetheless be applicable, most easily in the discrete form of Chapter 2, bringing order into otherwise unrelated regularities in the observed quantities. A search for causal mechanisms must be prepared to deal with scarcely visible clues, as long as the model can be tested.

The prediction of M from (7.15) assumes that within both the earlier and later period f was constant; that in each case the equilibrium appropriate to the level of f had been reached; and that in addition the parameter p was the same in both periods. Extracting the arrival rate f from data of the same year for which M is to be predicted introduces no chances of tautology; observations of f and M can be completely independent.[2] The accuracy of the predictions of M for the Episcopal church can be gauged from Table 4.3, which reports the estimate of p in each year as the ratio of observed M over observed f. For no one of the first years is the value of p matched closely by each of its values in the later years. Only two samples of chains were drawn for the Methodist church, for the 1920s and the 1930s; the values of p are 0.396 and 0.362 respectively. That is, the prediction of M for 1936–1937 from the f in that year and the p from 1922–1923 is within 10 percent of the observed value, a close fit in view of sampling variability. For the Presbyterian church, the estimate of p from 1922–1923, 0.460, is close to the value forty years later in 1959–1960, 0.436; prediction of M in later year, then, would again be close to the observed value.

Even though V cannot be measured, some estimated lower limit for the value of v, the total rate of movement per vacancy, is desirable as an independent check of the assumption that equilibrium is attained within a period of a year or so. In the Methodist church, it is clear that rate is very high. Vacancy chains of as many as thirty moves were completed between a given pair of years. In the Episcopal church the rate v is clearly lower. The median length of a group of precisely dated vacancies, reported in Appendix A, is 3.5 months (mean, 4.5 months). If this group were representative, the rate v would be about three moves per year. Representative estimates for the national samples can be inferred from Table C.1, where the number of vacancies which were actually listed as such in an annual is given. The ratio of this count to the total number of vacancies in the chains in each successive sample is 0.24, 0.16, 0.21, 0.15, and 0.23; the median ratio over all five decades is 0.21. For simplicity, assume that every vacancy has the same length; it must equal $1/v$, since that is the average rate at which a vacancy moves from a job. It is a reasonable approximation to say that a vacancy will be listed as such in an annual if the publication date falls within the period of the vacancy. If chains start at random times during the year, it follows that the publication date has a chance of falling within a randomly selected vacancy of the ratio of mean length of vacancy to length of the year, that is just $1/v$. The observed value of the chance is 0.21, so the estimated value of v is about 5. The average observed value of p is about 0.5; so pv is about 2.5 moves per year. It follows from (7.8) that $V(t)$ will be close to its equilibrium value within a year. A corresponding estimate can be made for the Presbyterian church from Table C.6; pv is about 0.6 per year. Several years would be required, after f achieved a constant value, for V to approach its equilibrium value there; the earlier use of (7.15) to predict M is not justified for the Presbyterian church.

It is reasonable to draw the following conclusions about the predictions of M, the total number of moves by vacancies. This binomial model does not predict well for the Episcopal church, which suggests that only a stratified model can be satisfactory. The single prediction made for the Methodist church, for a year in the 1930s based on parameter estimates from the 1920s, is accurate. In the case of the Presbyterian church, it is not legitimate to use the equilibrium form of the binomial model to make predictions.

Predictions for r, the rate of growth of the system, can be made from (7.11) in the same way and with the same kind of assumptions as can predictions for M from (7.15). "The system" is not the whole church, jobs, and men but just 1–1 jobs and their incumbents. The vacancy model requires this restricted definition, which is spelled out in Sections 2.1 and 3.2. However, most of the men and jobs and the great majority of moves within each church are encompassed in the system, as shown in Appendix C.

Consider r in its first form, given by (7.10). The prediction of r is based on the observed values of f_{job} and f_{man} in that year, only the parameters p and p_{job} being estimated from independent, earlier data. The first term on the right of (7.10), f_{job}, is assumed constant and, therefore, estimated by the observed number of jobs created in the whole year. The second term, the estimate of the number of jobs abolished, carries the whole burden of the prediction. The estimate of f used in the second term of (7.10) does not carry any of this burden, because the number of ending events equals the number of creations in each sample of vacancy chains, by its construction. The ratio p_{job}/p is unchanged if multiplied top and bottom by M; in fact, the concrete estimate from the earlier year for this ratio is just the number of jobs that leave the system divided by the sum of that plus the number of men who enter the system. Tables 5.10 and 4.15 supply the necessary Episcopal data and Tables 6.3 plus 6.1, for the Methodist church. The ratio p_{job}/p is fairly stable (see Table 7.1), and predictions of r will be fairly accurate in each church.

Estimates of the rate of growth from just the data in a given sample are worth reporting for their intrinsic interest. Estimates of rates of recruitment and severance from 1–1 jobs are derived in Appendix C from the samples of clergy indices, but the number of such moves in one sample was so small that only average estimates for all samples combined were attempted. The data on (weighted) vacancy chains in Chapters 5 and 6 can provide enough observations on terminations and beginnings, both for men and for jobs, to support estimates of growth rate during a year. The sampling variability is large, of course, since r is the difference between two rates, each of which is subject to large sampling fluctuations. Equation (7.10) is being used simply as a framework for reporting data on boundary crossings, not as a consequence or prediction from the vacancy chain model. The extra assumption is that the number of vacancies is fixed within each year so that the net growth rates for men and for jobs are the same. Table 7.1 reports the estimates for the Methodist and Episcopal

Table 7.1   Estimated Growth Rates for the Episcopal and Methodist Churches

Years	f	f_{job}	p	p_{job}	Sampling ratio[a]	Growth rate r in 1–1 jobs per year[b]
Episcopal						
1912–1923	34.573	16.959	.526	.178	10.8	+ 60
1933–1944	32.536	8.868	.611	.203	10.4	− 20
1954–1955	27.982	12.123	.448	.081	13.3	+ 100
Methodist						
1922–1923	34.199	14.757	.396	.204	76	− 220
1936–1937	14.689	7.231	.362	.188	76	− 30

[a] Since the values of f and f_{job} are from samples, they must be multiplied by the sampling ratio to compute r, which is for the entire system of 1–1 jobs in the church. Samples a decade apart are combined for the Episcopal church to increase the sampling base; the r is an average estimate over the two years. Sampling ratios are taken from Tables C.3 and C.5.

[b] Estimated from the observed values in the preceding columns using (7.10) as a format. As explained in the text, r is not a prediction or consequence of the vacancy chain model. The data is taken from the samples of weighted chains reported in Chapters 5 and 6.

churches. There are too few chains to justify estimates for the Presbyterian church. Each estimate is short term, for a period of a year or two surrounding the sample year. The clergy index samples are large enough to provide meaningful estimates of the total numbers of men in 1–1 jobs by year. The results for estimated numbers of filled 1–1 jobs are: 1912–1913, 4,070; 1922–1923, 4,050; 1933–1934, 4,040; 1943–1944, 3,850; and 1954–1955, 5,130. If the rates of growth at the sample years estimated in Table 7.1 are accurate, it must be that growth rates can fluctuate sharply over as little as ten years. In the Methodist church the estimated number of men in 1–1 jobs drops by 1500 in the fourteen years between 1923 and 1937. That drop would be consistent with a steady decline in the instantaneous rate of decrease in 1–1 jobs from the value of 220 estimated for 1923 to the later value of 30 (Table 7.1).

Predictions of M and r in any year are made from the arrival rate f during the year, and neither is assumed constant over long periods. Yet, it is assumed that f is constant over a period of two or three years and that the equilibrium formulas apply in each such period. In view of the fluctuations in f just inferred from Table 7.1, it is well to see if the model is sensitive to short-term changes in the arrival rate, f. Return to equation (7.3). Let the arrival rate grow linearly with time after the beginning, t_0, of a period:

$$f(t) = f(t_0) + \alpha(t - t_0) \qquad (7.16)$$

The solution to (7.3) is not (7.8) but

$$V(t) = \frac{f(t_0) - (\alpha/pv)}{pv} + \frac{\alpha}{pv}(t - t_0)$$

$$+ \left[V(t_0) - \frac{f(t_0)}{pv} + \frac{\alpha}{(pv)^2} \right] e^{-pv(t-t_0)} \qquad (7.17)$$

The last term on the right, the transient term, is very like that in (7.8) and decays at the same rate. As before, for $(t - t_0)$ exceeding $(3/pv)$ it is negligible. The first two terms can be rearranged, and (7.17) becomes

$$V(t) = \frac{f(t)}{pv} - \frac{\alpha}{(pv)^2} \qquad (7.18)$$

M, the total number of moves by vacancies in a year (the unit of time used in the equations), is to be predicted. Equation (7.15) no longer applies, but (7.14) does. If the year begins after the transient term has died out, the average value of $V(t)$ is

$$M = \frac{\overline{f(t)} - \alpha/pv}{p} \qquad (7.19)$$

where $\overline{f(t)}$ is the average value of $f(t)$ over the year. The predictions of M made earlier were based on the total number of creations f observed in the year, which is just $\overline{f(t)}$ even if $f(t)$ varies. In practice, the only difference between (7.15) and (7.19) for the prediction of M is the subtraction of α/pv in the numerator. This correction can be thought of as an inertial effect; V needs time to build up to a new level and perpetually lags behind the steady increase in $f(t)$. Suppose the growth is 10 percent a year; $\alpha = 0.1 \times f(t)$. For the Methodist church pv was found to be more than 10, and the prediction for M from (7.15) differs by less than 1 percent from the accurate prediction in (7.19). For the Episcopal church, pv is more than 2, and the error is still only a few percent. The same conclusions would be reached if $f(t)$ were declining linearly instead—just the sign of α need be changed. Similar conclusions could be drawn concerning slight variations over time in the parameters.

7.2 Bumper Chains and Vacancy Chains: Duality and Contingency

Vacancies need never be mentioned in the equations above, which can be read as statements about the interrelation of the number of men and the number of jobs in a system. The two powerful assumptions implicit in the use of $V(t)$ are that it is positive and that it is a gross, as well as net, measure of the vacant jobs in the system at time t. Stripped of one or both assumptions, the actual equations in $N(t)$ and $J(t)$ can suggest a great many models, two of which correspond to the bump chains and to the marriage processes of Chapter 1. Duality and contingency are the themes that guide one through the maze of possible models; it is through these themes that internal mobility can be related to the growth and decline of system size.

Replace the "transition" parameters for vacancies in the previous section with neutral labels:

$$a \equiv vp_{job} \qquad (7.20)$$

and

$$b \equiv vp_{man} \qquad (7.21)$$

Equations (7.4) and (7.5) in the interlinked rates of change of $J(t)$ and $N(t)$ are rewritten:

$$\frac{dJ}{dt} = f_{job}(t) - a(J - N) \qquad (7.22)$$

157

and

$$\frac{dN}{dt} = -f_{\mathrm{man}}(t) - b(N - J) \qquad (7.23)$$

Whatever interpretation is given these equations in a particular model, they should deal with the matching of men to jobs. The internal dynamics of the system described by the equations should tend to decrease any gap between N and J. It follows that both a and b should be positive. The signs of other quantities are problematic and on them hinges the particular interpretations of the equations.[3]

The only axiom is that J and N both are positive. Nothing about (7.22) and (7.23) precludes N being larger than J. If V is negative, the interpretation of the equations in terms of vacancies must be supplanted or enlarged by a discussion of bumpers, that is, surplus men. If one were mechanically to write down the simplest equations coupling rates of change of J and N, it would be natural to multiply J and N by different arbitrary parameters in a given equation. Only the concepts of the bumper or the vacancy suggest that the correct term is the "simple difference" of J and N, which acts as the irritant to produce changes in each variable which bring them back together.

The parameters a and b have concrete interpretations in terms of either vacancies or bumpers. It is not necessary to then assert a and b are positive simply on abstract grounds of tendencies in the system that are equilibrium seeking. In (7.22) the term containing a is the only rate that depends on the state variables J and N and, then, only on their difference. Suppose that J is greater than N, the flow of jobs responsive to this gap should certainly be to the outside. If jobs are in surplus, it is the number *abandoned* that should be in proportion to the size of the surplus. It would make no sense at all to add more jobs such that if the surplus doubled, for example, the corresponding flow of new jobs would also double. There may well be a large flow of new jobs into a system that already has a surplus of jobs, but that would not be caused by nor be proportional to the surplus; rather, it would be due to some exogenous need or plan and could only appear in the exogenous term f_{job}. When $J - N$ is negative there is a surplus of men, not of jobs. To the extent flows of jobs to and from the system are influenced by the gap between J and N, jobs should enter the system in response to a surplus of men. The product $-a(J - N)$ should be positive so that once again a must be positive. A similar argument applies to b in equation (7.23).

Both a and b have natural interpretations as rates per discrepant individual in the system. Let jobs be surplus: a is the average death rate of a surplus job, one much more exposed to the danger of termination because no incumbent need be considered. The job's vacant status is temporary while the search for the replacement goes on, but this is exactly the period when preconceived ideas about its dispensability would be put into effect as well as when a difficult search for a replacement would be allowed to lapse. When men are surplus, a is the average rate at which an extra man manages to create a job. Conversely, b is the rate of the disappearance of a surplus man; when jobs are surplus, b becomes the rate at which an unfilled job calls forth a recruit. It might be thought that equations (7.22) and (7.23) define a model that integrates the treatment of vacancies and bumpers. It is true that a and b remain positive, and the form of the equations need not be changed when the system switches from a state of surplus men to one of surplus jobs, back again, and so on; but the numerical size of a, or of b, cannot be expected to remain the same during such switches. A surplus man may in some sense "call up" a new job at a constant rate, but this value of a for $V < 0$ surely will not happen to coincide with the rate at which a vacant job leaves the system, the value of a for $V > 0$. The equations are tractable only when there tends to be either a chronic surplus of jobs or a chronic surplus of men in the system.

The complete solution of (7.22) and (7.23) for constant exogenous forces is given in Section 7.1. It is not restricted to $V > 0$; V is now simply an auxiliary variable, the gap between J and N, useful because its differential equation is self-contained. Since a and b are positive, it follows from (7.8) that V approaches an equilibrium value, given by

$$V_e = \frac{f_{\text{job}} + f_{\text{man}}}{a + b} \qquad (7.24)$$

The range of values of a and b found for the clergies may be fairly typical. Their equilibrium is reached quickly, and the transient terms in V and their contributions to the evolving values of J and N can be ignored. The rates of change of J and N are then the same, designated by r and specified in (7.11), which can now be rewritten

$$r = \frac{f_{\text{job}}b - f_{\text{man}}a}{a + b} \qquad (7.25)$$

159

7. Vacancy Models and Systems Evolution

If the exogenous forces are constant, V will not change sign over time, it will simply remain at the fixed size specified by (7.24). Its sign is the sign of $f_{job} + f_{man}$. If this sum is negative, the bumper interpretation of the equations is required and if positive, the vacancy interpretation. Positive f_{job} means the injection of new jobs while positive f_{man} means retirement of men in the equations, conventions which are natural since both processes create vacancies. The vacancy models of Section 7.1 and Chapter 2 seem more restrictive than necessary, since they require that both f_{job} and f_{man}, not just their sum, be positive. The converse model, of bumpers, requires both f_{job} and f_{man} to be negative.

Mixed signs for f_{job} and f_{man} do not disrupt the equations in this chapter, but they do produce extreme results. Suppose the sum is positive, then the vacancy interpretation applies. From (7.25) the rate of growth, r, is necessarily positive when f_{man} is negative; r is necessarily negative when f_{job} is negative, regardless of the sizes of a and b. Regard the last terms on the right of (7.22) and (7.23) as flows. Since a and b are positive, this pair always produce opposite flows of men and jobs—when $V > 0$, flows of jobs out and men in correspond to vacancy terminations; when $V < 0$, flows of jobs in and men out correspond to bumper terminations. Call these the "dependent" flows. The conventions for f_{man} and f_{job} dovetail— when both are positive, each is opposite to the corresponding dependent flow, since $V > 0$ follows from (7.24); if both are negative, they are also opposite to the corresponding dependent flows. Mixed signs for f_{man} and f_{job}, regardless of whether their sum is positive or negative, necessarily means that one of them represents a forced flow in the same direction as the dependent flow in that variable, forcing rapid cumulative change. Once V has settled down to its equilibrium size, the other state variable must also cumulate rapidly in the same direction.

A different kind of model of movements is needed when vacant jobs and jobless men are permitted to coexist in the system. Let $L(t)$ stand for the number of men without jobs loose in the system that the model is to describe. Let $V(t)$ now stand for the total number of vacant jobs. [$L(t)$ is set zero in the vacancy model and $V(t)$ is set zero in the bumper model.] Equation (7.1) now becomes

$$J(t) - V(t) = N(t) - L(t) \qquad (7.26)$$

where each side of the equation counts the number of filled jobs.

Three independent equations in rates of change of these four variables are needed for the model to be determinate. If they are to reflect causal mechanisms at the individual level, they may differ from the earlier equations in this section and in Section 7.1. There are a host of possibilities (see Section 8.4).

7.3 Retirement, Acceleration, and the Long Run

There is little reason to suppose that departures of men depend on the number of vacancies in the system at the time, but it does not follow that $f_{man}(t)$ is wholly arbitrary. The primary determinant of the number of retirements and deaths in a particular year is the size range of entering cohorts some forty years before. The latter, by the model, is proportional to the numbers of vacancies in those earlier years. It is impracticable to incorporate such extreme lags in the model, but some approximate representation of the determinants of $f_{man}(t)$ is desirable. The goal is a rough assessment of the evolution of system size in the long run, over many decades.

Total departures in a year are split equally between moves into pool and into limbo on the one hand and into death plus retirements on the other (see Table 5.8). Moves up to pool and limbo can be expected to grow or decline in proportion to the total number of incumbents, whether the moves are thought to reflect career decisions by individuals or pressures from central authorities. The total flow of men out of a huge system should be larger than that from a tiny system. In view of the difficulty of incorporating lagged terms for age effects, this comparative argument suggests the use of a simple proportionality between the total $f_{man}(t)$ and the $N(t)$. (The same proportionality is plausible in those organizations where substantial numbers of men voluntarily quit to take up other careers, although such rates may be sensitive to age and seniority, especially if rates were computed for separate strata.)

In equations (7.3)–(7.5) defining the vacancy model, let

$$f_{man}(t) = \rho N(t) \qquad (7.27)$$

where ρ is assumed to be constant. The whole approach to the equations must be changed. No longer is (7.3) for the number of vacancies independent of the others. There is no basis for assuming any simple relation between the flow of new jobs, f_{job}, and the size of the system. Results from the model will be for qualitative guidance, not for concrete prediction; to simplify the analysis, f_{job} will be assumed constant. Equation (7.4) is unchanged, while (7.3) becomes

$$\frac{dV(t)}{dt} = f_{job} + \rho N(t) - V(t)pv \tag{7.28}$$

and

$$\frac{dN(t)}{dt} = f_{job} - V(t)p_{job}v - \frac{dV(t)}{dt} \tag{7.29}$$

Differentiate (7.28) again:

$$\frac{d^2V}{dt^2} = \rho\frac{dN}{dt} - pv\frac{dV}{dt} \tag{7.30}$$

When (7.29) is substituted in (7.30) an equation involving only $V(t)$ results:

$$(d^2V/dt^2) + (pv + \rho)(dV/dt) + \rho p_{job}vV = \rho f_{job} \tag{7.31}$$

A new perspective on the vacancy model is opened up. Draw an analogy between V and the distance of a particle along a line from an origin in elementary mechanics. Equation (7.31) can be seen as a simple equation in forces. The role of acceleration is played by d^2V/dt^2 and mass, by $1/\rho$. The driving force is measured by f_{job}, the rate of injection of new jobs. There is also a frictional force that works against f_{job}; it is velocity dependent, like air drag. Finally, there is a restoring force proportional to the displacement, as in a spring or for the sweep of a pendulum.[4] The vacancy model stipulates that V shall not be negative, a limitation not usually found in analyzing the movement of a spring or pendulum in a viscous medium. It is clear, however, that the magnitudes of forces and parameters are such that V will not tend to return to zero or beyond. Equilibrium will be reached for some positive value of V, when the restoring force balances the driving force. Endless oscillation is prevented by the frictional force.

No analogy should be relied on, but it is interesting to see what parameters enter the terms acting like restoring and frictional forces. The product $p_{job}v$ corresponds to the stiffness of a spring or the effective weight of a pendulum; the larger the chance of a vacant job's being ended, the stronger the pull to bring V back to zero. The coefficient of the viscous force is $1 + pv/\rho$; as it increases, the drag opposing any given motion (any given rate of change of V) increases in proportion. Even if pv is zero, there is a damping term. If the origin of the coefficient is traced back, the unity term reflects the fact that V is not really an isolated variable but enmeshed in a larger set.

The analogy raises the question of units.[5] The only true units in the vacancy model are time and number. All the equations in this book must be and are consistent in these units. Every separate term in (7.21) has the units of number/(time)^2: ρ and v have as unit $1/\text{time}$; p and p_{job} are pure numbers; f_{job} is a rate with unit $\#/\text{time}$; and V of course has number as unit. Only a pure number is meaningful as the argument of a mathematical function like the exponential; whenever a quantity appears in that role, as in (7.8), it meets the test. Casting $1/\rho$ in the role of mass seems intuitively plausible; the faster the retirement of men, the less inertia there is in the building up of the rate of growth of vacancies.

The solution of (7.31) is[6]

$$V(t) = K_1\, e^{m_+ t} + K_2\, e^{m_- t} + \frac{f_{\text{job}}}{p_{\text{job}} v} \qquad (7.32)$$

where

$$m_{\pm} = \tfrac{1}{2}\{-(pv + \rho) \pm [(pv + \rho)^2 - 4\rho p_{\text{job}} v]^{1/2}\} \qquad (7.33)$$

The general behavior of $V(t)$ over time is completely determined by the values of m_+ and m_-. The constants K_1 and K_2 are arbitrary constants necessary to specify the initial size and rate of change of V. It is possible to settle the crucial issues about the values of m_+ and m_- without specifying numerical values for the various parameters, p_{job}, v, p, and ρ. Expand and rearrange the radical in (7.33):

$$(pv + \rho)^2 - 4\rho p_{\text{job}} v = (pv - \rho)^2 + 4\rho v(p - p_{\text{job}}) \qquad (7.34)$$

Since $p - p_{\text{job}} = p_{\text{man}}$, which is greater than zero, and any number when squared is positive, m_+ and m_- can have no imaginary component. $V(t)$ can exhibit no tendency to oscillate. The square root in (7.33) must be less in magnitude than the first term, by inspection. Thus, both roots are negative, and $V(t)$ must eventually move from any initial value to its constant component in (7.32). The magnitude of m_+ is less than that of m_-; so the speed of approach is limited primarily by the size of m_+.

From (7.27) the parameter ρ is a retirement rate per year per man in the system; it cannot be as large as 0.1, given average careers of even fifteen or twenty years. However, v is the movement rate per year per vacancy, which is at least 1.0. Moreover, p is larger than p_{job} and must be substantial if chains are to run their course within a year or so. Therefore, the second term in the square root in (7.33) is usually much smaller than the first term. The square root of a number close to 1 is just halfway between 1 and the number; hence, a good approximation

$$m_+ \doteq \left[-\frac{(pv + \rho)}{2} \right]\left[1 - \left(1 - \frac{2\rho p_{job} v}{(pv + \rho)^2} \right) \right] \doteq -\left(\frac{\rho p_{job} v}{pv + \rho} \right) \quad (7.35)$$

Since ρ is much smaller than pv, a further approximation can be made:

$$m_+ \doteq -\left(\frac{p_{job}}{p} \right)\rho \quad (7.36)$$

The parameter v, the rate at which a vacancy moves, has dropped out. When the retirement rate is small, the effective rate of approach by $V(t)$ to its equilibrium value is even smaller, according to (7.36). If average career length is more than ten years, it will take more than a decade for the system to get even halfway to its steady state.

Equation (7.27) is only a crude approximation to the true dependence of retirement rate now on size of the system before, when the men retiring had entered the system. The approximation makes sense since the equations do not predict decisive changes in variables in periods shorter than the average career. Equilibrium is predicted after sufficient time, not only in the number of vacancies but also in the numbers of men and jobs; by (7.32)

$$V_e = \frac{f_{job}}{p_{job} v} \quad (7.37)$$

The parallel with (7.9) in Section 7.1 is informative. The number of vacancies, the heart of the circulatory process, adapts to the driving force in the same way, but retirement no longer is included in the driving force. Instead retirement adjusts to the size of the system, it provides a safety valve that permits the system to stabilize. From equation (7.28) the size of $N(t)$ in equilibrium is

$$N_e = \left(\frac{p_{man}}{p_{job}} \right)\left(\frac{f_{job}}{\rho} \right) \quad (7.38)$$

The variation of N_e with parameters makes sense: the bigger the p_{man}, the bigger the inflow of recruits; therefore, the bigger N_e must be, for given ρ and the ratio of job input to job output, in order to generate an equal outflow of retirements. Mobility can also be predicted by using (7.7). At equilibrium, the in-mobility rate is

$$\mu = \frac{\rho(1 - p_{job})}{p_{man}} \tag{7.39}$$

It is roughly the retirement rate per man measured against the chance a vacant job will call a new recruit. The rate for a man moving out of his job in a year is almost the same as the in-mobility rate and depends neither on the rate of creation of jobs nor on the speed of movement of vacancies.

A look at some data for the churches will be instructive, even though the driving force and the parameters fluctuate quite a bit. In the Episcopal case, the average value of f_{job} in eleven samples over five decades, multiplied by the sampling ratio, is 145 new jobs per year. The average values of p_{job} and p_{man} are 0.152 and 0.372. The retirement rate in the same fifty years averages 0.05 per man this year; that is less than one fortieth of pv, amply justifying the approximation in (7.36). Fifty years is required for the system to get halfway to the equilibrium size, after f_{job} and the parameters assume constant values. The span of fifty years in the observations is not a large one by this standard. The observed size of the system of 1–1 jobs in 1954–1955 is 5100, and the predicted size in equilibrium is 7100. The estimated size in 1913 is just under 4000. The trend is toward the predicted equilibrium, but the system of 1–1 jobs in the Episcopal case in 1955 is nowhere near equilibrium, according to this simplified model of long-run behavior.

Similar estimates for the Methodist church are based on two samples only fourteen years apart, but the value of $1/m_+$ is only twenty-two years. The predicted value of $N(t)$ at equilibrium is 9100, and the estimated values in 1923 and 1937 are 12,700 and 11,100 respectively. In the Methodist church, the system of 1–1 jobs is declining but has not declined to anywhere near equilibrium, according to the projection afforded by the simplified model of long-run behavior.

The moral suggested by this glance at the long run is simple: a large system of men and jobs is unlikely ever to be near equilibrium, though for a few years the size may remain steady. It takes a very long time for a system to reach the dynamic equilibrium compatible with given structural characteristics and input rates; meanwhile, the inputs or the characteristics will have shifted again. In view of this conclusion, it is not necessary to analyze the distributions of seniority and age implied by the retirement model. The emphasis in Chapter 2 and Section 7.1 on separate treatment of cohorts of vacancies, with the initial states of the system treated as data to be observed, appears to be the sensible course (further evidence will be presented in Section 10.1).

7.4 Basic Stratified Model in Continuous Time

Chapter 5 demonstrated the greater predictive power of a stratified model, and the continuous time analogue will now be spelled out. All variables have s components, one for each stratum, and are written as row vectors. As in Chapter 2, let q_{ik} be the fraction of vacancy moves from stratum i which go to stratum k, and place it in the ith row and the kth column of a square matrix Q. The remaining fraction of moves from stratum i must go to the outside. Array these termination fractions down the diagonal of a square matrix P whose other entries are zero. The off-diagonal elements in the kth column of Q determine moves of men to all other strata from the kth stratum. The diagonal elements are irrelevant to interstratum moves, but it is convenient instead to keep track of total moves out of a stratum. Call the resulting matrix O:

$$O_{ii} = -\sum_{k \neq i} q_{ik} \quad \text{and} \quad O_{ik} = q_{ik}, \quad i \neq k \qquad (7.40)$$

Two equations for the stratified model are exactly parallel to (7.1) and (7.4):

$$\mathbf{J} = \mathbf{N} + \mathbf{V} \qquad (7.41)$$

and

$$\frac{d\mathbf{J}}{dt} = \mathbf{f}_{job} - \mathbf{V}vP_{job} \qquad (7.42)$$

but $\mathbf{V}$ as a row vector must precede a parameter matrix in any product. The exogenous forcing term and its components for men and for jobs are now specified by stratum and written as row vectors. Specifying the rate of change of vacancies by stratum—the analogue

166

to (7.3)—leads to a new form of equation because accounts must be kept for interstratum moves:

$$\frac{d\mathbf{V}}{dt} = \mathbf{f} + \mathbf{V}v(O - P) \tag{7.43}$$

Since the matrix O is in an average sense zero, the parallel of (7.43) to (7.3) is quite close.

An important identity among the matrices of parameters follows from the definition of O:

$$Q - O + P = I \tag{7.44}$$

where I is the identity matrix with unity in diagonal entries and zero elsewhere. Equation (7.43) can be rewritten as

$$\frac{d\mathbf{V}}{dt} + \mathbf{V}v(I - Q) = \mathbf{f} \tag{7.45}$$

Equation (7.45) could have been written down directly by inspection, but it is less transparent than (7.43) since the transactions with the outside are not kept distinct from the sums of internal moves. Either equation constitutes a coupled set of simultaneous linear differential equations of first order in the numbers of vacancies by stratum. The logic and structure of the solution[7] is parallel to that for an earlier pair of coupled equations, (7.28) and (7.29).

Let the component of the forcing term $\mathbf{f}$ in each stratum—the total rate of creation of vacancies in that stratum—be a constant, independent of $\mathbf{V}$ and $\mathbf{J}$. If there exists an equilibrium solution for $\mathbf{V}$, it can be found by setting the rate of change of $\mathbf{V}$ equal to zero. The result is

$$\mathbf{V}_e = \mathbf{f}[v(I - Q)]^{-1} \tag{7.46}$$

The result is strongly reminiscent of equation (2.10) for the stratified model in Chapter 2. The time-dependent part of the solution for $\mathbf{V}(t)$ consists of exponential terms in t, in which the decay rates are solutions of the determinantal equation:

$$|mI + v(I - Q)| = 0 \tag{7.47}$$

Equation (7.47) will be solved numerically with the Q estimated for the Episcopal church in Table 5.1. A cubic equation is obtained.

After terms are collected, and the equation is divided by v^3, the result is

$$x^3 + 2.256x^2 + 1.642x + 0.382 = 0 \qquad (7.48)$$

In (7.48) x is the ratio m/v. It can be shown that all three roots are real.[8] All the coefficients in this equation are positive; it is obvious that no real roots can be positive. Thus the time-dependent part of $\mathbf{V}(t)$ is transient, and $\mathbf{V}(t)$ will approach the equilibrium vector in (7.46) without oscillation. One root is $(-\frac{1}{2})$, as can be verified by substitution. By Newton's rule, no real root of (7.48) can be larger than that value. Thus the most persistent component of the transient part of $\mathbf{V}(t)$ will decay at a rate of about $\frac{1}{2}v$. That result is close to the one found in Section 7.1 for the binomial model. Since the value of v estimated in Section 7.1 was 5 per year, the transient part of $\mathbf{V}(t)$ will practically disappear within a year. As in Section 7.1, the equilibrium predictions of the model are applicable shortly after the input of vacancies changes to a new level.

It is not necessary to make numerical predictions of mobility based on (7.46) because such predictions will be identical with those reported in Section 5.2. One assumption has been left implicit. The same total rate of movement of a vacancy, v, has been used for each stratum. If there is a different rate for each stratum, the only change needed in the equation is an interpretation of v as a diagonal matrix like P. The position of v in each product in each equation as written is correct. Symbolize the matrix form by brackets around v. Equation (7.46) can be rewritten as

$$\mathbf{V}_e\{v\} = \mathbf{f}(I - Q)^{-1} \qquad (7.49)$$

where the ith component in the vector on the left side now contains v_i, not an overall v. In practice the only quantity to be predicted is the number of moves per year from a stratum, not the number of vacancies in a stratum at a given time. This prediction is affected neither by the sizes of the individual v_i nor by their average size.

7.5 Stratified Model with Retirement

The number of men leaving a stratum for the outside per unit time is assumed to be a constant, ρ_i, times the number of men in the stratum, N_i. Define a diagonal matrix R, parallel to P, with the retirement rates ρ_i on the diagonal. Then

$$\mathbf{f}_{\text{man}} = NR \qquad (7.50)$$

and, again, f_{job} is assumed constant. The search for an equation for V in isolation is parallel to that in Section 7.3, as is the result:

$$\frac{d^2\mathbf{V}}{dt^2} + \frac{d\mathbf{V}}{dt}[v(I - Q) + R] + \mathbf{V}vP_{\text{job}}R = \mathbf{f}_{\text{job}}R \qquad (7.51)$$

By analogy to the results in Section 7.3, it is clear that equilibrium will be reached only slowly, perhaps after decades.

The number of vacancies in equilibrium is

$$\mathbf{V}_e = \mathbf{f}_{\text{job}}[vP_{\text{job}}]^{-1} \qquad (7.52)$$

Each stratum can be treated as a separate system (using the binomial model of Section 7.3) when it comes to finding the equilibrium stock of vacancies. The real point of the model is the sizes of the different strata in equilibrium, and here strata do interact. Return to (7.45) and substitute (7.50). In equilibrium N must be

$$\mathbf{N}_e = [\mathbf{f}_{\text{job}}P_{\text{job}}^{-1}(I - Q) - \mathbf{f}_{\text{job}}]R^{-1} \qquad (7.53)$$

To understand the meaning of this result expand the formula for each stratum. Both a subscript i for the given stratum and a running subscript k for strata must be introduced, and it is then very clumsy to retain a subscript for "job." The latter appears always and only on $\mathbf{f}$ and P in (7.53); it need not be indicated explicitly. Similarly, the subscript e for equilibrium, which appears only on $\mathbf{N}$, is suppressed. The size of the ith stratum in equilibrium thus becomes

$$N_i = \frac{1}{\rho_i}\left[\frac{f_i}{p_i} - \sum_{k=1}^{s} \frac{f_k}{p_k} q_{ki} - f_i\right] \qquad (7.54)$$

If all terms in the bracket with the subscript i are brought together, the result is

$$\frac{f_i}{p_i}(1 - q_{ii} - p_i)$$

By definition of the transition fractions

$$(1 - q_{ii} - p_i) = p_{i,\text{man}} + \sum_{\substack{i=1 \\ k \neq i}}^{s} q_{ik} \qquad (7.55)$$

and (7.54) can be rewritten as

$$N_i = \frac{f_i p_{i,\,\mathrm{man}}}{\rho_i p_i} + \frac{1}{\rho_i} \sum_{\substack{k=1 \\ k \neq i}}^{s} \left[\frac{f_i}{p_i} q_{ik} - \frac{f_k}{p_k} q_{ki} \right] \qquad (7.56)$$

In (7.56) f_i and p_i are understood to be only the "job" component, while $p_{i,\,\mathrm{man}}$ is the fraction of vacancy moves which terminates the vacancy by introducing a new recruit. The first term on the right of (7.56) corresponds exactly to the result in (7.38) for the binomial model. Thus the size of the ith stratum in equilibrium differs from what it would be if there were no other strata by the amount shown in the second term on the right side of (7.56). The interaction effect of other strata upon the size of the given stratum is easy to interpret; it is simply a weighted measure of the degree of asymmetry in the transition fractions, q_{ik}.

Table 7.2 lists the predicted value of N_i for each stratum in equi-

Table 7.2   Predicted Sizes of Job Strata in Equilibrium[a]
for Episcopal and Methodist Churches

Stratum	Rates and parameters by stratum[b]			Size of stratum i, N_i	
	f_{job}	p_{job}	ρ_i	Observed in latest year	Predicted in equilibrium
Episcopal, 1912–1955					
Big	3.2	.048	.032	2100	290
Medium	43	.114	.056	2100	2600
Small	99	.242	.069	900	2500
Methodist, 1922–1937					
Big	4.2	.064	.057	3800	[c]
Medium	480	.132	.073	5400	20,700
Small	350	.408	.163	1900	[c]

[a] Numbers of filled jobs from (7.54). Rate and size estimates from the samples in Chapters 4–6 have been multiplied by the appropriate sampling ratios; each figure refers to the total system of 1–1 jobs in a church.

[b] The unit of time is a year. The estimated values of q_{ik} are reported in Table 5.1 and Table 6.1 for the Episcopal and Methodist churches.

[c] The numerical figures from (7.54) are negative: -6750 for the upper stratum and -860 for the bottom stratum.

librium and the values of $\mathbf{f}_{\mathrm{job}}$, p_{job}, and ρ, for each church together with the latest observed sizes of strata. The differences between prediction and observation seem too large to be attributed entirely to how far each church is from reaching equilibrium or to how much the f_{job} and the parameters fluctuated in this era. Lower limits on the numbers of vacancies, of jobs, and of men in a stratum are inherent in the application of the vacancy model. Equation (7.54) can yield negative values of N_i, as it does for the strata of big and small jobs of the Methodist church; the model should terminate the applicability of the equation before any N_i becomes negative [see equations (7.12) and (7.13)]. It is not only the predictions below zero in Table 7.2 that create uneasiness. The pattern of equilibrium sizes for Episcopal strata is puzzling. The total size in combined strata is not as unreasonable, but it is not the same as that for the binomial model (see Section 7.3).

7.6 *Job Evolution and System Size in the Long Run*

Individual parishes do not remain fixed in wealth or size. Assignments of jobs to strata change independently of moves by men. Predictions of the number of jobs in a stratum in the long run must include such changes, and the possibility of reaching equilibrium depends on them. Unfortunately the importance of change in job size from year to year was not appreciated at first; and tabulations of successive sizes were made for only a few of the national clergy samples. Equilibrium sizes of the strata will therefore be calculated for whole ranges of rates defining job evolution. The sensitivity of these predictions will become apparent and will be compared with the sensitivity of stratum size in equilibrium to the rate of creation of jobs.

The simplest assumption, and a plausible one, is that the number of jobs which move from stratum i to stratum j in unit time because of changes in number of communicants is a constant rate, g_{ij}, times the number of jobs in stratum i. The same rate applies whether the job is filled or is temporarily vacant. Enter the parameter g_{ij} in the ith row and j^{th} column of a matrix G. No rate is defined when $i = j$; in the diagonal cell of the ith row of G enter instead the sum,

$$\left(-\sum_{\substack{j=1 \\ j \neq i}}^{s} g_{ij} \right)$$

The matrix G is exactly parallel in structure to the matrix O defined in (7.40), although the elements in the former are not constrained in size. The net rate of change in number of jobs in stratum i, due to evolution of job sizes, is the ith entry in the vector JvG.

The addition of simple terms containing G to the equations of the model seems innocuous, but it greatly increases the difficulty of obtaining concrete solutions. Unlike the matrix O, the matrix G appears in the equation for rate of change of jobs, as well as in those for men and vacancies. The defining equations for the stratified model with fixed retirement rates per man, R, and with fixed evolution rates per job between strata, vG, are (7.1) plus

$$\frac{dV}{dt} = f_{job} + NR - Vv(I - Q - G) \qquad (7.57)$$

and

$$\frac{dJ}{dt} = f_{job} - VvP_{job} + JvG \qquad (7.58)$$

No longer can an equation with V as the only state variable be extracted as in Section 7.5. Yet terms in G would have little impact on the model in Section 7.4, where f_{man} is assumed constant rather than proportional to N.

Equations (7.57) and (7.58) can be solved by standard techniques[9] for given values of all the coefficients in the matrices and of the exogenous flows f_{job}. These equations are a coupled set of $2s$ linear, first-order differential equations in $2s$ variables, with constant inhomogeneous terms. A determinantal equation for the allowed transient rates m could be written down parallel to (7.47), but the calculations are difficult. Assume that the time-dependent parts of the solutions for V and J are transients and that each vector approaches its equilibrium value. In equilibrium the equations can be solved for Vv in terms of N:

$$Vv = (f_{job} + NR)(I - Q - G)^{-1} \qquad (7.59)$$

$$Vv = (f_{job} + NvG)(P_{job} - G)^{-1} \qquad (7.60)$$

Equating these two formulas for V yields an equation in the equilibrium vector N. Since inverses of sums of matrices enter the equation, it does not yield qualitative insight of the sort obtained from (7.56).

The form of the matrix G must be simplified in order to obtain manageable formulas for N in terms of job evolution rates. Numerical estimates for all the other parameters, known from Chapters 5 and 6, must be used. The familiar three strata by number of communicants are used for each church. Two different simplifications of G will be used, each of which reduces the number of independent rates to two.

The general structure of G is the same for all three churches. All the rates g_{ij} are small compared to the corresponding q_{ij} (and g_{ii} is zero by definition). The sum of all the evolution rates from a stratum is therefore also small compared to the termination rate q_{io} for vacancies. A job never jumped from the low to the high stratum, or conversely; mergers and splits are treated as endings and creations of jobs. The corner rates, g_{13} and g_{31}, are zero. Only four nonzero rates are left, all small.

It is the net result of opposite flows of jobs between two strata which is the contribution of job evolution to stratum size. One reasonable approximation is the replacement of a reciprocal pair of rates, g_{ij} and g_{ji}, by a single reduced rate in the direction of the net flow of jobs by evolution. This direction is affected by the sizes of the two strata as well as the rates, and the approximation can only be valid when initial stratum sizes are not remote from the equilibrium sizes.

In the Episcopal church fragmentary evidence showed jobs moving in considerable numbers from the low to the middle stratum but less often in the reverse direction, from the middle stratum, in spite of its larger size in the period studied. Both the flow of newly created jobs and the termination rate are much larger for the low than the middle stratum (Table 7.2). They balance out, and it is consistent to assign the net direction of flow from low to middle. The direction is even clearer between the top and middle strata. The top stratum loses few jobs to and gains many from the middle stratum. The flow of newly created jobs to the middle stratum is far greater and the termination rate only moderately greater. The matrix G will first be assumed to have the form

$$G = \begin{pmatrix} 0 & 0 & 0 \\ \alpha & -\alpha & 0 \\ 0 & \beta & -\beta \end{pmatrix} \frac{1}{1000\,v} \qquad (7.61)$$

where the number on the right is inserted to simplify later calculations. The net effect of job evolution using this approximation is to push jobs from the bottom stratum into the middle stratum and from there, into the top stratum.

The initial guess, on the basis of a few tabulations of changes in size of churches in successive years, was that the net percentages of jobs in a stratum changing to another stratum per year was about one percent; specifically,

$$\frac{\alpha}{1000} = 0.01 \quad \text{and} \quad \frac{\beta}{1000} = 0.02$$

These both correspond to a net flow of jobs, for stratum sizes as in the 1950s, of about twenty jobs per year. With v about 5, as for the Episcopal church, the elements in G are then small enough to be negligible in comparison to elements of P_{job} or of $I - Q$. Equations (7.59) and (7.60) can each be simplified by dropping G in the inverse matrix on the right side.

With these approximations, the equation in the equilibrium size of $\mathbf{N}$ becomes

$$(\mathbf{f}_{job} + \mathbf{N}R)(I - Q)^{-1}P_{job} = \mathbf{f}_{job} + \mathbf{N}vG \qquad (7.62)$$

Only the solution for the Episcopal church is treated, and numerical estimates of parameters are taken from Tables 5.1 and 7.2. After considerable manipulation, formulas for separate components of $\mathbf{N}$ in terms of the parameters α and β are derived:

$$N_1 = 281 + \frac{5165}{1 + 4.5/\alpha} + \frac{8920}{(1 + 4.5/\alpha)(1 + 14/\beta)} - \frac{237}{1 + 14/\beta} \qquad (7.63)$$

$$N_2 = \frac{2565}{1 + 0.222\alpha}\left(1 + \frac{1.72}{1 + 14/\beta}\right) \qquad (7.64)$$

$$N_3 = \frac{2520}{1 + 0.072\beta} \qquad (7.65)$$

When $\alpha = \beta = 0$ these equations reduce to the predicted values found in Table 7.2 before G was introduced.

Table 7.3 reports predictions of $\mathbf{N}$ in equilibrium for various pairs of values of α and β. All are small enough so that neglect of G in the inverses in (7.59) and (7.60) has made a negligible difference in the predictions. The total size is not affected by changes in α and β to the same extent as are the relative sizes in the three strata. Comparison of the second with the third column in Table 7.3 suggests that predicted size in any stratum varies by a smaller percentage than the percentage change in the parameters α and β themselves. Even for α and β both 100, corresponding to *net* flows of one-tenth of the jobs

Table 7.3   Some Predictions of Strata Sizes in Equilibrium when Jobs only Grow in Number of Communicants[a]

	$\alpha=\beta=0$	$\alpha=2,\ \beta=10$	$\alpha=2.1,\ \beta=12$	$\alpha=10,\ \beta=20$	$\alpha=100,\ \beta=100$
N_1	280	2920	3100	7350	12,600
N_2	2565	3040	3100	1600	270
N_3	2520	1460	1350	1030	300
Total	5370	7420	7550	9980	13,200

[a] From equations (7.63)–(7.65); using the following parameter values for the Episcopal church

(I)

$$
G = \begin{pmatrix} 0 & 0 & 0 \\ \alpha & -\alpha & 0 \\ 0 & \beta & -\beta \end{pmatrix} \frac{1}{1000v}
$$

where different values of α and β are used in each column and v does not affect the predictions.

(II) $\mathbf{f}$, $\mathbf{p}_{\text{job}}$, and ρ_i from Table 7.2.

(III) Q from Table 5.1.

in each stratum to the next higher stratum per year, the predicted sizes are not unrecognizably small or large. The numbers of vacancies in equilibrium can be predicted from (7.60) using Table 7.3. Only for $\alpha = \beta = 0$ are the numbers of vacancies comparable to the numbers of men and filled jobs. Vacancies are much more numerous in the lower two strata, relatively and absolutely, as could be expected.

There is a major weakness in the α, β form for G. The matrix G is useful for long-term prediction only if its components are constant. There is certainly downward movement of jobs by loss of parishioners as well as upward movement across stratum boundaries. The net flow may always remain up; if the relative sizes of two strata change drastically over time, it is implausible that the net flow remains a fixed fraction of the size of one of them. It cannot do so if the reciprocal rates g_{ij} and g_{ji} do stay constant. The practical implication is that equations (7.62)–(7.64) are meaningful only for values of α and β that predict equilibrium distributions of sizes not too dissimilar to the observed distribution of men among strata. The values of 2.1 for α and 12 for β can be seen, from Table 7.3, to yield a predicted $\mathbf{N}$ proportional to the observed $\mathbf{N}$ in the data on the Episcopal church for 1955, reported in Section 7.1. A unit change in α or β corresponds to a change of 0.001 in the actual net rate of change of jobs between strata per job per year. Thus an increase of α from 2 to 3 means an increase in the net flow of jobs to the highest stratum of about only 3 jobs per year, but the increase in the equilibrium size of N_1 is 1000 jobs.

Downward flow of jobs across stratum boundaries, as some parishes lose members, must be allowed for in the matrix G. An alternate approximation for G, then, is needed. For simplicity the parameters—the rates of flow across boundaries per job per unit time—will be assumed the same in different strata for the same direction. The new form of G, G', is

$$G' = \begin{pmatrix} -\delta & \delta & 0 \\ \varepsilon & -\varepsilon - \delta & \delta \\ 0 & \varepsilon & -\varepsilon \end{pmatrix} \frac{1}{1000 \ v} \qquad (7.66)$$

When G' is substituted in (7.62), equations relating predicted stratum sizes to δ and ε result. The form of G' is more intricate than the form of G; and the equations are more complex and will not be solved for N_i as an explicit function of δ and ε. The equations in predicted stratum sizes for the Episcopal case are

$$(0.032 + 0.0144\delta)N_1 - (0.0144\varepsilon + 0.0025\delta)N_2 + 0.0025\varepsilon N_3$$
$$= 9.7 \quad (7.67)$$

$$-0.0127\delta N_1 + (0.056 + 0.0127\varepsilon + 0.0071\delta)N_2 - 0.0071\varepsilon N_3$$
$$= 145 \quad (7.68)$$

$$-0.0051\delta N_2 + (0.069 + 0.0051\varepsilon)N_3 = 175 \qquad (7.69)$$

It is easy to find the predicted values of N_i for given numerical values of δ and ε. Table 7.4 reports some results.

The predictions for zero rates in the first column of Table 7.4 are from the first column of Table 7.3. In the next two columns of Table 7.4, the down rate δ and the up rate ε are taken equal. The naive supposition would be that the effects of down and up rates then cancel, but these two columns differ from the first column. The predicted size of the top stratum in particular is grossly increased by inclusion of nonzero, though equal, up and down rates. In the last column of Table 7.4, a new calculation is made with the form for G used in Table 7.3, and the net rates up from the bottom and middle

Table 7.4   Further Predictions of Strata Sizes in Equilibrium[a]

	$\alpha=\beta=0; \delta=\varepsilon=0$	$\delta=\varepsilon=10$	$\delta=\varepsilon=20$	$\varepsilon=20, \delta=10$	$\alpha=10, \beta=10$
N_1	280	1870	2020	3950	6300
N_2	2565	2180	2220	2340	1360
N_3	2520	2380	2360	1730	1460
Total	5370	6430	6600	8020	9120

[a] From the same basic equations and parameters used in Table 7.3, except that predictions in the middle three columns here are based on a different form for G,

$$
G' = \begin{pmatrix} -\delta & \delta & 0 \\ \varepsilon & -\varepsilon-\delta & \delta \\ 0 & \varepsilon & -\varepsilon \end{pmatrix} \frac{1}{1000v}
$$

which leads to equations (7.67)–(7.69).

strata are taken equal, $\alpha = \beta = 10$. In the next to last column, values for G'—$\varepsilon = 20$ and $\delta = 10$—are used that could be expected to yield the same predictions. Instead predictions in the last two columns are markedly different.

The overall conclusion is that evolution of jobs in size, as members join and leave parishes, is bound to have major effects on predicted stratum sizes—effects that are difficult to estimate. Two qualitative assertions are justified: the equilibrium size (1) of the top stratum will be larger and (2) of the bottom stratum smaller in the Episcopal church than would be predicted if the effects of job evolution are ignored.

These numerical explorations are based on specific estimates of parameters in the vacancy model for the Episcopal church. The estimates are subject to sampling variability; and different values of f_{job}, p_{job}, R, and Q can be anticipated for other organizations. It is natural now to observe how sensitive the predictions of equilibrium size are to changes in the vacancy parameters, in comparison to the sensitivity of the predictions to job evolution parameters exhibited in Tables 7.3 and 7.4. The parameters most likely to change over time and between organizations and most subject to sampling variability, are the components of $\mathbf{f}_{job}$, the rates of introduction of new jobs to various strata.

The estimate of $\mathbf{f}_{job}$ in the Episcopal church, averaged over fifty years, is given in Table 7.2—(3.2, 43, 99) new jobs per year. For comparison, the net flow of jobs per year into each stratum in equilibrium as a result of job evolution can be calculated: the sum of these net flows over all strata is zero. Equation (7.61) is used for G with values $\alpha = 2.1$ and $\beta = 12$ to estimate net flows:

$$(+7, +10, -17) = \mathbf{J}v G$$

$$= (3100, 3100, 1350) \begin{pmatrix} 0 & 0 & 0 \\ 0.0021 & -0.0021 & 0 \\ 0 & 0.012 & -0.012 \end{pmatrix} \quad (7.70)$$

The net flows due to job evolution in that situation are substantial fractions of the flows of new jobs from outside; they probably exceed any possible errors in the estimate of $\mathbf{f}_{job}$ due to sampling variability.

If job evolution is neglected, $G = 0$; then $\mathbf{f}_{job}$ is increased by the flows in (7.70); and the equations for the model in Section 7.5 yield the result

$$N = (2615, 3000, 1650)$$

in equilibrium, given

$$\mathbf{f}_{job} = (10, 53, 82)$$

For comparison, the original result in Table 7.2 is

$$N = (280, 2565, 2520)$$

from

$$\mathbf{f}_{job} = (3, 43, 99)$$

The vacancy model is sensitive to changes in parameters, but not unreasonably so. The only dramatic change in N is for the first stratum, where the assumed value of $\mathbf{f}_{job}$ has been more than tripled.

The model is not as sensitive to changes in $\mathbf{f}_{job}$ as it is to changes in evolution rates. The prediction from the original $\mathbf{f}_{job}$, but with job evolution included, at rates that yield the same flows of jobs into strata as the increased $\mathbf{f}_{job}$, is

$$N = (3100, 3100, 1350)$$

from Table 7.3. Part of this difference in sensitivity reflects the difference in the path of the system over time. The increase in $\mathbf{f}_{job}$ assumed is a constant term operating continuously from time zero. The effect of evolution rates depends on the sizes of the strata as they evolve over time from arbitrary initial values.

In the Methodist church, the pattern of job evolution observed is different than that for the Episcopal church. The yearly flow of new jobs—always defined to include jobs split off from compound parishes and jobs filled after long being empty—is largest to the middle stratum and is a substantial fraction of the total size of each stratum. The fragmentary data available for the Methodist church suggests that jobs also evolve in size faster than is common in the Episcopal church, and most notably in the middle stratum. A form for G different from either of the idealizations used for the Episcopal case would, of course, be necessary to represent this pattern.

7.7 Stochastic Models for Individuals in Continuous Time

Variability in the spacing in time between moves by a vacancy is to be expected. That problem was sidestepped in Chapter 2 by the use of conditional transition probabilities, and it did not arise in the deterministic models for aggregates in this chapter. A variety of stochastic processes for individuals incorporating assumptions about spacing will be surveyed here. It will be argued that the use of such processes contributes little to vacancy models, whether at the individual level, the aggregate level, or for study of interaction effects.

The original model for moves by a vacancy in Section 2.1 can be seen as imbedded[10] in a Markov process in continuous time. A Markov process is also the simplest generalization of the deterministic models of previous sections to deal with moves by individual vacancies. The probability of a move in the next instant is independent of how long the individual has been in its current state so that the distribution of times between moves is a negative exponential in a Markov process.[11] In the special case when the mean rate of making moves, v, is the same whatever stratum the vacancy is in, the vacancy model is close to that for the generalized Poisson process.[12] There must be $s + 1$ states in the latter, since the "outside" must be treated as a stratum which is an absorbing state. Chain length distributions could be found by computing the distribution of the number of moves required to first reach stratum zero starting from a given other stratum; that is closely related to the calculation of "absorption probabilities" and of "first passage times." Special provision would have to be made for the transitions from a stratum back to itself that are allowed in the vacancy chain model, that is, for moves from one job to another in the same stratum. A variety of techniques for carrying out such calculations are known, which are also applicable when the average rate of movement depends on which stratum the vacancy is in and for more general time distributions than the negative exponential.[13]

The average rate of movement by a vacancy may vary not only with its initial stratum but also with the destination stratum. Much more complex models are needed in this case. The semi-Markov process[14] can be used only if no transitions are possible from a stratum back to itself. The Markov renewal process[15] permits such transitions. In other respects the two are equivalent. Both admit general forms of distributions for time to the next move. They reduce for one special form of the time distribution to the Markov process and for another, to the conventional Markov chain for fixed intervals. When there is only one state, corresponding to the binomial model in Section 2.1, they reduce to a renewal process.[16]

Lack of data on exact times of vacancy moves precludes the actual application of any of these stochastic processes. However, one can ask whether the procedures used earlier to estimate the conditional transition probabilities are consistent in principle with such processes. Apparently the most general process consistent with estimating transition probabilities from observed frequency counts of moves is a generalized Markov process: This is a special case of the Markov renewal process in which the distribution of times to next move between a given pair of strata is the product of a constant transition probability, such as q_{ij}, times a general time distribution that depends only on the initial stratum; the latter distribution may be estimated from the distribution of observed times spent in a given stratum.[17]

The main argument against the use of those stochastic processes to describe moves of a vacancy in continuous time, whether or not data is available, is that they do not contribute additional insight. At the individual level, the main issue in vacancy models is the determinants of successive destinations in moves of a vacancy and, especially, whether the choice of next stratum is independent of all except current stratum. Exact timings of moves are essentially irrelevant.

Length distributions of vacancy chains have been the principal focus in tests of the models of Chapter 2. It is instructive to calculate these distributions again from the simplest Markov process, a stochastic analogue in continuous time of the binomial model of Section 2.1.[18] A replacement is called to a vacant job by a complex process in which many men must communicate and make decisions. Sometimes the selection is nearly decided upon before the actual vacancy arrives, and in other cases considerable delays ensue. The process is not so stereotyped that the delays cluster closely about some average value. If the upper limit set by the coding rules on the stay of a vacancy in a job is ignored, it is plausible to assume the conditional probability of a jump in the next instant is the same at all times. Then the distribution of times between jumps by a vacancy follows a negative exponential curve. More precisely

$$e^{-vt}v \, dt$$

is the probability a jump is made in the instant between t and $t + dt$, given that no jump has occurred between 0 and t. It is appropriate to use the symbol v from Section 7.1 in the exponent here, since it is the mean rate—the reciprocal of the mean delay between jumps—in this negative exponential distribution.

The total rate of moves is split into a rate for terminal moves, pv, and a rate for internal jumps qv. These two jumps are assumed to occur independently of one another; and the spacings for each, separately, should follow a negative exponential distribution. If a vacancy remains in the system for a time interval of length u, the probability that exactly n internal jumps take place is

$$\frac{(qvu)^n \, e^{-qvu}}{n!}$$

the Poisson distribution, easily derived from the negative exponential distribution for individual jumps. The probability that a vacancy persists for a long period u and then departs between u and $u + du$ is

$$e^{-pvu}pv \, du$$

since the average rate of termination is pv. The probability that a vacancy chain lasts a period u and is of length $n + 1$ (n internal jumps and one external jump) is simply the product of these two expressions. Hence the probability that a chain is of length j is

$$P_j = \int_0^\infty e^{-pvu} pv \, du \left[\frac{(qvu)^{j-1} e^{-qvu}}{(j-1)!} \right] \tag{7.71}$$

This can be converted to

$$P_j = q^{j-1} p \int_0^\infty \frac{w^{j-1} e^{-w}}{(j-1)!} \, dw \tag{7.72}$$

since $p + q = 1$, and vu is 0 or ∞ when u itself is.

The definite integral is just unity,[19] and equation (7.72) reduces to equation (2.3). Variability in spacing of jumps makes no difference to the predicted length distribution, as long as the spacings follow a negative exponential distribution; now a chain may in principle take an infinite time to run its course. Intuition should suggest that length of chain is affected little by how regularly the jumps are spaced in time, as long as the fraction of the jumps that are terminal, p, is fixed. The identity between (2.3) and (7.72) demonstrates that the length distribution of the chains is the same when the spacing is random as when it is left arbitrary.[20] At the aggregate level, the main issue in vacancy models is total numbers of moves. Those are little affected even by average rates of moves, much less by detailed timings.

Vacancies are a construct introduced to deal with interaction among moves by a population of incumbents in a system of jobs. The main interaction between men's moves is subsumed in the chain of moves by a vacancy. It would be hard to rederive the vacancy construct starting with stochastic processes for moves by *men* among jobs (as can be seen from the queuing models for whole systems described in Section 9.5).[21] Interaction among moves by vacancies themselves is unlikely to be much affected by exact timing. All the stochastic processes in continuous time described earlier apply only to moves by independent individuals. Since vacancies are assumed to be few in comparison with jobs and incumbents, there can be little in the way of the congestion effects treated by queuing theory, unless there are strong constraints on candidacies. Vacancies also do not multiply, and there can be no threshold effects of the kind found in stochastic models of epidemics.[22] Interaction among vacancies, with and without candidacy constraints, is assessed in Chapter 11. It will not be feasible to develop explicit stochastic models embracing the interlocking timings of moves by vacancies, but the allocation models developed suggest that interaction between vacancies is not very large.

There is a further reason for avoiding the use of stochastic processes in continuous time. For physical phenomena like cosmic ray showers, it may be reasonable to treat time as an ordered metric isomorphic to the real number system. Great precision in the treatment of probability distributions in time, as for the Markov renewal process, may be justified. In social processes there exists no variable parallel to this physical time. Simultaneity cannot be defined by a clock as it depends on the perceptions of different people as well as on communication among them. People sleep at varying times and work only part of their waking time. Seasons, weekends, and holidays each mark off special kinds of social time. The distance between June and September is unlike the distance between October and January. In any case, dates and times can only be obtained from the persons and records studied; manipulation of many kinds, often legitimate, is common in such reports. Time order and rates can be used and are essential, but elaborate treatments of probability distributions defined for continuous time do not seem justified.

7.8 How to Define a System and Estimate Parameters

The equations that define the vacancy models of Chapter 2 refer to moves, not to chains. Vacancies do jump repeatedly between jobs until they leave the system, but nothing in the equations overtly states that each particular vacancy can be traced. Rather, the explicit assumption in the equations, whether applied to one vacancy or to a cohort of independent vacancies, is that vacancies are conserved during moves within the system. As long as each job included in the system maintains a fixed number of incumbents, except for temporary vacancies during the calling of replacements, this assumption is satisfied. Such jobs were named "fixed jobs" in Chapter 1. There is an additional empirical assumption in the stratified models. Vacancies in fixed jobs behave as—that is, have the same transition probabilities as—vacancies in 1–1 jobs in the same stratum. It is unlikely that the mere presence or absence of job titles for individual incumbents will affect a job's replacement opportunities as much as the variation found within the stratum. Extension of the vacancy model to include fixed jobs makes plausible broader applications, such as the analysis of large fractions of national occupational systems to be suggested in Chapter 9.

The clergies of Protestant churches are unusual organizations. There are few fixed jobs that are not 1–1 jobs; the entrepreneur is still the norm. In the coding rules of Chapter 3 most of these exceptional jobs were included in the tracing of vacancy chains. Only if more than one man left or entered such a job in a given year was it coded as a pool job (in that chain). For other organizations it will be worthwhile to code moves of vacancies in terms of all fixed jobs. Predicted length distributions of vacancy chains can no longer be tested, but the model can be validated by the kinds of aggregate predictions studied in Sections 7.1 and 5.2. Procedures for estimating parameters from samples of isolated moves will be described later.

The ability to identify particular vacancies as each hops from job to job is the necessary and sufficient condition for tracing vacancy chains. If no more than one man ever enters or leaves a job during a single time period, chains can be traced. However, multiple jumps from a given job in a single year are bound to occur sometimes when several occupants are assigned to its roster. A diagram of moves in a year among a set of jobs can contain many graphs that cannot be uniquely decomposed into chains.[23] Figure 7.1 is a simple example of such a graph. There are various sets of chains that are consistent with the observations:

I. Possible decomposition into two chains, length of each, $j = 2$.
   Retirement $\underset{A}{\rightarrow}$ Job x $\underset{B}{\rightarrow}$ Job y $\underset{D}{\rightarrow}$ Recruitment
   Retirement $\underset{C}{\rightarrow}$ Job y $\underset{E}{\rightarrow}$ Job z $\underset{F}{\rightarrow}$ Recruitment

II. Possible decomposition into two chains, length of one, $j = 3$; length of the other, $j = 1$.
   Retirement $\underset{A}{\rightarrow}$ Job x $\underset{B}{\rightarrow}$ Job y $\underset{E}{\rightarrow}$ Job z $\underset{F}{\rightarrow}$ Recruitment
   Retirement $\underset{C}{\rightarrow}$ Job y $\underset{D}{\rightarrow}$ Recruitment

In principle, the frequency of occurrence of various particular graphs could be predicted by the model and tested on the observations, but the calculations and sample sizes required would be formidable.[24]

Even though individual chains cannot be treated, vacancy moves can be counted, transition probabilities estimated, and turnover predictions made. These procedures are not rigorously self-consistent; in principle there has been an important change in the context for moves. Since an individual vacancy cannot be traced, a cohort of newly created vacancies should not be treated as a set of independent entities. No longer is it legitimate to derive the model for an individual vacancy and then simply use the expected value as the prediction for the average results observed for the cohort (as is done in Chapter 2). It appears that something similar to the Einstein-Bose statistics for indistinguishable particles should replace the usual multinomial (Maxwell-Boltzmann) statistics.[25]

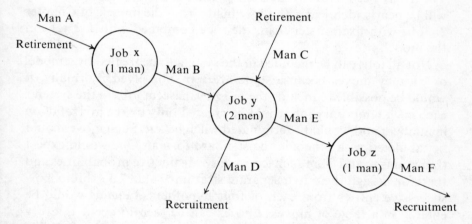

Figure 7.1   Graph of Vacancy Moves among Fixed Jobs. Each move of a vacancy is represented by an arrow, from initial job to subsequent job. The number of incumbents in each job's roster is given. Each man moving as a replacement is labeled by a capital letter. The number of arrows coming into a job must equal the number going out, since vacancies are conserved within the system of jobs.

Expected values often are not affected greatly by the subtleties shown to be required in principle. Using the models of Chapter 2 is equivalent to supposing that a complex graph, such as Figure 7.1, is decomposed into separate chains. Since the number of vacancy moves into a job always equals the number of moves out, at least one such decomposition is always possible. Artificial decompositions have already been used in Chapter 3 to deal with compound chains. The problem there was a similar but simpler one; that is, two vacancies might enter, but only one will leave a job, or vice versa. About 15 percent (by weight) of all chains reported in Chapters 5 and 6 are secondary ones from compound chains. For graphs, like Figure 7.1, it is hard to derive decomposition rules that reflect the actual priorities in moves, and no observed set of chains is obtained to compare with the predictions. If decomposition works well for compound chains, it is reasonable to retain as much as possible of the models of Chapter 2 when the graphs of moves are more complex.

An independent line of argument yields the same conclusion. The continuous time models developed in Sections 7.1 and 7.4 are deterministic and describe total populations of vacancies and moves. They can legitimately be applied even when vacancies are not identifiable. Yet it has been shown that their predictions of expected mobility will be nearly identical with those made from the models of Chapter 2. Jobs with fixed rosters can, then, be combined with 1–1 jobs in the model.

Not all jobs can be included in the system to be treated by a model of vacancy moves because some are too short-lived. Formally, it would be possible to include the most evanescent jobs in the system; each such temporary job would be created only by the arrival of an incumbent and would be terminated when he left. Such moves could be tabulated with others in the standard format. One would expect transitions to and from such jobs to have distinctive probabilities and therefore assign them to a separate stratum. Table 7.5 exhibits how successive entries from each of four hypothetical chains would be entered in a table of moves. Entries can be seen to occur in every cell in the row and in the column for the special stratum; it is possible that the estimated transition probabilities are much like those for a normal stratum.

The flaw in these proceedings is that moves to and from the special stratum cannot have the Markov property. Consider the first move in chain A of Table 7.5, designated A_1; it shows that a man is recruited from stratum 2 to fill the special new job. The point is one *knows* that such a move—any move of a vacancy from the special stratum to another job stratum—is the first move in a chain. Similarly a move, such as X_3 in the special column must be the next-to-last move in a chain. Any move in the diagonal cell for the special stratum, like B_1, must be both the first and penultimate move; that is, it necessarily lies in a chain of length $j = 2$. Such knowledge is a violation of the Markov assumption that the probability of a vacancy moving to a given other stratum depends on only the stratum it is presently in. A vacancy currently in the special stratum can jump to any stratum of jobs (including special) if it has entered by a job creation, but it can go only to the outside otherwise.

Table 7.5 Tabulation of Moves in Chains that Pass through Temporary Jobs[a]

Vacancy from	Vacancy to			
	Stratum 1	Stratum 2	Special stratum	Outside
Outside	X_0		A_0, B_0, C_0	
Stratum 1		X_1	X_3	
Stratum 2	X_2	A_2		A_3
Special stratum		A_1	B_1	B_2, C_1, X_4

[a] Each move is designated by the letter for its chain with a subscript indicating its order in the chain. Possible concrete interpretations of each chain are:

Chain A: A new temporary job is defined by the entry of an incumbent from a job in stratum 2, which is thereupon filled by the incumbent of another stratum 2 job, which a new recruit then occupies.
Chain B: A man moves from one special job, which thereupon ends, to a new one.
Chain C: A man in a special job retires.
Chain X: The vacancy created by retirement of incumbent in a job of stratum 1 is filled by an incumbent from a job in stratum 2, which manages to lure the incumbent of another job in stratum 1, which in turn is filled by a man from a temporary job, which vanishes with his departure.

Special jobs, and pool jobs as defined in Chapter 3, can be included in a residual category with empty jobs. The size of this category can be treated as a state variable. There is a two-way flow of jobs from this category to jobs subject to the model, and there is a two-way flow to the "outside" that is harder to measure.

Men, like jobs, can be in pool status. Data on the numbers of men in pool and in other marginal statuses are given in Section C.3. Men move from one residual status to another, although without setting off chains of moves. That mobility can be measured directly from the appropriate cells in Table C.7 and its parallels. Extrapolation to the future could be done best by a conventional Markov chain model for exposure of men to fixed probabilities of movement.[26]

Those high authorities who are interested in men in these residual statuses are also interested in the residual category of jobs. Innovations in types of jobs usually begin with jobs from the residual category and, similarly, many creative men spend much time in marginal statuses. Chronically empty jobs are a worry but so is the provision of future personnel needs. Sometimes jobs are left empty for a while deliberately. Pool statuses may often deliberately be used to "store" men, whether as recruits not yet called by a vacancy or as men in midcareer for whom no appropriate opportunity is available at the time. Mobility among fixed jobs is, according to the models tested earlier, a rigid process. One can expect to find techniques that dampen this rigid coupling of moves, such as beginning or ending chains of moves by moving jobs or men in or out of the residual categories.

Let the number of men in pool jobs and in limbo be $L(t)$. The part of the net rate of growth of $L(t)$ derived from moves to and from fixed tenures is, in the binomial model,

$$f_{pool} + f_{limbo} - V(t)v[p_{pool} + p_{limbo}]$$

Estimates of these quantities for the Episcopal church are given in Tables 5.6 and 5.10. Summed over the whole set of samples, the departures balance the arrivals to within 10 percent. The balance is also close for pool taken separately (17.816 weighted moves of men to pool statuses versus 17,838 for departures) and for limbo taken separately (16.240 versus 18.259). On the average, positions in pool and limbo do function as intermediate storage for men in the mobility generated by the movement of vacancies through the system. It need not follow that they are intermediate resting places in individual careers, since the men who enter pool and limbo status from the system of fixed jobs need not coincide with the men who go the other way in roughly equal numbers. Even if a pool job is typically an intermediate stage in individual careers, it is not likely that periods in pool either greatly enhance or depress an individual's standing. Not only in the system as a whole but also within each stratum the number of moves of men into pool and limbo from fixed jobs matches the number of men moving out, approximately. Episcopal and Methodist figures, summed over all decades, are given in Table 7.6.

Coding rules must precede estimation of parameters when applying these vacancy models to a new set of organizations. The important aspect that the rules must show is which jobs are in the system treated by the model and which are not in the system. For some jobs, the decision will be difficult. Moves of vacancies into a fixed job normally number the same as moves out during a year. Empty periods will occur, and every job must be born and eventually die. The crucial property of fixed jobs, as pointed out, is that moves by vacancies through a given job have the Markov property. Some pool

Table 7.6 Arrivals and Departures of Men to and from Pool and Limbo Status, by Stratum for Episcopal and Methodist Churches[a]

Stratum	From fixed jobs to pool and limbo $(F_{pool} + F_{limbo})$	To fixed jobs from pool and limbo
Episcopal Church		
Big	4.532	6.217
Medium	18.609	16.649
Small	10.915	13.232
Methodist Church		
Big	2.910	2.311
Medium	5.894	7.980
Small	6.389	3.516

[a] Figures are calculated from Tables 5.8 and 5.9 for the Episcopal, and Table 6.3 for the Methodist church.

jobs may be well-paid and prestigious when the incumbent is highly regarded, but none are persistent individual entities, that is, independent pieces of social structure in their own right; the logic of contingent moves by vacancies does not fit them. Often the mere title of a type of job will suggest the right answer to the coding question. If the title is modified or misstated often or if "temporary" or a synonym appears in the title, that type of job is probably a pool job. Other subsidiary indicators, such as pension contributions during incumbency, vary with the particular organization. The main criterion is stability, and lack of stability in a type of job is usually signalled by the casual and variable way in which it and its incumbents are listed in official reports.

The coding rule for which men to include is really the same as for the decision on what organizations or parts thereof to include. Unless the system is large enough to encompass much of the careers of a majority of the men in it at any given time, the model will have little predictive power because chains will be short and boundary crossings the main feature. Yet there is no advantage to coupling organizations, or classes of jobs within an organization such as blue collar and administrative, between which there is little movement. Boundaries will not often be as obvious as they are for clergies. Given the organizational boundaries, the system proper includes only jobs with fixed rosters and their incumbents, but the usefulness of vacancy models depends on the size of this system relative to the number of men in pool jobs and marginal statuses. The latter are linked by frequent moves to the system proper, and accounts must be kept for them too.

Given the coding rules, estimation of transition probabilities from samples of single moves is not too difficult. What is needed is an unbiased sample of all vacancy moves to enter in a cross-tabulation like that for Table 4.12. If moves are inferred from successive annual reports, as for the churches, four types of samples must be drawn. A

Table 7.7 Vacancy Moves from Samples of Moves by Men and Moves by Jobs in Five Decades, in the Episcopal Church[a]

Origin stratum	Destination stratum					
				Outside		
	Big	Medium	Small	Recruits pool, and limbo	Job end	Total number of moves
Outside new jobs	0.833	11.200	25.915			
death, pool, limbo	$6 \times \frac{11}{5}$	$11 \times \frac{11}{5}$	$10 \times \frac{11}{5}$			
Big	12	7	0	$4 \times \frac{11}{6}$	1.444	27.8
Medium	6	23	25	$15 \times \frac{11}{6}$	9.329	90.8
Small	2	11	9	$15 \times \frac{11}{6}$	16.784	66.3

[a] The integer entries are counts of moves by men in all eleven samples from the Episcopal clergy indices. New jobs (f_{job}) and job ends are kept separate within "outside"; the estimates for these are taken from Tables 5.8 and 5.9 for weighted chains. Counts of deaths are from k' samples alone and of recruits, from k samples alone; those are multiplied by the fractions shown to keep the sampling ratio the same in every cell.

random sample from a population list of men in the system in a year can be traced either forward or back. As explained in Section B.3 both traces must be combined to obtain unbiased estimates for origins and destinations of men who move. These two samples suffice for the counts of all vacancy moves, except those corresponding to creation of and death of jobs. Forward and back traces of samples of jobs are necessary to estimate the numbers of those events.

Table 7.7 illustrates the procedure. The moves by men tabulated are just the sample entry moves from which vacancy chains were traced in the Episcopal church, in all five decades. Counts of deaths (f_{man}) by stratum are the actual counts from k samples, doubled; counts of recruits and so on are the doubled counts from k' samples, as explained in Section C.3. That part of Table 7.7 is just a refinement of Table C.7 to show strata separately. Tracing men produces no counts of new jobs (or end jobs), unless the earlier status of the job is looked up. Then, the trace of a vacancy chain is begun, and the weighting problem for vacancy chains must be faced. A shortcut is taken, since it is tedious to draw large enough random samples of jobs to yield reliable estimates of creation and extinction. The samples of weighted chains give unbiased estimates of the numbers of new jobs and end jobs, using the same sampling ratio as for the counts of moves by men; these weighted estimates are used in Table 7.7.

Table 7.8   Comparison of Estimated Transition Probabilities from Single Moves and from Weighted Chains

Origin stratum	Destination stratum			
	Big	Medium	Small	Outside
	Single moves[a]			
Big	.43	.25	0	.32
Medium	.07	.25	.27	.41
Small	.03	.16	.14	.67
	Weighted chains[b]			
Big	.33	.30	.07	.30
Medium	.05	.27	.18	.50
Small	.04	.17	.15	.65

[a] Calculated from Table 7.7.
[b] Reproduced from Table 5.1, rounded.

Table 7.8 shows the estimates of transition probabilities made from Table 7.7. For comparison, the corresponding estimates from weighted chains in Table 5.1 are repeated in Table 7.8. (They are not independent estimates since the sample entry moves are also counted in the chains.) There are a total of 185 moves (27.5 of them from end jobs) in the three rows of Table 7.7 used to estimate the twelve transition probabilities, while those rows of Table 5.1 are based on chains containing a raw total of 632 moves. With only 15 moves per cell on the average, Table 7.8 cannot be expected to yield accurate estimates, and the figures have accordingly been rounded to two places. The agreement between the estimates from single moves and from weighted chains is good.

The vacancy models are applicable not just to 1–1 jobs but also to all jobs with fixed rosters: that is the main conclusion. Practicable procedures for estimating the parameters have been specified and the coding rules clarified. However, the structure of moves cannot be unambiguously decomposed into individual chains, and no direct test of the validity of the Markov assumption has been suggested to replace the prediction of chain lengths. One other caution is in order: fixed jobs neither imply nor are implied by fixed marginals; that is, the sizes of strata may remain constant from one year to the next, whether or not they are composed of jobs with fixed rosters. The vacancy models are based on assumptions about individual moves, not on global assumptions about the behavior of aggregates.

Chapter 8
Mobility Models with Interaction

In Chapter 7, the emphasis shifted from analysis of particular chains of moves among 1–1 jobs to patterns of flow across stratum boundaries. Fixed jobs were shown to be a sufficient basis for the models, and application to whole sectors of an occupational system could be entertained. It is natural to compare vacancy models in that broader context with other classes of mobility models. Some comparisons were made in Section 7.2, and Chapter 9 is a detailed analysis of the linear, single-flows models of careers that have been most commonly used in mobility studies. This chapter briefly examines a broader spectrum of models that all include some type of interaction among careers.

8.1 Prices and Exchange

Hiring men and accepting jobs seem comparable to market processes for which economic theory is a natural framework. The underlying question is whether the presuppositions of economic theory are appropriate for processes of matching, such as those implicit in the mobility of men among jobs. It is difficult to find treatments of economic theory which specify its postulates in abstract form. The discussion here will rely on the formulation of Tjalling C. Koopmans: "... the derivation of all results from prime postulates throws a clear light on the limits of their applicability. ..."[1]

Formation of prices and quantities, especially in competitive markets, is the traditional focus of economics. Maximation under constraints by actors concerned with various types of goals is the guide for specifying individual choices. The objects of choice by actors are commodity bundles, each a vector in the space of n commodities considered, which include labor of various kinds. The standard interpretation is that the amounts of commodities chosen are constant rates of flow. In the system considered as a whole, the sum of the vector choices of all actors should be zero, so that the markets are cleared. Prices are the mechanism by which choices of each actor are decoupled from choices of other individuals and turned to the market as a whole. Constraints on the choice bundle of a producer can be related to technology and constraints for a consumer, to limitations on his labor capacity. Further stipulations are needed: each of these constraints and all prices are independent of the choices made by every actor; each consumer has a complete preference ordering on the set of commodity bundles to which his choice is restricted. Each producer's set must be convex, excluding increasing returns to scale in production. Each consumer's preference ordering also has to be convex; that is, if commodity bundle, A, is preferred to another bundle, B, then any bundle that is a linear mixture of the two is also preferred to bundle B.

Indivisibility both in productive resources, whether physical or entrepreneurial, and in commodities is excluded in the theory of markets sketched above. It is well recognized that indivisibility is essential to an understanding of such basic facts as increasing returns to scale and of even the sheer existence of cities and other inhomogeneities of location. However, ". . . in regard to the allocation problems raised by indivisible commodities, with or without locational distinctions, theoretical analysis has not yet absorbed and digested the simplest facts established by the most casual observation."[2]

Not only men but also jobs come in discrete units. These units are not atoms, because units of each type are distinguishable; indeed, mobility need not be studied if the substitution of one man for another in a job made no difference. It is because these dual sets consist of individualized entities that divisibility cannot be assumed as a reasonable approximation. There is some parallel to the inadequacy of indivisibility for location theory, although there the issue is inhomogeneity in concentration, not contingencies in reshufflings of units. Once indivisibility is allowed, efficient allocation by a price system is rendered dubious whatever the other assumptions of the model.

If commodities are infinitely divisible there are no natural units, and in economics the terms of trade are open. In mobility there is at most one man to a given job in large fractions of the system, given the facts of social structure; there the physical terms of matching are given. All matchings have aftereffects built in, whereas divisible commodities are simply consumed. At some later time, each matching will be broken, casting a job or a man or both into a flow or pool of candidates for matchings.

Exogenous flows to or from the system have no place in the economic model. Economics deals with possibilities, that is, it explores the mutual elicitation of one flow of commodities by another. The market determines the flows, not the flows the market. In mobility, death is independent of matching to jobs (if extreme Malthusian states are ignored) and generates a true exogenous flow of available jobs in the system. Like men, all jobs are mortal. New jobs and recruits may be pressed into the system. Flows can no longer be thought of as elicited from bottomless wells in amounts that can be determined through the interplay of bargaining reflected in a system of prices in markets.

Men and jobs could be described as commodities in an economic model for labor markets. If there exist powerful men who control labor or jobs or both, these men could be seen as the actors. Their powers would have to be pervasive indeed for the flows of men and jobs to behave as commodities do in the economic model. Not many training institutions would claim that their "production set" was convex, nor would many heads of organizations have complete, convex preference orderings for numbers of bureaucrats. If such were the case, it is doubtful that mobility of men among jobs would be worth analyzing. Men and jobs would be passive, and they could be moved in arbitrary flow patterns much like regular commodities bought and sold by economic actors. Transfers from one job to another could be ignored since men could be seen as equivalents and jobs as transient. Net flows of jobs and men would constitute the market.

Markets and prices are concepts that are not germane to a mobility process for matching individual men and jobs. They deal with net, not gross, flows in amounts that are treated as continuous variables and in amounts that are not dependent on the rates of processes exogenous to the model. Many observed markets in durable goods exhibit some of the properties of the mobility process, yet the economic model is often applied to these with the claim that it is a reasonable approximation. It is instructive to sketch the approach to a durable goods market suggested by its similarities to the mobility process.

The market in automobiles is to be formulated in terms exactly analogous to those in vacancy models for mobility of men among jobs. New car sales in a year are taken as given and not explainable within the model. They play much the same part as the flow of new jobs in the mobility model. The point of the model is to explain the turnover in cars already owned—the used car market. Car owners are the population of men in the system. Most own one car, but multicar families can be included if the number of cars owned by a family is regarded as fixed. Owners die, leave the country, or otherwise withdraw from the system for reasons independent of their ownership. The resulting stream of available cars is another exogenous flow, as are jobs vacated by death, to be combined with the flow of new cars. A man who buys a used car is analogous to the priest called to a vacant parish in the course of a vacancy chain. Strata of cars can be defined in a variety of ways, perhaps best by price and make together. The main difference from the mobility model is that cars move systematically from one price range to another as time goes on. In Section 7.6, the mobility equations were extended to cover the case of jumps of jobs between strata, and this extension can be adapted to cover the case of steady drifts.[3]

The operative assumption in the model is that the next owner is recruited in fixed proportions from owners of cars in various strata, with a fixed proportion recruited from men without cars and a fixed proportion of "vacant" cars being scrapped. The latter two proportions added together are the analogy to the termination probability in Chapter 2. Several restrictions are built into the operative assumption. Let similar symbols be used as in the vacancy chain model, with j' as subscript for cars and m' as subscript for owners. A fraction $p_{j'}$ of new cars, as of all other vacant cars, will be scrapped. This minor effect can be thought of as new cars not sold that year. In comparison with the number scrapped because they cannot be sold by the former owner who has bought another vehicle, few cars are abandoned while in active use, and the error in prohibiting scrapping of cars actively in use is probably not serious. Men do not "push" into ownership of a car, recruits are called in to buy cars left vacant. That assumption is one about the behavior of a population and need not be construed to mean that no individual goes out on his own initiative to buy a car whether or not he knows of an available one. It does seem likely that most persons first buy a car only because some are known to be available, usually older and cheaper ones. As in the mobility model, the most fundamental restriction is the Markov property. Chains of changes in ownership analogous to vacancy chains can be traced, at least in principle, even with existing registration data; and predictions of length distributions can be tested as in Chapters 5 and 6.

Prices are not the focus of the model. They are descriptive parameters, with some customary structure that changes, slowly, by mechanisms not considered in the model. The number of new cars sold per year is allowed to fluctuate arbitrarily. Little of the fluctuation seems to be attributable to price changes in reality, taste changes and mood factors apparently bulking large in any explanations offered; however, response of $f_{j'}$ to prices need not be excluded. Imbedded in the model is the assumption that cars and men are distinguishable, as well as indivisible. No one who has bought a used car will argue that point, and even new cars are so variable in specific features as to be unique items. The price is an important parameter, but it does not constitute a complete description of all items in a class.

The analogy is imperfect. Automobiles are a pale substitute for jobs. There is no real analogy to the job controllers. Each owner of a given car may act in turn as a salesman, but no men have a persisting interest in it. Few jobs are filled through mass media, whereas cars are often traded to a new car dealer who then disposes of them in used car lots.[4] A large number of men may put their cars on the market and then each explore for another one among that very set. The vacancy model may not be adequate for the automobile market, but the orthodox economics model will not be appropriate either; a model such as the Holt-David one in Section 8.3 may be what is required.

8.2   Real Labor Markets

Orthodox economics in the form of price theory might apply to general labor markets even though conventional price theory is unsuitable logically to the analysis of mobility in systems of 1–1 jobs. In 1951 Lloyd Reynolds published a general assessment, *The Structure of Labor Markets: Wages and Labor Mobility in Theory and Practice*, based in part on empirical studies for particular cities. His main idea is that mobility and wages in fact have little to do with one another. Some of his conclusions are strikingly parallel to assumptions used in vacancy models, while others call for a matching model of the kind discussed in Section 8.3. These conclusions, for convenience labeled V and M, respectively, can be reported as a series of quotations.*

(M)   The effective labor supply at any time seems to include three main groups: new entrants to the market, laid off and discharged workers, and workers who have become sufficiently dissatisfied with their jobs to quit of their own accord. During a period of prosperity a dissatisfied worker can sometimes line up a new job before leaving his old one. The more usual procedure, however, is to quit the job and then start a serious search for new employment. (p. 211)

(V)   Main reliance is placed on tips received from relatives and friends . . . the worker usually accepts the first job he finds which meets his minimum standards . . . Jobs come into the market and are filled so rapidly that a worker who pursues the bird in the bush too diligently may find himself permanently unemployed . . . the worker is usually not in the position of choosing between two or more alternate jobs. (p. 212)

(V and M)   In actuality an employer can usually expand and contract employment at will without altering his terms of employment. The main reason is the existence in most urban areas of a pool of unemployed which is continuously replenished. (p. 227)

Reynolds goes on to propose a revision of labor market theory.

(V)   . . . occupational wage differentials seem to have been considerably larger than would be required to induce upward movement of labor . . . A worker does not get an opportunity to learn a job until a vacancy develops. Adaptation of labor supplies follows and is induced by changes in demand, rather than the reverse . . . if differentials are larger . . . vacancies in these occupations have to be rationed among those who want them. *The existence of job rationing . . . is one of the most familiar facts of industrial employment.*† (p. 239)

(M and V)   Opportunity must be added to willingness before any actual *movement* will occur. (p. 240)

* (Harper & Row, 1951). Reprinted by permission of the publishers.
† Italics added for emphasis. Job rationing corresponds to the idea of job controllers calling men to vacancies in the models of Part I.

(V) . . . the better jobs being filled mainly by intraplant promotion. (p. 242)

All the career models of movement by men (Chapter 9) are based on the concept of individual propensity to move. Reynolds rejects this concept as a basis for predicting amounts of movement.

(V) The amount of movement, then, is determined basically by circumstances external to the worker rather than by workers' average propensity to move. *Differences* in the propensities of individual workers, however, help to determine the *incidence* of movement . . . These personal characteristics help to determine *who* will move into a particular vacancy; but they have little influence on *how many* vacancies there will be or on the total amount of movement. (p. 244)

(V) Differentials in opportunity can thus produce movement even in the absence of wage differentials. The converse proposition, however, does not hold. (p. 245)

(V) Some jobs are very much better than others, and vacancies on these jobs are rationed among a chronic surplus of applicants. (p. 246)

In the area of labor mobility, Reynolds rejects the orthodox economic theory of clearing markets by a price system. Some of his conclusions support the Holt-David theory. Most of Reynolds' conclusions and his proposed revision of labor market theory amount to a call for vacancy models. The missing idea is the multiplier effect—the chain of moves that can be set off by creation of a vacancy. A sense of that gap in his ideas may account for Reynolds' extraordinary proposal, in discussing objectives of labor market policy, that "Retiring workers should be replaced mainly by hiring new entrants to the labor force" (p. 267).

8.3 Holt-David Model

In 1966 the National Bureau of Economic Research (NBER) published *The Measurement and Interpretation of Job Vacancies*, the report of a conference funded by the U.S. Department of Labor to bring together American economists interested in developing job vacancy data and economists from countries with more experience with such data. C. Holt and M. David contribute the only explicit model for the use of such data in labor market theory.*

> We start by focusing on the two important stocks in the labor market, unemployed workers and job vacancies. Then we consider the interaction between these stocks and the corresponding flows, and determine how the flows and stocks influence each other and how the market reaches equilibrium. (p. 74)

In their stochastic model of the labor market

> the heart of the process is the random interaction between unemployed workers and job vacancies . . . The complex random process of job seeking and finding arises from the non-standardization of jobs and workers and the lack of perfect knowledge. This accounts for the *simultaneous* existence of unemployed workers and job vacancies, a situation not contemplated in classical economic theory, in which there may be excess supply or excess demand but not both. (pp. 94 and 101)

Holt and David work in the framework of management science and operations research; yet like other economists in this style, they try to maintain some linkage to classical theory. They find a conventional supply schedule for labor to be irrelevant and misleading (see their discussion of their figure 3 in the NBER report). Instead of dropping the idea entirely, they try to adapt it by making an extra assumption about change in the wage acceptable to a man as length of unemployment increases (their figure 4). There also is ambiguity in their treatment of jobs, which is induced by a desire to adapt classical ideas of demand schedules for labor by relating wages to departures from an ideal size of the stock of labor (their figure 2).

Figure 8.1 here is a replica of their figure 1 for flows and stocks in the labor market. Merely from the pattern of arrows it is clear that Holt and David do not treat jobs and men symmetrically. *Vacant* jobs are discrete entities parallel to unemployed men, and the labor market is the place where these dual entities are matched; but a continuous variable, man-hours of work, is used instead of the number of filled jobs. Unfilled demand for man-hours is then converted into a *net* flow of new vacant jobs. It seems odd that a job

---

* "The Concept of Job Vacancies in a Dynamic Theory of the Labor Market." Excerpts reprinted by permission of the publishers.

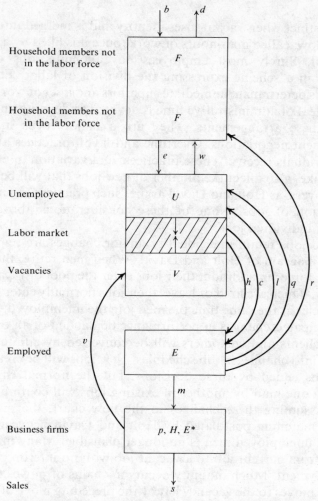

F = number of family members not in work force; b = births; d = deaths; e = entries to work force; w = withdrawals from work force; U = number of unemployed workers; V = number of job vacancies; v = net new job vacancies; h = new hires; l = layoffs plus terminations and other separations; q = quits; r = retirements; E = number of employed workers; E^* = desired number of employees; m = man-hours; p = production of finished goods; H = finished goods inventory; s = sales of finished goods.

Figure 8.1   Labor Market Flows and Stocks.

SOURCE: C. Holt and M. David, "The Concept of Job Vacancies in a Dynamic Theory of the Labor Market," in *The Measurement and Interpretation of Job Vacancies* (National Bureau of Economic Research, 1966), p. 79. Reprinted by permission of the publishers.

that is distinct when vacant loses identity and is merged into a continuous flow, called man-hours of work, once it is filled by a distinct individual. Surely most employees have definite jobs—definite positions in a scheme expressing the division of labor. Each employee has determinate immediate superiors and a set of workmates. A great deal of administrative time is devoted to defining and maintaining these arrangements. They are a major focus in union-management negotiations. Overtime and layoff practices affect the pay individuals receive. These practices, and variation in efficiency and the like, also affect the number of new jobs that will be created by employers, as Holt and David argue; such practices can also lead to abolition of jobs. None of these considerations abrogate the reality of individual jobs.

If filled jobs retain their identity, major changes are required in the flow diagram of Holt and David. When men retire, they leave the labor force; in addition, their jobs enter the pool of vacant jobs. Similarly, if men are fired or leave, their jobs normally enter the pool of vacancies at the same time the men join the unemployed. Current and anticipated changes in performance demanded of an organization by clients and customers will be converted by administrative decision into changes in job schedules. New jobs will be created and some jobs ended by these decisions, but the normal rhythm of replacing one man by another in existing jobs will continue all the while. Assuming these changes in the flow chart, the process of random matching postulated by Holt and David between vacant jobs and unemployed men is no longer plausible. Many men move directly from current job to a vacant job with no interim period of unemployment. Much mobility occurs in chains of moves in which one man moves to the vacancy left by the preceding move of another man.

Holt and David themselves are ambivalent about the random interaction between unemployed workers and vacant jobs at the heart of their model. The following pair of quotations come from successive paragraphs.

> For example, an employed person may search the job market, quit his current employment, and move almost immediately into a job vacancy. (p. 92)

> The likelihood of filling vacancies depends on the number of unemployed workers with the necessary qualifications, on the

effectiveness of their search in finding the available vacancies, and on their willingness to accept the jobs at the wages offered. (p. 93)

In their reply to comments on their paper, Holt and David go so far as to outline a chain of replacements beginning with a vacancy for an economist and ending with a move by a ditch digger to a job as floor sweeper (p. 139). However, their subsequent comments only deal with upgrading by unemployed workers.

The feeling persists that the desire to bring in classical economic theory may have led Holt and David astray. Consider their description of the variable E^* in their flow chart (Figure 8.1).

> . . . a useful concept of desired work force (E^*) is formulated, i.e., the level of the work force which would be most profitable. The size of the desired work force depends on the existing work force, the forecast of future roles, the present level of finished inventory, the backlog of unfilled orders, labor productivity, and wage rates. A work force either above or below E^* is less profitable, and the firm can be expected to take corrective actions to change the size of its work force. (p. 82)

Most of the NBER conference dealt with problems of how to define and collect data on job vacancies. The basic paper, "Job Vacancy Data and Economic Analysis," by J. T. Dunlop, points out three major difficulties with the development of job vacancy measures.

1. Employers do not themselves think in terms of vacancies, and most of their answers to questionnaires on the subject would be unrealistic.
2. Job vacancies claimable by outsiders arise normally only in selected jobs in an organization, most movements being promotions within the unit.
3. There are no sets of job titles and occupational groups applicable across employers with any demonstrated reliability or validity.

In response to comments emphasizing the relevance of Dunlop's second point, Holt and David redefine their paper as one dealing solely with the labor market external to the firm and claim that internal mobility is a separable problem (p. 138). It is hard to see how a model that includes layoffs of workers in unionized firms can claim to be confined to the external labor market.

8.4 Matchmaking Models

We now return to the matchmaking system described in Chapter 1. Chains of contingent moves do not occur. Since a man always spends a period being unemployed before going into any new job, the occurrence of a vacancy in some other job cannot "pull" him out of his current job.

In the vacancy model, all moves depended on flows across the system boundaries. In the matchmaking case mobility takes place even in a closed system, and exogenous flows are of secondary importance. Let all jobs be lumped in one stratum, parallel to the binomial model of Section 7.1, and all men be treated as equals. Let N_0 and J_0 designate the fixed numbers of men and jobs in the system. Interest centers on the number of men unemployed, on L for limbo, and on the familiar variable V, the number of vacant jobs. The first model below and its solution were proposed by Scott Boorman, an undergraduate at Harvard.

Let the number of tenures be T. The closed system can be described in terms of this one variable, since

$$L = N_0 - T \tag{8.1}$$

and

$$V = J_0 - T \tag{8.2}$$

Because dissolution is a spontaneous event, the simplest assumption is that each of the T tenures has the same fixed chance β of breaking up in a unit time. The rate of formation of new tenures, however, must depend on both L and V; the simplest assumption is a rate, α, proportional to the number of possible matches—the product of L and V. A single equation defines the dynamics:

$$\frac{dT}{dt} = \alpha(N_0 - T)(J_0 - T) - \beta T \tag{8.3}$$

The right side is a second order polynomial in T and thus can be factored into two linear terms:

$$\frac{dT}{dt} = \alpha(T - T_+)(T - T_-) \tag{8.4}$$

Here T_+ and T_- are combinations of the constants determined by the usual quadratic formula

$$T_\pm = \frac{1}{2}\left\{\left(N_0 + J_0 + \frac{\beta}{\alpha}\right)\right.$$

$$\left.\pm\left[\left(N_0 + J_0 + \frac{\beta}{\alpha}\right)^2 - 4N_0J_0\right]^{1/2}\right\} \quad (8.5)$$

The expression taken to the $\frac{1}{2}$ power can be rewritten to yield

$$T_\pm = \frac{1}{2}\left\{\left(N_0 + J_0 + \frac{\beta}{\alpha}\right)\right.$$

$$\left.\pm\left[(N_0 - J_0)^2 + 2\frac{\beta}{\alpha}(N_0 + J_0) + \left(\frac{\beta}{\alpha}\right)^2\right]^{1/2}\right\} \quad (8.6)$$

All terms in the expression taken to the $\frac{1}{2}$ power in equation (8.6) are positive, and both T_+ and T_- are real. In equation (8.5), it is clear that the square root cannot be as large in magnitude as the first term. Hence T_- as well as T_+ must be positive, and T_+ must be less than $N_0 + J_0 + \beta/\alpha$.

Either T_+ or T_- is an equilibrium value for T, since dT/dt is zero at either value. When T is between T_- and T_+, its rate of change is negative, and it approaches T_-. When T is below T_-, its rate of change is positive, and, again it approaches T_-. When T is greater than T_+, dT/dt is positive, and T increases indefinitely. Only T_- is a stable equilibrium. One substantive constraint has remained implicit:

$$T < \min(N_0, J_0) \quad (8.7)$$

since there cannot be more tenures than men or than jobs. T_- is below this limit. From the original equation (8.3) dT/dt will be negative for a range of values of T below the smaller of N_0 and J_0 because of the term $-\beta T$ and, by equation (8.4), T_- is the lower bound of these values. By similar reasoning it is clear T_+ must exceed both N_0 and J_0.

A few special cases will indicate the range of likely equilibrium values in this model. Suppose the numbers of men and jobs in this closed system are equal, that is, $N_0 = J_0$. Then if $\beta/\alpha = N_0$, the equilibrium value T_- will be $0.38 N_0$, from equation (8.6). If the dissolution rate is only a fourth as large, $\beta/\alpha = \frac{1}{4}N_0$, the equilibrium size rises, as one would expect, but only to $0.60N_0$. For more than

8. Mobility Models with Interaction

90 percent of the jobs and men to be combined in tenures, in equilibrium, the ratio of dissolution rate β to formation parameter α would have to go down to $\frac{1}{100}N_0$.

If the numbers of men and jobs differ widely; specifically, if

$$(N_0 - J_0)^2 \gg (N_0 + J_0)\frac{\beta}{\alpha} \tag{8.8}$$

equation (8.6) can be closely approximated by a binomial expansion. The result for the equilibrium number of tenures is

$$T_- \doteq \min(J_0, N_0)\left(1 - \frac{\beta/\alpha}{|J_0 - N_0|}\right) \tag{8.9}$$

In other words, if J_0 and N_0 differ widely compared to the size of the ratio β/α, then T_- will be very close to the number of men or of jobs, whichever is less.

By the construction of the model the mobility rate—the fraction of tenures formed and dissolved per unit time—in equilibrium is just the parameter β. The size of the system in filled jobs quickly[5] reaches an equilibrium value that is a large fraction of the number of men or jobs in the system for reasonable values of the parameters β and α. Addition of outside flows, exogenous or dependent, need make little difference in these qualitative predictions, although there will then be three dynamic variables and the equations will be much more complex mathematically. Outside flows are simply added on to a dynamic system that will achieve a reasonable equilibrium in size and mobility without them. The contrast is great between the evolution of a system described by a vacancy model and one described by a matchmaking model. Equilibrium is reached slowly, if at all, according to vacancy models (Chapter 7), and the size and growth of the system is very sensitive to the sizes of the exogenous flows.

Arbitrariness is a major weakness of matchmaking models. It is unsatisfactory to treat all jobs and all men as equivalent. Strata must be introduced, and the rate of formation of tenures can no longer be made proportional to the simple product of total number of vacant jobs and total number of unemployed. A myriad of possible assumptions is opened up, each requiring arrays of new rate parameters; and there is little theoretical basis for choice among them. Even if attention is confined to the single stratum model of equation (8.3), questions arise about the form of the parameters.

It can be plausibly argued that β should be proportional to V, because men are more likely to leave a job if there are a lot of vacant jobs around. With this change, $\beta = \psi V$, equation (8.4) becomes

$$\frac{dT}{dt} = \alpha(J_0 - T)\left[N_0 - T\left(1 + \frac{\psi}{\alpha}\right)\right] \tag{8.10}$$

If N_0 is equal or close to J_0, the stable equilibrium value of T is given by $N_0/(1 + \psi/\alpha)$. It can be shown that this result is quite different from the equilibrium size of T predicted from equation (8.3) for comparable values of the parameters. Illustrative values used earlier were $N_0 = J_0$ and $\beta/\alpha = 0.01N_0$, which produced an equilibrium T over 90 percent as large as N_0. To produce at equilibrium a dissolution rate equal to β, ψ/α must be $0.01N_0/V_0$. Given $N_0 = J_0$, this leads to a quadratic equation:

$$\left(\frac{\psi}{\alpha}\right)^2 = 0.01\left(1 + \frac{\psi}{\alpha}\right) \tag{8.11}$$

Hence, the comparable value of ψ/α is 1.005, and the equilibrium T predicted is only $\frac{1}{2}N_0$. Other plausible arguments will lead to other forms for dependence of β or of α on the state variables. For example, it can be argued that men are fired more readily when there is a large pool of unemployed; therefore β should be proportional to L. Each of these forms can lead to sharply different predictions for the equilibrium size of T, even though rates at equilibrium are matched.

8.5 Epidemic, Predation, Exchange, Matching, and Vacancy Models

Initially models of epidemics, whether of disease or of a fad or innovation, resemble matchmaking models. Proportionality between a rate of change and the product of two state variables is an almost invariable feature of such models. Epidemiology has a well-developed set of models from which it would be valuable to be able to borrow.[6] Unfortunately models of epidemics cannot be construed to deal with formation of compound objects from dual entities. Whether it is disease or information that is spread, the focus of the model is on transition of individuals from one category to another. Imitation is the paradigm for the process, whether it is avowed copying or catching an infection. Epidemic models are even more unlike vacancy models, being typically concerned with irreversible change in a closed system.

8. Mobility Models with Interaction

A. Epidemic (closed system)

B. Predation (open system)

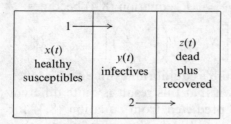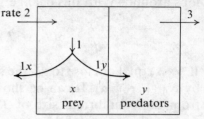

rate $1 = \beta xy$
rate $2 = \alpha y$

epidemic complete when $\dfrac{\beta}{\alpha} > y(0)$

rate $2 = \alpha x$ (natural growth)
rate $1x = \beta xy$ (loss from predation)
rate $1y = \beta' xy$ (gain from predation)
rate $3 = \alpha y$ (death from starvation)

C. Economic

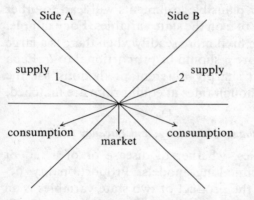

I. Market (open system with no stocks)

rates of flows 1 and 2 elicited are determined by a price system reflecting production constraints and demand preferences (see Section 8.1)

II. Combat (closed system)

rate $1 = \alpha y$; $\alpha' yx$; or α''
rate $2 = \beta x$; $\beta' yx$; or β''

Figure 8.2 Characteristic Flow Pattern and the Dependence of Rates on State Variables in Epidemic, Predation, and Economic Models.

208

Ecological competition between species also leads to models resembling the matchmaking models but only superficially. It is not the formation of compound animals but the growth of the predator and decline of the prey species that are proportional to the product of the number of predators and prey in ecological models. Human warfare, however, is symmetric in that both sides lose men as the result of combat.[7] Since the combat is between organized armies, combat models (associated with the name of Lanchester), usually do not assume quadratic interaction proportional to the potential number of encounters of pairs but rather a constant or linear interaction.[8] Thus combat models resemble economic theories of exchange but for closed systems and with terms of "trade" fixed differently.

Not mobility but sizes of flows or categories are the natural focus of all those models. It is only in vacancy models that mobility underlies the sizes of flows, rather than being a byproduct of them. A series of diagrams is the best way to clarify the similarities and differences among these various models. Three models—epidemic, predator, and economic—are designed for continuous variables rather than discrete entities. Only in more complex stochastic versions, such as the ones for threshold phenomena in epidemics, are the state variables counts of individuals.[9] Figure 8.2 shows the characteristic flow patterns and the dependence of rates on state variables in these three models. Both a closed system (combat) and an open system (market) version of the economic model are included; in neither is a unique form of the dependence of flows on state variables assumed. Stratification and other refinements of the state categories, such as according to geographical location, have not been carried very far in any of these literatures. Figure 8.3 diagrams the matchmaking and vacancy chain models. In both, discrete entities rather than continuous variables are essential to the logic of the model since marriages of dual units is the central process. The matchmaking model is shown as an open system, but the internal flows 3 and 4 are the core of the model (as shown in Section 8.4). The vacancy chain model, however, is structured around external flows.

In this book mobility is seen as chains of transfers of men between jobs, corresponding to flows 7 and 8 in Figure 8.3B. There are no analogous kinds of flows in the other models, only dissolutions and formations, exchanges, or simple shifts from one attribute category to another. An enormous range of particular models can be devised by varying assumptions about rates and by cross-breeding some of those models. The Holt and David model in Section 8.3, for example, is an attempt to combine the economic model with part of the match-making model. None of the other models or their variants appear able to deal with chains of contingent moves, which play a large part in observed mobility.

This comparative discussion will be continued in Chapter 9 where a special class of models that have been widely used in studying mobility are examined in detail. Those models resemble the epidemic model in that movements are only by persons and between

A. Matchmaking (open system)

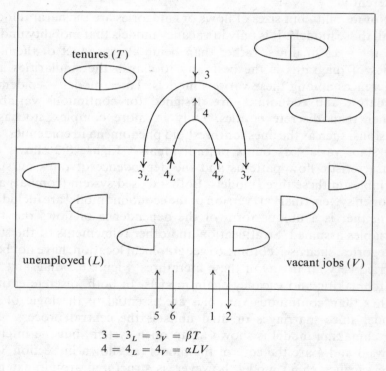

$$3 = 3_L = 3_V = \beta T$$
$$4 = 4_L = 4_V = \alpha L V$$

various possible assumptions about
the rates for flows 1, 2, 5, 6, and
whether the flows are exogenously
or endogenously determined

Figure 8.3   Characteristic Flow Patterns and the Dependence of Rates on State Variables in Matchmaking and Chain Models.

categories, and most often the system is taken as closed. But rates of movement per person are assumed constant rather than proportional to the population of the destination category, the number of categories is enlarged, and two-way flow of persons between any pair of categories is allowed. All models in Figures 8.2 and 8.3 have flows influenced by some form of interaction between the numbers of entities in different categories, whereas the models in Chapter 9 are essentially models of careers of individuals in isolation.

8.6 Mobility among Committees and Other Generalizations

Memberships in committees can be an important determinant of status and influence and independent of the particular job held.[10] Casual observation suggests standing committees may be most important both when 1–1 jobs are very stable and clearly defined, as for rectors of churches, and when 1–1 jobs are hardly discernible, as

B. Vacancy Chain (open system)

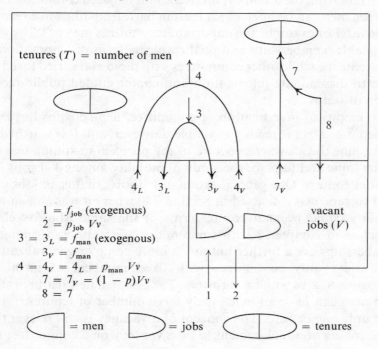

tenures (T) = number of men

$$1 = f_{job} \text{ (exogenous)}$$
$$2 = p_{job} Vv$$
$$3 = 3_L = f_{man} \text{ (exogenous)}$$
$$3_V = f_{man}$$
$$4 = 4_V = 4_L = p_{man} Vv$$
$$7 = 7_V = (1 - p)Vv$$
$$8 = 7$$

vacant jobs (V)

= men   = jobs   = tenures

in university faculties. In both cases, memberships are likely to be relatively independent of the job held. When 1–1 jobs are especially stable and clearly defined it seems to follow that they are grouped in fairly broad strata of equivalence with little explicit structure of authority or interrelated specialization within; and there is little basis for correlating particular jobs with particular committees. Even in government and business bureaucracies, where authority structure to coordinate interdependent specialists is developed more explicitly around 1–1 jobs, there is considerable flexibility in creation of committees and choice of membership. Decisions about change in the size and structure of an organization seem especially likely to be taken in committees, which become the foci whereby conflicts and change can be seen most clearly.[11]

Both policies and implementation are often settled by committees, and investigation of the structure and determinants of membership is important. Overlaps in membership permit inferences from incumbencies at one cross-section in time, which are impossible in the case of 1–1 jobs.[12] The study of mobility is available to the outside observer as an additional probe that is needed to sort out the important from the unimportant. Relations between committees and between men can be inferred, at least in part, from objective records of moves. For example, the important committees may be those with very stable memberships and predictable patterns of co-optation of replacements, while other committees with rapid and varied turnover serve to disseminate information and confer graded public recognition of status.

No empirical investigation of committee memberships has been carried out. Data is readily available, however, and it is worthwhile to examine the abstract structure of the problem to stimulate work on the topic and to place the study of mobility among 1–1 jobs in a broader context. One generalization of 1–1 jobs, that is, to jobs with fixed rosters, was discussed in Section 7.8, where it was shown that mobility could be analyzed in terms of the same Markov chain model as in Chapter 2 with some minor adaptations. Committee memberships are a further but much more complex generalization.

Consider only committees with fixed numbers of members, analogous to jobs with fixed rosters. The essential new feature is that each man can have an indefinitely large number of tenures, rather than only one or zero. The concept of a vacancy is still relevant, as is the calling of a replacement to fill a vacancy on a committee. But the movement of a man to a vacancy no longer implies the automatic creation of a vacancy in another committee to which the man already belonged. Although symmetry suggests the logical possibility of a committee system in which a man is limited to a fixed number of committees, it is hard to think of an empirical instance. Thus the concept of a vacancy chain is irrelevant for the committee problem.

The matchmaking model for mobility among 1–1 jobs is, instead, the natural special case from which to generalize to the committee problem. The simplest assumption to have any plausibility is that all men in the system, whatever the number of committees on which each is already a member, are available as partners to match with vacant memberships on committees. As in the matchmaking model of Section 8.4, the essentials of the mobility process are internal movements in the system. Death or retirement from the system may play a significant role in initiating vacancies, but there need be no immediate pressure for recruiting new men into the population of men eligible for committees.

There would be at least as many difficulties as in Section 8.4 in developing a determinate model with strata defined for committees and for men, but some differentiation of men and committees by eligibility and status would be essential. Even without stratification the problem of developing a coherent model of mobility for committees is difficult. Combinatorial mathematics, of the sort used in Chapter 11, would seem to be the natural approach.[13] Sheer counts of the possible incumbencies of men in sets of committees at a given time are difficult, even without touching on mobility.[14]

Several variants on the basic concept of the 1–1 job have now been suggested. Figure 8.4 sketches the interrelations of those variants that may be relevant empirically for the systematic study of mobility. Each variant is given a label with appropriate connotations and is identified by an ordered pair of counts. The first symbol in the parentheses counts the number of jobs or positions held by each man in the system, the second symbol counts the number of men occupying each job or position in the system. Where the number is fixed and is the same for all cases, a numeral is entered. Where the number is fixed but varies from case to case, the symbol n_i is used in the first place and n_j in the second. Where the number is variable, the symbol x is used. Many other variants are conceivable, and for the committee and ex officio[15] cases the sheer counts of men per position and positions per man are not likely to be the important constraints in the system.

All of these variants assume some matrix of formal organization. Somewhat similar concepts are relevant in the study of more fluid social situations. For example, a kind of "position" is defined by the aggregation of people into groups or social cliques; there the social "position" has no independent, continuing identity as an entity.[16] Mobility models leading to predictions of size distributions of cities could be handled either in terms of such positions or by analogy to pool jobs.[17]

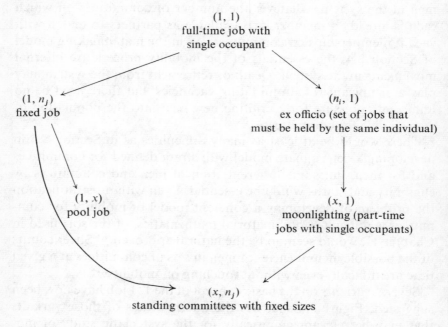

n_i = fixed number of jobs or positions held by each man
n_j = fixed number of men occupying each job or position
x = variable

Figure 8.4   Some Variations on the Basic Concept of the 1–1 Job.

Yet another type of mobility study is that of movements by men among categories defined in abstract cultural terms, that is, attribute categories. If several attribute "dimensions," each with several possible categories, are considered, the kind of incumbency is essentially different from any of those in Figure 8.4. There can be an unlimited number of men x in any "committee," and a man is on a fixed number of committees, d, for the number of dimensions, so that (d, x) would seem the appropriate designation in the terminology of Figure 8.4. There is an exclusion principle added by which each man is on exactly one of the set of committees corresponding to each dimension. There is a huge literature on measures of association in cross-tabulations that have been developed to describe such attribute incumbencies for a population of individuals.[18]

Chapter 9
Single-Flows Models of Mobility

Flows of jobs interact with flows of men in the vacancy models. The two are converted into flows of a compound entity—the vacancy. In Chapter 8, vacancy models were treated as a special case of models that explicitly match flows of two types. Here they will be compared with a variety of models of flows in a single kind of entity—single-flows models. Sections 9.1–9.3 show that all the devices used in the vacancy models are also used in various single-flows models, although not in the same combination. The contribution of the vacancy model is not the development of new mathematical tools but a new conceptualization of the nature of mobility as a dual process. Section 9.4 contrasts substantive implications of the single-flows models with those of the vacancy models. Section 9.5 is the final result; it develops the simplest way to introduce jobs into single-flows models of mobility and thereby clarifies the assumptions implicit in them. Queues are the device used, and the models are parallel to the stochastic models for continuous time in Section 7.7.

Most models discussed are based on a matrix of coefficients of flow, assumed to be constant over a considerable period; that is, the flows from a given origin category to various destinations are assumed to remain in fixed proportions to one another whatever the total outflow from the origin category. When flows are composed of individuals, the latter are assumed not to interact; the matrix consists of rows of transition probabilities, that is, it describes a Markov chain.

Some of the models describe closed systems but others are for open systems, which obscures the similarity of the tools. The empirical systems are in reality open, and the closed systems can be viewed as an approximation or a degenerate case. In some of the models time is continuous and in some, discrete intervals are used; in terms of applications this difference is superficial, as has been shown in Chapter 7.

Matrices of fixed flow coefficients are used in models for fields far removed from social or job mobility. This chapter does no more than touch on models where origins and destinations are described in terms of continuous variables rather than discrete categories; that is, on fluid flow and diffusion models of the kinds familiar to the natural sciences.[1] Diffusion models are highly developed but also very specialized. Powerful assumptions are made about the topology of the space of states, usually Euclidean; and flows can only proceed through a succession of neighborhoods in the space. Random walk models are also much more intensively developed than mobility models, but they are even more of a special case. Those models are diffusion models for a space in which states are discretely spaced; in mobility models, flows can in general proceed directly from any state to any other state. Like most diffusion and random walk models, the mobility models deny historical effects within the given framework of states, although they may permit explicit time dependencies to enter the parameters. Even in the simple model of Section 7.3 a natural role for lagged effects was manifest; the restriction is a serious one, which is ameliorated only slightly by the introduction of higher order Markov chains.[2]

Single-flows models differ in emphasis on one of three mathematical tools. Of these three, only the multiplier matrix $(I - Q)^{-1}$ appears in the input-output model of Leontief (Section 9.1). Careers as a mathematical concept, the second tool, presuppose flows made up of individual entities described in probabilistic terms. Demographic models are the oldest example, and the distribution of life expectancies can be seen as an analogue to the chain lengths in earlier chapters. The third tool, turnover—the composition of groups by past membership—appears in models of attitude change in terms of the transition matrix raised to a power. In the vacancy models all three tools are relevant. Comparison with the single-flows models shows which aspects of the vacancy construct are essential to which aspects of the vacancy model.

9.1 The Multiplier Equation in Leontief's Input-Output Model

If we disregard the interaction of men and jobs, we can consider vacancies as entities in their own right. The basic equation for the mobility generated by an initial cohort of vacancies was derived in Section 2.2

$$\mathbf{M} = \mathbf{F}(I - Q)^{-1} \tag{9.1}$$

where the vector **M** specifies total moves and **F**, original arrivals of vacancies by stratum in a year. Multiply by $(I - Q)$ and rearrange to produce an equation that can be called the multiplier equation

$$\mathbf{M} = \mathbf{M}Q + \mathbf{F} \tag{9.2}$$

A direct interpretation of this equation makes sense: Let **M** on the left be the total count of arrivals by stratum. On the right, **M**Q counts by stratum the arrivals of vacancies that departed from other strata; some of the departures are not included because they are terminal moves to the outside. The term **F** must be added on the right of equation (9.2) because some of the arrivals are directly from the outside. Instead of tracing chains out step by step as in Chapter 2, the cumulated result they must produce is formulated in a set of simultaneous equations in interlinked variables.

Equation (9.2) can be used as the general prototype for any contingency or multiplier effect. It is unimportant whether actual individual chains can be traced. The contingency effect is present in equation (9.2) whether the model is regarded as purely aggregative or as based on a parallel law at the individual level. If it does reach to the individual level, it does not matter whether this is as a stochastic or as a deterministic model. The term "multiplier" indicates that equation (9.2) appears in Keynesian economics.[3]

Equation (9.2) is a close analogue to the central equation of the Leontief input-output model.[4] Redefine q_{ij} as the amount of the jth good required to produce a unit amount of the ith good. Redefine **F** as the amount of each good to be consumed, that is, sent out of the system. Redefine **M** as the total amount of each good that must be produced to generate the consumption specified. Equation (9.2) must be turned inside-out in time:

$$\mathbf{M}' = Q\mathbf{M}' + \mathbf{F}' \tag{9.3}$$

Here the primes indicate the vectors must be written as column vectors, in accordance with the laws of matrix multiplication. As in the vacancy model, **F**′ is an exogenous flow imposed on the system. It is not the cause of production in a physical sense; it is a normative demand. Hence **M**′ on the left is a count of total "departures," not arrivals.

Leontief adds an extra variable and equation. Labor, call it M_0, is an input demanded from the environment. It is assumed to be a fixed linear function of the amounts of goods to be produced:

$$M_0 = \sum_{i=1}^{s} q_{0i}M_i \qquad (9.4)$$

The analogue of this equation in the vacancy chain model is obvious: the total number of moves by vacancies to the outside, call it M_0, is a linear function of the number of appearances, that is, of arrivals, of vacancies in the various strata:

$$M_0 = \sum_{i=1}^{s} M_i q_{i0} \qquad (9.5)$$

The analogy between the two models is not complete. The q_{ij} in Leontief's system are ratios of, say, coal to steel or coal to coal fixed by the rigid, unique technology assumed. There is no sensible way they can be interpreted in stochastic terms, and the Leontief system is intended solely for the level of aggregates. The M's and $\mathbf{F}$ are rates but not of denumerable entities such as vacancies.

In formal terms, the equations for the vacancy model appear to be a special case of the Leontief system. Prices can be introduced into that system. The natural numeraire good is labor: the price of a unit of labor is 1, or all other prices are expressed in units of the price of labor, P_0. It is clear intuitively that the price of the jth good is just the total amount of labor needed to produce a unit amount of it, both the direct labor and the labor used in making the amounts of all goods used in producing one unit of good j.[5] The prices must be fixed in terms of the labor input coefficients, q_{0i}, amplified by the indirect labor requirements. Writing the q_{0i} as a row vector, $\mathbf{q}_0$, and the prices, P_j/P_0, as a row vector $\mathbf{P}$, then

$$\mathbf{P} = \mathbf{q}_0(I - Q)^{-1} \qquad (9.6)$$

Since each equation of the vacancy model is the inverted form of the analogous Leontief equation, the "prices," whatever they may mean in the vacancy model, should be given by

$$\mathbf{P}' = (I - Q)^{-1}\mathbf{q}_0' \qquad (9.7)$$

Primes denote column vectors as before, and in the notation of Chapter 2, $\mathbf{q}_0$ was written as $\mathbf{p}$.

The vacancy model seems a special case because there are constraints on the coefficients q_{ij}, whereas the q_{ij}'s in the Leontief model can each have any numerical value, independent of what the other q_{ij}'s are. (In a feasible technology $q_{ii} < 1$ is required, and, indeed the size of various strings of subdeterminants of $(I - Q)$ must be positive; these are mere inequalities.)[6] Since the q_{ij} apportion a collection of vacancies among a set of $s + 1$ possible destinations (whether as probabilities or as transition fractions),

$$q_{io} + \sum_{j=1}^{s} q_{ij} = 1 \qquad (9.8)$$

In vector terms,

$$\mathbf{q}_0' = (I - Q)\mathbf{1}' \qquad (9.9)$$

where $\mathbf{1}'$ is a column vector whose s components are each unity. Equation (9.9) can be substituted in equation (9.7):

$$\mathbf{P}' = I\mathbf{1}' = \mathbf{1}' \qquad (9.10)$$

that is, every "price" in the vacancy model is unity. Simple logic validates the result: the total amount of "labor"—the number of terminal moves of vacancies from all strata allocated to "produce" a unit of "consumption," the arrival of one vacancy in stratum j—must be unity. What goes in must come out.

The Leontief model has no more degrees of freedom than the vacancy model, since the prices (relative to labor price) are rigidly fixed. The only real difference is that in the Leontief system the unit in which a good is measured is arbitrary. The "terms of trade" between goods are fixed in both the Leontief system and the vacancy model. With appropriate choice of units for goods, prices in the Leontief model, as in the vacancy model, are all unity.[7]

The Leontief literature suggests some new ideas about the vacancy model,[8] but the motivation for this section lies elsewhere. Indivisible individuals are not the construct used in Leontief models, nor is interaction between two kinds of flows of "goods" a process studied. Yet predictions of total flows from exogenous flows can be derived in analogous ways in the two models. Hence the contingency (or regenerative or multiplier) aspect of the vacancy model, and its dependence on flows across boundaries, are shown to be separable from the underlying specification of vacancy formation and jumps in terms of individual men and jobs.[9]

9.2 Demographic Models

Unlike Leontief models, demographic models for survival of a population deal with discrete individuals. However, the same kind of multiplier equation, (9.3) or (9.2), applies. The main difference is the additional interpretation in terms of individual careers justified for the demographic model, one step closer to the vacancy models, but no more than that.

The interpretation of **M** in equation (9.2) is, now, the number of man-years of living, in the various years of age, generated by a cohort of recruits counted by **F**; the s strata are the years of age a baby can attain. Usually interest would be focused mainly on M, the total number of man-years generated at whatever year of age; unless immigration to the population were large, the recruits would be babies and only the first component of **F** would be appreciable. The ratio of M/F is called the life expectancy in such a population.

The transition matrix Q must have a very special form. All entries must be zero except those on the diagonal just above the principal diagonal:

$$q_{i,j} = 0 \tag{9.11}$$

for $j \neq i + 1$, where i and j range from 1 to s. Equation (9.1) is still the solution; the inverse matrix $(I - Q)^{-1}$ must be calculated from the given values of $q_{i,i+1}$. As in the vacancy chain model the q's are treated as probabilities for individuals. .There must be a set of residual fractions, $q_{i,0}$, that give the death rates. Residual fractions do not appear explicitly in the equations, but since the sum of all the fractions from a stratum is unity,

$$q_{i,i+1} = 1 - q_{i,0} \quad i \leq s - 1 \tag{9.12}$$

When $i = s$, $q_{ss} = 0$ so that $q_{s,0} = 1$; that is, men must die at age s, if not before. Age can be seen as a continuous variable, and a first-order differential equation in age is more natural than the Markov chain formulation.[10]

The probability distributions for length of life of individuals, entering at various ages, are given by equation (2.5). The demographic model can be seen as a Markov chain for individuals. Career distributions are particularly simple, in view of equation (9.11); the number of moves made in an individual's lifetime is defined by the state from which he leaves. Turnover—the composition of the group of men in a stratum according to their strata at an earlier time—is an immediate consequence of the definition of age, not a concern of this model as it is of the social mobility models treated next.

As outlined so far, death is the subject of basic demographic models. Individuals are considered purely in terms of physical survival. Demographers may treat any subpopulation as an independent entity, down to a size below which age-specific data on deaths would be too small to be reliable. In this way causal factors affecting death, which can be represented in terms of differences in attributes of individuals such as in social class, can be included in the model. However, interaction between survival of different individuals or subpopulations is ignored. Causes of death include starvation, epidemics, and accidents, all of which depend in part on population density and may depend on more subtle characteristics like the age structure of the total population. Such dependencies are hard to include in the model. Naturally it is unlikely that death rates, even the age-specific death rates q_{io}, for a specific subpopulation, will remain constant over long periods. Projections to the future are difficult. Instead, demographers often summarize the existing state in one year in terms of an artificial cohort, describing the life expectancies that would be observed if a new cohort of men were exposed to the same age-specific rates observed that year in the collection of cohorts alive now. Equations (2.5) and (9.2), with constant Q, do just that. Usually an elaborate scheme of numerical computations is used to generate the "life tables," but a number of mathematical demographers have emphasized the greater clarity of the formulation as a Markov chain.[11]

Births are the source of essentially all new entries when the total population of a nation is treated. It is obvious that births should be roughly proportional to the size of the population at fertile ages rather than being a completely arbitrary exogenous variable. The specification of $\mathbf{F}$ as the product of rates times the population exposed to movement is a new feature with no analogue in the vacancy chain models of Chapters 2 and 7. Bisexual reproduction has proved remarkably difficult to incorporate into the models.[12] The standard procedure is to focus on the female population and define age-specific (age of mother) birth rates for this sex only. An additional vector for the rates, $\mathbf{b}'$, can be defined. The demographic model is now one of renewal of a total population rather than survival of a cohort. Instead of the equilibrium equation (9.2) for a cohort, an equation in **W**, the total female population by age, is needed:

$$\mathbf{W}(t + 1) = \mathbf{W}(t)Q + [\mathbf{W}(t)\mathbf{b}']\varepsilon_0 \qquad (9.13)$$

Here ε_0 is the unit vector $(1, 0, 0, \ldots, 0)$; the second term, $[\mathbf{W}(t)\mathbf{b}']\varepsilon_0$, merely adds to the total population the number of births the previous year.[13]

The equation (9.13) can be solved explicitly by standard methods for a balanced, stable growth, in which $\mathbf{W}(t + 1) = r\mathbf{W}(t)$.[14] It can be proved that the population will reach equilibrium in that sense. The (scalar) constant growth rate r is called the "intrinsic rate of natural increase." The percentage distribution of the population by age remains constant. The rate r is not parallel in meaning to the rate r in Section 7.1, which refers to changes in the dual populations underlying the population of vacancies exposed to Q, whose population is constant in size. Unlike the retirement rates ρ in Sections 7.3 and 7.5, the birth rates $\mathbf{b}'$ apply to the population exposed to Q. In general the population **W**, unlike the populations **N**, **J** (and **V**) of Section 7.5, cannot be constant.[15] There is no analogue to the birth process in the vacancy or other social mobility models. There may be an analogue in the von Neumann model for an expanding economy, which can be seen as a generalization of the Leontief model for a closed system.[16]

Vacancy models and other social mobility models should describe open systems whose inputs and outputs of men are ultimately derived from demographic processes of birth and death. The mobility models described in later sections investigate mobility of men among a set of social categories of men. The only satisfactory way of describing outputs and inputs would be by a cross-classification of these categories by age categories: work by J. Matras along these lines is discussed in Section 9.7.[17]

9.3 *Attitude Turnover*

Three models using Markov chains to describe social mobility appeared nearly simultaneously in the early 1950s. This section treats a model of attitude change derived from the work of T. W. Anderson.[18] Change in attitudes may, initially, seem too personal a matter to subsume under the rubric of social mobility. Anderson's model is most often applied to time series data on political party preference or the like, wherein categories are matters of public definition, known and accepted by the individuals studied. The tincture of prestige differentiation that adheres to the phrase "social mobility" can well apply too. The structure is the same as for other single-flows models of social mobility: men move among defined categories of unrestricted size according to fixed transition probabilities.

Turnover is here taken to mean the distribution of the present population of each category among all categories in a subsequent year. The resulting total may be smaller because some of the people have left the system in intervening years, and they need not be included explicitly in the distribution. In social mobility, turnover measures the extent to which present membership of a social group will disperse over time and indicates the extent to which its anticipated future will diverge. Reverse turnover measures the composition of the present population of a category by membership in an earlier year; entrants to the system since the earlier year can be counted as coming from an "outside" category. In social mobility, reverse turnover has a bearing on the homogeneity of experience and possibly on cohesiveness in a social group.

In Anderson's model the calculation of turnover is no longer the trivial matter it was in the demographic model. Sections 2.6 and 2.7 specify and discuss turnover for a model like Anderson's ("constant turnover" model) except that death is allowed in the former. Turnover over various periods is represented in terms of corresponding powers of a fixed matrix of transitional probabilities. Anderson himself discussed in detail turnover during only a single time interval[19] and therefore did not make full use of his time series data on attitude change in a panel of respondents. He concluded that the matrix of transition probabilities for the panel changed twice.[20] The main point is that if turnover were calculated for vacancies rather than for men in the vacancy model in Chapter 2, the formulas would be identical with those for turnover of men in a model like Anderson's.

In a closed population like Anderson's, the normal interpretations of career (see Section 10.1) are useless, since men never enter or leave the system. One can look instead at the distribution of the population over the possible sequences of states (including complete immobility) during an arbitrary period of time.[21] However, the only measure of careers studied for the demographic or vacancy models, that is, length, is not relevant for that kind of population distribution.

The total amount of movement in each stratum is a major concern of the vacancy model. Initial movement caused by new arrivals regenerates itself repeatedly, in accordance with the fixed transition matrix, to form the final mobility totals for vacancies. In Section 9.1, the multiplier equation (9.2) was shown to be a shortcut to the same result; only the properties common to the Leontief model and the vacancy model can be relevant to the formula for total movements, $\mathbf{M}$. Whatever the nature of a flow, whether it consists of entities and if so, whether or not they are compound entities, total flows into strata must equal the allocations of parts of the same totals as out-flows into the various strata plus the fresh flows from the outside into strata. This solution by a logic of self-consistency is a simultaneous equation. It has great intuitive appeal, but it seems to depend entirely on the existence of an external flow. Mobility is also important in closed systems like Anderson's. The question of what becomes of the multiplier equation there is answered in the following discussion.

Some preliminary clarification for the open system is needed. Equation (2.10) prescribes total rate of movement for only a special case in which the total population is a single cohort. Vacancies are presumed to disappear within a year, and vacancies arrive only in a bunch at the beginning of a year. The total population of vacancies never contains more than one cohort at a time. The same is true for goods and consumption orders in the Leontief scheme. In general, the multiplier equation (9.2) cannot describe movements per unit time by total populations in an open system.

The demographic model for deaths of a cohort was converted into the model for a total population subject to birth and death in Section 9.2. The multiplier equation had to be dropped in favor of equation (9.13), which, quite aside from the special form the birth term takes, is completely different from the multiplier equation. Equation (9.13) is not an equation in total movement but in total size of population. It is not a self-consistent equation for equilibrium values but a difference equation specifying a later, in terms of an earlier, state vector $\mathbf{W}$, where $\mathbf{W}$ measures the total population. If the source of the new cohort $\mathbf{F}(t)$ is not specified, equation (9.13) can be written in a general form applicable to the total population $\mathbf{W}(t)$ of any open system governed by a matrix Q:

$$\mathbf{W}(t + 1) = \mathbf{W}(t)Q + \mathbf{F}(t) \qquad (9.14)$$

If equilibrium were reached, the equation for $\mathbf{W}_{eq}$ would be exactly parallel to the multiplier equation. Equilibrium could be reached only if the cohorts were constant in size so that the losses implied by a Q whose determinant was less than unity could exactly balance each new arrival cohort. In that case, moves into each stratum would exactly balance moves out of it, and the total movements in a year, $\mathbf{M}$, for the total population could be found from the multiplier equation (9.2). Otherwise, total movements can be calculated only from the size of total populations determined by equation (9.14).[22]

In general, the multiplier equation in an open system defines the total lifetime movements of a given set of individuals and not the movements per unit time of the total population in the system during that interval. A slight generalization of the multiplier equation is possible. Consider an arbitrary population $\mathbf{W}(0)$ in an open system at some time labeled "zero." Suppose additional cohorts, counted by $\mathbf{F}(t)$, enter the system at a finite number of subsequent epochs, so that $\mathbf{F}(t)$ is zero for all t greater than some fixed time T. Define $\mathbf{L}$ as the vector counting the total numbers of moves made by the initial population and the additional cohorts during their entire lifetime in the system subsequent to time zero:

$$\mathbf{L} = \mathbf{L}Q + \mathbf{W}(0) + \sum_{t=1}^{T} \mathbf{F}(t) \tag{9.15}$$

The left-hand side of the equation counts the number of moves into statuses in the system. The first term on the right counts the moves into statuses made by individuals already in the system. The final term counts the arrivals of subsequent cohorts. The second term on the right counts the appearance of the initial population in the system at time zero as a set of formal "moves." If these moves are to be disregarded, the vector $\mathbf{L}$ calculated from equation (9.15) is interpreted as the total numbers of moves out of statuses after time zero by the whole population. $\mathbf{L}$ does not count moves in a fixed time interval by a fixed population, and it is not a count germane to the usual measurement of mobility as a rate of movement.

One additional qualification applies to the preceding discussion of the multiplier equation. In the vacancy model, each individual vacancy is required to move. In other mobility models, an individual may not move at all during a given interval; the probability of immobility is given by the diagonal entry q_{ii}. In such cases, the diagonal entries in the matrix Q should be suppressed in the multiplier equation but not in equation (9.14).[23]

Anderson's model is one for closed systems and one in which individuals do not move during every interval. The general multiplier equation (9.15) is applicable to closed systems, but there are two special features. All $\mathbf{F}(t)$ are zero, and the determinant of Q is unity, since each row sum is unity. The size of $\mathbf{L}(t)$ is indeterminate, since $(I - Q)^{-1}$ is undefined. The concept of total movement during the lifetime of an individual is meaningless because the lifetime is infinite. Total movements by the population per time unit can be found by applying the off-diagonal rates q_{ij} to the population vector $\mathbf{W}(t)$, and mobility rates can then be calculated. The main point is that the multiplier effect does occur in this as in all the other systems describable in terms of a fixed matrix of transition probabilities. At bottom the multiplier effect simply says that a new string of moves is generated in a system every time an individual is added.

Anderson skips directly from discussion of turnover to evolution of stratum sizes. The basic dynamic equation in the model of a closed system is

$$\mathbf{W}(t + 1) = \mathbf{W}(t)Q \tag{9.16}$$

which adds to each stratum the difference between inflow and outflow.[24] The main theoretical result is that $\mathbf{W}(t)$ will approach an equilibrium distribution vector independent of its initial form $\mathbf{W}(0)$, as long as it is possible, at least indirectly, to go from each stratum to every other stratum. The equilibrium vector $\mathbf{W}_e$ is simply that distribution of the total number of people in the system, $|\mathbf{W}(0)|$, which satisfies

$$\mathbf{W}_e = \mathbf{W}_e Q \tag{9.17}$$

When formulated in terms of Markov chains, as Anderson's are, the equations are interpreted in terms of probabilities for an individual, with the fixed size of the population, $|W(0)|$, being unity. The advantage of this formulation is that variabilities in predictions for a population are made explicit—marginals vary around their expected values according to a multinomial distribution.[25] The disadvantage lies in the rigid assertions of the independence and sameness required concerning the individuals. The treatment in Chapter 7 of the evolution of the distribution of vacancies $\mathbf{V}(t)$ in a system parallels Anderson's approach, although for an open system in continuous time; but the probabilistic interpretation is largely suppressed.

Choice of states is as difficult a problem with Anderson's attitude categories as it was for job strata in Chapters 4 and 6. A stochastic process may appear Markovian for one choice of states but not for another; if Markovian for either of two choices, the transition probabilities may be constant for one but not the other. Anderson considered second-order chains in which each state is defined by the particular attitude held at each of two neighboring epochs.[26] If estimated transition probabilities differ according to the next-to-last attitude held, this is evidence against the Markovian character of the first order chain. The Markov property could also be tested by comparing observed and predicted distributions of the population over possible sequences of states, but the test is harder to apply correctly than the analogous test in the vacancy chain model. There the measure of sequence structure is sheer length of a vacancy's total career in number of jobs; since a chain can be traced through individual jobs, transitions within a stratum count toward career length.

9.4 Mobility of Men as Markov Chains

The focus now shifts from comparison of the formal structures of models to the contrast between single-flows models and vacancy models in their substantive implications. Sample survey techniques developed for the study of voting and other attitudes were soon applied to social mobility. In the 1954 compendium on British stratification and mobility edited by D. V. Glass, a national sample of men was cross-classified by own and by father's occupational prestige category.[27] This new data stimulated S. J. Prais to propose a Markov chain model of intergenerational mobility.[28] The greater depth and flexibility of questioning possible in a sample survey as opposed to a census permitted two decisive improvements: (1) prestige of occupations could be assessed and used to group them in categories sufficiently coherent to sustain interpretation as states in a Markov chain; and (2) each respondent could report occupational standings of other individuals with ties to him.

Surveys were made in a number of other countries[29] at the time of and subsequent to the Glass studies, the main ones being for Denmark and the United States. There is no time series for a panel of individual respondents in one country because of the long time spans expected for substantial mobility in occupational prestige. A generation was the only possible time unit to be used for estimating transition probabilities, and a family the natural unit in the flow. The data on grandfathers and more remote ancestors of respondents was so fragmentary that no time series and, hence, no test of the Markov assumption or of constancy of parameters was or is possible even for the artificial time unit of a generation. O. D. Duncan has demonstrated the unreality of treating the fathers of an existing population of men, even in a given age range, as an earlier cohort in the occupational system, even if it were possible to eliminate biases from multiple counting and omission of men in the "fathers' cohort."[30] Prais himself pointed out the artificiality of confining attention to male descent in putative "families," which is reminiscent of the single-sex demographic model.

In spite of these differences in the nature of the data, Prais's is a single-flows model closely parallel to the attitude turnover model in Section 9.3, and most of that commentary is relevant here. Prais's system is closed too, not because his time spans are too short for disappearance and creation of new units (male family lines) to be relevant but because of limitations of data. Prais emphasizes the individual interpretation less than and the aggregate interpretation of the model more than Anderson. Prais neglects variability calculations in favor of attending to the construction of measures. A proliferation of unsatisfactory measures is a characteristic of the measurement literature on stratification. Prais proposed a group of new measures which had the great advantage of being based on an explicit model of the process of mobility flow, rudimentary and artificial as it may be. The idea of a natural standard, a society with perfect equality of opportunity for mobility but with the same distribution of men by stratum as the actual society, is used extensively by Prais in constructing measures. There is no parallel for attitudes,[31] and the measures derived by Prais therefore constitute more than a simple transposition from notions of turnover, careers, and marginal change in models of attitude change.

The crucial difference between models of attitudes and of mobility should be in the determinants of the sizes of categories. The vacancy model derives from the idea that jobs are not created, or shifted in status, by the will of the mobile individual. Prais recognizes that the distribution of positions by stratum may be determined by economic and social forces exogenous to the mobility process, although the marginals he used for the equal-opportunity standard society are the equilibrium marginals that would be generated by repeated application of the Markov chain. Measures of association between initial and final status in social mobility have usually been based on the same idea of "removing" the effect of, or "standardizing," the marginals (see Section 11.5). In a limited sense, all the Markov models for men are based on standardization of marginals, since the transition parameters are probabilities or rates per individual of the origin category which are assumed to be independent of the initial and final sizes of the categories.

Prais, in an appendix, proposes to eliminate the effects of changes in marginals on observed transition probabilities in order to obtain true propensities to move. Any procedure for "standardizing" column marginals in the Markov chains is arbitrary unless based on an explicit model of how men, positions, and opportunities to move fit together. Prais merely divides the mobility matrix into two factors: the first matrix transforms the observed initial marginals to the final marginals and the second then applies hypothetical true mobility propensities to these marginals. Thus the second matrix must have the column marginals as its equilibrium distribution ("fixed point" vector). To obtain a unique matrix of propensities, the first matrix, which implicitly represents the effects of economic and other forces, must be fully specified. Since the number of men is fixed, positions must be reallocated by the first matrix from the categories that decline to categories that grow. Prais uses one of the simplest possible assumptions:[32] a category that grows draws the growth from the nearest (in prestige) category that declines.

In a paper on combinatorial models of intergenerational mobility, this author suggests an alternative approach.[33] As Prais pointed out, there is no evidence for large departures from equal opportunity. Most of the degrees of freedom left when marginals are taken as fixed by exogenous forces are not used. Two forms that might be taken by the actual biases are barriers preventing extreme mobility jumps and inertial forces restraining sons from leaving their father's stratum, for example, inheritance of jobs. These two forms are polar opposites among the symmetric biases that might be imagined, and there is little sign of asymmetric biases (for example, ones that work on upper but not lower strata or on upward but not downward moves). When entries in the appropriate cells are fixed for each form of bias, the entries in the remaining cells expected by chance, given the observed row and column totals, can be computed. The chance process is the selection at random of an allocation of available men among available jobs; it is a problem in restricted permutations. Both Glass's data and a corresponding mobility table for Denmark are more nearly consistent with an inheritance bias than with a barrier bias.[34]

In the combinatorial model, shifts in marginals have ramifications throughout the mobility table so that men's mobility propensities for individual cells are no longer meaningful. Yet this model or, more specifically, the inheritance model is a precursor of the vacancy chain model, which specifies, for an open system, the way changes in marginals trigger chains of moves. The inheritance model thus permits the reintroduction of propensities (of vacancies) to move from one stratum to another but on a new basis. In another paper, this author makes a slight change in the combinatorial calculations that yields a modified model of inheritance whose kinship to the vacancy model is much clearer.[35] All the combinatorial models depend on preassigned column marginals and therefore cannot be extended to predict mobility in subsequent generations.

James S. Coleman has proposed a model that, like the revised inheritance model, assumes that (unobserved) intragenerational career mobility of the sons generates the observed intergenerational cross-tabulation.[36] Men are allowed to move only to strata adjacent in the prestige ordering,[37] which therefore is assumed to approximate a true ordered scale. This step-by-step mobility process is represented by a set of interlocked differential equations of a kind common to queuing and random walk models. The algorithm for inferring the instantaneous transition rates between adjacent strata is approximate,[38] and the algorithm provides no means of assuring a fit to the observed column marginals. Coleman reports the fit between predicted and observed tables for Denmark and Britain is not good.

I. Blumen et al. dealt explicitly with intragenerational mobility for an artificially closed population moving among a set of unordered categories (industries).[39] In an attempt to match prediction with observation for tables of long-run turnover, they revised the simple Markov model by treating a population as if it were split between movers—whose behavior is described by a constant Markov chain—and stayers—who never leave the origin category. In one paper, this author has shown how these mover-stayer models are related to the modified inheritance model and, thus, how both can be interpreted, if the column marginals are treated as external constraints, as a step toward the vacancy chain models of opportunity flows.[40] Section 10.2 discusses ways to distinguish men by attributes in a vacancy model.

In their Chapter 7, Blumen et al. suggest a variety of extensions of the mover-stayer models. They distinguish three sources of variable liability of men to movement: proneness, experience, and instability. The first two are natural generalizations of the differential propensity to move at the heart of the mover-stayer model.[41] The third, instability, includes changes in exposure of all individuals to movement that result from fluctuations in general economic conditions.[42] If concrete reference to jobs is substituted for the reference to general economic conditions, it resembles the idea in the vacancy models that amount of movement is dependent on creation of vacancies and on rates of termination of vacancies. Still missing is the idea of mobility as a regenerative process in which initial moves trigger chains of subsequent moves, so that mobility is proportional to vacancies created times a multiplier matrix.

The fundamental differences between the vacancy chain model and the mover-stayer models of Blumen et al. can be seen in the kinds of data suitable in each model. Blumen et al. use observations of where given men are employed during successive quarterly intervals, although they would prefer data on employment at successive points in time.[43] In either case, they could not observe all moves made, but they do not see this as a fundamental problem. They show that "... we can ignore the number of movements made by individuals between the points of time at which we take our observations" at least in some simple forms of their models.[44] In the logic of the vacancy chain model, a move by a man is part of a series of moves generated by creation of a vacancy, and it cannot be understood apart from this dependency. In earlier chapters, samples were drawn: they were samples of complete chains, not of isolated moves. Any move could appear in the sample, not only moves by given men observable at preassigned points in time. In a closed system, there could be no mobility because there are no vacancy creations.

9.5 Queues, Blocking and Vacancy Chains

Single-flows models of mobility tend to assume men choose where to move without constraint, their stable average preferences being recorded in a table of transfer coefficients among strata. In one major variant, the inheritance model, mobility is not an independent process but an adaptation to preassigned terminal distributions. Allowing a queue at each stratum is the simplest way of introducing the reality of job opportunities in the single-flows models while preserving the basic assumption that movers' tastes are the prime determinant of mobility. The implicit assumptions in single-flows models are thereby made visible.

Yet queue length at each stratum must be limited. Men elsewhere are then blocked from obeying their urge to move to a stratum when all jobs and the line there are already filled. As men subsequently leave that stratum, the queue is reduced below the limit, and the blocking of mobility urges is removed temporarily. When there are normally more than enough men in the system to fill the jobs, it is obvious that blocking replaces urges to move as the decisive factor in mobility. A blocked movement to one stratum is removed by a departure and then reimposed after a new arrival, whose departure removed temporarily the blocked movement to his origin stratum, and so on. The focus of attention shifts from the blocked urges to move of the bulk of the men to the shifts of blocking from one stratum to another. The choice of the individuals to fill the few vacancies rather than of the latent urges to move held by the bulk of the population at any given time is the issue. In the limit when allowed queue length is zero, the blocking model resembles the vacancy chain model but still suffers from its focus on hypothetical urges to move.

Models of mobility among strata with queuing are extremely complex. Fortunately, in a recent paper, "Closed Queuing Systems," W. J. Gordon and G. F. Newell analyze properties of abstract queuing systems with arbitrary crossovers allowed among various stages of parallel servers.[45] In a second paper, "Cyclic Queuing Systems," they treat a special case of a system with blocking, that is, with maximum queue lengths.[46] Their results are not exhaustive, especially in "Cyclic Systems," but they are sufficient for expository purposes. Instead of Markov chains describing moves at fixed intervals, Gordon and Newell postulate a Markov process in continuous time in which the probability distribution of time in a job is negative exponential, as is customary in the literature on queuing. This shift in framework is actually an advantage in exposition, for it will clarify the meaning of probabilities on the diagonal of the matrices for the single-flows models. The simultaneous treatment of open and closed systems in both papers will also prove instructive.

We now return to a system of men and 1–1 jobs. Let there be r_i permanent jobs in the ith of s strata. Suppose a man quits his job because of some chance trigger event at a rate μ_i for a job in the ith stratum; the distribution of tenure lengths is a negative exponential with mean value $1/\mu_i$. Once he has left, the man instantly chooses the stratum in which to seek a job according to fixed probabilities p_{ij}; his path through the system of stages is random. At the destination stratum, the man must wait in line for the first available job unless one is already vacant. By these identifications, the mobility problem is converted into Gordon and Newell's abstract closed queuing system. Jobs in strata become a stage of servers in parallel, and men become customers. "Service" is the realization of a man's urge to leave his present job, and fixed transfer coefficients describe the likelihood of his then going to various strata as destinations. All men are equivalent, their desires to leave and their choice of destination being distinguished only according to the stratum of their present job.

That abstract queuing system is a natural vehicle for extending the kinds of single-flows models developed by Anderson, by Prais, and by Blumen et al. The fundamental assumption in those models is that the wishes of men to move determine movement without reference to the existence of opportunities, that is, of vacant jobs. This assumption is built into Gordon and Newell's definition of the "service" process, and yet permanent jobs are introduced into the system as independent entities. The flexible queues allowed at each stratum reconcile fixed numbers of jobs with independent moves by men. Instead of each departure by a man being conditioned on a preceding departure from a destination job, there is a delay in a man's entry to a job conditional on the size of the queue waiting at that stratum for incumbents to leave their jobs. The only restriction is that while men are in queue, they are not exposed to urges to move to other strata but remain patiently in line until an opening occurs. When the number of jobs r_i in each stratum is infinite, queuing is irrelevant; the system behaves like the single-flows models of men moving among categories.

Results are derived in Gordon and Newell's closed system for only equilibrium probability distributions of the population of customers among stages of servers. This is the equivalent of Prais's main goal.

Turnover and career lines of men are not considered. Queue discipline can be left open; that is, whether it should be head-of-the-line, random, last-in–first-served, and so on. Similarly, the histories of particular jobs in a stratum are not dealt with, and the principles of assignment of an arrival to one of several empty jobs need not be specified. Whatever the discipline assumed, predictions for careers and turnover would obviously be different from those in any single-flows model because periods spent in queue would depend on the overall dynamics of the system.

Let new men be attracted to the system only when it contains fewer than N_0 men, where N_0 is a fixed ceiling. Introduce an artificial new stratum, labeled 0, which is identified as the station for arrivals from outside the system. Define $\mu_0 r_0$ as the maximum rate at which the new men arrive, the rate being $(r_0 - 1)\mu_0$ when there are already $N_0 - r_0 + 1$ men in the system and falling to μ_0 when there are $N_0 - 1$ men in the system. A new arrival joins the queue at stratum j with probability $p_{0j}, j = 1, 2, 3, \ldots$; and p_{00} is zero. Conversely, a man leaving stratum i leaves the system with probability p_{i0}, $i = 1, 2, 3, \ldots$. That is Gordon and Newell's "open" system described in their "Closed Queuing Systems." That system matches the logic of the single-flows models of mobility, although all of them are actually models of closed systems, as has been emphasized in previous sections. The entrance of men to the system is a process nearly independent of the state of the system, being reduced below a fixed average rate $r_0\mu_0$ only when the system is filled to near capacity. That capacity N_0 is arbitrary and is not dictated by the numbers of jobs, since any queue can be indefinitely long. Not only is the input nearly constant but men also leave the system according to fixed average rates determined by the strata of their jobs.

The open system is not analyzed directly in "Closed Queing Systems"; it is, instead, equated to a hypothetical closed system in which stage 0 is now part of the system and has its own queue of men. The arbitrary capacity N_0 becomes the fixed number of men in the closed system. The p_{0j} have the same interpretation as in the open system. The p_{j0} define the fraction of movers from j joining stage 0 as opposed to leaving the system; the stream of arrivals from the outside at station 0 is replaced by streams of arrivals to stage 0 from other stages determined by the p_{j0}. In short, the closed system is identical with the queue system as initially described except that another stage is assumed. Solutions for only a closed system are

9. Single-Flows Models of Mobility

presented hereafter, and the index numbering for stages is begun with 1 rather than 0. If the solution is to be interpreted like one for an open system, however, the probability distributions must be summed over all values of the size of the queue used as a substitute for the arrival process.

The reason for the particular variation chosen for arrival rate with number of men in the open system near capacity in "Closed Queuing Systems" now seems clear. Only that choice, not particularly plausible empirically, leads to equivalence with a closed system (which is easier to solve). The hypothetical queue at stage 0 in the closed system is just such as to generate the same pattern of arrivals as is assumed for the open system. Blumen et al. attempted to develop an analogous equivalence[47] and in fact used a closed system for their Markov chain model of labor mobility. The difficulty in handling an open system realistically evident in both "Closed Queuing Systems" and Blumen et al. seems to stem from the population they treat. If all men in the system are moving, and by their own volition, inputs from the outside are logically a minor part of the mobility pattern. The inputs are exogenous flows that are hard to combine with intrinsic rates of movement by men in the system.

In a given state of the system, let the number of men in stratum i, including those in queue, be denoted by n_i. The total number of men in the closed system, in any state, is N_0. The number of jobs in stratum i is r_i; denote the total number of jobs by J, where

$$J = \sum_{i=1}^{s} r_i \qquad (9.18)$$

When the closed system is in equilibrium, the joint probability distribution can be written in a simple form:[48]

$$P(n_1, n_2, \ldots, n_s) = \frac{\prod_{i=1}^{s} (y_i/\mu_i)^{n_i}[(1/\beta_i[n_i])]}{\text{(sum of the products above over all sets of } n_i \text{ that sum to } N_0)} \qquad (9.19)$$

Two auxiliary fractions appear here: first, the fixed-point vector $(y_1, y_2, \ldots, y_s)$ of the matrix of transfer coefficients $\{p_{ij}\}$, whose components are determined from

$$\mathbf{y} = \mathbf{y}\{p_{ij}\} \qquad (9.20)$$

second, a counting formula,

$$\beta_i[n_i] = n_i! \tag{9.21a}$$

when $n_i \leq r_i$ and

$$\beta_i[n_i] = r_i! r_i^{n_i - r_i} \tag{9.21b}$$

when $n_i \geq r_i$. The analogue of the single-flows models of mobility is the case when each r_i is infinite, that is, when the number of jobs in each stratum is infinite so that no one ever waits in queue. It is easy to see that the joint probability depends on r_i only through the counting formulas (9.21a) or (9.21b).

Suppose an actual queue system is approximated by a single-flows model through setting each r_i equal to infinity rather than to its observed value. Each counting function (9.21a) or (9.21b) is unchanged for small values of n_i but is increased for the larger values, for $n_i > r_i$. The product in the numerator of equation (9.19) corresponding to a given state is thereby decreased; of course, products in the denominator sum in equation (9.19) are also decreased. In all states of the closed system, the total number of men is fixed, at N_0. Hence not every factor in the product is decreased in most states; and if N_0 is smaller than the total number of jobs J, there are some states for which the numerator product in equation (9.19) is unchanged. The relative decrease for a state tends to be greater and, hence, the actual value of the joint probability is reduced more for those states which have large numbers of men in strata with few jobs.

Intuition confirms that conclusion. If the queues in a system are ignored, then all men in a stratum are assumed to be moving out at the given rate μ_i, and the total departure rate from the stratum is overestimated. Since the system is closed, the average change in the departure rates over all strata will not affect the equilibrium distribution and simply enhance the arrival rates to all strata. Those strata with few jobs can be expected to have the largest queues and the largest overestimates of departure rates; the probabilities of states with large numbers of men in these strata will therefore be underestimated when queues are ignored.

The preceding arguments are rigorous only when the matrix of transfer coefficients has constant columns—when the y_i are equal—and when the rates μ_i are all the same. Effects of inequalities in the matrix of transfer coefficients on changes in the joint probability distribution resulting from changes in the r_i are hard to assess.

Derivation of a marginal distribution—the probabilities of various numbers of men being in a given stratum whatever the overall system state—is difficult because the sum of the numbers in all strata is constrained to be N_0. Simple asymptotic formulas are derived in "Closed Queuing Systems" for large and uniform systems, in which both N_0 and s are large and in which the ratios $y_i/\mu_i r_i$ are of the same general size. The probability that n_i men are in stratum i is approximately[49]

$$P_i(n_i) \doteq \frac{(y_i^*/\mu_i)^{n_i}[1/(\beta_i[n_i])]}{\text{(sum of the numerator over all } n_i \text{ from 0 to } \infty)} \qquad (9.22)$$

In (9.22) the asterisk on the y_i indicates that all the components of **y** have been divided by a renormalization constant chosen such that the sum of the expected values of the n_i will equal N_0. When the observed values of r_i are replaced by infinity, the counting formulae $\beta_i[n_i]$ are changed in the numerator as before; another factor in the numerator, the $(y_i^*)^{n_i}$, now changes too. Nonetheless, it is a reasonable approximation to say that the probability of a large number of men in a stratum with few jobs is markedly underestimated when queues are ignored.

Models that ignore queues will do somewhat better in practice than those comparisons suggest. If queues are really present, the data is such that men are identified with strata by criteria that do not include specification of definite jobs held at the given time. The rates μ_i are likely to be estimated as gross averages, that is, the number of men who left in a unit period divided by the average number in the stratum in that period. Even if the probability distribution of time in a stratum is sought, the resulting average over individuals will include the period spent in queue. Therefore, if queues are ignored, the values used for the μ_i in the model will be changed. Presumably the sizes of the errors just described will thereby be decreased on the average, although the shape of the marginal distribution will remain distorted. It is the defects in logic in single-flows models of mobility that are the main focus.

To establish a correspondence between the Markov chain models and the queue system with limitless jobs per stratum, parameters must be matched. The "service rate," μ_i, is the average rate at which individuals in jobs make moves out of stratum i; when jobs are unlimited, μ_i is the rate for each of the n_i men in the stratum. The corresponding rate in the Markov chain model is $1 - P_{ii}$, if the same time unit is used, since the probability of a move out of the stratum in the unit time is $\sum_{(j \neq i)(j=1)}^{s} P_{ij}$. The transfer coefficients in "Closed Queuing Systems," the p_{ij}, are transition probabilities that are conditional upon a move being made. Diagonal probabilities p_{ii} are allowed, but they refer to cycling back to the same stratum after quitting one server in it and are best disregarded here as irrelevant. To equate a single-flows model of mobility that uses Markov chains with the queue model with unlimited jobs (queues disregarded), a transformation of parameters is needed. The off-diagonal probabilities P_{ij} are each divided by $1 - P_{ii}$ and only then equated with the p_{ij}. The service rate μ_i is equated with $1 - P_{ii}$. With these identifications, the two models are, on the average, equivalent.

The queue system itself has no logical defects as a model for interdependent moves, but it is inadequate on empirical grounds. There are several reasons. Most obviously, it makes no sense for the queue of men irrevocably committed to waiting for a job in a given stratum to be indefinitely long. The first task is to investigate the effects of limiting allowed queue length.

In "Cyclic Queuing Systems," Gordon and Newell develop a model for a system of queues of limited length. The system is closed, although, as in "Closed Queuing Systems," there is an equivalent open system with a rather baroque arrival process. There can be no question of ejecting customers who arrive at a full queue from the system. (If customers were ejected at full queues, the arrival process, which would have to be assumed in the equivalent open system, would be strange indeed.) Instead, the "service" process is suspended for potential customers when a queue is already full. This, however, creates a quandary: in the closed queuing system, men in jobs in any stratum are potential customers to any other stratum, in amounts fixed by the p_{ij}, and only a few strata may have full queues at a given instant. The quandary is resolved in the cyclic queuing system by the expedient of restricting p_{ij} to a special form, the matrix representing a complete permutation. The system of stages is now arranged in a circle so that men leaving a stratum go only to the next stage in the circle, which receives men from only this predecessor stage.

The quandary now reappears in milder form. When a queue is filled, service is suppressed in all servers in the preceding stage. However, when the queue has room for just one more man only one

239

server in the preceding stage can be permitted to resume operation (if two or more did so, they might happen to release men simultaneously and then the queue would be forced over the limit). Such a model would be hopelessly complex. Another expedient is introduced by Gordon and Newell in "Cyclic Queuing Systems": only one server is allowed per stage, $r_i = 1$.

The limited queue model in that paper is by no means simple, even though p_{ij} is restricted to a permutation matrix and all r_i are restricted to unity. Blocking, that is, suppression of service in one stage when the queue is at its limit in the next, is the central phenomenon. Let the maximum number of men allowed in stage i, both in the server and the queue, be m_i. Equations in the rates of change of probabilities of the various states of the system are written down in "Cyclic Queuing Systems," and the equilibrium equations discussed but no solution obtained.[50] By appropriate summations, equilibrium equations are also obtained for marginal distributions, that is, for the unconditional probabilities of number of men in a stratum. Those equations couple marginal distributions in successive stages, as well as linking the probability of x men in stratum i with the probability of $x + 1$ men there, and no solution is obtained for them either. Setting the limits m_i not only constrains the allowed values of the n_i but, through blocking, also introduces formidable interlinkings among probabilities in the state equations.

One advantage of the simple circular structure of stages is that a rate of flow of men through a server can be defined simply in terms of the marginal probability distribution for a stratum and for its predecessor.[51] In equilibrium, the expected rate of flow is the same at each stage, F. The cognate parameter for the individual man is the expected speed in terms of stages passed per unit time, which is Fs/N_0.

The main interest in "Cyclic Queuing Systems" focuses on cases in which blocking is most frequent, that is, cases in which the number of men N_0 is close to the maximum number of "places" for men in the system, $\sum_{i=1}^{s} m_i$. Tracing movements of "holes" is a natural idea in a system near saturation. At any time, their number in stage i is $m_i - n_i$. The duality between movements of men in the cycle and the movements of holes in the opposite direction is formulated explicitly in Gordon and Newell's discussion of cyclic systems.

The simplest case is the one in which the number of holes in the system, that is, $\sum_{i=1}^{s} m_i - N_0$, is no greater than the number of places in the smallest stage, the minimum m_i. Then there can be no blocking of holes, just as the limitations on queue size are irrelevant when the total number of men N_0 in the system is *smaller* than the smallest m_i. The solutions for systems with unlimited queues in the paper on closed systems can be used, that is, equations (9.19) and (9.22). Because the r_i are all unity all the $\beta_i[n_i]$ are unity; since the $\{p_{ij}\}$ is a permutation matrix, the y_i are all equal. Of course, in the resulting formulas the number of holes in a stratum, i, and the number of men there, is in the power to which the service rate μ_{i-1} is raised for the preceding stratum.[52]

Precisely that condition of nonblocking of holes is the most relevant case when the model is applied to mobility of men among jobs. The restrictions of r_i to unity and of transfers to a pure cyclic structure cripple the scope of the model; but the assumption that the number of places in each stratum of jobs defined should exceed the maximum number of holes in the whole system at any given time is entirely plausible. The point is the system, when near saturation, becomes much simpler; there is *no* interaction between different holes.

When each m_i is set equal to r_i, here unity, and therefore no queue at all allowed, the restrictions on holes are like those on vacancies in the models of Chapter 7. However, since only one job is allowed per "stratum," the hole model is analogous to a special case of the binomial model—the model for vacancy moves among jobs all lumped in a single stratum. It is also analogous to the special case in which a rigid cyclic order in filling jobs is assumed, that is, a case in which the jobs are arranged in a linear hierarchy. The asymptotic equation for "speed," V, in "Cyclic Queuing Systems" for this special model[53] is consistent with the equation for mobility in Section 7.1, even though the latter is a model for an open system, with a fixed arrival rate. [The parameter in Section 7.4 that corresponds to μ_i is $v(1 - Q_{ii})$.]

The Markov chain model in Chapter 2 dealt in principle with moves by a single vacancy, although there, and in Chapter 7 for the deterministic model in continuous time, the model was extrapolated to small sets of vacancies. As an analogue to the vacancy model, the potential advantage of a hole model is in specifying effects of interaction among holes. In "Cyclic Queuing Systems," Gordon and Newell allow only one job per stratum; to be comparable to the vacancy chain, no queues can be allowed. Therefore, all m_i are unity. The minimum m_i is unity, and if there are even two vacancies in the system, there will be blocking of vacancies. The simple solution in "Closed Queuing Systems," transformed to dual form, is no longer applicable. A simple, direct solution is given in the paper on cyclic systems when all μ_i are equal as well as the m_i being unity.[54] There prove to be no interaction effects. The real need is investigation of interaction between holes in a model with the restrictions on r_i removed (similar to that for vacancies in Chapter 11).

Queue systems are unsatisfactory models of mobility because limits cannot be set to queue lengths, except in very special systems. Introduction of queues to single-flows models removes a logical inconsistency, but the inconsistency reappears when queue lengths are limited. The root of the trouble lies in the axiom on which the queue system is based: Men have an urge to move, and that is what drives the mobility process. The vacancy models are not special cases or dual forms of the queue system with queue lengths set zero because vacancy models are based on a different axiom:[55] Job controllers have an urge to fill vacancies, which are created by forces exogenous to the mobility process. Not only is the atomic rate of movement μ_i defined with respect to a different kind of entity, but the compound nature of that entity leads to a natural place in the model for flows from and to the outside, flows of both men and jobs.

9.6   Bartholomew's Model for Constant Marginals

While at work on Chapter 9, the developments of D. Bartholomew in stochastic models of social processes were brought to my attention.[56] His chapter 7 introduces a concept of vacancies in a model for moves of men between hierarchic grades with constant sizes. In its abstract structure, his model is closely related to the second model of Gordon and Newell in "Cyclic Queuing Systems" and Bartholomew's model is subject to the same fundamental limitations as are theirs.

In his second chapter, Bartholomew reviews the models for closed systems treated in Section 9.4 here. His main interest is in a different tradition, one of stochastic models for movements of men in organizations which focus particular attention on recruitment and severance in an open system. That tradition is closely allied to actuarial studies, and Bartholomew devotes special attention to distributions of men by seniority as influences on promotion chances and termination rates. Recruitment is sometimes taken as a given stochastic function, and sometimes it is derived from a stipulated growth rate for the organization (as in the models in n. 63 in this chapter). Bartholomew surveys a variety of such models in his chapters 3–5, and provides an excellent bibliography. The simplest model (his section 3.2) is very similar to the constant turnover model defined in Section 2.6 here. In his chapter 6, Bartholomew develops his own general purpose model for assessing overall recruitment and wastage for a bureaucracy.

The views of potential users are given great weight in structuring these actuarial models. Personnel managers naturally focus on careers and worry about length of service and about departure rates. Bartholomew shows that such thoughts should be recast in terms of more refined measures, after introducing more realistic models and inputs for an organization. This work takes for granted that aggregation of careers is the core problem. The elaborate apparatus and special functions are geared to that task. A main argument in this book is that the metabolism of a large system can be understood better through the paths of local disturbances, that is, through the vacancies defined by interaction among men and jobs.

Bartholomew's chapter 7 is a new departure. He is dissatisfied with earlier mobility models because they turn the numbers of men in various grades in an organization into a dependent variable. The main objection here is parallel: such models ignore the independent reality of jobs. Bartholomew then goes to the other extreme and stipulates that the number of men in a grade of an organization remains constant over time. Thus a man can move only to fill a vacancy. Only departures of men from the organization can create vacancies, by hypothesis.

Bartholomew's key assumption is that the dynamics of movement must be defined with respect to men. In this he retains the viewpoint of the earlier models he surveys. Men can only move to fill vacancies in another grade, but it is still the moves of men that are being studied. Densities of events in time are defined on the basis of men, usually as subclassified within a grade on the basis of seniority.[57]

Bartholomew's chapter 7 is similar to the Gordon and Newell paper on cyclic systems. Men correspond to customers. A stage of servers corresponds to a grade in a hierarchy. The fact of a constant number of servers in a stage corresponds to the fact that the number of men alloted to a grade is constant. The chance of movement by a man out of his grade in the next instant corresponds to the chance the customer finishes service in the next instant.

Once they let maximum queue length be fixed, at zero or any other figure, Gordon and Newell were forced to add a pair of extremely restrictive assumptions. In order to obtain a consistent model, they had to stipulate a fixed cyclic order of stages and a single server per stage. Bartholomew writes his equations in terms of a single vacant position at a time and does not explicitly consider interactions between men's moves, which raise some problems of consistency. Intuition leads him to consider a pure hierarchy in which men move from one grade only to the next higher. (Bartholomew does consider more general forms of distribution functions than the negative exponentials used by Gordon and Newell in "Cyclic Queuing Systems.") In effect Bartholomew forbids more than one vacancy in a grade at a given instant, and he too assumes the equivalent of one server per stage. That is, at most one man in a grade should be designated for exposure to mobility at a given instant, the other $m - 1$ constituting in effect a queue (designations both of the most senior man and of a man chosen at random are considered). Bartholomew insists that the queue be kept filled to its maximum; this corresponds to a focus by Gordon and Newell on the operation of the system when it is kept nearly saturated.

Bartholomew's vacancy is equivalent to Gordon and Newell's "hole," not to the free-moving vacancies of the vacancy chain models. When men's states are defined by seniority and only the most senior man is exposed to mobility, queues of finite size can be allowed in the restatement as Gordon and Newell's model. If their equations can be solved, some insight into interaction effects will result, but only for the special case of the perfect hierarchy of grades.

9.7 Conclusions and Discussion

Duality between men and jobs must lie at the core of a consistent theory of mobility. If mobility is to be seen as a single flow, it must be the flow of a compound entity which represents an interaction between men and jobs. Flow of men alone will not follow any simple, lawful pattern; flow of vacancies may. In particular, successive moves of vacancies between jobs or clusters of jobs may exhibit the Markov property. Parameters such as rates of flow and transition probabilities for vacancies can be defined only on a population of vacancies, not of men or jobs. Vacancies cannot be seen merely as holes, that is, as missing men; nor can mobility be treated separately for subpopulations of men defined on the basis of attributes. Transactions with the environment, in men and jobs and in both births and deaths, have a special status as the sources and destinations of vacancies. The causes of mobility, its active source as opposed to the structural constraints by which it is determined, are to be sought in those transactions. Such a theory provides a framework for supplementary hypotheses about principles of selection of particular men and particular jobs in the mobility process.[58]

These are conclusions suggested by the survey of models in this chapter.[59] Their most general significance is to suggest a need for revisions in theories of social structure and process. Jobs are a simple, concrete case of social positions. They go only one step beyond the use of categories and attributes to represent social structure. Such a step is crucial, for it forces serious attention to duality between enactment of structure and structure itself. A by-product is the renewed attention it suggests to the field of demography, conceived now more broadly as the interpenetration of movements of different kinds of entities. Further developments to encompass the relational aspects of social structure were suggested in Section 8.6.

Substantive implications for the study of mobility in large social systems can be drawn. J. Matras, in his useful survey of existing single-flows models,[60] derives a fundamental dichotomy between social structure—represented by the distribution of men among categories at a given time—and social mobility—represented by the matrix of men's transition probabilities used by Anderson, by Prais, and by Blumen et al. That dichotomy is a false one for the vacancy chain model. Both the transition probabilities for vacancies and the distribution of jobs among categories are aspects of social structure; the patterns and variation over time in transactions with the environment is the nub of mobility. Vacancy models have been tested only for special systems, but it seems reasonable to use them as a guide to new studies of mobility in total societies.

The concept of generations obscures the true structure of mobility. Recruitment of men should be studied as a continuing process in coordination with deaths of jobs, and conversely.[61] A second basic dichotomy Matras points out in his review, between structural mobility and exchange mobility, should also be revised. "Structural mobility" is the minimum shifts of men between two periods needed to produce the observed changes in distribution of men among categories; "exchange mobility" is the residual.[62] To draw this distinction is to fall into the analogue of the ecological fallacy. Jobs like men have life histories; they are not only born, they die. In even the most stable system, with unchanging marginal distributions, there is a constant turnover of particular jobs. If structural mobility is to denote mobility necessitated by changing objective needs in productive activity, gross rather than net changes in jobs should be considered. That is, flows of new jobs must be kept separate and not balanced off against departures of jobs, and the changes should be measured in absolute numbers and not in percentages. It is probably useful to expand the definition to include the need for replacements to men who die and disappear. Exchange mobility should be replaced by chain mobility, the mobility described by the multiplier effect. The latter is not a residual concept; it is mobility lawfully dependent on structural mobility, using the revised and expanded definition of the latter. Exchange mobility suggests invisible hands or secret cabals that arrange closed cycles of moves.

Specific systems of jobs, composed of all or parts of one or more formal organizations, are the basis for the models of vacancy chains in this book. Applications to other organizations, both industrial and government, are needed. There is a literature on personnel mobility in other organizations, in particular for military services,[63] but it is based on the kind of single-flows models surveyed in this chapter and is not comparable to vacancy models.

Part III
Foundations: Duality and Networks

Chapter 10
Careers, Attributes, and Replacements: Refining the Markov Chain

Men's careers are by-products, not generators, of mobility in the vacancy model. The single-flows models of mobility of Chapter 9 took the opposite view. Interaction among men's moves among jobs is the heart of the vacancy model, and its Markov chain describes "careers" of vacancies rather than of men. Section 10.1 transforms results for vacancies, in the probabilistic format in imbedded time from Chapter 2, to predictions about careers of men. Only one simple aspect of careers, the distribution of length in number of jobs held, is treated. The system is assumed to be in an equilibrium sustained by constant flows of new vacancies. The simplest assumption, random selection, is made about allocation of calls to men within a stratum, partly because no mechanism for distinguishing between men has been built into the vacancy model thus far. The results force a reappraisal of the usefulness of careers as measures of mobility, a topic taken up again in Section 10.8.

Tenures can be differentiated by attributes of the incumbent men as well as by the job strata used so far in the vacancy chain models. The corresponding elaboration needed in the Markov chains is discussed in Section 10.2, as well as the difficulties in finding useful data on attributes for the clergy. If personal attributes of men in a stratum affect their chance of receiving a call, career predictions obviously must be affected, but the simple model without attributes may still be valid for vacancy moves and amounts of mobility. The real issue is replacement effects, whether the kind of man called to a vacant job depends not only on the kind of job but also on the personal attributes of the prior incumbent. Replacement effects in vacancy chains are discussed in the abstract in Section 10.5; they are assessed for the Episcopal church in Sections 10.6 and 10.7 for a special kind of attribute, seniority.

Whether or not men are distinguished by attributes in the Markov chain model, movements of jobs between vacant and filled statuses can be traced only through use of a second-order version of the

Markov chain for vacancy moves. Job moves are obviously most complex and interesting when tenures are differentiated by attributes of their incumbents. Formulas for job turnover in that case are developed in Section 10.4. The ground is laid in Section 10.3, which explicates the asymmetry between job turnover and man turnover in vacancy chain models. The same asymmetry, but in reversed form, appears in the bump chain models of Chapter 1.

10.1 *Career Lengths from Vacancy Chains: Random Selection*

An individual career is the sequence of statuses traced out by a new man during his stay in the system. The same concept can be applied to a derived entity like a vacancy. In aggregate form, or treated in probabilistic terms, career refers to the distribution of a new cohort over all possible sequences of statuses. Thus career is a generalization of turnover (Sections 2.6 and 2.7) as applied to new entrants. Sequences of status are so complex to represent that the length of career in number of statuses (jobs), according to the category of entrance, is the only measure of career treated extensively here and in the earlier chapters, either for vacancies per se or for men. The career length of a vacancy is the length of its chain, which even on the average need not equal the career lengths of men.

The main difference between transition matrices for men and those for vacancies is the meaning of the diagonal elements. In the vacancy model, q_{ii} is not a residual parameter—a measure of inertia—it is merely the probability that the new job to which the vacancy moves is in the same stratum as its current job. In a transition matrix for men, the diagonal probabilities include the large chance of no move being made in a given interval. For this reason calculation of career length, as number of statuses held, is not as simple a matter for men as for vacancies. This is true whether the Markov chain for moves by men is stipulated directly and refers only to changes among broad strata (as in the models of Sections 9.3–9.4) or whether it is the chain derived from a vacancy model and refers to moves among individual jobs.

Principles for selection of the men "displaced" by vacancy arrivals in a stratum are not built in to the vacancy model. For purposes of predicting long-term turnover, the hypothesis of random selection was asserted in Section 2.7. In Section 10.2 the complex framework needed to handle other hypotheses about selection, selection in terms of attributes of the men found in a stratum, is sketched. It is prudent to try first the hypothesis of random selection in calculating career lengths. The main goal is to obtain a qualitative picture of career distributions; to see if predictions from the vacancy models are roughly consistent with observed distributions of career lengths and differ from predictions of reasonable alternative models. Section 2.7 contains a detailed discussion of the use of matrix operators to effect random selection.

Men's careers span successive eras of war, "normalcy," and depression; even within an era, sharp fluctuations of the number and distribution of vacancy creations, and thus mobility, are common. To produce a definite, if simplified, prediction for career lengths a second major assumption is made, similar to that in Section 7.5 on system size: the number of vacancy moves from a stratum each year is a constant fraction of the total number of men in that stratum. A third assumption is made about longevity: a man can remain in the system for an infinite time.[1] That simplifies the analysis without greatly affecting career length as measured in number of jobs held. As in Chapter 2, a man is assumed to move at most once in a given year, and new vacancies are assumed to appear in a group at the beginning of a year (see Section 10.4 for an alternative formulation).

The derivation is simple, with all these assumptions. Return to the notation of Chapter 2 and Chapter 7. Consider the binomial model first, with only one inclusive stratum of jobs. Vacancy moves are counted by origin, which is the destination of the corresponding moves by men. M is the number of moves made by vacancies in a year, assumed a fixed fraction of the total number of men in the system that year, N. The probability a vacancy move comes from outside the system is F/M, with $q = 1 - F/M$ being the probability of an internal jump. Only part of the moves from the outside, of number F_{man}, will correspond to departures of men; call the fraction d:

$$d = \frac{F_{man}}{M} < \frac{F}{M} = p \qquad (10.1)$$

A new entrant will remain in his job the next year with probability $(1 - (Md/N) - (M/N)q)$. The probability C_1 that his total career will be confined to one job is the sum of the probabilities he dies in his first job after j years in it:

$$C_1 = \sum_{j=1}^{\infty} \left(1 - \frac{Md}{N} - \frac{Mq}{N}\right)^{j-1} \frac{Md}{N} \qquad (10.2)$$

The geometric series is easily summed:

$$C_1 = \frac{(M/N)d}{[(M/N)(q + d)]} = \frac{d}{q + d} \qquad (10.3)$$

The probability a man remains i years in the first job, switches to a second job, remains j years in that job, and then leaves the system is a product of independent probabilities; the probability C_2 that he has a career of exactly two jobs is the sum of the product over all possible values of i and of j:

$$C_2 = \sum_{i=1}^{\infty} \sum_{j=1}^{\infty} \left[1 - \frac{M}{N}(q + d)\right]^{i-1}$$

$$\frac{Mq}{N}\left[1 - \frac{M}{N}(q + d)\right]^{j-1} \frac{Md}{N} \qquad (10.4)$$

As before, years are counted with the convention that all moves occur at the beginning of a year. The sums over i and j can be made independently; and

$$C_2 = \frac{qd}{(q + d)^2} \qquad (10.5)$$

The general formula for the probability of a career of length χ is clear:

$$C_\chi = \left(\frac{q}{q + d}\right)^{\chi - 1} \frac{d}{q + d} \qquad (10.6)$$

With only number of tenures, not duration in time counted, and with no upper limit on total duration, the career distribution is of the same form as the distribution of vacancy chain lengths, derived as equation (2.3). The career distribution is skewed to higher lengths, since $q/(q + d)$ is less than q. Each man's arrival coincides with the departure of a vacancy to the outside and conversely for departures of men, but there are, in addition, arrivals of vacant jobs that start chains and departures of vacancies that terminate jobs and thus end chains. There are more vacancy chains than careers begun or ended in any era; naturally, careers must be longer on the average.

Generalization to many strata parallels the development of turn-over equations for the vacancy model in Section 2.7. A major simplification is made here: the number of moves by vacancies to (or from) each stratum is assumed to remain a fixed proportion of the number of men in the stratum. The analogue to the q in the binomial model is like the "turnover coefficient" defined in equation (2.41):

$$v_{rc} = \frac{M_c q_{cr}}{N_r} \tag{10.7}$$

for the movement of *men* from stratum r to stratum c. This same definition is used when $r = c$ for movements to new jobs within the same stratum. Each of these parameters must be renormalized, corresponding to the passage from equation (10.2) to (10.3) for the binomial model. This divisor is

$$\sum_{r=1}^{s} v_{rc} + \frac{(fr)_{\text{man}}}{N_r}$$

The second term, the fraction of *men* in stratum r who leave the system per year, corresponds to the d in equation (10.1). It was designated t_{r0} in Section 2.7, and it too is assumed to remain constant throughout the period. Designate the renormalized coefficients with a prime:

$$v'_{rc} = \frac{v_{rc}}{\sum_{r=1}^{s} v_{rc} + t_{r0}} \tag{10.8}$$

Let $\mathbf{C}_\chi$ be the vector whose r^{th} component is the probability that a man who enters in stratum r will have a career exactly χ jobs in length. The formula is a straightforward generalization of equation (10.6),[2]

$$\mathbf{C}_\chi = (V')^{\chi-1}\mathbf{t} \tag{10.9}$$

There $\mathbf{t}$ is the column vector of the t_{r0}, the proportion of men in stratum r who leave the system each year; and V' is the $s \times s$ matrix of the v'_{rc}.

In equation (2.50) for turnover, a product of distinct matrices

$V(k)$, one for each year, corresponds to the power of V' in equation (10.9). Variability between the matrices $V(k)$ reflected the erratic fluctuations in the vector of vacancy creations from year to year. These fluctuations have to be suppressed to obtain manageable formulas in the case of careers; otherwise, as can be seen from equation (10.2), there would be no compression of the effects of duration of tenures into a simple normalization factor.

Estimates of all the parameters from (10.7) and (10.8) necessary to make predictions from equation (10.9) are supplied in Chapter 5 for the Episcopal and in Chapter 6 for the Methodist church. The prediction in (10.9) is a poor way to test the vacancy chain model, because exactly the same prediction would be made from the constant turnover model. The latter was defined in Section 2.6, and various special forms, usually for closed systems, were surveyed in Chapter 9. If men moved among strata according to fixed transition probabilities, that is, a constant Markov chain, it is obvious that the form of the equation for career length distribution would be just the one in (10.9). Further, when explicit operational measures for the parameters in (10.9) are stated in terms of observables, the numbers of moves a_{ij} in (2.19), it becomes clear that exactly the same numerical values would be used for a constant turnover model of careers. Comparison of prediction with observation would test only two things: (1) the constancy of effective transition rates for men across the given stratum boundaries defined by one attribute (size) of jobs; and (2) the hypothesis of random selection of individuals to make up these rates. The first is counter to one of the main ideas in the vacancy model, and relaxation of the second assumption is the topic of Section 10.2.

Observed career length distributions for the Episcopal church will be reported in Chapter 12. It is not necessary to compare them with the simplified prediction, (10.9), from the vacancy model. Therefore the observations will be for whole careers, including periods in pool jobs and in limbo, rather than for segments of time in 1–1 jobs, the aspect of careers to which (10.9) refers. An equation like (10.9) could be derived for the constant turnover model of men's careers and extended to cover total careers, using the data in Appendix C on movement into, within, and out of pool and limbo jobs; once again it would not be necessary. Career length distributions will, instead, be treated simply as data and compared for two different classes of clergy in Chapter 12. Section 10.8 will discuss another approach to the analysis of careers, outside the framework of explicit models of mobility.

In the vacancy chain model, careers of a given cohort of men interact with careers of other cohorts. Opportunities generated each year by new vacancies are shared among cohorts. Since careers span long periods, they should reflect both yearly fluctuation and longer term changes in opportunity flows. A conclusion should be drawn from the difficulty in obtaining realistic predictions of career lengths: if the vacancy chain model is correct, careers are a poor way to assess mobility.[3] Men's careers cut across the natural grain of mobility flows. Only in a chaotic and jumbled way do careers reflect the history of mobility in a system. That conclusion is only reinforced if the Markov chain model is elaborated to differentiate men by attributes. In succeeding sections, this elaboration will be carried out in order to improve the model of mobility, not to give a basis for refinement of career predictions.

10.2 Substrata for Men's Attributes

Differences in personal attributes have been ignored thus far in vacancy chain models. Even in the single-flows models of men's mobility in Chapter 9, a man's status is defined by his current job rather than by his intrinsic attributes. Let m categories of men be distinguished, in terms of education, for example. Within each job stratum, filled jobs can be divided into m substrata. There are two problems, one structural and one practical, in using these refinements of the job strata in the Markov chain models of vacancy chains.

The structural problem is in the treatment of new jobs, considered as flows of vacancies from the outside into job strata, counted by the vector $\mathbf{F}_{job}$. In the first move of the chain initiated by a new job, the vacancy jumps from the job stratum corresponding to the size of the new job. Obviously there is no incumbent retiring from this new job, and the vacancy must be assigned to a special substratum for jobs without incumbents. In moves within the system, the vacancy moves only to filled jobs, since its move is defined by the call of an incumbent to the job initially vacant. It seems artificial to have a special substratum that can only appear in the initial move and only for chains started by new jobs.

That artificiality seems to disappear if each vacancy move is split into two parts: (1) arrival in a filled job in the substratum defined by the incumbent's education, followed immediately by (2) transition to the special substratum for vacant jobs in that stratum. Moves by vacancies then come in pairs: (1) a move from a substratum for vacant jobs to one of the m substrata of filled jobs in some job stratum, followed automatically by (2) a switch to the substratum for vacant jobs. The concrete effect on predictions from using a Markov chain with this doubling of vacancy moves would seem to be nil, since the automatic switch would be accomplished with a probability of unity. There really are, however, two possibilities. If states of the Markov chain were defined simply by which substratum the vacancy is in just before it moves, as in the "first-order" Markov chains of Chapter 2, half of the effect of substratifying by men's attributes would be lost. The transition probabilities for a vacancy moving from a given job stratum would be the same despite the attribute of the previous incumbent in the vacant job. Calls from vacant jobs in a stratum to men in a given other stratum would depend on the attributes of the replacements, but the possibility of a direct relation between their attributes and the attributes of the men they were replacing would be excluded.

Vacancy chains could be renamed replacement chains if the personal attributes of the man called depend on the personal attributes of the man he replaces, rather than simply on the characteristics of the jobs in which each starts. The Markov chain model should provide a test of that. If vacancy moves are split into two parts, a "second-order" chain must be used. The simplest way to present the second possibility is as a first-order chain with a doubling of the m substrata of occupied jobs in a job stratum: to each is associated a substratum for jobs just vacated by those incumbents. There must then still be an extra substratum for new jobs, which have no previous incumbent. A full circle has been traced on the structural problem. The seeming artificiality of a special substratum for new jobs cannot be eliminated.

There *is* a need for splitting each vacancy move into two parts and using the second-order Markov chain. It is not for predicting vacancy moves; whether or not there are replacement effects, one may as well define a first-order Markov chain for movement of vacancies directly between substrata of filled jobs. Section 10.5 surveys the main types of effects that might be found if such were done. The need is to provide a framework for the turnover of jobs. Once stratification by men is introduced, jobs can be seen as moving among the sub-strata for men. A job whose incumbent has left does not leave the stratum appropriate to its size when the abstract vacancy moves on. The job awaits the arrival of a new incumbent, which then moves the job back into one of the substrata defined by attributes of incumbents. Prediction of the turnover and distribution of jobs among these substrata is desirable and obviously requires the use of the second-order chain. The form of the calculations is complex. Section 10.4 will develop the equations for the special case where jobs are treated as equivalent entities (the one-stratum, binomial model of Chapter 2) moving among a set of m categories defined by attributes of incumbents.

The practical problem in subdividing job strata according to attributes of incumbents is the enormous number of parameters needed for the Markov chain model of vacancy moves. With s job strata and m categories for men, there are $s(m + 1)$ substrata. A vacancy can jump from a job in any one of them to a tenure in any substratum including the initial one. (If each vacancy move were split into two parts, there would be $s(2m + 1)$ substrata, but half of the transitions would be forbidden.) Altogether $s^2(m + 1)m$ transition probabilities would have to be estimated in the enlarged Q matrix, plus an additional $s(m + 1)$ termination probabilities, the **p** vector of Chapter 2.

The problem is unmanageable if more than two or three job strata and two or three attribute categories are used, since tens of thousands of moves might be needed to give reliable estimates of all transition probabilities. The systems of jobs for which vacancy chain models were designed may not exhibit more than a thousand or so moves a year. In any case, only samples of a hundred or so moves in a year were drawn for any of the clergies studied.

Fairly complete biographical directories for the Episcopal church are published regularly, and large enough samples were drawn to support estimates of transition probabilities with two categories of men and two strata of jobs—$m = 2$ and $s = 2$. Unfortunately, the information on personal attributes did not prove very rewarding. Marital status and number of children change over time of course, and their relevance to a priest's suitability for a job depends in complex ways on the ideology and traditions of the parish and diocese concerned. Sons of clergy appear to be more successful in the jobs they obtain than are other Episcopal priests. The directories' reporting of parental background is not reliable, and the fraction who are sons of clergy is too small to justify a split into two categories. The most interesting and relevant data is on education: graduation from or attendance at college or private preparatory school or seminary or any combination. However the data was too incomplete and unreliable to be useful. Education was omitted from many entries, and many others were ambiguous as to length and status of attendance at an institution and as to whether a degree was obtained.

Date of ordination is a personal attribute known with certainty for almost all priests, but this attribute is difficult to treat. Seniority, by definition, changes systematically with time and it is best handled as a numerical variable. Section 10.6 analyzes the data on seniority outside the framework of strata for the Markov chain, whereas Section 10.7 looks for replacement effects in moves between strata.

The main conclusion is a negative one. The Markov chain is not an appropriate technique for analyzing mobility among a large number of states, whether they be pure job strata or, as here, a refinement of job strata by men's attributes. The only exception is when the transition probabilities can be fixed or reduced to functions of a few basic parameters on theoretical grounds.

In Section 7.8, the Markov model for vacancy moves among job strata was shown to be applicable even when jobs were not 1–1, as long as the number of incumbents in a job was fixed. However once job strata are subdivided by men's attributes, the Markov chain for vacancy moves allows for replacement effects. Then vacancy chains must be traced through 1–1 jobs in order to determine which individual replaces which prior incumbent in that stratum.

10.3 Dualities in Chains and Strata

Dualities in mobility are varied and subtle. Jobs are dual to men; vacant jobs, to surplus men; internal moves, to moves across boundaries; births of jobs, to deaths of men; as well as deaths of jobs, to births of men. Tenures as compound entities are dual, in some sense, to single entities like men or jobs. Earlier events are dual to later events; in a different way, exogenous events (beginnings of chains) are dual to endogenous events (endings of chains). Period of birth is dual to seniority. Vacancies, as distinct from particular vacant jobs, are dual to bumps, as distinct from particular surplus men;

both, as complex contingent entities, are dual to concrete compound entities like tenures. A number of these dualities are interlocked in the duality between vacancy chains and the bump chains defined in Chapter 1, and this duality requires an asymmetry between the stratification natural to vacancy chains and that natural to bump chains.

In the vacancy model there are no excess men in the system at any time, by hypothesis; a stratification of men is simply a stratification of tenures—man-job pairs—by attribute of the man in the job. By definition, a vacancy can exist only in a job. A vacancy moves, within the system, from a job without incumbent to a job with incumbent. Even when the jobs are treated as equivalent, that is, lumped in one stratum as in the binomial model, and tenures are stratified by men's attributes, moves by a vacancy are defined in terms of jobs. Thus the length of a vacancy chain is the number of moves the vacancy makes among 1–1 jobs.

In bump chains, men rather than jobs are in surplus. A bump chain model with a single stratum was defined in Section 7.2. Jobs in the system are, by definition, always filled. The "bump," the state of being in surplus, is defined for only men. A bump moves within the system from an individual without a job to the incumbent in a job. When men are assigned to attribute categories, these are states in the Markov chain for bump moves. Stratification of tenures by job size can be superimposed on the attribute categories, just as substratification by men's attributes was introduced for the vacancy model in Section 10.2. But the length of the bump chain is defined by the number of departures of the bump from individual *men*.

A chain of changes inferred by comparing tenures in a system in two successive years may be interpreted in terms of either a bump chain or a vacancy chain. The number of moves in the corresponding Markov chain can be different depending on whether the changes are interpreted as moves of a bump or moves of a vacancy. Two extreme examples are diagrammed in Figure 10.1.

A beginning event for a vacancy chain is the end event in the dual interpretation as a bump chain, and conversely. Cause precedes effect; and the vacancy chain interpretation must be preferred where as in Chapters 5 and 6 retirement (or arrival of a new job) at one end of a chain of changes occurs before the retirement of a new man (or death of a job) at the other end. If the duration of a chain of changes is but a few months long, only its structure, not its directionality, can be inferred from comparing successive annual lists of incumbencies. Decision as to interpretation as a bump chain or as a vacancy chain—often decision as to the length of the chain—requires knowledge of the time order of neighboring moves in a chain of changes.

A.		B.
Outside (new job)		*Retired*
	Trinity	Edward
Charles		Redeemer
	Epiphany	Samuel
Outside (end job)		*Recruitment*

Figure 10.1   Dual Interpretations of Chains of Changes: Vacancy Chains versus Bump Chains. *A:* as *vacancy chain*—two moves by the vacancy created by the new job (the move from Trinity to Epiphany and from Epiphany to Outside); as *bump chain*—one move by the bump created by abolishing Epiphany (the move from Charles to Outside). *B:* as *vacancy chain*—one move by the vacancy created by Edward's retirement (the move from Redeemer to Outside); as *bump chain*—two moves by the bump created by Samuel's entry (the move from Samuel to Edward and from Edward to Outside).

Each move by a bump can be split in two [(1) move from a jobless man to an incumbent, followed instantly by (2) a switch with the latter to jobless status]. That split is analogous, a kind of dual, to the split defined in the Section 10.2 for vacancy moves. As was necessary there, a second-order Markov chain must then be used. Predictions of bump moves are unchanged by that elaboration of the framework. Careers and turnover of men among categories of jobs can, however, be traced only through use of the second-order Markov chain. The duality between bump chains and vacancy chains is manifest: it is turnover of jobs among categories of men in the vacancy chain model that requires use of second-order Markov chains.

10.4   Job Turnover: A Second-Order Markov Chain

Jobs, unlike vacancies, do not move between one job stratum and another. (Long-term evolution of jobs in size, and thus stratum, treated in Section 7.6, is ignored here.) Hence the essential structure of job turnover among categories of men can still be seen when jobs are treated as equivalent, the binomial model, and the formulas are then greatly simplified. Let each filled job be assigned to one of m categories according to the attribute of its incumbent. When a filled job in category i loses its incumbent, treat it as shifting instantaneously to a twin category i for vacant jobs. The second-order Markov chain introduced in Section 10.2 becomes a first-order chain in terms of this set of $2m$ categories. The move by a vacancy from one filled job to another is split into two parts, and the transformations of jobs associated with vacancy moves can then be traced. Before the turnover formulas can be derived, the model must be specified in more detail and the numbers of jobs in the $2m$ categories in equilibrium must be found. Only equations for expected values will be derived, as in Section 2.7 for turnover of men among job strata.

Complete vacancy chains were traced out by comparing successive annual clerical registers. The convention adopted in the model of Chapter 2 was that vacancies were created in one bunch at the beginning of a year and the chains ran their course before the next year. Men move in the opposite direction to vacancies, and this convention led to no additional difficulty in developing turnover formulas for men. Jobs move in parallel to the abstract vacancies, however, and turnover formulas for jobs are simpler if creations of vacancies are divided evenly among successive waves of moves. All moves are treated as occurring in coordinated waves, each wave being defined by an application of the matrix of transition probabilities to the vector giving the distribution of the population among states. The time unit is the constant interval between successive waves.

The rate of creation of vacancies in each category will be assumed constant. Let η be the vector counting the number of vacancies created on each wave, by category. Part of these represent departures of men from the system. Each death of an incumbent in a tenure in attribute category i shifts his job to the twin category i for vacant jobs. Count these creations of vacant jobs in the twin categories by the vector η_{man}, parallel to the F_{man} vector in Chapter 7 but with components defined in terms of attribute categories. Arrivals of new jobs also create vacancies but not in one of the twin categories. Since jobs are not differentiated by strata, there is no need for recording their arrival in a special category for new jobs. On the next wave after its arrival, the new job will acquire an incumbent who is in some attribute category, forcing his job to that twin category. Arrival of new jobs will be counted at that time, defining a vector η_{job}. Both η_{job} and η_{man}, as well as their sum η, are assumed constant.

Let the vector $\mathscr{V}(t)$ count the expected number of vacant jobs, between the waves of moves at t and at $t + 1$, in each of the m categories defined by attribute of previous incumbent. All vacant jobs in the system move on the next wave. Let E_{ij} be the fixed probability that a vacant job from twin category i moves to tenure category j. Arrival of the vacant job in category j to claim a new incumbent instantly forces his former job into vacant category j. Thus E, the matrix of transition probabilities, applies to movements of an abstract vacancy from one twin category to another as well as to the transfer of the vacant job to a new tenure. E is then parallel to the Q in Chapter 2, except that E's states are defined by attributes of incumbents rather than jobs. It follows that the expected numbers of vacant jobs in the various twin categories after the wave of moves at $t + 1$ is

$$\mathscr{V}(t + 1) = \mathscr{V}(t)E + \eta \tag{10.10}$$

$\mathscr{V}(t)$ is analogous to the vector $\mathbf{V}(t)$ counting vacant jobs in Chapter 7. The latter is a count by job strata, and it is defined at an instant so as to fit a differential equation approach. With these restrictions, equation (10.10) is a parallel to (7.45).

Turnover formulas will be derived only for periods after the system is in equilibrium. Successive application of (10.10) shows that after a long enough period, the expected numbers of vacancies in various categories will reach constant values:

$$\mathscr{V}(0) = \eta(I + E + E^2 + \cdots + E^n) + \mathscr{V}(-n - 1)E^{n+1} \tag{10.11}$$

The absolute value of E is less than unity, since all vacancies eventually leave the system, either as new recruits come in or as vacant jobs are abolished. Hence the last term in (10.11) becomes negligible if the initial time, $-n - 1$, is pushed far enough back. Summation of the series yields a familiar form for the relation between $\mathscr{V}$ in equilibrium and the constant input vector:

$$\mathscr{V} = \eta(I - E)^{-1} \tag{10.12}$$

Equation (2.10) has the same form but a different interpretation. It gives the total expected numbers of moves made by a given annual cohort of new vacancies, counted by $\mathbf{F}$, assumed to run their course before the next cohort arrives, with the numbers of vacancies decreasing wave by wave.

Let $\mathcal{N}(t)$ be the vector counting the expected number of filled jobs by category at time t; the term is analogous to the $\mathbf{N}(t)$ in Section 7.4 in the same way that $\mathcal{V}(t)$ is analogous to $\mathbf{V}(t)$. The counts in $\mathcal{N}(t + 1)$ are not changed from those in $\mathcal{N}(t)$ by the moves of jobs between categories counted by the $\mathcal{V}(t)E$ term in (10.10). Each job transferring into a filled category knocks out exactly one job to the twin vacant category. Similarly, the claiming of incumbents by new jobs, counted by η_{job}, knock those jobs into the twin categories and do not change the counts of filled jobs. The numbers of filled jobs are, however, decreased by deaths of incumbents, counted by η_{man}. However, some of the jobs vacant at time t, counted in $\mathcal{V}(t)$, are filled by new recruits and have not been counted in the $\mathcal{V}(t)E$ term. Let the probability that a vacant job in twin category i claims a recruit who belongs to attribute category j be H_{ij}. Then

$$\mathcal{N}(t + 1) = \mathcal{N}(t) - \eta_{\text{man}} + \mathcal{V}(t)H \qquad (10.13)$$

since the last term is a vector counting the numbers of tenures formed by calls of new recruits to vacant jobs.

Once the numbers of vacancies have reached equilibrium, the numbers of filled jobs will stabilize if and only if

$$\eta_{\text{man}} = \mathcal{V}H = \eta(I - E)^{-1}H \qquad (10.14)$$

This constraint on H is assumed to be satisfied. Its significance can best be understood in the special case where the attribute categories are collapsed into one, yielding the familiar binomial model of Section 2.1. In that case, the matrix E reduces to the probability q that a vacancy jumps to another job. The vector η reduces to the count of new vacancies F. The matrix H reduces to the probability that a vacancy is filled by a new recruit, that is, to p_{man} in the notation of Section 7.1. Hence (10.14) reduces to

$$F_{\text{man}} = F\left(\frac{1}{1 - q}\right)p_{\text{man}} \qquad (10.15)$$

This is just the condition derived in Section 7.1 for $N(t)$ to be a constant [see (7.11)], since

$$1 - q = p = p_{\text{man}} + p_{\text{job}} \qquad (10.16)$$

263

10. Careers, Attributes, Replacements

Similarly, when categories are collapsed, (10.13) becomes the transcription of (7.5) into a difference equation. [In the stratified analogues to (10.13) and (10.14), appropriate to Section 7.4, the matrix H would be replaced by the diagonal matrix P_{job}.]

The preliminaries are now complete. Formulas for turnover of a population of jobs among men's attribute categories will be derived for a system in equilibrium. The constant numbers of vacant jobs in the twin categories are given in terms of the constant flows of new vacancies by (10.12). The number of filled jobs in each category remains constant at its initial value by (10.13) and (10.14). Let the corresponding vector be rewritten as the entries in a diagonal matrix, $\mathcal{N}_D$, parallel to the N_D defined in Section 2.7. Define B as the turnover matrix for one wave, analogous to the matrix B for turnover of men in one year in Section 2.7: the entry B_{ij} counts the jobs that were in category i for filled jobs at time 0, which are in filled category j at time 1. Altogether, jobs to the number $\mathcal{V}_i$ are knocked out of category i for filled jobs by the wave of moves at time 1: $(\mathcal{V}E)_i$ of them, by transfer of vacant jobs to claim their incumbents; $(\eta_{man})_i$ of them, by deaths of incumbents; and $(\eta_{job})_i$, of them, by arrival of new jobs to claim their incumbents. All of these jobs move into the twin categories for vacant jobs, and cannot appear in the counts B_{ij} for turnover among categories for filled jobs. Within a category, the filled jobs eliminated are selected at random; the numerical chance of a given filled job being pushed out on any wave is given by $\mathcal{V}_i/\mathcal{N}_i$. Let D be defined as the diagonal matrix whose entries are the probabilities that jobs in various categories will not be moved:

$$D_{ii} = 1 - \frac{\mathcal{V}_i}{\mathcal{N}_i}$$

$$D_{ij} = 0, \quad i \neq j \tag{10.17}$$

It follows that B is a diagonal matrix:

$$B = \mathcal{N}_D D \tag{10.18}$$

The main point in job turnover is that jobs pushed out return to filled categories after two intervals, following a stay in the twin categories for vacant jobs. The jobs pushed out on the first wave are selected out by the operator $I - D$: their number is $\mathcal{N}_D(I - D)$. Let $B^{(2)}$ be the turnover matrix across two waves.

$$B^{(2)} = \mathcal{N}_D[(I - D)(E + H) + D^2] \tag{10.19}$$

The matrix E traces returns of the jobs from vacant status to claim incumbents from filled jobs; the matrix H traces returns to filled categories through calling new recruits; a third portion of the eliminated jobs leaves the system and does not enter the turnover count. After the third wave, the turnover matrix is

$$B^{(3)} = \mathcal{N}_D[(I - D)(E + H)D + D^3 + D(I - D)(E + H)] \tag{10.20}$$

The first term counts the jobs knocked out on the first wave, retrieved on the second wave, and untouched on the third wave. The second term counts the jobs untouched on any wave. The third term counts the jobs untouched on the first wave, knocked out on the second, and returned on the third wave. Note that since a diagonal matrix does not commute with a nondiagonal matrix, the third term is not, in general, equal to the first term. Note also that the flow of new jobs, η_{job}, makes up part of the numerators in the numerical fractions on the diagonal of D, even though the actual new jobs cannot, by definition, appear in the turnover table for the initial population of jobs.

The general form of the turnover operator, the expressions in brackets in (10.18)–(10.20), is seen most easily in an enlargement of scope. Consider turnover among all $2m$ categories taken together. List first the m categories for filled jobs and then the m twins for vacant jobs. The turnover operator is a matrix with $2m$ rows and $2m$ columns that transforms the initial population of jobs distributed among $2m$ categories into a turnover table for the $2m$ categories. Call this enlarged turnover operator T:

$$T = \begin{pmatrix} D & I - D \\ E + H & 0 \end{pmatrix} \tag{10.21}$$

where the 0 represents an $m \times m$ matrix each of whose entries is zero. The turnover operator among the $2m$ categories after k waves is simply T raised to the power k. The turnover operator among just the first m categories, for filled jobs, is just, for each power k, the upper left block of size $m \times m$ in T^k:

$$\begin{pmatrix} \mathcal{N}_D & 0 \\ 0 & 0 \end{pmatrix} T^k = \begin{pmatrix} B^{(k)} \cdots \\ \vdots \end{pmatrix} \tag{10.22}$$

10. Careers, Attributes, Replacements

Since the submatrices of which T is composed in (10.21) do not, in general, commute, there is no simpler way to express $B^{(k)}$ than as in (10.22). By computing the first three powers of T, with due regard to the order of factors in each product, the reader can verify (10.18)–(10.20).

The matrix D commutes with any other matrix in one special case—when all the diagonal elements are equal. By (10.17) the D_{ii} are equal when the ratio of vacancies to filled jobs is the same in each category in equilibrium; call this ratio ξ and then

$$D = (1 - \xi)I \tag{10.23}$$

Equations (10.22) and (10.21) can then be converted into difference equations. The solution is

$$B^{(k)} = (\mathcal{N}_D) \sum_{\chi=0}^{h} \binom{k - \chi}{\chi}(1 - \xi)^{k - 2\chi}\xi^{\chi}(E + H)^{\chi} \tag{10.24}$$

where

$$k \text{ (odd)}: h = \frac{k - 1}{2} \qquad k \text{ (even)}: h = \frac{k}{2} \tag{10.25}$$

Equations (10.18)–(10.20) reduce to (10.24) when D satisfies (10.23). The form of the integer coefficient

$$\binom{k - \chi}{\chi}$$

is easily deduced from a combinatorial argument.

The simplest possible case of job turnover is when $m = 1$, that is, when all men as well as all jobs are treated as equivalent. Then as in (10.16) the matrix E becomes simply the binomial probability q and the matrix H becomes simply p_{man}. Hence

$$E + H = q + p_{\text{man}} = 1 - p_{\text{job}} \tag{10.26}$$

The operator D from (10.17) is simply a number, $1 - V/N$. Hence (10.23) and (10.24) are applicable, with

$$\xi = \frac{V}{N} \tag{10.27}$$

[By (10.12) and (10.15), V is equal both to η/p and to η_{man}/p_{man}, but the constant value of N is arbitrary.] The turnover table $B^{(k)}$ reduces to a simple number $b^{(k)}$, and $\mathcal{N}_D$ is simply N. The fraction of the initial population of filled jobs which are filled k waves later is

$$\frac{b^{(k)}}{N} = \sum_{\chi=0}^{h} \binom{k-\chi}{\chi} (1 - \xi)^{k-2\chi} \xi^{\chi} (1 - p_{job})^{\chi} \qquad (10.28)$$

where h is defined in (10.25). That fraction approaches zero for large k, as it should, when p_{job} is not zero.

In the binomial model of Section 2.1, time is measured in years and not in the distance between waves; vacancy creations are not spread evenly over all waves; and the moves M rather than the number of vacancies is counted. In the binomial model of Section 7.1, time is treated as a continuous variable. All three versions of the binomial model are essentially equivalent. Equation (10.28) describes job turnover in the binomial model for vacancies when selection of filled jobs from which incumbents are called is random and when the system is in equilibrium with a constant flow of new vacancies. Turnover of men, however, is almost meaningless in the binomial model for vacancy chains. If men are in the system at all, they are in filled jobs. With neither jobs stratified nor men assigned to attribute categories, there is nothing to keep track of except the reduction in the initial population of men by a constant fraction at each wave.

In the empirical study of the three clergies, no satisfactory way to define categories for clergy by personal attributes was found. Unfortunately the job turnover formula for the one-category case, equation (10.28), also cannot be tested adequately against the data. As explained in Section 7.1, the number of jobs vacant at various dates in a year can only be inferred roughly from data based primarily on successive annual registers.

In some systems in which mobility is studied, bump chains may prove appropriate. Then all jobs in the system are filled, and it is men who are surplus and engender the chains of moves. With obvious translations in the meaning of the symbols, the equations in this section, rather than those in Sections 2.7 and 2.6, are required to predict turnover of men among job strata from bump chains. Such chains among job strata are the proper dual to vacancy chains among categories of men; turnover of men in the former, like turn-over of jobs in the latter, require the use of second-order Markov chains. By similar logic, the study of careers of men moving among strata of jobs requires a second-order Markov chain if mobility occurs in bump chains.

10.5 Replacements and Quotas

The kind of man called to fill a vacancy could depend solely on the attributes of the man being replaced. There would still be the coupling in Chapter 2 between the type of job vacated and the type of job from which the new incumbent came, but it would be inde-pendent of the coupling between attributes of the former and the new incumbent. Amount of mobility would still be determined in terms of job strata, but the kinds of men called would be interrelated in terms of the attributes of successive movers in vacancy chains.

Consider, for example, the ideologies of ministers. In the Epi-scopal church, the most noticeable split is between High churchmen, devoted to the Catholic tradition and associated elaborations of ritual, and Low or Evangelical churchmen, devoted to the Protes-tant tradition in the church and simplicity of ritual. Most priests take some intermediate stand of course, but a reasonable dividing line could be drawn between High priests and others.[4] It is possible that a parish tends to call a new priest of the same persuasion as his predecessor; it is also possible the typical parish will try to achieve a balance by an alternation of type. In either case the choice of ideo-logical type may be completely independent of the size of the parish. If so, the transition probabilities, Q_{ij}, for vacancy moves between the size strata would still be valid even when substratification by incumbent's ideological type is introduced. The transition proba-bilities in the refined cell for moves from stratum i to stratum j could be written as products. Table 10.1 shows such pure replace-ment effects.

Since the sum of the two probabilities in either row of the refined cell is just Q_{ij}, the dynamics of vacancy moves among job strata would be unaffected by the ideologies of the men involved, as long as there were sufficient men of each persuasion in each stratum to fill all the calls. Conversely, to obtain estimates of α and β, one could simply cross-tabulate each replacement in a 2×2 table by ideo-logies, ignoring which job strata are involved. (The amount of mobility could only be determined in terms of job strata of course, since it depends essentially on the termination probabilities, p_{i0}, from recruitment and from deaths of jobs, which both vary by strata.

Table 10.1   Pure Replacement Effects Seen in Substratification of a Cell in the Matrix of Transition Probabilities by Ideology of Priest[a]

Stratum i	Stratum j	
	High	Other
High	αQ_{ij}	$(1 - \alpha)Q_{ij}$
Other	$(1 - \beta)Q_{ij}$	βQ_{ij}

[a] The same parameters α and β would appear for every combination of initial and final job strata, i and j, of the vacancy.

One, therefore, must also know the arrival rates F_i, including the creations of new jobs that would not appear in the 2×2 table for replacements.) If α and β were 1, the replacement would always be of the same ideological persuasion as his predecessor; if α were 0, High priests would always be replaced by Low priests, and so on. The existence of these separable factors α and β in the refined transition probabilities can be said to indicate pure replacement effects. Section 10.6 looks for evidence of such effects for the attribute of seniority.

Intermediate between pure replacement and random selection is selection of new incumbents by quota. Return to Table 10.1. If $1 - \beta = \alpha$, then the attribute of the previous incumbent has no effect on the kind of man chosen as a replacement (except in the sense that variability is reduced by the stratification). The quota of High priests chosen in filling vacancies is α, regardless of the ideology of the predecessors. The quota α may well vary with the initial stratum i and with the destination stratum j, and it is natural to give it subscripts, α_{ij}. The question is whether α_{ij} is different from the fraction of all priests in stratum j with that attribute, which will be the expected fraction with random selection of priests to fill vacancy calls (for any i). Section 10.7 looks for evidence of such quota effects as well as for replacement effects in the attribute of seniority. The form of the refined transition probabilities corresponding to quotas is as in Table 10.2. The dynamics of vacancy moves and thus the amount of mobility is not affected by the existence of quotas. The transition probability of a vacancy from job stratum i to stratum j remains Q_{ij}, regardless of the types of men who are moving.

Table 10.2   Quota Effects Seen in Substratification of a Cell in the Matrix of Transition Probabilities by Ideology of Priest

Stratum i	Stratum j	
	High	Other
High	$\alpha_{ij}Q_{ij}$	$(1 - \alpha_{ij})Q_{ij}$
Other	$\alpha_{ij}Q_{ij}$	$(1 - \alpha_{ij})Q_{ij}$

Size of job is not logically related to ideological persuasion, nor is there a strong empirical correlation. The discussion has so far avoided the most confusing case, wherein jobs are stratified on a basis similar to that for men. Let the stratum of a job now be determined by the ideological persuasion of its parishioners and vestry. Pure replacement effects (Table 10.1) are then highly unlikely, but quotas of some kind may be discernible (Table 10.2). If stratification of jobs by size be retained, let categories for men be assigned on the basis of salary; again, pure replacement effects are highly unlikely. Substratification of tenures by an attribute of incumbents may not reveal much additional structure unless the attribute is very different from the property of jobs used for stratification. In that case, stratification of a job simultaneously by two different properties may do as well in revealing fine structure in transition probabilities. Still another possibility is stratification of tenures according to an attribute determined by the combination of man and job. Normally salary is such an attribute.

The main point is that the particular criteria used for stratification of jobs and substratification by men will often be interrelated, and interpretation of differences between transition probabilities as "replacement" or "quota" effects may be ambiguous.[5] Return to the ideological example. Suppose High churches normally recruit High priests, and Low churches call Low priests. The match between jobs and men in ideological views may become so close that it is hard to separate one from another. Adequate predictions could be made either from job strata, men being treated as equivalent, or from categories for men using the binomial model for job strata.

The classical distinction between ascription and achievement is difficult to apply to men moving in a system of 1–1 jobs. A man's achievement is most naturally measured by the status and type of job he is in. The vacancy model with random selection is a model of pure achievement in that sense. Where transition probabilities based on stratification by jobs predict mobility volume and career evolution, there is no role left for men's attributes. Astute choice of job strata, perhaps multidimensional stratification on several attributes of jobs, may always be able to yield an adequate account of the mobility data. Replacement and quota effects may disappear if the framework of job stratification is elaborated enough. It is difficult to see how to assign causal importance to a man's background characteristics in his mobility experience in such a system. This issue will appear again in Section 10.8 and in Chapter 12, where direct analyses of men's careers are taken up.

10.6 Seniority Differences in Vacancy Chains

Seniority, the number of years elapsed since ordination, is the only data on priests that is reliable and relatively complete in the clergy studies. Because vacancy chains run their course within a year or so, seniority can be regarded as a fixed attribute of a man for vacancy models of mobility. In models of careers such as those to be taken up in Section 10.8, the corresponding concept is the cohort to which a man belongs. There the fates of different cohorts, much less men, are not interlinked, and the cohort defines a subpopulation rather than an attribute of men within an interacting population.

Replacement effects in terms of the attribute of seniority may reasonably be expected in sizeable organizations and may be larger than for any other attribute. In the language of Table 10.1, one might expect α to be large, high seniority men tending to be replaced by other senior men, quite independent of the size of the job involved. One special type of replacement effect is unavoidable: men entering jobs must, on the *average*, be less senior than men leaving jobs, by a margin equal to the average length of a tenure.

Seniority comes closer to being a meaningful interval scale than other variables like size of jobs. It is plausible that a man with ten years seniority is as much senior, in the ways relevant to mobility, to a man with five years seniority as the latter is to a new recruit. At the upper end of the scale, this property may not hold. A man with twenty-five years seniority may be handicapped in getting a call to a good job, with respect to a man with fifteen years seniority, to just the same extent as a young man with five years' experience. Even if such a "fold-over" property is true, the numerical spacing of years of seniority remains significant. Therefore it is wasteful to throw away the numerical values of seniority and simply assign men to a few gross categories of seniority.

To the extent seniority is an interval scale, it is reasonable to suppose replacement effects can be discerned in terms of the *difference* in seniority between the new incumbent in a job and his predecessor, independent of the absolute levels of seniority. Regular promotion through successive grades of jobs in a large organization may lead to a concentration of seniority differences for replacement events around a few values, which may be independent of what size job is involved in a replacement. Section 10.7 will revert to the categorical approach, in which replacements are cross-tabulated in terms of the seniorities of predecessor and follower. There the frequency of each possible difference in seniority between a prior incumbent and his replacement in a job will be examined as possible evidence for replacement effects. Jobs are treated as equivalent, that is, the binomial model is assumed.

Table 10.4 reports for the Episcopal church the distribution by seniority difference of all replacement events observed in the samples of vacancy chains from five decades. Table 10.3 reports distribution of Episcopal priests by seniority. Naive inspection of Table 10.4 suggests there is little trace of replacement effects. There is not the pronounced bulge in the distribution near a positive difference of seniority which would indicate a strong tendency for the call for a replacement to go to a man a certain number of years junior to the man departing. Nor is there a peak at a positive difference matched to a peak at a negative difference of seniority as would result from an alternating pattern of replacing older by younger man, then younger by older man, and so on.

A null distribution is needed for comparison, that is, a distribution of seniority differences that would be predicted if the seniority of the departing man has no bearing on the seniority of the man called as replacement. To make this calculation a distribution of priests by seniority is needed. The first column of Table 10.3 reports the percentage of Episcopal priests in each ten-year interval of seniority. (Index samples of priests drawn in various decades have very similar distributions and are combined in Table 10.3.) The Episcopal church

Table 10.3   Percent Distribution of Episcopal Priests by Seniority[a]

Seniority[b] by ten-year intervals	Priests stable in 1–1 jobs in sample years	Priests moving into or out of 1–1 job in sample years
30+	17	16
29–20	25	17
19–10	27	18
9–0	26	39
Unknown	6	10
Totals	100	100
	($N = 431$)	($N = 89$)

[a] Five clerical index samples from three decades combined; samples from 1943–1944 (war years) omitted. See Chapter 5.
[b] Year for which that clergy sample drawn minus year of ordination to diaconate.

has been quite stable in size, and it is not surprising to find the distribution of priests by seniority is almost rectangular, about 25 percent in each of the first three ten-year intervals of seniority. If ordered pairs of priests are drawn at random from this rectangular distribution and the differences in seniority computed, the resulting null distribution is quite close to that observed (shown in Table 10.4).

Replacement effects are measured by the association between the attribute of the man leaving and the attribute of his replacement. Replacement effects should not include biases in the types of men who move, that is, the marginal distributions are to be taken as given in computing the association. Hence the relevant null distribution of seniority differences is not that calculated from the distribution of all priests by seniority, as above, but from the observed distributions of seniority for priests who leave and for priests who enter jobs. An approximation will be made here, because the sample sizes are not big enough to permit estimation of seniority distributions separately for men moving in and for men moving out of jobs. The second column of Table 10.3 reports a combined distribution of seniority for priests who move, whether into or out of jobs, in index samples of Episcopal clergy. The distribution of seniority differences for ordered pairs drawn at random from this combined population will be computed. The mean value of this symmetric distribution must be zero. The correct null distribution should have a mean value equal to the average length of a tenure, since priests moving out of jobs must be on the average that much older than priests moving in. The correct null distribution can thus be approximated by shifting the symmetric distribution so that its mean equals the average length of a tenure. From Table 4.6 the average length of tenures in 1–1 jobs is seen to lie between six and seven years.

The observed distribution of seniority among movers in the clergy sample can be approximated by a simple step function: at each value from 0 through 9 years of seniority there are 4 percent of the movers, and in the range from 10 through 39 years there are 2 percent of the movers with each value. This step function can be seen as the superposition of two rectangular distributions, one from 0 through 39 years and one from 0 through 9 years of seniority.

It is easy to derive the expected distribution of differences in seniority for ordered pairs drawn at random from a rectangular distribution. The lowest value of seniority is 0 years, and designate the highest allowed value as $U - 1$. There are U possible values of seniority, and each has probability $1/U$. Since the pairs are drawn at random, each particular ordered pair of seniorities has the same probability, $1/U^2$. The probability of finding a seniority difference of Δ is just the number of ordered pairs with that difference times $1/U^2$. There are $U - |\Delta|$ ordered pairs in which the seniority of the first minus the seniority of the second is Δ. For example, if $\Delta = -5$, the seniority of the first man drawn, say F, may take any value from 0 through 34 years, and the seniority of the second man is then fixed as F + 5, so that there are 35 such pairs. In short, the probability of a seniority difference of Δ is

$$P(\Delta) = \frac{U - |\Delta|}{U^2} \tag{10.29}$$

where Δ can assume any of $2U - 1$ values:

$$-U + 1 \leq \Delta \leq U - 1 \tag{10.30}$$

The sum of $P(\Delta)$ over all the allowed values of Δ is, of course, unity.

The distribution of seniority differences in pairs drawn randomly from the observed step function for seniority among movers can be computed by appropriate combination of differences from the two rectangular distributions into which the step function can be decomposed. The result is

$$P(\Delta) = (0.8)(0.8)\frac{40 - |\Delta|}{(40)^2}$$

$$+ (0.6)(0.2) \times \begin{pmatrix} \dfrac{40 - |\Delta|}{10.30} & \text{if } 39 \geq |\Delta| > 30 \\[2ex] \dfrac{10}{10.30} & \text{if } 30 \geq |\Delta| \geq 10 \\[2ex] \dfrac{|\Delta|}{10.30} + \dfrac{10 - |\Delta|}{10.10} & \text{if } 10 > |\Delta| \end{pmatrix} \quad (10.31)$$

The sum of (10.31) over all 79 possible values of the seniority difference Δ is just unity, as it should be.

The observed distribution of replacement events according to seniority differences is reported for the Episcopal church in the second column of Table 10.4. All eleven national samples from four decades were combined, but even so the sample size requires grouping of seniority differences. Seven-year intervals are used. Six years is chosen as the center value of the principal interval to correspond roughly to the average length of tenure, since, on the average, that is the amount by which the seniority of the predecessor in a job exceeds the seniority of his successor.

Altogether 456 seniority differences were observed, which is smaller than the total number of moves observed in the vacancy chains (see Chapters 4 and 5) for two reasons. In a little under 10 percent of the replacements, the seniority of one or the other man was unknown; and many of the moves in vacancy chains are creations or terminations of jobs, which do not define replacements of one man by another.

An indirect test for replacement effects can be made by comparing the distributions for weighted moves and for unweighted moves. The two should differ if there are replacement effects. For example, large negative values of the seniority difference should then occur disproportionately often in long chains. The most likely replacement effect is choice of a new man many years junior to the incumbent; and if that is the tendency, long chains can occur only if there is a sharp reversal, that is, replacement of a young by an old man, in the chain. In fact, the distribution by seniority difference of the raw number of replacements is almost identical with the distribution when a replacement is given the weight $1/k$, the sampling weight of the chain in which it appears. The distribution in Table 10.4 is for unweighted moves.

Table 10.4   Predicted (P) and Observed (O) Distributions of Replacements by Seniority Difference   (percent)

Seniority difference[a] by seven-year intervals	P[b] (in random pairs)	O[c]
−40 and lower	0	0
−39 to −33	0.1	0.9
−32 to −26	2.8	1.8
−25 to −19	6.1	3.5
−18 to −12	8.1	4.8
−11 to − 5	10.1	10.5
− 4 to + 2	13.7	20.2
+ 3 to + 9	18.1	25.0
+10 to +16	13.7	14.2
+17 to +23	10.1	9.8
+24 to +30	8.1	4.8
+31 to +37	6.1	2.6
+38 and higher	2.9	1.8
Total	99.9	99.9
		(N = 456)

[a] Year of ordination to the diaconate of departing incumbent minus ordination year of his successor in that job.
[b] Drawn from a step function, an approximation to the observed distribution of all movers in the eleven samples by seniority. See equation (10.31). The origin is shifted to six years, the observed average length of tenure.
[c] For the Episcopal Church. All replacements in eleven national samples of vacancy chains in four decades are combined, unweighted, except that subsidiary chains are excluded.

The predicted distribution of seniority differences appears in the first column of Table 10.4. It was computed from (10.31) using the seven-year groupings and shifting the origin to six years, the average tenure length. In view of the sampling variability in the observed distribution and the approximate nature of the model from which the predicted distribution is derived, little weight should be given to small differences in the two distributions. The main conclusion is clear: the observed and predicted distributions are strikingly similar in qualitative features—each is symmetric but tapers off slowly from its mode—and they even agree approximately in numerical terms. Seniority differences between predecessor and replacement in vacancy chains are distributed nearly randomly. There is little evidence for replacement effects in the attribute of seniority.

10.7 Seniority in Replacements among Episcopal Clergy

Priests are now to be categorized as either old or young in the sample year. Fifteen years seniority is taken as the dividing line. Half the priests who move out of 1–1 jobs are more senior than that and half have fifteen years seniority or less. One cannot deal with fine discrimination in seniority and calculation of seniority differences in replacements, as in Section 10.6. In particular, it is not possible to see if very old priests and very young priests tend to be interchangeable. The size of the predecessor's job can be held constant in analyzing replacements.

Probabilities of replacement of priests in one seniority category by priests from another will be estimated separately by stratum of jobs. The sample sizes are big enough, with only two categories used, to support separate estimates from samples in different decades. The results for the Episcopal church are reported in Table 10.5. There appears to be no consistent pattern of change in replacement probabilities over time; the tables are consistent with the idea that replacement probabilities among seniority categories, with predecessor's job size held fixed, are constant over time.

Those replacement probabilities are not the same as transition probabilities for vacancies when tenures are substratified by seniority of incumbent (see Sections 10.2 and 10.5) for two reasons. First, the size of job from which the replacement comes is not specified, and the replacement probability lumps together moves of vacancies to various destination strata of job size, including moves to the outside coincident with arrival of new recruits. Second, moves of vacancies which correspond to filling new jobs or to ending vacant jobs are not included because they do not define a replacement of one priest by another in that job. In terms of the probabilities laid out in Table

10.1, the replacement probabilities in a column of Table 10.6 are the average value of the αQ_{ij} in the row i or of the $(1 - \beta)Q_{ij}$ in the row i, where "High" is equated with "Old."

Table 10.5   Probability that Vacancies are Filled by Older Men, by Seniority[a] of Predecessor and Size of Job, in the Episcopal Church

	Sample years		
Stratum	1912–1923 (4 samples)	1933–1944 (4 samples)	1953–1954 (3 samples)
Big			
Old man[b]	0.52	0.38	0.42
Young man[c]	0.29	0.16	0.24
Medium			
Old man	0.32	0.52	0.39
Young man	0.40	0.29	0.17
Small			
Old man	0.35	0.31	0.61
Young man	0.44	0.21	0.30
Total weighted[d]	36.20	27.78	45.46
Total raw	166	97	219

[a] Seniority is year sampled minus year of ordination to the diaconate.
[b] Old defined as greater than fifteen years seniority.
[c] Young defined as less or equal to fifteen years seniority.
[d] Probability estimated as the weighted number of moves of vacancies to (and thus replacement of predecessor by) older men divided by the total weighted number of replacements. Replacements do not include vacancy moves from new jobs and from jobs thereby abolished; and the totals are therefore less than those in the tables of Chapter 4.

The main question is whether probability of replacement by an old priest is different according to the seniority of the predecessor, with the size of job held fixed. That is, the upper and lower probabilities in the first column should be compared for a given stratum in Table 10.6, where the separate samples in Table 10.5 are combined. The difference is large in the big stratum and decreases in the two lower strata, and the pattern over time in the latter two differences is seen to be irregular in Table 10.5. It seems that the kind of man called to a vacancy in a job of given size does not depend on the kind of predecessor in the job, when kind is defined in terms of seniority, with one exception: an older man leaving a big job is more likely than a younger man to be replaced by an older man. Of course this exception might disappear if the big stratum were refined into several components, since it may simply be that the very big jobs go mainly to older men.

The main conclusion is that there is rather little coupling between characteristics of predecessor and successor in jobs of a given size, to the extent that these characteristics are reflected by seniority. This conclusion supports the use of the term vacancy chain rather than replacement chain for the observed sequences of moves traced. Additional evidence is reported in the column for raw moves of Table 10.6, which is exactly parallel to the first column except that

Table 10.6 Probability that Vacancies are Filled by Older Men, by Seniority of Predecessor and Size of Job, for all Episcopal Samples Combined

Stratum	From weighted moves		From raw moves	
Big				
Old man[a]	.43	(19.39)[c]	.46	(96)
Young man[b]	.24	(7.09)	.31	(39)
Medium				
Old man	.39	(25.20)	.33	(99)
Young man	.27	(32.18)	.30	(152)
Small				
Old man	.38	(12.64)	.48	(46)
Young man	.34	(12.93)	.28	(50)
Total		109.43		482

[a] Old defined as greater than fifteen years seniority.

[b] Young defined as less than or equal to fifteen years seniority.

[c] 1 minus the probability that vacancies are filled by older men is the fraction of replacements who are younger men. Base numbers are given in parentheses; they are the denominators in the estimates of the probabilities.

all moves in the observed chains are weighted equally (raw moves) rather than being given the sampling weight $1/k$ for the vacancy chain in which each occurred. In effect the second column of Table 10.6 gives disproportionate emphasis to replacements found in long chains. The pattern of differences in replacement probabilities within the three strata changes. The one consistent tendency in all the evidence is for big jobs, in which older men substantially more often than younger men are replaced by older men.

In Table 10.7 all jobs are lumped together in one stratum. The overall probability of an older man being replaced by an older man, 0.40, is appreciably larger than the fraction of the time a younger man is replaced by an older man, 0.28. The probabilities are almost identical (0.41 and 0.29) if calculations are based on raw moves. The row and column totals of weighted moves are also shown in Table 10.7. The column total must be larger than the row total for younger men since on the average men are moving out of jobs about six years after they move into jobs.[6] Also indicated are the weighted number of replacements in which one or both of the ordination dates were unknown; altogether less than 10 percent of the moves are not classifiable.

Table 10.7   Replacement Probabilities for Episcopal Priests Classified by Seniority[a]

Predecessor	Successor		Number of moves[c]	Additional moves, seniority unknown
	Old[b]	Young		
Old[b]	0.40	0.60	57.23	2.44
Young	0.28	0.72	52.20	1.88
Number of moves[c]	37.91	71.52	(109.43)[d]	
Additional moves, seniority unknown	0.67	4.68		(1.16)[e]

[a] All eleven national samples combined.

[b] More than fifteen years seniority.

[c] Excluding moves from new jobs and from jobs thereby ended, which do not define replacements of one man by another.

[d] Total weighted number of moves in which seniority of both predecessor and successor is known.

[e] Number of moves where seniority of neither party is known.

Since replacement effects are not large, the main question becomes whether there are quota effects (see Table 10.2) not consistent with random selection; that is, random selection, within a stratum, of men called to vacancies in another stratum. The sample sizes are not large enough to justify substratification of both initial stratum and final stratum in vacancy moves by seniority of the men involved, nor is the distribution of all priests by seniority available for separate strata. By combining the two seniority rows for each stratum in Table 10.6, the overall fraction of calls to each stratum which go to older men can be computed. These fractions are nearly the same in the three strata: 0.38, 0.32 and 0.36, respectively, for weighted moves. If, as seems likely, different strata have similar seniority distributions, the evidence is consistent with random selection.

This chapter has shown how complex it is simultaneously to control for attributes of jobs and of men in analyzing vacancy moves. However, these last two sections suggest that it may not be very important to distinguish men by attributes when applying the Markov chain model to a large system. Random selection of men seems a reasonable first approximation. Section 10.1 suggests that men's careers cannot provide robust measures of social processes because they are exposed to complex, irregular changes in the system over time. Section 10.8 examines an approach in which men's careers are analyzed in terms of background attributes with no attempt being made to specify the causal processes that generate careers.

10.8 Duncan's Interpretation of Careers

O. D. Duncan rejects models of successive moves between categories by men of the kind surveyed in Chapter 9. He argues that the use of Markov chains oversimplifies the influence of much earlier statuses on later status of a man and, in particular, the definition of status by gross category omits too much information. Duncan turns from models of explicit processes to statistical analyses of observed career sequences of cohorts.[7] Status is converted somewhat arbitrarily into a continuous metric to permit the use of regression techniques, in particular, the method of path analysis.[8] Observed correlations over time of men's attributes are the focus of analysis.[9]

Vacancy models argue the importance of interaction among different men at the same time. It is vacancies, not men, that are free to move between categories according to fixed transition probabilities. Careers of men are chaotic by-products of the dynamics of vacancies over long periods, as sketched in Section 10.1. According to Sections 10.2–10.7 it may be sufficient to identify men only by stratum of current job when predicting where vacancies move.

The strengths of Duncan's analyses are weaknesses in the vacancy models and conversely. The two approaches are more complementary than inconsistent. Duncan defines his problem as describing the impact of earlier characteristics and achievements on eventual status of men; vacancy models describe the causal processes at work at a given time in mobility in a system of men and jobs.

Duncan speaks of "causal interpretation" but does not deal with cause and effect in the normal scientific sense, since no attempt is made to specify the actual mechanisms and processes of movement. Just because Duncan says nothing about mechanism his interpretations of career sequences, unlike the models of Chapter 9, may be consistent with complex interactions among men and jobs in mobility. Duncan cannot predict amounts of movement; and he cannot interpret his parameters—path coefficients—in terms of actual moves. There is no reason to expect these parameters to remain fixed over long periods.[10] A system of men and jobs, not cohorts of men, is the subject of vacancy models. Tests are largely confined to sequences of events terminating within a year, and validated models may well be insensitive to correlations between men's statuses some years apart. Long-term projections are made but of the size of the system in men and jobs, not of correlations within individual careers.

Duncan works directly with data on huge national systems whereas the vacancy models in their present form are applicable only to restricted systems of jobs for single incumbents. Even the total populations of the latter would be too small to support intercorrelations on as many attributes as Duncan considers—family background, education, sex, age, ethnicity, and so on in addition to job status at various times. The overriding importance of men and their careers is taken for granted in Duncan's work, which can be seen as a sophisticated reformulation of the distinction between ascription and achievement.[11] In vacancy models, concern is with the system of men and jobs as such, with the ways in which local disturbances appear and move through a system.[12]

Chapter 11
Interaction among Vacancies

Only a vacancy is free to move among 1–1 jobs, since two men cannot occupy the same job. The same man cannot occupy two different jobs, and two vacancies cannot move to the same job. That interaction is neglected in the model of Chapter 2 for independent moves by cohorts of vacancies. The error may be appreciable when vacancies are numerous relative to candidates for them.

Assessment of interaction at one time among potential moves by a population of vacancies will be divorced from the sequential dependence among moves by men that is built into the vacancy model. Too complex a model would be needed to embrace both. Instead, constraints on simultaneous allocations of vacancies among candidates are estimated. Overlaps among particularized individual candidacies, the realistic case, are dealt with after the interaction measure is developed for homogeneous candidacies from random selection.

11.1   Random Selection

The simplest assumption about candidacies is that any man may be called to any vacancy, selection of the quota for a stratum in one wave of moves being by random choice. This is the assumption used in Sections 2.7 and 10.1, although the vacancy model itself does not specify a principle for selecting the particular men called. A slightly different assumption is suggested by the mover-stayer model of Section 9.4: only a subset of all men are interested in moving at a given time, but each may be called by random selection to any of the vacancies. Intuition suggests interaction should be small given random selection of a man from the whole population for each vacancy. In particular, a measure of interaction, in addition to ranging between conventional limits of 0 and 1, should be proportional to the ratio of vacancies to men when the ratio is small.

An indirect kind of interaction among potential moves by a population of vacancies was suggested in Sections 7.2 and 8.4: the rate of formation of tenures should be proportional to the number of conceivable pairings of unemployed men to vacant jobs in the next instant. The only constraints considered on likelihoods of pairings were based on categories defined by attributes of men and of jobs. Available men were considered to be those in limbo rather than all incumbents in jobs, but as in the vacancy models only one move at a time in the population is considered. No evidence was found in Section 4.6 for dependence of transition probabilities for a vacancy on total numbers of incumbents in various strata.

Section 9.4 introduced a different viewpoint, allocation of a whole population of men among a population of jobs, again with only categorical constraints. Instead of focusing on intervals so small that only one move takes place at a time, attention is given to what populations of moves could be arranged, in effect simultaneously. Interaction among moves emerges implicitly from the necessity of a complete match of men to jobs. Continuing inputs and outputs of men and jobs are ignored; so the populations to be matched are fixed. An appropriate illustration is the game of musical chairs considered in Section 1.4, where each person has the same chance of ending in any chair. Another kind of illustration could be sets of the simultaneous chains considered in the same section.

An exact assessment of the interactions among vacancies would require a more general viewpoint incorporating both these two. But it is extremely difficult to treat a series of single moves where at each step the populations of vacancies and of eligible candidacies changes slightly.[1] The allocation viewpoint captures the main aspect of interaction among vacancies, the constraints on filling each vacancy implicit in calls to the same candidates issued by other vacancies. When each allocation has the same a priori probability, the count of allocations with a given property, for example a given split of calls among strata, is proportional to the probability of that property in a random allocation.[2] Counts of allocations, then, are a natural basis for a measure of interaction.

First the number of possible allocations of vacancies to candidates is calculated with a given structure of overlaps. Then it is computed for the same total number of candidacies, but with no overlaps allowed, so that no man is in more than one candidacy. The difference between these two counts reflects the interaction among vacancies. Since all moves are treated as simultaneous, it is irrelevant whether incumbents who move leave vacant jobs behind them. The men in candidacies need not be identified by the jobs they hold, and new recruits can be included among candidates.

Counts of allocations for populations yield numbers so large as to be cumbersome. Logarithms are a convenient and natural transformation of such counts in many applications of combinatorics, for instance in information theory.[3] The measure of interaction among vacancies, call it I, will use the ratio of logs of the numbers of allocations:

$$I = 1 - \frac{\log \text{(allocations with overlaps)}}{\log \text{(allocations without overlaps)}} \tag{11.1}$$

Natural logarithms, for the base e, are used. Given that at least one allocation is possible,[4] the maximum interaction corresponds to an I of unity and negligible interaction to an I of zero.

Consider the binomial model with all jobs lumped in a single stratum. Let each of the N men in a system be candidates for each of the V vacancies then open. The number of possible allocations of candidates to vacancies is

$$\frac{N!}{(N - V)!}$$

Now, suppose there are enough new recruits to make up the same total number of candidacies, namely NV, but with no man a candidate for more than one job. The number of possible allocations is

$$N^V$$

where there are no overlaps among candidacies. The Stirling approximation for factorials can be used in the count with overlaps; if the number of vacancies is small compared to the total number of men, the log of the count can be approximated as[5]

$$V \log N - \tfrac{1}{2}(V + 1) \frac{V}{N} + 0\left[\left(\frac{V}{N} \right)^2 \right]$$

the third term indicates the terms neglected are of the order of $(V/N)^2$ or less, the largest being $[-\tfrac{1}{2}V(V/N)^2]$. The measure of interaction defined in equation (11.1) is clearly close to zero and can be approximated as

$$I \doteq \frac{V + 1}{2N \log N} \quad \text{for} \quad \frac{V}{N} \ll 1 \tag{11.2}$$

The same result holds if the random selection is confined to a subset of men as long as the subset is still large compared to V.

With random selection and candidacies of all men for all vacancies, the measure I is seen in (11.2) to be proportional to V/N, as anticipated, when V/N is small. Random selection is the principle of random sampling, and the difference between allocations with and without overlap parallels the difference between sampling from a finite population with and without replacement. It is widely accepted that finite population corrections for sampling without replacement can be neglected in statistical inference when the ratio of sample to population, here V to N, is small.[6] When V/N is less than say one tenth, and when N is greater than 1000 as for all the churches studied, the interaction measure I is less than 0.007, from (11.2). Similar results would be obtained for a stratified vacancy model, corresponding to stratified random sampling.

When the number of vacancies is comparable to the number of men available, interaction should not be negligible, although as long as all men are eligible for any vacancy there will be no real bottlenecks. A model without interaction should still be a reasonable approximation. Consider the special case where $V = N$. The number of allocations with overlaps is simply $N!$, and the interaction measure is

$$I = \frac{1}{\log N} + 0\left(\frac{1}{N}\right) \quad \text{for } V = N \tag{11.3}$$

(Note that the approximate formula (11.2) for small V/N is still accurate to within a factor of 2.) For N of the order of 10^3 to 10^4, as in the churches studied, the measure I ranges between 0.14 and 0.11; I declines to zero when the population size N goes to infinity. That corresponds to both the belief that overlaps of candidacies have no effect in an infinite population, even though jobs and candidates are equal in number, and the fact that sampling theory for infinite populations need not take any account of sample size.

The simple ratio V/N is an adequate measure of interaction effects with unlimited candidacies. Intuition alone suggests that small V/N then implies little interaction.[7] The need for the measure I is in the more realistic case when particular overlaps among individual candidacies are important rather than the gross ratio of total vacancies to total men candidates for all vacancies. Intuition suggests that interaction effects will be much larger.

11.2 *Overlapping Individual Candidacies*

Systematic data on candidacies for particular vacancies is not available for the churches studied. Instead interaction will be assessed for various, rather extreme, assumptions about overlaps between candidacies. In this section, a lower bound is derived for the interaction measure defined in (11.1). In subsequent sections, exact calculations are made for special cases, and the problem is recast in terms of standard topics from combinatorics.

Men may hope for jobs far beyond their reach, and a vestry may scout candidates who would never consider that job. The first simplification is to admit only candidacies who are realistic from the points of view of both man and job controllers. A candidacy can then be viewed as a symmetric link between man and job, a potential move as seen by both sides as well as by a higher authority or an outside observer. The second simplification is to treat all candidacies as equivalent in likelihood of being realized.

Strata and substrata themselves become superfluous once moves are restricted to candidacies defined between individual incumbents and vacant jobs. Candidacies are an alternative way to refine the binomial model for vacancy moves. Each vacant job has, so to speak, its own stratum to which to send calls. The reality of networks of influence and information among particular men is recognized, whereas the vacancy models in previous chapters grouped men into equivalence categories of the nature of social classes.

The structure of candidacies can be represented in an incidence matrix, call it C. Let each of V vacancies be assigned a row; each of n men who are candidates be assigned a column; and let the entry in a cell be unity if that man is a candidate for that vacancy, the entry being zero otherwise. Designate the entry in row i and column h as C_{ih}, so that the row sum, c_i, states the number of candidates for vacancy i and the column sum $c_{.h}$ states the number of candidacies for man h. The total number of candidacies is the sum of all entries in the matrix, call it simply c.

The number of allocations of men to vacancies can be computed as the permanent of the matrix C, given the trivial restriction that available men outnumber vacancies, $n \geq V$. The permanent is simply the sum of all possible products of V entries with one from each row and no two from the same column.[8] In the count of allocations for the denominator of (11.1), overlaps in candidacies

287

are excluded; and the number of men, n, is inflated to equal the given number of candidacies, c. It is obvious that the count then is the product of all the row sums

$$\prod_{i=1}^{V} c_i.$$

With overlaps in the incidence matrix, the calculation of the permanent is in general exceedingly complicated. When the matrix is square, $n = V$, the permanent is like a determinant without the alternation of signs in summing products, but evaluation is much more difficult. Given $n = V$, it is possible to establish an upper bound for the permanent and thus a lower bound for the interaction measure I from (11.1). That case is a natural one on which to focus. The number of men n is unlikely to be less than V; it can, at most, equal the total number of candidacies c, in which case there is no overlap in candidacies and thus no interaction among vacancies. Intermediate values of n, for a given c, should correspond to less interaction than for $n = V$, which therefore provides a conservative estimate of interaction effects.

An upper bound on the permanent of the square matrix with entries of 0 and 1 is[9]

$$\prod_{i=1}^{V} \frac{c_i + (2)^{1/2}}{1 + (2)^{1/2}}$$

The corresponding lower bound for the interaction measure is

$$I \geq \frac{V \log 2.41 - \sum_{i=1}^{V} \log[1 + (1.41/c_{i.})]}{\sum_{i=1}^{V} \log c_{i.}} \tag{11.4}$$

Vacancies with only one candidacy can be subtracted from V and ignored since they contribute zero to both the numerator and denominator of (11.4). In the special case where the number of candidacies is the same for each vacancy, the number of vacancies drops out:

$$I \geq \frac{\log 2.41 - \log[1 + (1.41/k)]}{\log k} \tag{11.5}$$

when

$$c_{i.} = k \quad \text{for } i = 1, 2, \ldots, V \tag{11.6}$$

Table 11.1 reports the lower bounds for selected k; when there is variability in c_i, I from (11.4) will be some average of these values.

Normally there will be only a handful of realistic candidates for a vacancy; so the small k are the important ones in Table 11.1. The lower bound for the interaction measure will lie in the range from $\frac{1}{3}$ to $\frac{1}{2}$ when $n = V$. Interaction effects must be much larger than with random selection from the whole population for each vacancy, corresponding to $k = n$; in (11.3) where $V = N$, I was only about 0.1.

Table 11.1   Lower Bounds for the Interaction Measure I with Equal Numbers of Vacancies and Men and the Same Number k of Candidacies for Each Vacancy[a]

k	2	3	4	5 ...	10 ...	10^3 ...	$n \to \infty$
Lower bound for I	.51	.45	.42	.39	.32	.13	$\dfrac{0 \cdot 88^{b}}{\log n}$

[a] From equation (11.5). The number of vacancies, V, does not appear. I is defined in (11.1).
[b] When $k = V = n$, the actual value of I is given as $1/\log n$ by (11.3).

It seems clear that candidates outnumber vacancies in most applications. I will then be less than found with $V = n$, just as for random selection, I dropped from 0.14 to 0.007 when the ratio of V to N was reduced from unity to one tenth. If the lower bound on I found in (11.4) is a tight one, such that values for most incidence matrixes will be close to the lower bound rather than near unity, it is plausible that interaction effects where k is small, but with V much less than n, will be small enough for the model of independent vacancies to be a good approximation. The last column of Table 11.1 reports one piece of evidence: the lower bound estimated for very large k is within 15 percent of the actual value calculated from (11.3). In Section 11.3, exact calculations of I are made for several other incidence matrices with $V = n$, after translating the count of allocations into a familiar combinatorial problem.

11.3   Systems of Distinct Representatives for Finite Projective Planes[10]

Conceive of the candidates for a given job as members of a committee. Each vacant job defines a committee of arbitrary size. Each man may be a member of any number of committees. Assignment of

289

men to vacant jobs is isomorphic to the well-known problem of committee chairmen. Filling all vacancies corresponds to selecting a system of distinct representatives for the committees, such that each committee has one representative and no man represents more than one committee. Let SDR stand for system of distinct representatives and thus for an allocation that fills all vacancies from the given candidates.

There is a well-known necessary and sufficient condition for an SDR to be possible:[11] every subset of the population of vacancies, whatever its size or membership, must contain in its candidacies at least as many different men as there are vacancies in the subset. The model of Chapter 2 admits an enlargement of the definition of candidacies which guarantees fulfillment of this condition in a trivial way. Each vacancy is allowed to leave the system by a formal move corresponding to termination of that job or leaving it empty. Define a corresponding "candidacy" and "man," then each job has at least one candidate unique to it. The boundary values asserted for the measure I defined in (11.1) depended on at least one allocation of men to fill all vacancies being possible; the justification should now be apparent.[12] In Table 11.1, the case of exactly one candidate for each job, $k = 1$, was excluded. If the one candidate is in fact unique to the job so that no overlaps are possible, then exactly one allocation of men among vacancies is possible. The measure I becomes

$$1 - \frac{\log 1}{\log 1}$$

which can reasonably be defined as zero in conformity with intuition.

Translating allocation into SDR makes accessible computations in the literature for certain incidence matrices. The incidence matrix for an SDR is the same as for the corresponding allocation, as is computation of the number of SDR from the permanent. Suppose first the number of different men, n, equals the number of committees, V. Suppose also every committee has exactly k members, as in (11.6) and Table 11.1, with k equaling, at most, $V - 2$.

The main restriction is that every pair of committees has exactly λ men in common, with λ at least 1 but less than k. When translated into candidacies, that defines a very strong kind of overlap since every one of a possibly large number of vacant jobs must share with each other job λ men as mutual candidates. The interaction measure for that overlap should be close to an upper bound for matrices with the given number of vacancies V and total candidacies kV.

An incidence matrix with those properties defines a (V, k, λ) configuration, one of the symmetric balanced incomplete block designs treated in the statistical theory of experimental design.[13] Although much attention has been given to these configurations, not much is known about the permanents. Even the existence of configurations for particular values of v, k, and λ is problematic in general, although necessary conditions are known.

Counts of SDR are known for a few particular configurations of special importance in several related areas of combinatorics. When $V = 7, k = 3$, and $\lambda = 1$ a configuration is known that is equivalent to the unique projective plane of order 2.[14] The number of SDR for this configuration, the value of the permanent, is 24. The product of the committee sizes, that is, the number of allocations of men to fill all vacancies given the same number of candidacies but without overlaps, is just k^V, here 3^7 or 2187. Hence the interaction measure I from (11.1) is 0.59, not very far from the lower bound of 0.45 for $k = 3$ in Table 11.1. In Table 11.2 results are quoted for that and two other projective planes.

It seems clear from Table 11.2 that as the number of vacancies

Table 11.2   Interaction measure I when Each Pair of Vacancies Share One Candidate[a]

Order of projective plane[b]	V	k	I	Lower bound for I from (11.5)[c]
2	7	3	.59	.45
3	13	4	.54	.42
4	21	5	.49	.39

[a] Exact result from (11.1). As in Table 11.1, the number of men equals the number of vacancies V, with exactly k candidacies for each vacancy; so the denominator is log k^V.

[b] From whose incidence matrix the number of allocations with overlap, that is, the number of SDR, is calculated as the permanent. Each of these projective planes is also a (V, k, λ) configuration with $\lambda = 1$.

[c] See Table 11.1.

grows large, the lower bound in (11.5) is also a reasonable asymptotic estimate of I for $n = V$, even when candidacies are so interlinked that every pair of vacancies shares a candidate. In actual applications, the number of men who are candidates presumably will be much

larger than the number of vacancies and interaction effects substantially smaller. If the drop in I is comparable to its drop between
(11.3) and (11.1) for across-the-board candidacies, it is reasonable to
conclude that the model of Chapter 2 for independent vacancies is
an acceptable approximation.

11.4 Chains from Activated Permutations

A crude model for vacancy chains incorporating interaction among
vacancies will now be developed. Individual moves in the chains are
treated as effectively simultaneous. The model reverts to random
selection from homogeneous candidacies, but only for a group of
n^* incumbents in jobs who are assumed to constitute a separate
small neighborhood of acquaintances. The new model is an adaptation of the combinatorial model for intergenerational mobility of
Section 9.4. Instead of the system of men and jobs being closed,
deaths of men initiate chains and recruitment terminates them. The
small neighborhoods replace division of jobs among gross strata. As
in Chapter 2, the distribution of chain lengths is the main concern.
This distribution proves to be qualitatively different from that for
the corresponding binomial model for single vacancies.

Suppose each man's preference for his next job is confined to a
small circle of n^* jobs whose incumbents constitute a clique of
acquaintances. The jobs are not distinguished in status so that
preference depends on personal tastes for change. A man does not
retain a preference that conflicts with that of another man. Assume
the structure of preferences at a time has evolved so that it can be
represented as a permutation on the set of n^* incumbents. Each node
has exactly one arrow leading out to choice of next job and conversely receives exactly one choice.[15] The preferences fall into a set
of disjoint cycles. In the next year, let d of the n^* men depart from
the system by death or other independent event. Each disappearance
permits realization of the preference to move in that cycle of the
next man, whose move opens up the next link in the cycle, and so
on. A chain of moves runs until it reaches a job that was the
preference of a man who has left the system; assume, then, this job
is filled by a new recruit, terminating the chain.

The result of the d deaths is creation of a set of d realized vacancy
chains, the cycles that death does not enter remaining latent. The
lengths in the set of d chains will depend both on the structure of the

permutation and on where death occurs. Suppose each possible permutation is equally likely and deaths strike men at random, independent of their position in the permutation. A probability distribution of chain lengths can be calculated in stages. The probability of each possible initial permutation, that is, a set of cycles, can be calculated.[16] For each such set, the probability of each possible set of locations for the d deaths can be computed[17] and the corresponding set of d vacancy chains specified by lengths. Probabilities of various ways of creating a given set of chain lengths are then added together. Each possible final set of chain lengths caused by d deaths among the n^* men is assigned an overall probability, the sum over all sets of being unity. Finally, the probability of a single vacancy chain selected at random in a given year being of length j is computed; it is the sum over all final sets of the probability of the set, times the fraction of chains in that set that are of length j.

Cycles of unit length are not allowed in the original permutation. They correspond to a man's wishing to remain in his current job, and the number of such men need bear no relation to the likelihood of unit cycles when unrestricted permutations are considered. Since only incumbents who wish to move are counted in n^*, it must be assumed that men aim for a job only if the incumbent desires to move.

Consider illustrative calculations for the case where $n^* = 9$ and $d = 3$. The ratio d/n^* is the analogue to the termination probability p in the binomial vacancy chain model of Chapter 1. A p of $\frac{1}{3}$ is in the range found for the three churches studied.[18] The probability that the permutation is a set of three cycles with lengths 5, 2, and 2 is 0.0680. After three deaths have been assigned at random to the nine men, the conditional probabilities of various sets of lengths for the resulting vacancy chains are

Initial set of cycles	Final set of chain lengths	Probability	Any complete cycles remaining
	3, 1, 1	.0595	2, 2
	2, 2, 1	.0595	2, 2
	4, 2, 1	.2381	2
5, 2, 2	3, 2, 2	.2381	2
	5, 2, 2	.2381	0
	5, 1, 1	.1190	2
	2, 1, 1	.0476	5
		.9999	

The last column specifies the lengths of any cycles not hit by deaths and thus not opened up into vacancy chains. When similar calculations for all possible sets of initial cycles have been combined, there are twenty-four different final sets, when lengths of any complete cycles are specified. The probability of at least one complete cycle remaining in the final set is 0.3043. The overall probability that the three vacancy chains in the final set are of lengths 5, 1, 1, for example, is 0.0243.

Table 11.3 reports the probability a single chain selected at random from a final set will be of length j. Results for $n^* = 9$ and $d = 3$ are compared with results for $n^* = 6$ but the same chance of death, with $d = 2$. As a possible clue to the incidence of loops, reported in Section C.2 for the churches, complete cycles have been included on

Table 11.3   Distribution of Chain Lengths from Permutations among n^* Men Activated by d Deaths[a]   (percent)

| | $n^* = 6, d = 2$ | | $n^* = 9, d = 3$ | |
| | | Complete | | Complete |
j	All chains	cycles	All chains	cycles
1	15.4		22.0	
2	34.3	6.6	29.7	5.0
3	22.4	2.0	20.3	1.9
4	18.9	0.7	13.5	0.7
5	9.5		8.4	0.2
6			4.3	0.04
7			1.6	

[a] Randomly selected permutations, except unit cycles, and randomly assigned deaths.

the same footing with vacancy chains. In each case, the chance of finding a loop is less than 10 percent of the chance of finding a vacancy chain.[19] The distribution of chain lengths for $n^* = 9$ is seen to be close to that for $n^* = 6$ and to have a slightly smaller mean value, 2.65 compared to 2.70. Intuition would suggest these distributions depend primarily on the ratio d/n^*. To model an actual system, it would have to be considered as a collection of neighborhoods of men aiming for each others' jobs, and the length distribution would have to be averaged over the neighborhoods, each with its own value of n^* and of d/n^*. For the assumption of equally likely permutations to be plausible, the value of n^* must always be small.

Interaction among vacancies in earlier sections is analogous here to the fact that random deaths may bunch in the same cycle of the permutation, splitting it into several chains. The interesting feature of the distributions in Table 11.3, which distinguishes distributions from the prediction of equation (2.3) for any binomial model, is the existence of a peak at $j = 2$. This suggests that interaction among vacancies should change the shape of the distribution of lengths predicted from the models of Chapter 2. Hence the tests in Chapters 5 and 6 may be sensitive to interactions among vacancies as well as to non-Markovian influences in a given chain.

11.5   Measures of Association: Levine's View of Matchmaking

O. D. Duncan's path analysis (Section 10.8) is a statistical assessment procedure that sidesteps weaknesses in single-flows models of careers (Chapter 9). J. H. Levine avoids the conundrums in explicit matchmaking models (Chapter 8) by a new assessment procedure for cross-classifications.[20] Neither his procedure nor the ones in Chapter 8 define explicit mechanisms. Exogenous flows have no causal role, and the systems studied can be considered closed. Duncan analyzes correlations between earlier and later statuses of independent individuals; Levine, it will be argued, assesses relative attractiveness of different categories of "men" and "women" for each other in matchmaking. When vacant jobs are numerous relative to incumbents (as well as when pools of free men and jobs in the system are available for matchmaking) the models for independent vacancies break down; Levine's procedure may be a sensible way to assess the results of interaction.

The sizes of destination categories impose constraints on amounts of movement. Levine proposes to measure "true" interactions between origin and destination categories by factoring out the marginal totals in a cross-tabulation. C. F. Mosteller discusses the provenance of this idea in a recent survey article on contingency tables in general: "... think of a contingency table as having a *basic nucleus* which describes its association and think of all tables formed by multiplying elements in rows and columns by positive numbers as forming an equivalence class—a class of tables with the same degree of association ... an index of association that is invariant under these row and column multiplications is the cross product ratio."[21] In a

2 × 2 table, that index, also called the "odds ratio," is simply the product of the two entries in diagonal cells divided by the product of the counts in the two off-diagonal cells. Other definitions are possible for invariance of interaction under changes in marginals, and Levine develops a number of arguments in support of the multiplicative criterion.

The special problem in assessing mobility tables is the treatment of men who do not change in status. The most arbitrary part of Levine's analysis is his treatment of entries in the diagonal cells, the immobiles.[22] If only moves are tabulated, explanation of total amounts of mobility is outside the scope of the assessment; and special techniques are still necessary to deal with empty cells on the diagonal. L. A. Goodman,[23] Y. M. M. Bishop and S. E. Fienberg,[24] and this author,[25] as well as Levine, have proposed such techniques. The focus tends to shift from assessing interaction among particular pairs of rows and of columns to predicting all off-diagonal entries from the given marginals on the hypothesis that interaction is constant throughout the tables.[26]

One image Levine has used is flows of water from an upper row of tanks to a lower row through pipes of varying apertures connecting each upper tank to each lower tank.[27] That image corresponds to the case of total mobility, where every man moves; and it is for that case that Levine's model is most appropriate. In his survey article, Mosteller describes a baseline model for preferential marriage in two steps that he and A. K. Romney developed. They find use of the cross-product ratios with multipliers to construct the observed marginals yields a good approximation to the expected numbers of marriages on the model.[28] The predictions deal only with cases of equal numbers of men and women in which all marry. Levine's model can be seen as an analogue in which men, categorized by present status, are matched to an equal population of vacant jobs, also categorized by status.

Levine assesses interactions between categories in the complete matching of one population with another in a closed system at a given time. Real processes, whether or marriage or mobility, are spread over time, in systems open to an environment, and do not yield complete matchings. Levine's work differs from the models in Chapter 8 as well as from the vacancy model on one or another of these criteria. Yet, when the real processes are too complex to be dealt with, Levine supplies a way to interpret relations among categories. The transition probabilities among strata, the q_{ij}, report these relations in the vacancy models. When vacancies are too closely coupled to be treated as independent individuals, estimates of q_{ij} can no longer be interpreted as transition probabilities. It may be possible, instead, to interpret cross-tabulations of vacancy moves through a modified form of Levine's cross-product ratios.

Chapter 12
Localism, Elites, and Tenure Networks

Vacancy chain models are blind to particular ties among men. Moves between jobs for particular individuals are shaped by networks of acquaintances and sponsors which evolve over long periods in overlapping neighborhoods. Variation in vacancy chains by locale is demonstrated in Section 12.1. Section 12.2 suggests that elite subsystems are woven into the fabrics of the clergies. Particularism of these kinds can be explicated only from patterns in moves over long periods.

To make progress, the problem must be recast in new terms. Stratified models appear to give satisfactory accounts of the gross pattern and amounts of mobility among categories of jobs. What is missing is insight into "inbreeding" in the system; that is, tendencies toward one man following in the footsteps of another, toward certain arbitrary jobs marking the occupant for eventual success or failure, toward small sets of jobs capturing the whole careers of certain sets of men, and so on. In Section 12.3 a new framework is developed appropriate for measures of inbreeding. Dynamics is no longer the focus and vacancies are no longer the actors.

Random walks would have to replace Markov chains as the formal framework for vacancy dynamics in order to use transition probabilities referred to individual sites rather than to equivalence classes. The difficulty is that very little is known about the structure of acquaintance networks in any social context, much less about how the spread of influence and information is shaped by the structure.[1] Random walk models give useful results only when the topology of the network—the structure of overlaps between neighborhoods centered on different men—is extremely simple, say if people are arrayed at the corners of a regular grid of ties.[2] Even when moves between jobs are assumed to be constrained to adjacent levels in a tree representing a simplified authority structure, the calculation of vacancy chain lengths has proved very complex.[3]

Small delays between choices of men by jobs and jobs by men shaped the analysis in earlier chapters and lead to the focus on vacancies because system dynamics were assumed to be determined by the immediate past. Men do have memories. The maintenance of traditions, elites, and localism may depend on direct interaction among events widely separated in time. Interaction among moves may ramify beyond overlaps among candidacies at one time and beyond the sequences of opportunities realized in single vacancy chains. Section 12.4 develops representations of the assignments of men to jobs over long periods and suggests measures of both particularism and interaction across long periods.

12.1 Diocesan Samples of Vacancy Chains

Ignore, now, the stratified models. Think of vacancy chains simply as records of the tracks of disturbances moving through a large system. Even though the topology of ties among men and jobs is unknown, it is clear that one important influence on association is belonging to the same local unit of clergy and churches. Regular meetings and common financial responsibilities as well as geographical contiguity and common leadership define the most potent local unit, called the "diocese" in the Episcopal church and the "annual conference" in the Methodist church. The question is how vacancy chains are related to these local units. Different perspectives will emerge from both different sorts of evidence and different measures on the same evidence.

The first evidence used is distributions of lengths for all vacancy chains that impinge on a diocese in a given year. The longer the chains, the more extensive is the scope of contingencies in mobility for that diocese. Few enough chains touch a particular diocese in a year for an exhaustive inventory to be feasible. Nonetheless, to achieve comparability with national samples, weights must be assigned chains to correct for differential exposure resulting from differential spread of chains across dioceses and across annual registers. Section B.3 explains three different sampling schemes used, identified by the symbols D, D'', and d'. These diocesan samples were actually the first ones traced.

Tables 12.1 and 12.2 report weighted length distributions for the Episcopal church scattered over an eighty year period. Dioceses of different ideological persuasions and degrees of urbanization as well as from different regions have been chosen (see Section 5.4 for background). Nonetheless, they are not a probability sample; only if results for all dioceses were combined could one be sure to obtain

Table 12.1 Lengths of Vacancy Chains that Touch a Given Episcopal Diocese, Complete Inventories (percent)

j	Massachusetts		La.	Wyo.	Chicago
	D^a 1958–1959	D 1876–1877	D'' 1957	D'' 1956–1959[b]	D'' 1957
1	30.0	55.1	39.7	23.2	14.7
2	48.8	11.2	28.3	11.6	35.9
3	10.2	19.2	7.6	24.4	27.3
4	4.7	7.5	9.4	7.4	3.3
5	1.3	5.5	7.9	18.0	7.8
6	3.7	0	1.9	5.0	7.1
7	0.8	1.5	2.7	3.7	1.4
8	0		0	0	0.8
9	0		0	5.0	0
10	0		1.0	1.8	1.7
11	0.5		0		
12			1.4		
	$N_w{}^c = 15.02$	$N_w = 8.22$	$N_w = 8.82$	$N_w = 7.20$	$N_w = 10.19$
	$J_c{}^d = 2.17$	$J_c = 2.03$	$J_c = 2.54$	$J_c = 3.60$	$J_c = 2.96$
	$J_m{}^e = 3.02$	$J_m = 2.97$	$J_m = 4.25$	$J_m = 5.03$	$J_m = 4.04$
Official number of clergy	286	144	82	39	192
Official number of parishes and missions	201	95	85	51	133
Raw number of chains	(36)	(22)	(19)	(26)	(31)
Raw number of 1-year vacancies	(30)	(27)	(20)	(28)	(40)
Raw mean length	(3.11)	(2.64)	(4.75)	(4.73)	(4.10)

[a] Section B.3 explains how chains are discovered and weights computed for each sample type. Chains are traced as in Chapter 3.

[b] To obtain a sizeable base in this small diocese, lists of appointments and resignations for four years were combined. Chains which had entries in two of the lumped years were counted twice. N_w should be divided by 4 to compare with official size data and with other dioceses.

[c] In this and all subsequent tables in which it appears, N_w represents weighted number of chains.

[d] J_c represents mean length (weighted).

[e] J_m represents mean length (weighted) as context for moves; see Appendix B.

distributions representative of the national church like those in Chapter 5. No aggregate tallies of moves by strata across these selected dioceses have been made since the resulting estimates of transition probabilities would have no definite reference population.

Table 12.2   Lengths of Vacancy Chains Containing Resignations in a Given Episcopal Diocese,[a] Sample Type d'

j	Massachusetts				New York
	1958	1954	1950	1949	1921
1	7.4	25.0	21.1	43.0	41.1
2	51.6	31.0	23.7	7.2	37.7
3	27.0	21.6	32.9	12.9	12.2
4	4.9	15.2	10.5	0	1.7
5	1.8	3.1	7.9	18.5	1.7
6	6.3	2.0	3.9	14.4	3.2
7	0	0		4.1	2.4
8	0	2.0			
9	0				
10	0				
11	0.9				
	$N_w = 13.56$	$N_w = 8.08$	$N_w = 6.33$	$N_w = 3.49$	$N_w = 15.01$
	$J_c = 2.68$	$J_c = 2.57$	$J_c = 2.76$	$J_c = 4.01$	$J_c = 2.04$
	$J_m = 3.42$	$J_m = 3.39$	$J_m = 3.37$	$J_m = 5.15$	$J_m = 2.96$
Official number of clergy	286	266	271	259	420
Official number of parishes and missions	201	199	200	204	297
Raw number of chains	(25)	(16)	(16)	(13)	(28)
Raw number of 1-year vacancies	(32)	(16)	(16)	(21)	(20)
Raw mean length	(3.48)	(3.31)	(3.25)	(4.92)	(2.82)

[a] See Section B.3.

Section A.4 explains systematic biases to which the d' samples but not the others are exposed; results from the former should be compared only with each other and are reported separately, as Table 12.2.

Comparison of the first two columns in Table 12.1 suggests that the vacancy dynamics related to a local area can be quite stable across very long periods.[4] Comparison of the last three columns with the first suggest there may be substantial differences among dioceses, with newer or smaller ones tending, perhaps, to participate more in longer chains. A better idea of the stability in length distributions in nearby years for a given diocese is given by the first four columns of Table 12.2, which indicate that variability over time in means for one diocese need not obscure differences between dioceses. As explained earlier, the absolute values of parameters in Table 12.2 are biased upward: compare the first columns of Table 12.2 and 12.1. The column in Table 12.2 for New York, the largest and one of the oldest dioceses, shows, as expected, smaller values of mean lengths than for Massachusetts; Massachusetts, itself quite large and old, has in turn smaller lengths than the other dioceses shown in Table 12.1.

Chain lengths for the Methodist conference in Table 12.3 have decreased substantially over three decades, during which there has been a merger and a trend toward a more educated ministry. Chain lengths are clearly longer than in the corresponding Episcopal dioceses, where, if anything, the mean length has been overestimated. The one distribution shown for a Presbyterian synod is, as expected, quite similar to the one in Table 12.1 for the most similar Episcopal diocese, Massachusetts (1958–1959).

The perspective from within the diocese, the chains as they would be seen by, say, the bishop, has been slighted by the weighting procedure. The raw distribution corresponds to what a diocesan might see. Long chains will tend to cross many dioceses and therefore play a bigger role in perceived chain length than the short ones. The bottom row in each table gives the mean lengths of the raw distributions; that is, the sum of the lengths of chains that touch a diocese divided by the raw number of such chains, shown in a row above. Inevitably the raw mean is larger than J_c, the weighted length. The raw mean is also distinct from J_m, which measures chain length as seen by the average move, including all moves inside and all moves outside the given diocese (see Appendix B).

The weighted distributions for dioceses can be compared with the national sample results given in Chapters 5 and 6 (and in Appendix C for J_m, the mean contextual length). However, it is not practicable, from differences in the distribution of relevant creations among strata, to assess the extent to which variation of dioceses from national results can be explained using the stratified models.

Table 12.3 Lengths of Vacancy Chains that Touch a Given Methodist Conference or Presbyterian Synod, Complete Inventories, D Sample[a]   (percent)

	Methodist	Methodist Episcopal (North)		United Presbyterian (USA)
	New York Annual Conference[b]			New England Synod
j	1954–1955	1936–1937	1921–1922	1959–1960
1	45.0	41.1	24.8	46.7
2	27.5	29.4	49.6	24.9
3	10.0	11.8	4.1	10.9
4	9.1	0	0	5.0
5	0	5.9	6.2	6.2
6	0	5.9	6.2	2.3
7	2.5	0	0	1.7
8	0	0	2.1	2.3
9	0	0	0	
10	2.5	0	0	
11	0	0	0	
12	3.5	0	0	
13		0	2.1	
14	0	0		
15	0	0		
16		5.9	0	
17			0.7	
18			4.1	
	$N_w = 20.03$	$N_w = 17.00$	$N_w = 24.17$	$N_w = 5.36$
	$J_c = 2.5$	$J_c = 2.94$	$J_c = 3.34$	$J_c = 2.24$
	$J_m = 5.0$	$J_m = 7.2$	$J_m = 8.1$	$J_m = 3.54$
Official number of clergy	227	259	283	183
Official number of parishes	188	209	0	85
Raw number of chains	(27)	(18)	(28)	(16)
Raw number of loops	(0)	(4)	(4)	(0)
Raw mean length	(3.22)	(2.89)	(4.03)	(3.44)

[a] See Section B.3.
[b] The southern and northern branches merged in 1940, but membership in the New York conference was little affected.

Regional variations in transition or termination probabilities could always be postulated to account for the length distributions, however difficult actual estimations would be.[5] The issue of inbreeding in a network structure is not really confronted.

Consider three successive "neighborhoods"; the diocese, the larger set of jobs linked by vacancy chains to the diocese, and the whole national system. The larger set is unlikely to include whole dioceses. Vacancy chains, over a period of years, could be used to map the network of jobs in the mobility neighborhood of a given arbitrary set, here a diocese. J_c measures the mean length of chains, much of which lie outside the diocese in the larger set. Suppose just the moves within the diocese were fitted together to make complete chains. Using logic and equations parallel to those in Section B.7, the mean length expected in such a set can be computed, once using beginning events and once using ending events. The differences between these and J_c is an indication of the extent of homogeneity in chains within the larger set. The formulas and calculations are intricate and will not be reported. In all the dioceses studied (D sample only), except the Presbyterian one, the two means calculated from sample entries were close to and bracketed the value of J_c.

Another type of evidence concerns the extent to which a diocese is tied by vacancy chains to other dioceses. The differences between the churches are so clear-cut and dioceses within a church so similar in this respect that no tables and detailed definitions of measures are required. More than half the Methodist chains that touch a diocese are contained wholly within the diocese. In the Episcopal and Presbyterian churches, however, in more than half the chains that touch a diocese, only one move in the chain is within the diocese.

The encapsulated nature of a Methodist conference is reflected in the coding rules developed in Section 2.2 for length of vacancies. Because the bulk of chains are wholly within a conference, short delays between successive moves in a chain are possible. It is reasonable to terminate a chain at a listing of a job as vacant in one annual. As one would expect, mean length is little affected if chains are traced through one year vacancies as for the Episcopal data. For example, in the sample for 1936–1937 in Table 12.3 the increase in J_c is only from 2.94 to 3.13. In all cases, the values of J_c and J_m are increased by less than 10 percent. The same conclusions can also be reached by simply computing the number of dioceses per move in weighted

chains from the national samples in Chapters 5 and 6. For the
Methodist church, it is obvious that models of moves among gross
national prestige strata or regional strata cannot give the full
picture of constraints on vacancy moves, although their predictions
in terms of these strata are satisfactory. The full picture would
require a model that at least dealt with moves between individual
sites, like a random walk.

12.2   Bishops versus Priests: Chains and Careers

Filling the job left vacant by a newly elected bishop has a cachet that
may persist for several moves down the vacancy chain. The length
distribution for such chains is unusual. Table 12.4 reports all

Table 12.4   Lengths of Vacancy Chains from Promotions
of Principal Diocesan Bishops Incumbent in 1962
in the Episcopal Church   (percent)

j	Total	Chains ended by recruitment from seminaries
1	1.3	0
2	19.5	0
3	19.5	4
4	7.8	24
5	14.3	8
6	14.3	32
7	11.7	24
8	6.5	4
9	2.6	4
10	2.6	
Number[a]	(77)	(25)
Mean	(4.95)	(5.8)

[a] No sampling weights are needed since the chains are
drawn from a well-defined population of initial events.

seventy-seven chains containing the promotions to principal bishop
of an Episcopal diocese of the men incumbent in 1962. Not only
are the chains long, the mean and the median being five jobs, but
also the shape of the distribution, rectangular or possibly twin-
peaked, is very unlike any of those for national samples reported in
Chapter 5.

12. Localism, Elites, Tenures

A secondary use of such data is to provide a rough operational measure of the "height" of the clergy, that is, of the number of moves between 1–1 jobs to get from the bottom to the top of the church. For this purpose, only chains that terminate by recruitment of a newly ordained young man should be used. That subset is reported in the second column of Table 12.4. The variance of the distribution is quite small, and there is only one chain of length 3 or less, which suggests that more than three strata should be discriminable in the analysis of mobility.

It could be that a refined Markov chain model with many strata would yield a predicted length distribution for chains begun in the top strata, which is much like that observed for bishops. It may also be that the bishops' chains reflect a new kind of interaction in mobility. An elite subsystem of men and jobs may be hidden within the gross national system. Moves of "comers" may be confined to special earmarked jobs, and the corresponding chains may, to some extent, be planned by informal cliques of men of power in the church.

One fragment of evidence is the use of coadjutor status. Half of the men were elected via this "trainee" status, under the authority of the incumbent but with automatic right of succession, usually realized within a year or two. Presumably such elections, under the eye of, and at a time chosen by, the incumbent, provide more scope for planning and arranging attendant choices of men and moves. Another bit of evidence is the frequency with which suffragans—assistant bishops without succession rights—and missionary bishops—elected by the House of Bishops rather than a diocesan convention of priests and laity—appear in the chains. In one chain, three bishoprics appeared, not counting coadjutors, and in another four appeared; altogether fourteen subsidiary bishoprics appeared in the seventy-seven chains. Moves among bishoprics will probably increase now that "translation" of the ordinaries themselves is permitted by revised canon law. A third indication of selectivity, incompatible with a model incorporating only gross strata of jobs and substrata by men's attributes, is the frequency of appearance of deanships. In the seventy-seven chains, most of which ran in the late 1940s or mid-1950s, nineteen cathedral chairs appear, two twice; that is, more than half the deanships appear in the seventy-seven chains, although the total number of jobs of comparable pay and seniority is in the hundreds. Finally, the incidence of one-year vacancies in the chain traces, ninety-nine among the seventy-seven chains, is compatible with unusually short vacancies in these chains, since the average number of moves per chain is five. Short vacancies suggest there might be considerable advanced planning in the chains.

Careers furnish more decisive evidence for the existence of an elite subsystem. Table 12.5 compares careers of the seventy-seven bishops

Table 12.5   Career Lengths of Episcopal Bishops and Priests[a]   (percent)

Length[b]	Bishops (Ordinaries) incumbent in 1962	Priests Class of 1912[c]	Priests 1960 retirees[d]
1	0	4.3	3.9
2	0	17.4	10.4
3	0	16.0	18.2
4	5.2	16.0	13.0
5	15.6	11.6	11.7
6	23.4	13.1	10.4
7	28.6	7.3	10.4
8	14.3	4.3	7.8
9	11.7	7.3	5.2
10	1.3	0	2.6
11		1.4	1.3
12		1.4	0
13			2.6
17			1.3
18			1.3
Number	(77)	(69)	(77)
Mean $\bar{y}$	(5.7)	(4.6)	(5.5)

[a] Traced from the annuals, aided by self-reported career in Stowe's Directory.

[b] Number of 1–1 jobs held during entire career plus the number of periods spent in some one or succession of pool and limbo or both positions. On the average, both for bishops and for priests, only about 40 percent of the careers have any periods in pool or limbo. Note that the χ defined in Section 10.1 refers only to a continuous succession of 1–1 jobs unbroken by periods in pool and limbo.

[c] Every other name in the official list of diaconates for 1912 in the *Triennial Journal of the General Convention*, except five men who spent their whole careers as foreign missionaries and one who was a missionary to the deaf.

[d] One retired priest from the clergy list of each diocese in the 1960 annual.

incumbent in 1962 with careers of priests. One sample of priests consists of every other man in the group ordained deacon in 1912, close to the period when most of the seventy-seven bishops were ordained. The other sample of priests consists of one priest on the retired list of each diocese as of 1960. Those two samples yield distributions of career lengths both of which are quite similar and have a mean near that for bishops. The interesting fact is the very small variance of career lengths for bishops as compared to priests. Only 6.5 percent of the bishops' careers had lengths of 4 or less or 10 or greater, whereas 55 percent of either sample of priests had careers that short or that long. The long tenure enjoyed by many bishops is not sufficient to explain the difference in variance, since long tenures are also common for older priests. Nor does it matter whether all jobs or only 1–1 jobs are counted in career lengths, although it is true bishops have had somewhat fewer periods in pool and limbo—less than 6 percent of the total career lengths—compared with 10 percent for the samples of priests.

Common sense suggests that certain young men are marked even in seminary as future bishops, and the common phenomenon of successive generations of bishops in a family suggests still earlier attributions. "Correct" careers could be planned in advance for such young men, careers with just the right number of moves. But the data in Table 12.5 is retrospective and does not deal with whether and how recruits were earmarked for later success. It could be that only those men who happen through luck to have "correct" careers are elected bishop. Credulity is, however, strained by the thought that happenstance alone shapes successful careers. The knowledge of which career is correct surely filters back through the system, influencing not only ambitious young men but also older men searching for likely protégés.

A final type of evidence is overlaps in jobs between the set of careers of bishops and the set of vacancy chains tied to their elections. Only in the extreme case of a pure linear hierarchy of jobs topped by a given bishopric would one find the jobs in a given bishop's career identical with the jobs in his vacancy chain. If there is an elite sub-system, jobs should exist that are recognized as stepping stones for future bishops in general—these jobs should tend to be restricted to men thought of as bishop caliber—and there will be considerable overlap between jobs in the set of chains and jobs in the set of careers.

A rigorous derivation of the number of overlaps expected by chance would be complex, because one would have to allow for a given job appearing several times in the set of careers and in the set of chains or in both as well as for the overlap between the two sets. Consider instead the overlap between the set of distinct jobs from all careers and the similar set from all vacancy chains. First, the bishoprics themselves must be excluded since, until last year, no principal bishop was allowed to translate to a different diocese. With this exclusion, the number of distinct 1–1 jobs in the seventy-seven bishops' careers is 278. (The total count of 440 tenures for bishops from Table 12.5 is the sum of that plus the seventy-seven bishoprics, plus thirty-eight coadjutor statuses, plus twenty-six periods in pool and in limbo or in both, plus twenty-one multiple appearances of a given job in two or more careers. The latter figure seems small, but it could merely reflect the fact that most of the bishops are of similar age and therefore would tend to be in jobs of a given status at the same time, thereby barring many overlaps.) When the bishoprics and multiple appearances of jobs are excluded from the total of 380 1–1 jobs in bishops' vacancy chains, a total of 282 distinct 1–1 jobs remain. The total number of 1–1 jobs in the Episcopal church in the 1950s can be estimated from Tables C.3 and C.7 as 5100. A crude estimate of the number of career jobs that can be expected, by chance, to appear among the vacancy chain jobs is

$$\frac{278}{5100} \times 282 = 15 \tag{12.1}$$

where it is assumed that all the jobs that appeared in bishops' careers are still in existence in the 1950s. Any attempt to correct for this assumption, or to allow for possible effects of regionalism or clustering of bishops' careers in high-status jobs, would only tend to increase the number of overlaps expected by chance.

The observed number of distinct jobs that appear in both one or more careers and one or more vacancy chains is surprisingly small, namely thirty. That is so close to the crude calculation of chance expectancy, it is unlikely that more refined calculations could change the main conclusion: there is no evidence for an unusual degree of overlap in jobs between careers and vacancy chains. (Excluded from the count of thirty are seventy-seven automatic overlaps in tenures between careers and vacancy chains, namely the jobs from which the seventy-seven bishops were promoted, each of which must appear in both that bishop's vacancy chain and career.)

If there is an elite subsystem, it must take a different form from reservation of earmarked jobs for promising young men. The simplest possibility is that favored men are elected bishop because of personal attributes or friendships, regardless of what jobs they have held; but that would not account for the unusually small variance in number of jobs in career demonstrated in Table 12.5. A more subtle form would be interrelation of particular cliques of men in their movements through jobs, the particular jobs important for later elite status differing over time and from one clique to another.

A new, more detailed framework of analysis is necessary to search for such subsystems. The framework must encompass the whole system if it is to show the distinctiveness of some parts. It should be general enough to permit a search for effects of localism of the sort treated in Section 12.1.

12.3 Tenure Networks

Return to Figure 1.3, the diagram of a chain of moves among tenures. Consider only sequential order in time; disregard all dates and all measures of duration. Spread out the ovals representing tenures in two dimensions so that each move by a job from one man to another is represented by a horizontal arrow to the new tenure. The arrows for moves by men remain vertical; use broken lines to distinguish them further. It is natural to wish to extend the diagram to include earlier and later moves by the men and the jobs in the vacancy chains. Further jobs and men appear, and their moves in turn can be recorded. See Figure 12.1 for an illustration.

The resulting diagram for a whole system of men and jobs over a long period is a graph representing a tenure network. Each node is a tenure, a continuous incumbency of a man in a 1–1 job. Exactly one solid arrow enters and exactly one leaves each node, and similarly for the dotted arrows representing transfers of men. The conventions for terminal moves are the same as in Figure 1.1. In the language of graph theory, each node in the directed graph has the same local degree for each type of link—an in-degree of 1 and an out-degree of 1. Links of each kind can be grouped into individual classes. A sequence of vertical links defines a man's career. A sequence of horizontal links defines successive incumbents in a job during its history. The topology for a tenure network, the way in which the neighborhood of one node overlaps the neighborhood of neighbor nodes, is the main issue.

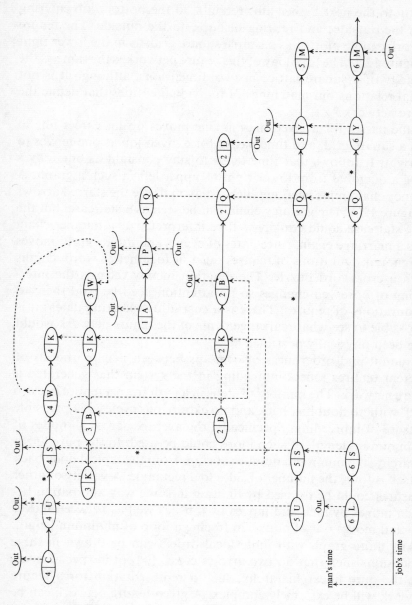

Figure 12.1   Part of a Tenure Network. Men are represented by capital letters, jobs by numerals, and tenure by ovals. Dotted arrows trace a man's career. Initial tenures are on the left of job lines (solid arrows). Arrows marked by asterisks are events in the first part of the vacancy chain begun by U's retirement. (See Table 12.6 for another representation of a tenure network.)

In one special case the topology is very simple. Consider a pure linear hierarchy, with a single job in each rank. Let promotion be strictly to the next higher job; recruits, to the bottom job entering from the outside; and retiring bishops, to the outside. The tenure network can be plotted as a simple square grid, as in the lower right of Figure 12.1. The topology of this tenure network is the same as the topology of a square lattice in two dimensions, although it is not spatial relations but matchings of individual entities that define the tenure network.[6]

Time passes for a given man as one moves up his career line in such a square grid, and time passes for a given job as one moves to the right. It follows that time tends to stay constant as one moves along a diagonal from lower right to upper left in such a graph. A vacancy chain must lie along such a diagonal; see the starred arrows in Figure 12.1. The vacancy chain can be seen as a staircase, but the same staircase could equally well be interpreted as a bumper chain or as a marriage chain, since dates of events and durations of moves are ignored. Durations of tenures must fit together as word lengths do in a crossword puzzle. The diagram merely records the inter-linking of observed changes so no attention need be paid there to the durations of tenures. There is a cost in overlooking dates: it is impossible to see what rearrangements of the tenure network would have been physically possible.

Amount and orderliness of overlaps between neighborhoods of different tenures reflect inbreeding in the system that generated a tenure network. The number of steps in a path from a tenure back to itself, with no doubling back and no extraneous cycles, is a plausible measure of inbreeding. Specifically, the average across all nodes of the minimum length of such loops could be used. In the pure linear hierarchy, the minimum number of steps from the typical node back to itself is four, the number of sides to a rectangle. A variety of other measures could be devised by limiting in some way alternation be-tween moves by men and moves by jobs, as well as between moves into and moves out of nodes, in tracing a loop of minimum length.

Any finite graph with finite local orders can be drawn in three dimensions such that no two arrows cross. Except in special cases, like the pure linear hierarchy, such a representation for a tenure network will be extremely complex. A given tenure network can be drawn in a huge number of ways which appear quite different to the eye. If both moves by men and moves by jobs between tenures are recorded in a graph in a fully dual way, the result is too complex to be manageable; it is hard to supply dates for tenures in this representation. These graphs can be suggestive, but a different kind of representation is essential for work with real data.

12.4 Representations and Measures

Abandon the idea of representing moves explicitly. Return to the annual registers, the basic source of data described in Chapter 3. Construct a rectangular array to report the assignments of men to 1–1 jobs in all annuals. Lay out the list of jobs as a row of column headings. Each job and its column is identified by a distinct integer. Assignment of integers to jobs can be arbitrary, but the row of headings is arranged in ascending order. Successive rows in the array are allotted to successive annuals, identified by year. Name each man by a distinct letter, arbitrarily assigned. In the row for an annual, enter a man's letter in the column for the job he holds that year. At most, one letter appears in each cell since the jobs are 1–1. Table 12.6 shows ten rows in an array for a hypothetical system of just ten jobs; the first six columns correspond to the graph in Figure 12.1.

All the information for a tenure network can be extracted from such an array by routine procedures. The job histories in the graphs of Section 12.3 correspond to job columns. In a job column, each block of cells containing the same letter defines a tenure. A transfer by a man corresponds to a shift of his letter from one column to the adjacent row in some other column. A chain of moves between two years can be traced in the array just as it was from two annuals. The array is isomorphic to the job lists in a stack of successive annuals.

The array for a given church could be stored in a large computer. In practice, the main difficulty would arise in coding the annuals. Pool jobs must be distinguished from 1–1 jobs, and so on. A program could be written for tracing chains of moves in the array. As in the annuals, an index of men would simplify the tracing procedure.

Indexes of men in the annuals correspond to a dual form of the array. Columns are assigned to men, arranged in the alphabetical order of their letter names. In the row for each year, the numeral for a job is entered in the column of the man occupying it each year. An efficient computer program for tracing chains of moves or other

313

kinds of paths in the tenure network will presumably require storage of both forms of the array.

Arrays for tenure networks are similar to Latin rectangles, which are used in experimental design, graph theory, and combinatorial analysis.[7] A given letter appears at most once in a row of the array.

Table 12.6   Portion of a Tenure Array for a Hypothetical, Small System of Ten Jobs[a]

Years	In	Jobs										Out
		1	2	3	4	5	6	7	8	9	10	
$t + 10$		O	D	W	K	M	R	G	J	T	V	P, E
$t + 9$	V, D	P	O	K	W	M	E	R	G	J	T	Y
$t + 8$	J	P	O	K	W	Y	M	R	G	E	T	B
$t + 7$	M	P	B	K	W	O	Y	R	G	E	T	
$t + 6$		P	K	B	W	O	Y	R	G	E	T	S
$t + 5$	G	P	K	B	S	O	Y	W	R	T	E	A, U
$t + 4$	P, E	A	K	B	U	S	O	Y	W	R	T	
$t + 3$		A	K	B	U	S	O	Y	R	W	T	C
$t + 2$	T	A	K	B	C	U	S	O	Y	W	R	L, I
$t + 1$	S, Y	A	B	K	C	U	L	O	W	I	R	
t												

[a] Each man is identified by a capital letter, which is entered in the column for the job he is in during the year designated by a given row. New recruits are listed in the "in" column of the year before their first job, and departures are listed in the "out" column for the year after their last job. Ten years for this system of ten jobs are shown, during which twenty men have tenures. By the logic of Chapter 3, ten vacancy chains would be inferred from this array, ranging from length $j = 7$ to $j = 1$, plus five loops, each of $j = 2$. No jobs are created or destroyed in this example since there are no blank stretches in the columns.

Exclude the rare events, when a man returns to a job for a second tenure. Then a given letter appears in at most one continuous block of cells in a given column of the array. If all tenures were a year in length, an array would be isomorphic to a Latin rectangle, except for certain boundary effects. However, the two "outside" columns used to keep track of entries and exits of men have no analogue in the Latin rectangle. In addition, jobs may be vacant for a year or terminated or not yet founded, whereas every cell in a Latin rectangle contains a letter.

Latin rectangles and tenure arrays are similar enough for results concerning one to guide analysis of the other. Chains and paths have not been considered in work on Latin rectangles, but a great deal is known about the number of distinct Latin rectangles of given sizes. Distinctness can be defined at several levels. If one rectangle can be converted into another simply by repeated exchanges of names (of men, jobs, and years) they are isomorphic, and it is reasonable to say they have the same structure. In the analysis of tenure networks too, one would not wish to distinguish arrays which differed only in names of individuals. A still less restrictive definition of distinctness, called isotopy, is used for Latin rectangles and might be suggestive for tenure networks.

Algebraic analyses of tenure arrays will be more useful than counts of arrays, important though the latter may be for establishing chance expectations. The main problem is developing generalized measures of inbreeding in the system as a whole. This is analogous, in part, to the problem of discerning what prescriptive rules of marriage and descent, if any, underly observed genealogies. Job lines could be regarded as analogous to descent lines, and careers, to marriage cycles. The data for tenure arrays is simpler than for kinship as long as only 1–1 jobs are studied, but one is less likely to find simple and clear-cut clusterings of nodes and ties into equivalence classes guided by explicit norms. Recent work by J. P. Boyd suggests how to formulate such clusterings in terms of homomorphisms on a semigroup generated by two binary relations, in his case, the graph of marriage ties and the graph of descent ties on a given population.[8] Extinction and creation of men and jobs, as of men and women, requires adjoining a zero operator to such a semigroup.

Many other algebraic approaches may be relevant, and there are other partial analogues to tenure arrays. It might be possible to infer partial orders among men or jobs or both and clusterings of men within such partial orders, using techniques suggested by M. F. Friedell in recent work on models of authority structures as semilattices.[9]

This chapter like the last has been exploratory and will receive little attention in the concluding chapter. The main point to be made is that stratified models of vacancy chains cannot be the full explanation of mobility patterns, however well they work at a gross level. A major effort will be required to develop and apply more detailed frameworks for looking at interactions of individual candidacies and at involution in tenure networks resulting from constraints on knowledge and from personal ties among men. In the end, there may prove to be disjunct levels of coupling within a social system as reflected in mobility of men among jobs. Vacancy models reflect short-term coupling caused by logical constraints on opportunity. Constrained within accurate predictions from stratified models for independent vacancies may be localized interaction among candidacies of particular men at a given time. Ascribed characteristics quite independent of current job may shape the result of those localized interactions. Perhaps most interesting for the theory of social structure is that there may also be long-term coupling of the moves of particular sets and neighborhoods of men, not in terms of particular earmarked jobs but in terms of similarities across job lines and careers of each set of men.

Chapter 13
Use and Meaning of Vacancy Models

"We have to deplore the many changes that have occurred, and that are perpetually occurring among our clergy. Partly, it is owing to want of liberal maintenance on the part of parishes, partly owing to the uneasiness of the clergy themselves, and partly to the novelties that disturb our peace. The effect is serious, beyond our estimate: unfortunate to the clergy who change, or are changed, and detrimental to the prosperity of the Church, as hindering many from seeking the privileges they might profit by."

—*Manton Eastburn, Bishop of Massachusetts, from his summary statement on the State of the Church, to the General Convention of the Protestant Episcopal Church in the United States, page 441, Appendix I,* Journal, *1871.*

A new perspective is required by vacancy models. Personnel managers and operations analysts may think of optimum assignments for a pack of IBM cards—the company's men—among slots in the organization table.[1] Each man may scheme and gossip about building a career, getting ahead through credentials, "know-how," and "know-who." A system evolves by its own logic, neither controlled by putative central authorities nor amenable to manipulation by its members. Even the boundaries for a system of interrelated men and jobs evolve, much of the time, out of sight and control, although they are recognized from time to time in reorganizations, mergers, splits, formation of professional societies, creation of specialized journals, and the like.

New principles emerge from that new perspective, but there is no need to assume a new level of social reality and no need for a Durkheimian concept of a social reality *sui generis*. Interaction among local events in a system of matched entities is the reality to be understood. Each immediate linkage is transparent and well understood in everyday life.[2] The problem is the ways the immediate linkages cumulate into longer chains of cause and effect. Mobility is neither a simple addition of local events nor the combination of men's careers. It is the dynamics of local disturbances, their creation, movement, and demise—disturbances defined in terms of dual entities: men and jobs.

13. Meaning of Vacancy Models

Individuals can learn from the new perspective what degrees of freedom remain to them within the overall system and avoid failure from strivings in terms of unreal folk pictures. Men with some measure of power may come to grips better with the endless search for arrangements more broadly satisfying. The networks of contingencies spread so widely that arrangements optimum in all aspects are a dream, but change that is constructive in its overall results, not just its immediate targets, is possible. There is no reason to continue echoing either the sterile cry of Bishop Eastburn that mobility is too much with us or the simplistic alternatives to this cry.

13.1 Fields for Application

Men and jobs are not the only dual entities constituting matching systems of interest in social science.[3] Chains of moves by families among houses, reminiscent of vacancy chains, were reported by F. S. Kristof in 1956.[4] A survey of moves set off by occupancy of new housing units has been completed at the Survey Research Center of the University of Michigan. One of the research team, C. W. Clifton, is developing a theory of the housing market resembling the generalized form of the vacancy model in Chapter 10.[5]

There may well be work on other analogues of vacancy chains in the literature or in process.[6] A little thought or perusal of newspapers suggests a variety of possibilities.[7] Jobs, as a category, could be replaced by offices in formal organizations—political parties,[8] honorary societies, and so on. Changes in rankings, such as seedings in tennis, could also be interpreted in terms of opportunity chains of various kinds. Considerable modifications would be required in the particular models suggested here to adapt them to such new contexts. Various generalizations of the abstract idea of vacancy chains, relaxing the assumptions about 1–1 matching, have already been sketched in Sections 7.8 and 8.6.

The vacancy models of Chapters 2, 7, and 10 should be applicable to a wide variety of systems of men and jobs. Specific definitions of strata must be developed anew in each case, as in Chapter 4; but Chapter 6 suggests it may be possible to use general guidelines transferable from one case to another. Similarly, the logic of differentiating pool and limbo as special marginal statuses outside the system proper may be quite widely applicable.[9]

318

J. Kahl suggested in 1957 that the mobility effects of technological change in a national economy could only be understood in terms of chains of replacements, each step corresponding to a modest upgrading in skill.[10] The present work was stimulated in part by this suggestion, which Kahl attempted to support by a hazardous procedure of subtracting known causes of intergenerational mobility from observed total amounts.[11] To adapt vacancy models for a national economy, considerable changes would be needed;[12] but, as suggested in Section 9.7, the basic ideas should carry over. A multiplier matrix would formalize and elaborate Kahl's idea about the multiplicative effect of novel jobs and at the same time extend it to include all new jobs plus deaths, and so on. Demography would control the entry of new persons into the job-holding ages, but the actual entry of persons into jobs would be treated as a process dependent on calls to vacancies. The author would anticipate that even the numerical values of transition probabilities for clergies, which encompass the whole career of most ministers, could be a reasonable approximation for a national system of jobs grouped in a few broad strata. Sections 7.3, 7.5, and 7.6 suggest how sensitive expansion and contraction of the job system would be to variations in the flow of new jobs.

Private corporations present a considerable challenge for vacancy models since little information on personnel is published systematically and the records are regarded as confidential. As in the study of housing markets, it will probably be necessary to trace vacancy chains directly using a national interviewing staff. Few companies, except the largest, will constitute apt choices for system boundaries. Better choices may be a set of people in a specialized role—accountants or plastics engineers—or in a more general role but within a specific industry or product line—sales managers for heavy electrical equipment. It may well prove advantageous to develop special functional strata of jobs which serve as entry ports, terminal jobs, and so on. Salaries should be more closely related to transition probabilities than in the case of clergies, and it might prove possible to relate differences between transition matrices as a whole to differences in the overall structure of salaries as reflected in Gini indices or other measures of size distribution.[13] New light may be cast on existing discussions of career structures for "middle management."[14] The high incidence of geographical shuffling of managers, within companies as well as during changes of employers, may be a by-product of pressures from vacancy chains running through compartment-alized systems.

The specialized techniques for tracing chains developed in Chapter 3 and in the Appendices will be applicable only for government or quasi-governmental bureaucracies that publish regular reports of assignments. Two advantages to those techniques are low cost and accessibility of the same data for checking by other analysts. Histori-cal scope is the great advantage in using the natural, self-generated data. There is little other possibility for building long time series, for comparing mobility dynamics in say 1900, 1930, and 1960.

Vacancy chains have been traced, using year-by-year inference from registers, for a variety of governmental units:[15] French Minis-try of Finances regional offices; British colonial and diplomatic services; Tenured members of English universities; U.S. Coast Guard; U.S. Forest Service;[16] Atomic Energy Commission; U.S. Foreign Service; Tennessee Valley Authority; U.S. Veterans Ad-ministration; U.S. Civil Service Interagency Finance officers. There appear to be few obstacles to the straightforward application of vacancy models in most of these cases. It would be especially inter-esting to apply vacancy models to the higher reaches of the British Civil Service, where careers have been examined with meticulous care by R. K. Kelsall.[17]

Comparative analysis of a large number of clergies, in the United States and in Europe, is the most obvious extension of the results reported earlier. Chains have been traced in more than a score of churches without encountering serious obstacles.[18] To establish vacancy models as an approach with wide relevance, however, it is essential to go beyond one class of organizations. Clergies, especially Protestant ones, may correspond only to special types of business or government organizations, such as a system of automobile dealers, a network of restaurants franchised under a special name, or some other arrangement of subcontracting. New, more abstract typologies of organizations as systems will be needed to discriminate classes of organization with different logics of mobility.[19]

13.2 Heuristics

Qualitative ideas and heuristics are important products of models, in addition to precise applications to particular systems. Even when the models fail, a new perspective on measurement remains. Chains record the passage of disturbances and thus information through a system at a given time. Length of chain from endpoint to a given job is a measure of the status of that job. Variance in chain lengths can be a measure of degree of hierarchization.

A system without deaths and new jobs is frozen, unable, according to the vacancy models, to provide normal circulation of men to more compatible jobs. A continuing influx of new jobs and abandonment of existing ones is an essential component of circulation, according to Chapter 7, and a requisite for simply maintaining the system. Demographic constraints ensure less flexibility in separation rates of men than creation rates of jobs, and the latter are likely to carry the brunt of attempts at control. Changes of retirement age and the like are not made easily even when bulges in age distributions resulting from rapid growth in earlier periods produce great pressures.[20] Retirements from and creation of high-status jobs are important not only directly, because of the greater power in such positions, but also obliquely, because of the longer trains of moves set off. Yet moves might be even more frequent in an egalitarian system wherein men accepted opportunities by whim undisciplined by a common perception of what is "advantageous."

The multiplier matrix relates moves quantitatively to boundary events. Once transition probability matrices for a range of periods and systems with comparable strata are available, variation of the multiplier with changes in the general environment could be investigated. An obvious beginning point is the termination probability for the lowest stratum, corresponding to the main input of new entrants to the system. Ease of recruitment, and thus indirectly the probability of terminating a vacancy chain with a recruit, will be tied to the level of salaries and other factors in the environment. Variations in the multiplier matrix with small changes in a transition probability can be derived and then, perhaps, a simple relation to variations in environmental factors uncovered. Prediction of transition probabilities from first principles appears much more difficult. Interaction among overlapping negotiations must be considered as well as the criteria used in a given negotiation between candidate and vacant job.

Some manipulation may be possible even with fixed transition probabilities and fixed schedules for retirements and new jobs. Pool jobs and limbo statuses are not subject to the same constraints as are the basic 1–1 jobs. A hard-pressed executive can create new chains by shifting men to flexible positions. Conversely, he can terminate chains by then calling such men back into regular jobs. The scope of manipulation is limited to delays and anticipations unless there are secular trends in the proportion of flexible jobs. Perhaps the burgeoning of staff jobs in industry is an example of the latter. Some fraction of these flexible advisory positions become institutionalized as 1–1 jobs but many remain floating, exposed to rapid elimination. The high levels of mobility found in recent decades among men in "line" jobs at middle levels might be subject to a surprisingly rapid decline if the proliferation of staff positions were to cease.[21]

Change is the norm within organizations if only because they must respond year by year to erratic fluctuations of transactions in men and jobs with the environment. Time spans are better reckoned in the duration of vacancy chains than in the duration of careers. Men last longer as stable entities than do systems. A perceptual framework accounts for much of the continuity attributed to organizations. Our culture provides flexible ways to endlessly recast selected events after the fact. We tend to capitalize on the accidental. We also try to maintain traditions and create trends by social fictions. The same rewriting of history goes on at the individual level. A career is often given an orderly interpretation in terms of the background and motives of a few individuals, rather than as a chaotic by-product of the path of a large system.

13.3 Models of Mobility Compared

Choice between alternatives for each of eighteen postulates about the system studied can differentiate among the main mobility models surveyed in this work. The formulation is such that six of the choices can be made independently of one another, the remainder being more specialized choices contingent on a positive choice on one of these six. Positive choice means that choice made in the Markov chain model of vacancy chains; the negative choice is formulated so that each of the models falls on one side or the other of each dichotomy (where it is applicable). Twelve models in four main groups are reported in Table 13.1. A negative choice on a given postulate for a given model (or inapplicability when choice was negative on a logically prior dichotomy) is indicated by an × in that cell and a positive choice, by no entry.

Table 13.1 Combinations of Postulates in Various Mobility Models[a]

marriage (8.4)	economic (8.1)	demographic (9.2)	stratified turnover (2.7, 9.3)	a.f.: with retirement (7.5)	a.f.: strata (7.4)	aggregate flows: binomial (7.1)	vacancy chains with rules (9.1)	combinatorial (11.4)	bump chain (1.4, 7.2, 10.3)	binomial v.c. (2.1)	stratified vacancy chain (2.2, 7.7, 10.2)	Postulates:
	×											1. bounded (infinite)[b]
		×										2. open (closed)
	×	×	×	×								3. exogenous input (dependent)
×												4. dependent output (exogenous)
						×				×		5. with localities (undifferentiated)
	×											6. with internal flows (without)
×	×							×				7. linear (interactive)
	×		×	×								8. dependent on current state (historical effects)
	×							×				9. constant rate parameters (fluctuating rates)
	×		×	×	×	×	×					10. stochastic process (deterministic)
	×		×	×	×							11. for discrete units (for continuous variables)
	×		×	×	×							12. distinguishable (indistinguishable)
		×	×									13. with contents of two kinds (with contents of one kind)
	×	×	×									14. with matching (indefinite)
×	×	×	×				×					15. surplus in only one kind (surplus in either)
×	×	×	×						×			16. jobs (men)
	×	×	×									17. any external flows in surplus only (also in matches)
	×	×	×									18. any internal flows in surplus only (also in matches)

[a] Markov model for vacancy chains used as the standard. In the cell from the column for a postulate and the row for a model: no entry = postulate as stated; × = opposite form, stated in parentheses.

[b] Negative choice in parentheses.

[c] Section numbers refer to the text where model is described.

13. Meaning of Vacancy Models

The empirical meaning of the same choice on a given postulate can be very different in two models from different rows of the table. The subject of one postulate pair is affected by what choice is made on another pair, even though any combination of choices on the two pairs is possible. In the turnover models, the lack of interaction within internal flows (postulate 7) means men move independently. Men's moves interact strongly according to the vacancy models, but the same choice is made on postulate 7 because the internal flows consist of vacancies rather than men, by the choice on postulate 18. Vacancies can move independently of one another even though men's moves interact because in the vacancy model only moves by the set of men in a given vacancy chain are assumed to interact.

The postulates are informal statements that cannot yield a rigorous formulation of a model. A brief tag is used to identify each postulate in the table. Longer descriptions, which can be filled out by reference to the main text, follow (with description of the negative choice set off in parentheses).

1. The system is bounded. (There is no definite limit to the contents of the system.)
2. The system is open. (The system is closed.)
   If open:
   3. flows into the system are exogenous, independent of the state of the system (flows in are endogenous)
   4. flows out of the system are dependent on the system's state (flows out are exogenous)
5. Localities are distinguished within the system, which may be a set of categories or ordered strata or locations in a network, etc. (The system is not differentiated.)
6. Movement inside the system is possible—it need not necessarily be defined in terms of locality. (There is no internal movement.)
   If movement inside is possible:
   7. flows are linear; that is, one part of the flow does not interact with other parts (there is interaction within the flows)
   8. the amount of movement is determined solely by the present state of the system (there are historical effects—time lag terms in the equations)

324

9. the parameters that appear in rates of flow are constant—whether or not the flows are linear (rate parameters fluctuate)

10. movement is a stochastic process (movement is a deterministic process)

11. Contents of the system are discrete units. (The contents are described by continuous variables.)
    If discrete:

12. units are distinguishable individuals (units are identical and indistinguishable)

13. Contents are of two kinds—whether or not localities are distinguished. (The contents are of one kind.)
    If of two kinds:

14. there is matching between the two kinds according to fixed criteria, within all localities, and therefore a definition of surplus (matching may exist but not with fixed criteria)
    If there is matching:

15. only one kind may be in surplus at any time (either or both kinds may be in surplus)
    If only one kind in surplus:

16. jobs (men)

17. any flows into or out of the system must constitute flows of surplus (simultaneous matched flows of the two kinds of content in the same direction are permitted into or out of the system)

18. only surplus can be free to move within the system and any moves of the two kinds of contents must constitute a flow of surplus (simultaneous, matched flows of the two kinds of content are permitted)

One important empirical difference between vacancy models (the first two groups of rows in Table 13.1) and the other models of mobility does not emerge clearly from the comparison by this list of postulates. All vacancies move often, specifically with spacings of the order of months. Some men in turnover or marriage models do not move for years. Vacancies, unlike men, cannot remain still because, by the definition of the system, surpluses are disturbances in equilibrium.

13. Meaning of Vacancy Models

A given row of postulate choices in the table will be satisfied by many variants of the particular model indicated in the stub. Like the stratified vacancy chain model, the fixed roster model of Section 7.8 assumes the positive form of each of the sixteen postulates in the table: although matching is not 1–1, it is fixed; although vacancies are no longer distinguishable from one another, jobs (and men) still are (postulate 12). Of course, models using different bases of stratification, such as those in Chapter 6, look the same in the table.

Only a few of the models treated in the text cannot be effectively described in the particular framework of postulates used in the table. The Holt-David model of Section 8.3, for example, is a hybrid between the marriage model (for matchmaking between vacant jobs and unemployed workers) and the economic model (for formation of a demand schedule for labor and thence net new vacancies). Jobs are distinct entities when first created but thereafter are merged into the continuous variable of demand for labor. Unemployed men and men departing the system are distinct entities, but employed men are not. The economic model itself does not deal with a system with an interior and so is defined only residually in terms of this set of postulates.

Auxiliary assumptions of a more purely technical character are not given a place among the postulates in the table. Treatment of time as a discrete variable is not differentiated from its treatment as a continuous variable. More generally it should be clear that mathematical style and complexity have little to do with the essential nature of a model. More often than not technical elaboration of a model is a blind alley that distracts attention from the main theoretical issues.

The same models of mobility can be compared in kinds of predictions possible. All yield some form of prediction of mobility rates for men. In addition there are some kinds of prediction distinctive to each group of models.

Vacancy models

Current amounts of internal movement are predicted from current sizes of a compound stream of transactions with the environment, namely, deaths of men plus births of jobs. New jobs create mobility rather than mobility calling forth new jobs as in turnover models. Parameters estimated from the data enter the prediction formula after a nonlinear transformation, as the multiplier matrix, the inverse matrix $(I - Q)^{-1}$. Instead of careers of men, the natural subject of prediction at an individual level is careers of vacancies, since vacancies, but not men or jobs, move freely within the system. In the *aggregate flow versions*, the natural topic for prediction is the evolution of system size in men and in jobs.

Models for turnover of men

Long-term turnover of men among occupational categories is the distinctive prediction. Men choose freely when and where to move. Flows of men are divorced from flows of jobs, and internal flows are divorced from flows to and from the environment of the system.

Economic and marriage models

Sizes of pools of men and jobs available for matching are the distinctive topic for prediction in the latter. Terms of trade in the matching of men to jobs are the distinctive prediction in the former, where the system is not bounded.

13.4 Higher Order Principles in Vacancy Models

Duality between men and jobs in a system is one higher order principle relevant to vacancy models. Duality means invariances in models of social structure and process under the interchange of men and jobs. In the models of vacancy flows duality is partial, since only jobs can be in excess. Duality there takes the form of symmetry between two alternative forms of flow, vacancy chains and bump chains (see Section 10.3). There is no explicit formulation of causal processes in time when the system is described as a tenure network (Chapter 12), but its structure is invariant under interchange of men and jobs.

Causality is another higher order principle which guided the construction of vacancy models. Vacancies are temporary local disturbances in matching, stipulated to be from an excess of jobs over men. Vacancies are thus a special case of the concept of disturbance in equilibrium. Vacancy chains are the tracks of movements by these local disturbances. Constant motion by the vacancies is axiomatic, enforced by the definition of inclusion in the system. Recruitment of men and abolition of jobs are assumed to be processes dependent on, in fact proportional to, the number of vacancies. Together they constitute the extinction process for vacancies and set the limits of causality. Creation of jobs and departures of men, which together add up to the creation of vacancies, are treated as the independent exogenous events that introduce disturbances. These exogenous events are the ultimate cause of mobility.

Causality is not a principle distinctive to vacancy models. All the models in Table 13.1 embody an explicit causal mechanism. Distinctive to vacancy models is a principle of contingency: events in one locale in a system are linked in chains of cause and effect to events in other locales, chains which are of short duration in time. That principle of contingency assumes both the earlier principles of duality and causality but adds to them a principle of equilibrium and a set of localized constraints in social structure. In vacancy models those constraints are of a very simple kind: exclusion of men from the system who are not in 1–1 matches (tenures) with jobs. The principle of equilibrium is familiar: the system will, in the absence of independent influences from the environment, move toward a state of equilibrium.

Causality, duality, equilibrium seeking, and exogenous flows from the environment can each be found in one or more of the other mobility models. Vacancy models are distinctive in a particular combination of these principles into the principle of contingency. Contingency in turn rests on the existence of local constraints in social structure. The core idea behind vacancy models is the need to trace social processes at a microscopic level of social structure to obtain valid causal theory.

13.5 Open Problems

Jobs have been taken as given. Their existence as stable entities in social structure (independent of, although complementary to, incumbents) is one open problem. Intertwined with it is the problem of system cohesion. Subsets of jobs and men within recognized organizations (clergies) constituted the systems in this book. Membership in these subsets was defined so as to justify the postulates about matching and movements. The models would be more cogent, particularly the postulates about constant transition probabilities for vacancies, if membership could be defined on criteria independent of matching and movement.

Jobs serve as static foci in a system with structured networks of ties which define interlocking duties and expectations of various incumbents. Neither jobs nor ties can be defined in isolation from one another. That is one kind of complementarity. A second kind is the complementarity between prescription on the one hand, in job and in tie, and realization on the other, in particular men as incumbents and in repetitive relations among particular men. A pair of concepts such as role and position cannot encompass both complementarities.

A third kind of complementarity is that between microsystem and macrosystem. Concepts such as role have little empirical relevance when referred to a pair or trio in isolation from an overall system. A given kind of role or a given kind of tie cannot be seen merely as a certain kind of contact repeated within one pair. A given role or tie is also a pattern of connections between numerous pairs in a whole population. Complementarity also figures in structures of ties and relations. Balance theory is the simplest example. The pattern formed by ties of one kind implies constraints on allowable configurations for ties of other kinds, both in a particular locale and across the whole system.

None of those concepts can be understood apart from mobility of men and changes in relations, unavoidable because of mortality and commonly far greater than the demographic minimums. One aspect is the ancient problem of descent, that is, of mechanisms for assimilating new humans into the social identities of predecessors. Descent can rarely be direct from a dying to a newborn human; no matter what the mechanism, demographic variability will confound any replacement of so orderly a kind. Reshufflings of many men and positions are needed to fill in after a death or open up after a birth— of a position as well as of a man.

Models of mobility are thus essential to the foundations of the theory of social structure. Vacancy chains are a reminder of the third kind of complementarity, and the stratified models identify those aspects of gross mobility which reflect structure in the system. Tenure networks provide, in the case of systems for 1–1 jobs, a framework within which the first two complementarities may be treated.

Jobs are only a special case of positions in social structure. One plausible hypothesis is that a structure of positions emerges as the skeleton deposited by, that is the residue in cultural terms from, repetitive enactment of orderly networks of relations among men.

That residue cannot reflect every detail of various networks of relations across a population, but it must reflect indirect interconnections among men implied by maps of manifest direct relations. Therefore, the residue must concern some kind of reduction of types of relations, direct and indirect, to some core of essential classes of ties among sets of men, when men in each set are essentially equivalent in their relations to men in any other such set. In technical language, homomorphic images of relation mappings on a population may constitute the essential skeleton of social processes, and the complementary equivalence sets of men may be the essential actors in social process.[22] It is reasonable to suppose the latter may be the genesis of social positions, including jobs. Only in Section 8.6 and Chapter 12 are these ideas broached. There is much to do and little guidance in the literature, with the notable exception of *The Theory of Social Structure* (New York, 1957) by S. F. Nadel. He understood enough to be baffled by the problem of even defining social structure. It is with one of his suggestions, that of defining structure indirectly through the analysis of recruitment patterns, that the current book is consonant.

Glossary of Major Symbols

Predictions for Vacancy Chains

j = length of a vacancy chain: number of moves by a vacancy from 1–1 jobs, including the terminal move outside the system

s = number of strata

$\mathbf{P}_j$ = by stratum of arrival, the probability a vacancy will trace a chain of length j while in the system

λ = by stratum of arrival, the mean length of chain

$j(t)$ = overall mean length in a cohort of chains

Vacancy Models (strata defined by jobs)

Flow vectors

Creation of vacancies:
$\mathbf{F}$—(per year)
$\mathbf{F}_{job}$: in new jobs
$\mathbf{F}_{man}$: by departure of men from system
$\mathbf{f}$ gives $\mathbf{F}$ as proportions

Total moves by vacancies:
$\mathbf{M}$—(per year)

Size vectors
(state variables)
$\mathbf{J}$ = jobs
$\mathbf{N}$ = men
$\mathbf{V}$ = vacancies

Turnover matrices B

Parameters
$s \times s$ matrix of transition probabilities in Markov chain for internal moves:
$Q : [q_{ij}]$
(When $s = 1$, reduces to a single fraction, q. Termination probabilities adjoined as q_{io}, or when $s = 1$ as p.)

Glossary of Major Symbols

Matrix of termination probabilities:

$P = $ diagonal matrix
P_{job}: in ended jobs
P_{man}: in new recruits

Retirement rates: R: a diagonal matrix, component ρ_i

Number of waves of moves per year: v

Sampling Frames

k, k', K: number of exposures of a vacancy chain to entry in certain types of national random sample of moves by men

D, D', D'': number of exposures of a vacancy chain in types of local inventories for vacancy chains which cross a given diocese

Observed Vacancy Chains

J_c = mean length of chains in a sample after weighting

J_m = length of chain in which the average move in a weighted sample is found

N_w = number of chains in a set after weighting in the frame symbolized by w

$a_{ij}(t)$ = the number of moves of vacancies from stratum i to stratum j for the cohort of year t; if the count is from a sample of vacancy chains weights are used; terminations are included as moves to stratum zero

Careers

χ = length of a man's career in 1–1 jobs

C_χ = by stratum of recruitment, the probability distribution of χ

Combinatorial Models

I = measure of interaction among vacancies based on counts of allocations

SDR = system of distinct representatives

c_i = number of candidacies for vacancy i
n^* = effective size of neighborhood
d = annual number of deaths in a neighborhood

Tenure Networks

(d, E) = the tenure defined by incumbency of man E in job d

Conventions

I = identity matrix
1 = column vector with each element unity
(i, h) = dummy indices identifying strata

Appendix A
Details of Coding Rules and Sources

The main task in this appendix will be to distinguish 1–1 jobs, pool jobs, and limbo statuses in each of the three churches used for the study. The first distinction determines the length of the chains, while differences in terminal events corresponding to the second distinction may clarify the causes of chain formation and chain ending. In stricter terms, it is tenures, not empty jobs or jobs in the abstract, that are being classified. Very brief tenures are ignored, even though they may be recorded in individual local journals, since they do not appear in national reports. The basic references for each church are the national annual reports.

A.1 Protestant Episcopal Church in the United States

The main reference for tenures in the Episcopal case is the *Episcopal Church Annual*, a semiofficial but highly reliable national compendium of information, gleaned not only from the official diocesan journals but also from a variety of regular, direct reports by various church officials to the editor. Before 1953, the *Episcopal Church Annual* was called *The Living Church Annual*, and under that title it absorbed several competitors. The *Churchman's Almanac* was published from 1830 to 1922, when it amalgamated with the *Churchman's Annual*, but no data have been taken from it. More important, until its absorption by the annual in 1909, was *Whittaker's Churchman's Almanac* (previously called the *Protestant Episcopal Annual and Directory* but still published by Whittaker), from which all data before 1909 have been taken for this study.

The second main reference is the *Triennial Clerical Directory*, which is an official publication based on the biographical information supplied by individual clergy. The entries are often fragmentary; even where they seem complete, there is a tendency to omit mention of minor jobs or of periods in limbo. Actual periods in major jobs as shown in entries in the annual report are often extended to account for these omitted periods. The job listings in the annual were therefore taken as definitive. It was possible to compensate for one weakness in the indexing of the data in the annual by the use of the directory. A priest who held an extra-diocesan job as a chaplain, national administrator, or so on, was not indexed by that job, and it often was not referred to after his name in the "nonparochial clergy" section of the diocesan list. The date of ordination to the diaconate was also obtained from the clerical directory. (The title has been *Stowe's Clerical*

Directory until recently and was *Lloyd's Directory* before 1917, but there have never been competing directories.)

The *Journal of the General Convention*, official report of the triennial national legislative meetings, was used when the other sources were incomplete. The journal contains the official list of ordinations and a necrology as appendices. These lists are inconveniently arranged for the nineteenth century, and two special tabulations were helpful there: E. H. Downing, comp., *List of Persons Ordained Deacons in the Protestant Episcopal Church, 1858 to 1885* (New York: Whittaker, 1886); Right Reverend George Burgess, *List of Persons Admitted to the Order of Deacons in the Protestant Episcopal Church in the United States of America, from A.D. 1785 to A.D. 1857, Both Inclusive* (Boston: A. William & Co., 1874). The general convention journal also contains the official canons of the church, which define various ecclesiastical terms of importance in tracing vacancy chains; various annotated editions of the canons have been published that are even more helpful in this regard.

One-to-one jobs

A 1–1 job is one in which the replacement of one priest by another can be traced.

Rector

Well over half the priests have the job of rector of a named permanent local church. There is at most one incumbent, and normally the job is kept continuously filled. This is the basic "line" job in the church, and the idea of a vacancy chain is most naturally applicable to it.

1. The first name listed after the church in the diocesan list in an annual is the rector. In earlier annuals, the rector's status is denoted by the abbreviation *r.*, but in later years this is usually omitted. Various other titles are used to specify the man in charge of a church; but for the purposes of coding vacancy chains, they are treated as identical. (Some of those other titles are vicar, priest-in-charge, incumbent, dean, minister.) In the Anglican church, names such as "vicar" originally had a restricted, well-defined meaning; such variation in title is now arbitrary, depending on local custom.

2. In some, mainly Southern, dioceses, individual churches are grouped into "parishes," usually on the basis of a geographical unit such as a county. The best known urban example is Trinity parish in New York; as many as ten individual churches (called chapels) and two dozen clergy have been listed under it. A common charter and large endowments encourage the continued existence of such joint urban parishes. In joint parishes, the incumbents in constituent churches are listed separately, and since these men move separately they are rectors for mobility purposes.

3. Churches differ not only in size but also in legal status. Some are

A. Coding Rules and Sources

"parishes in union with the diocesan convention," which normally means that they are fully self-supporting and of some years standing. However, some old, decaying churches retain that status even though they receive funds from the diocese. Other churches are parishes but not in union. Still others are organized missions, and there are occasional unorganized missions. The latter at least do not normally have a church building (even old and well-to-do parishes may not have a rectory, much less parish halls and other subsidiary buildings). The main distinction of relevance here is that the bishop has authority to appoint ministers to missions, and their vestries have correspondingly less power and autonomy (in addition they usually have fewer members and officers). In the diocesan list in the annual, however, churches are not categorized this way. In reality, the bishop's authority is neither as great as his formal authority in missions nor as little as his formal authority in "parishes in union." The balance depends on personalities, local circumstances, potential for growth, actual money raised, and so on. Hence each church in the diocesan list is treated on an equal basis in coding.

4. It is common for a set of small churches in a diocese (almost never in different dioceses) to be held by the same man. Those are the compound jobs discussed in Section 3.2. (In a few dioceses, mainly in South Dakota, mission churches to American Indians are listed separately, often grouped into "missions." Those jobs are clearly not comparable with normal churches. Some of the incumbents are Indian priests, in practice ineligible for other jobs. Job incumbencies are very fluid, and those jobs are uniformly coded as pool jobs. If such a priest holds a white as well as an Indian church however, the job is coded as 1–1.)

5. Churches marked as summer chapels are not counted as 1–1 jobs. When those are a man's only listed job, they are treated as a limbo status. Chapels attached to institutions (hospitals, schools, and so on) are not treated as churches. Usually, numbers of communicants are not given for them, and the incumbent is treated as in a 1–1 job only when he holds additional posts. Churches that minister to the deaf are in the diocesan lists as well as in a separate section of the annual. Ministers move in and out of this special field, and it is included as a regular 1–1 job.

6. The most difficult case is "colored" churches. In the past, many northern as well as most southern dioceses designated some churches as "colored" (in parentheses). The practice is not uniform however. In other areas, the use of an African saint's name usually, but not uniformly, designates a colored church. An official survey of "Negro work" was made in 1938, reported in Appendix XXIII to the *Journal of the General Convention*, 1940. At that time, there were 259 colored parishes, only 20 percent self-supporting, with 50,000 Negro communicants. Of the 165 parishes that answered, 31 had white priests. The total number of priests involved is

small, and individual identification by color very difficult. It is clear that often the priest is a white man, and one who moves from and to other white churches. No distinction has been drawn between white and colored churches.

7. A temporary rector, usually designated as *locum tenens*, is treated as in a regular 1–1 job if he remains two years or more. During wars, for example, an incumbent rector who becomes a chaplain is usually kept as official rector but rarely returns to his old job. For all practical purposes, the "stand-in" has a stable rectorship once he stays more than a year.

Other principal jobs

1. *Bishops* The prototype for the bishop is the "ordinary" of an established domestic diocese, who is elected by concurrent vote of the lay house and the clerical house of that diocesan convention. Until the 1960s it was illegal for a bishop to "translate," that is, accept election to another diocese, and an incumbency is usually of long duration. Other classes of bishops have the same sacerdotal powers and, with one exception, are also coded as 1–1 jobs. Suffragan bishops are elected by the diocese to assist the ordinary. Missionary bishops, whether principal or suffragan, whether for domestic missionary districts (dioceses) or overseas, are elected by the triennial national House of Bishops. All those bishops can change jobs.

The coadjutor bishop is a suffragan elected with the right to succession. Except in the rare cases where he dies or retires first, he automatically succeeds his ordinary. That position is not coded as a 1–1 job but rather as a "temporary" limbo status between last job and entry to the ordinary's job. Usually the delay is only one or two years, and the vacancy chain started by retirement of an ordinary is traced around this limbo status through the last regular job of the coadjutor. If that were not done, there would be the misleading picture of a high-status resignation setting off a very short chain ending in a job-end (since any new coadjutor would not be elected for ten or twenty years). That is the one case when an event of a later year is regarded as the cause of movements in earlier years.

2. *Professors* Only one type of teaching role is considered central enough to a church career to be a 1–1 job: named, or otherwise stably defined, professorships in the official seminaries that train Episcopal priests.

3. *Institutional heads* The head or the chaplain of official secondary schools (listed by the diocese that supports them) are coded as 1–1 jobs, when a priest regularly fills the post in that era (period of about a decade). The same applies to deans of Episcopal seminaries and to the presidents of the few official Episcopal colleges. Other jobs, varying with period and diocese, such as head of the New York City Missionary Society or of officially recognized monasteries or nunneries, are coded as 1–1 by the same

logic. They are stable jobs from which one can move on to other regular jobs, and they are filled by one priest at a time.

4. *Archdeacons*   Archdeacons are officials who initiate, direct, and encourage the development of mission churches in a defined area of a diocese under the authority of the bishop. In most dioceses and most eras, they are stable, well-defined jobs. They are coded as 1–1 unless the position is temporary and associated with the rectorship of a large church.

5. *National administrative officials*   When normally held by priests, the position of executive secretary or other department heads of the National Council is coded as a 1–1 job.

6. *Chaplains*   Most chaplaincies are pool jobs. When men are readily available, such jobs are often filled by more than one man. The exceptions are chaplaincies in major, long-established institutions. Prestigious Episcopal secondary schools and hospitals provide the clearest examples. The Episcopal church has always emphasized work in colleges, and a list of colleges and their chaplains has long been given in the annual. In most cases, those men are simply rectors of churches near the campus and such entries are ignored. A college chaplain is coded as a 1–1 job only when the chaplaincy has a history as a stable, full-time job. In many cases, that means the job is included in the diocesan list of churches, often with a named "foundation" attached.

Assistantships

Distinguishing between assistant rectorships that are stable enough to be coded as 1–1 jobs and those that are not is the most difficult single coding task. Unfortunately, it does not seem reasonable to code them all as pool jobs. A variety of documentary sources, particularly official reports on personnel in the printed journals of the triennial legislative conferences of the national church, show that since 1920 provision of assistant rectors in large churches has become an accepted norm and a widespread national practice. When an incumbent leaves such a job, a replacement is sought as quickly and as consistently as for the rectorship of a medium-size church and more consistently than for a typical small church. If one classes all assistant rector jobs as pool jobs, then rectorships of small churches (not amalgamated into sizeable compound charges) should be coded in the same way. Lengths are reduced but not very significantly, since minor jobs usually occur not in the middle, but near the end of chains.

Variation in exact titles is arbitrary and (as with rectorships) is ignored except in the case of the diocesan cathedral, where titles like canon are treated as distinct types of assistantship when they are stable over several years. Depending on diocese, era, and bargaining whim, the assistant may be called an assistant, an associate, or a curate, to either a rector or a vicar, and so on. For example, an older man who no longer wants a parish may take over the same duties a young assistant might but be given a more dignified title.

In the count of sample entries who are stable in their jobs, no great care need be taken with assistantships. When a church is above the median in size for any decade, any sole assistant is counted as a 1–1 job. If the church has over 800 communicants and no more than two assistants, the latter are counted as being in 1–1 jobs. Beyond 1000 communicants, any stable assistants numbering no more than three are coded as being in 1–1 jobs.

When an assistant appears in a church above median in size for the first time in some years, a new job is coded if the assistantship is kept filled for the next three years by him or successors. Otherwise, the job is coded as pool. A converse rule defines endings for assistantships, and the same cutoff points for size as above are used when there are multiple assistantships. The important issue is when to trace a vacancy chain through changes of assistant rectors.

1. When there are two or more assistants at one time and two or more of them move between successive annuals, the jobs are coded as pool. Each move is coded as a terminal (either beginning or ending) event. By reference to details in the diocesan journal, one can sometimes establish which of two new men is a replacement for which of two departing men—by either precise dating or seniority and pay—and thus trace out two distinct chains. Such cases are rare, however, and it seems wiser to use only the official national annual in the coding, to avoid problems of incompatability in coverage between diocesan journals.

Usually, only one assistant at a church changes in a given year, and indeed most churches have at most one assistant. A complex set of criteria is needed to cover the various cases.

2. If one man is dropped and another man added to the list of assistants in a large church between two successive annuals so that the number of assistants is unchanged, a vacancy chain is traced through their replacement. (The order of assistants may be alphabetical or may reflect seniority.) In some sense this replacement may be not in a 1–1 job but rather in a fixed roster of jobs (see Section 7.8); nevertheless, it is treated as an event in a vacancy chain.

3. If a sole assistant is replaced in the succeeding annual by a sole assistant in a church above median in size, the job is considered 1–1, and the vacancy chain is traced through it.

4. The remaining possibilities arise when no replacement of an assistant is listed in the adjacent annual. If there is more than one assistant, a vacancy chain is not traced through an intervening one-year vacancy in the job, as it is for principal jobs (except for the staff of a cathedral with individual stable titles). The basis for inferring a replacement event seems too slim.

In a church with one assistant, the job is assumed to be stable through a one-year vacancy, and a chain is traced through it if:

a. for two successive annuals before and two after the change, the single assistant is stable, or
b. any change in those four annuals is an immediate replacement without a one-year vacancy, or
c. in bracketing the move over an eight-year period, there is one assistant except for one-year vacancy periods.

By these rules, an assistantship can never be coded as empty; when it is not treated as a 1–1 job it is considered a pool job.

Pool jobs

Pool jobs are jobs other than 1–1 jobs that are accepted as worthwhile in a priest's career. They are the kind of jobs a man does not hesitate to list in his biographical entry in Stowe's. Yet they are jobs which are disposable in the sense that they may be added to or left unfilled without seriously affecting the main tasks of the church as generally perceived by the clergy. Explicitly, pool jobs include:

1. acting as *locum tenens* in a rectorship for a year
2. any assistant job (in a church) not stable enough to be 1–1 or any director of Christian education in a local church
3. domestic missionaries not assigned to specific churches (for example, members of city missionary societies, American Indian missions, missionaries-at-large in domestic dioceses, and so on); all jobs except bishoprics in overseas missionary districts and dioceses, even when the man is stable rector of a particular church—Hawaii, Alaska, the Virgin Islands, and the Panama Canal Zone, but no others, are defined as domestic dioceses for this purpose. [The reason for that distinction are (1) there is no real institutional pressure to keep those jobs filled, even though they may formally be 1–1 jobs; (2) a man often stays in overseas missionary work for his whole career, thereby remaining outside the main mobility patterns; (3) in most cases, some language skills are needed that the typical Episcopal priest does not have; (4) the channels of information about job openings and men eligible for jobs in the United States tend to be more restricted overseas than locally.]
4. in official institutions, all chaplaincies that are not stable enough to be 1–1 but are listed in the annual—in particular those at schools, colleges, hospitals, monasteries and nunneries; all chaplains in the Armed Forces (listed in a separate section of the annual), since a bishop oversees their work and in collaboration with diocesan committees both helps in their selection and arranges for their return to

normal jobs; chaplaincies at large institutions—prisons or hospitals—that are not official Episcopal establishments

5. professorships (except named chairs) in Episcopal seminaries and teaching jobs in official Episcopal schools; students for Ph.D. degrees in church-related fields who are ordained priests, since they normally move on into deanships or professorships
6. official jobs with the National Council, except department heads; any officially approved job with an ecumenical organization; full-time administrative positions, other than those listed as 1–1, in large dioceses—executive secretary, director of Christian education.

Limbo and the definition of priesthood

Limbo is a residual category for priests. A definition of how one enters and leaves the Episcopal priesthood is needed to understand the limbo state. There are two ways of entering.

Ordainment

Usually, even in the nineteenth century, ordainment follows graduation from a seminary, in the twentieth century a postcollege seminary. The formal requirement is passage by the Board of Examining Chaplains in what is agreed to be one's home diocese. There is an elaborate series of steps and requirements, pertaining to reputation and character as well as scholarly ability and vocation, that precedes that event. It is sufficient for our purposes that ordination itself is a meticulously recorded canonical act. In each triennial report of the national legislative convention, the registrar gives a numbered list of all ordainments with date, place, and the bishop who performed the rite. There are two levels—first diaconate and then full priesthood—that must be separated by at least six months and are currently separated by no more than a year. There are very few men who remain perpetual deacons, and they are not counted as clergy, since they do not participate in normal mobility or hold regular jobs. For all other men, seniority is measured from the date of the diaconate, since they may and often do hold a parish job from that time, even though they do not hold the full sacerdotal powers of a priest. (A small fraction of men enter the priesthood from other vocations, usually professional or executive, at an age well beyond the usual range of 25 to 30.) By the canon law of the church, a man cannot be ordained unless there is a job for him; and almost without exception, a priest cannot start off in limbo.

No attempt is made to trace men through seminaries or through various preliminary sacerdotal steps such as candidate and postulant, although there are records of these steps in diocesan journals. For purposes of this study, a man is "born" when he becomes a deacon. (Women may not be ordained in the Episcopal church.)

A. Coding Rules and Sources

Lay readers are not ordained, although they are officially selected. They have only limited local powers. Sometimes they are listed in italics at churches otherwise vacant but mostly not; they are ignored in tracing chains. Their number is growing and conceivably in the future they might come to play a significant role in the actual running of the church.

Reception

Priests in the Roman Catholic church and in other national churches of the Anglican Communion have always been recognized as having legitimate Episcopal ordainment. If there is a job for such a man in an Episcopal diocese, the bishop may "receive" him into full clerical membership of the Episcopal church. An official list of receptions is published in each annual as well as in the triennial convention journal. Ministers of other Protestant denominations are frequently admitted into the Episcopal church, usually by a pro forma ordination that amounts to a reception. The relevant point here is that a man who is received retains (in the eyes of others) a large measure of his seniority as a clergyman when it comes to being placed in a job.

The ways to leave the ordained state are:

Death

A reliable although sometimes delayed necrology is published in each annual. An official list is given in each triennial convention journal.

Deposition

Deposition is usually voluntary and for reasons not affecting a man's moral character. Occasionally, such a deposed man is "restored" to the normal exercise of his priestly office and can take a job again. Complex doctrines and regulations surround these events; here the important point is that the events are clear-cut in time and are published regularly in the annuals.

Transfer

Transfer to another (usually Catholic) church is a third way of leaving the priesthood. That is the converse of the reception of entry, but it is much rarer. It is usually the return of an Anglican after a period of ministry in the Episcopal church.

It is useful to define general categories for the statuses or jobs held by priests in limbo. Almost all priests in limbo (as well as half or so of those in pool jobs) are listed in the annual under the all-embracing heading "non-parochial clergy" for their diocese, immediately following the main list of parishes and their associated clergy.

Special List of the House of Bishops (SHB)

In any large organization, some men simply get lost. The SHB in each annual lists those men whose whereabouts or activities are unknown or who for other technical reasons cannot be listed as canonically resident in a diocese.

Retired

A priest does not lose his ordination because he retires from jobs. Until recently there was no fixed retirement age for either bishops or clergy, although a mandatory pension scheme has been in effect since 1917. Even after the present mandatory retirement age of 72, a man can hold a job on a year-to-year basis under certain conditions. Those ambiguities about age of retirement, as well as those about retirement on health grounds, are such that limbo rather than complete removal from the system seems the most appropriate categorization. In short, men do re-enter jobs from retirement in more than negligible numbers, especially during wars.

Part-time work

Priests who "supply" Sunday services in scattered parishes on short-term bases have no regular parochial position, no employer to pay pension contributions, are of low professional status, and so on. The same applies to men who work only at summer chapels in resort areas. Priests do not leave jobs because they are attracted by part-time work; so it is reasonable to define it as limbo.

Unofficial jobs

Many priests hold perfectly worthy jobs, such as instructors in schools and colleges, as editors, and so on, which are outside the recognized framework of jobs in the system. They are considered in limbo because they are relatively unlikely to come back into a regular Episcopal job.

Unemployed

Especially in the last century (possibly because more clergy then had private incomes) a considerable number of clergy apparently held no jobs at all for long periods, although they were not in ill health or aged. Others take thoroughly secular jobs, although usually voluntary deposition follows soon after.

Other statuses

There are a whole range of committees at all levels of the church. The clergy consider committee memberships important enough to list in their biographical entries. Most of the committees are ephemeral or minor, but others such as the standing committee of a diocese have major impact in helping the bishop make decisions and set policy. Rectors are automatically members of the clerical house of the diocesan convention, which determines local policy and elects new bishops. It also elects clerical deputies to the triennial national convention, the supreme legislative authority in the church. No attempt is made to trace such memberships or positions, although it would probably be desirable in a definitive study of the causes and meaning of mobility, especially in relation to prestige (see Section 8.6).

Dioceses and jobs

The geographical grouping of jobs is well-defined. The basic unit is the diocese. Dioceses usually fall within state boundaries, but their numbers have expanded so that many states contain three or more dioceses. (It should be noted that their names are not always derived from the state name.) Each diocese is controlled by a single bishop, the ordinary.

According to the canons of the church, every priest is attached to a particular diocese. A man may not formally take up a new post in another diocese until he has been accepted by its bishop and released by the bishop of his former diocese. Lists of such transfers (not completely reliable) are published in diocesan journals. Men holding regional or national Episcopal posts are normally listed under the heading "nonparochial clergy" for their "home" diocese as well as under the institution in which they serve. (Military chaplains and chaplains to the deaf are in separate lists but with their home diocese stated.) Occasionally a man will hold office (usually for a short time or in a missionary district) in one diocese but retains his canonical attachment to another. This is always indicated by a footnote in the annual. The important points for this study are:

1. A priest never has a parochial job in more than one diocese. Thus even where he holds a compound parish, his incumbency can be unambiguously assigned to one diocese.

2. A priest in a pool job, and even in some 1–1 jobs in regional institutions or in the national administration, will not necessarily be attached in a substantively important way to any diocese, even though he will be "canonically resident" in a particular one.

3. Regulations and customs concerning transfer are such that in practice any priest with a legitimate job offer from a parish or other institution in the diocese can be sure of automatically obtaining a transfer. A bishop may occasionally exert influence against a man but not to the extent of refusing a transfer once the authorities decide to make a job offer.

4. A priest in limbo is to some degree the responsibility of his bishop, to whom he will look for help in finding a proper job. He can therefore be meaningfully assigned to the diocese where he is canonically resident.

A.2 Methodist Churches

Coding rules for the Methodist church will be mentioned only when they differ from the Episcopal church. The same outline used in Section A.1 is followed. "Conference" is substituted for "diocese" as the basic unit. The main data reported in the text, for national samples, is from the Northern branch of the Methodist Episcopal church before the 1940 merger; comments on other Methodist churches is confined to a paragraph at the end.

The main reference for tenures in the Methodist church is the official *Minutes of the Annual Conferences of the Methodist Episcopal Church*. There is one volume for conferences whose annual clergy meeting is in the Fall, and another for Spring conferences. Each volume contains a separate statistical section reporting size and financial data for each parish (called "Quarterly Conferences"). Definitions and regulations are taken from the official *Doctrines and Discipline of the Methodist Episcopal Church* for various years. Supplementary information, including biographical sketches of officials, comes from *The Methodist Year Book*. Also useful, although incomplete, is *Who's Who in Methodism* (Chicago: A. N. Marquis Company, 1952).

One-to-one jobs

   Minister

   4. Since the seat of a compound job is not explicitly listed, the largest congregation is treated as the seat in tracing compound chains, except that no move is coded for an incumbent who retains some part of the compound job after a split or merger. Only rarely are the constituent congregations in a tenure listed separately in the job list of the conference, but the entire list must be scanned to pick up these exceptional cases.

   7. When the minister's name opposite a job is in italics, he is usually still on probationary status ("received on trial"); the district superintendent, a subordinate of the bishop, may have made the official appointment. Such tenures may continue for years. Probationers are numerous, since the probationary period is often prolonged; they often hold sizeable jobs. The pattern of their movements is much like that for other ministers. These incumbencies are treated as valid tenures, and vacancy chains are traced through them.

   Other principal jobs

   1. Each bishop is elected by the General Conference, the national legislative body, and presides over several conferences. The exact assignment of bishops to conferences was obscured until the 1930s because of the ideology that they functioned as a collegial unit, each able to "travel" to any conference.

A. Coding Rules and Sources

4. District superintendents are the analogue to archdeacons. Jobs as professors, institutional heads, national administrative officials, and chaplains were not listed systematically in the minutes, either under particular conferences or in separate sections. Therefore it was impossible to trace chains through them. The casual treatment of these jobs justifies classifying them as pool.

Assistant jobs

Assistant rectorships are much less common in the Methodist than in the Episcopal church. Nonetheless the same rules are applied when appropriate.

Pool jobs

The principles and even the specific list of jobs for the Episcopal church apply here. A few additional jobs, such as field agent for a Methodist charity, can be added. The equivalent of the "nonparochial clergy" list for an Episcopal diocese, following the list of regular parishes, contains mostly men in pool jobs. The separate lists for various types of limbo are indicated below.

Limbo and the definition of priesthood

Ordainment

Reception on trial by a conference is the functional equivalent of the Episcopal diaconate, but it lasts longer and often coincides with much of the man's theological training. The latter is often a course of study under a conference board instead of formal seminary training. Admission-into-full-membership is the functional equivalent of ordainment as Episcopal priest. (The formal levels of the Methodist ministry are deacon and elder.)

Local preachers, usually men without higher education, are the analogue to the Episcopal lay reader. Some, called supply pastors, receive pay from time to time for leading small congregations.

Reception on credentials

Reception on credentials is possible from a number of other churches and from all other conferences.

The ways of leaving the ordained state in the Methodist church are much as in the Episcopal.

Death

A list of deaths in a conference, as of the other entry and exit events, is given in each year's minutes in answer to one of the traditional disciplinary questions, which provide the rubric for much of the minutes.

Expulsion and withdrawal

Expulsion and withdrawal are the nearest analogues to deposition, but ministers may also have their conference membership terminated by voluntary location, by involuntary location, or by discontinuance (for probationers). These actions, like ordainment and reception, are by the authority of the collegial body of ministers constituting a conference. The bishop may achieve much the same result by not assigning a job to a minister, in which case he becomes supernumerary.

Transfer

Transfer to another church is a special kind of voluntary location. Transfer to another conference is routine.

A separate list of retired priests is printed for each conference in answer to another of the disciplinary questions. That is one general category distinguished within limbo in recording terminal events of vacancy chains. Another category (corresponding roughly to part-time work, unofficial jobs, and unemployment for the Episcopal church) are all the men "located" or otherwise suspended, as described above. A third category are the many men "left without appointment to attend one of our schools."

Conferences, jobs, and vacancies

Every statement made under the heading of "diocese and jobs" for the Episcopal church is also valid in the Methodist church. The crucial difference is that the Methodist bishop has complete formal authority to reassign every man in the conference each year, at the annual meeting. Relatively few ministers from outside the conference are offered a job within it, although it is easy for them to obtain permission to transfer out of their home conferences if they are offered a job. Hence the great majority of job changes are within a conference and are announced on the same day (the last of the annual meeting of ministers in the conference) by the bishop. A chain of replacements does not spread out through the records in several successive annuals; and there is little need to allow for one-year vacancies in coding.

Other Methodist Churches

Some of the chain samples drawn in individual conferences (Chapter 12) are from the merged Methodist church after 1940. Publication of the *Minutes* and *Discipline* is continued in much the same form for the merged church. Bishop Nolan B. Harmon, from the former Southern branch, gives one account of the merger and its results in *The Organization of the Methodist Church*, 2nd rev. ed. (Nashville: Methodist Publishing House, 1962). For other views see J. M. Moore, *The Long Road to Methodist Union* (New York: Abingdon-Cokesbury, 1942); and J. M. Straughn, *Inside Methodist Union*

A. Coding Rules and Sources

(The Methodist Publishing House, 1958). A few changes in coding conventions must be made for the later era, mostly in interpreting seniority and data on congregation size.

A.3 United Presbyterian

The following paragraphs concentrate on those aspects and areas of coding for the Presbyterian church (Northern branch) that deviate from the rules laid down for the Episcopal and Methodist churches. The differences will be outlined within the same framework as used for the other churches.

The main reference used is the annual *Minutes of the General Assembly of the Presbyterian Church of the U.S.A.* This publication has been issued in several parts; the data used in this study are taken from *Statistical Tables and Presbytery Rolls*. Legal definitions are taken from *The Book of Church Order*.

One-to-one jobs

Pastor

There is normally one incumbent and the job of pastor is kept continuously filled (for exceptions see the next section). However, presumably due to the complete decentralization of the Presbyterian church, there are many more one-year vacancies (and one-year limbos abutting them) than in the Episcopal church.

1. The first name after the church in the presbytery list is that of the pastor. His status is always denoted by the abbreviation P.

4. When a man holds two (or more) churches in the Presbyterian church, neither (none) is explicitly designated as the main seat. It was therefore found necessary to adopt the arbitrary rule that when one church is substantially larger than any of the others it is treated as the seat; in other cases, the church a man retains is considered the seat.

7. Temporary pastors designated by SS (stated supply) or TS (temporary supply) are treated in the same way as temporary rectors in the Episcopal church; that is, when they remain for two years or more, they are treated as in a regular job.

Other principal jobs

There are no bishops in the Presbyterian church, and the various clerical officials such as stated clerk are elected from the clergy for a short term only. Most priests do not leave their churches on being so elected but hold the two posts simultaneously. Almost all officials therefore have the job of pastor of a named local church, and vacancy chains are coded solely through the latter.

348

Assistantships

Many large churches have one or more assistants, designated AP. The problem of distinguishing between assistantships that are sufficiently stable to be coded as 1–1 and those that are not, is treated in exactly the same way as in the Episcopal church, with one exception. Copastors must be distinguished from other assistants, since a copastor is elected with the right to succession, in the same way as an Episcopal coadjutor bishop. As in the case of the latter, vacancy chains are traced around that status, through the last regular job held by the copastor but only when that post was held by him not more than five years earlier. When a man has been copastor for more than five years his status is coded as pool.

Pool jobs

The list for pool jobs for the Presbyterian church is much the same as for the Episcopal and Methodist churches, with a few additions. Copastor is a pool job when the post is held for more than five years. Related to this are a few cases in which two men are listed as pastor in a given church. That is an acceptable situation in the laws of the church. No cases were found of replacement of a second pastor, only cases in which one man was replaced by two or a second man came in to join the original pastor. It was therefore decided to code a joint pastorship as a pool job.

Limbo

All teaching jobs are listed as limbo. This is partly because there are very few (church) educational institutions in the Presbyterian church but mainly because no distinction is made between teachers in church institutions and those in secular colleges, in the clergy list.

Synods, presbyteries, and jobs

There are two basic units: the synod and the presbytery. Synod boundaries are fairly stable, but the boundary lines of the presbyteries, into which the synod is subdivided, change frequently. All priests (including those in pool and limbo statuses) as well as churches are listed under and are under the jurisdiction of a presbytery rather than a synod. It is therefore essential to keep track of changes in presbyteries when coding chains. The task is feasible only because churches, like priests, are listed in a separate index. If "presbytery" is substituted for "diocese" the comments about residence for Episcopal priests apply here too.

A.4 True Lengths of One-Year Vacancies

In some years some Episcopal diocesan journals supply exact dates for each event in the lists of resignations and appointments. These lists however are not exhaustive (see Section A.5), making it impossible to dispense with before-and-after inference. Such inference is more easily carried out from the national annuals than from the journals of the numerous dioceses, but it is possible to show the exact sequences of dates of events in at least parts of some of the chains derived from the annuals. The specific validity of the abstract reasoning in Section 3.2, used to justify tracing chains through one-year vacancies, can be tested.

All the data in the Table A.1 are for incumbencies in the Massachusetts diocese that appear in two sets of vacancy chains: those traced from the 1954 list of resignations (d' sample), and those traced from comparison of all incumbencies in 1958 with those in 1959 (D sample). In those two sets of chains, approximately half of the total number of transitions from one incumbent to the next in a job can be dated. Table A.1 lists the pairs of dates for the resignation of the old and the appointment of the new incumbent. The corresponding actual length of interim vacancy in months is given on the right. In about two-thirds of these changes, the new incumbent is listed in the next succeeding annual, and there is no one-year vacancy in the chain inferred from the national annual. The pairs of dates for changes for which there was a gap, when for one intermediate annual no incumbent is assigned to the job, are listed in the bottom section.

Two facts stand out. The distribution of actual delays in filling a job, when the job is listed as vacant in one annual, overlaps the upper part of the distribution of actual delays for jobs never listed as vacant in an annual. Secondly, with few exceptions, it is resignations in the winter or fall that lead to jobs being listed as vacant in one annual, whether or not the actual delay is exceptionally long. When a job has the new incumbent listed in the next annual with no one-year vacancy, the resignation is likely to have been in spring or summer.

The first fact supports the idea that a job listed as vacant in just one annual has not usually been vacant for a full year. The actual delays in replacement do not fall outside the range for replacements when no one-year vacancy appears. The second fact has two implications. Firstly, the publication date of the annual falls in late winter, and jobs emptied shortly before then will be listed as vacant though a replacement comes in within a few months, that is, in spring. Secondly, jobs emptied in fall or winter take longer to fill than those emptied in other seasons. Again, two factors serve to explain the latter difference. Negotiations, trips of inspections, and so on may take longer in the winter months; quite apart from this, it is unlikely that a minister who has agreed to accept a new job will actually take it up until he has completed the active part of the church year, through Easter, in his existing incumbency.

(It should be noted explicitly that the cognate delay between the time a man leaves one job and moves into his next is typically very short: usually one day and never more than one month for the moves studied in Table A.1.)

Date of resignation	Date of appointment	Months job vacant
Jobs filled in each successive annual		
7/31/53	8/1/53	0.03
7/9/53	9/10/53	0.03
10/13/53	11/8/53	0.8
9/1/53	10/1/53	1
6/1/53	8/1/53	2
7/1/53	9/15/53	2.5
9/10/53	12/1/53	2.7
9/1/53	1/1/54	4
2/18/54	7/1/54	4.5
2/1/54	7/1/54	5
1/154/	9/5/54	8.2
8/1/58	7/1/58	−1.0
7/1/58	7/1/58	0
7/31/58	8/1/58	0.03
8/31/58	9/1/58	0.03
9/30/58	10/1/58	0.03
6/5/58	7/1/58	0.8
7/1/58	8/1/58	1
3/31/58	6/31/58	2.3
7/1/57	9/15/57	2.5
7/31/58	11/1/58	3
3/31/58	7/1/57	3
4/22/58	8/1/58	3.3
4/30/58	9/15/58	4.5
4/30/58	9/15/58	
Jobs vacant in one intermediate annual		
11/30/53	3/24/54	3.8
10/16/53	2/15/54	4
11/30/53	5/1/54	5
10/4/53	5/1/54	6.8
12/31/53	8/1/54	7
11/2/53	7/1/54	8
11/1/58	2/1/59	3
9/2/57	1/1/58	4
10/15/57	4/23/58	6.3
12/15/58	8/31/58	8.5
9/30/58	7/1/59	9
11/1/57	8/1/58	9
11/11/57	9/1/58	9.6
8/31/58	8/1/59	11
3/31/58	7/1/59	15
2/22/58	9/1/59	18

[a] Dates from diocesan journals for turnover of jobs in vacancy chains inferred from national annuals.

351

In short, men prefer to leave old and take up new jobs in the summer, and then delays are short at that time. After a few such changes in tandem, however, delays have accumulated so that a resignation comes in the fall or winter. It is hard to find a replacement till the next summer, but the annual has gone to press with a vacancy necessarily listed for this job. The coding rule to trace vacancy chains through one-year vacancies in Episcopal annuals seems justified. Many more errors would be made by treating them as chronic vacancies that are difficult to fill.

It is worth reporting what happens to one set of vacancy chains when one-year vacancies are treated as terminal events, that is, are coded as empty. Consider the k' sample of vacancy chains (from a national systematic sample of the clergy index) for 1955 traced back to 1954. The mean length of (weighted) chains is $2.62 = J_c$, the parameter $J_m = 4.68$ (see Table C.2) and 31.9 percent of the moves are in (weighted) chains of length $j = 6$ or greater. (See Appendix B for sampling weight schemes.) Naturally, long chains tend to be broken up when the tracing of a chain from the entry event is terminated upon reaching any one-year vacancy. Indeed, there are none of length $j = 6$ or greater. However, the effect on the *average* length of chains is not as great, for there is a compensating factor in the change of sampling weight.

Because the number of entry events is unchanged, the raw number of chains can, at most, be reduced by the number of secondary branch chains, here a reduction from 27 to 22 chains. However, the *weighted* number of chains should increase (since the k' tend to be smaller) and does, from 7.24 to 10.67. The weighted number of *moves* should of course be about the same whether they are traced through one-year vacancies or not, and indeed 19.03 moves changes to 19.73 moves. It follows that the mean length J_c decreases from the 2.62 value to 1.84. The other mean length of chain (as context for moves) J_m naturally decreases even more, from 4.68 to 2.52.

One byproduct of that account is a demonstration of the proper performance of the sampling weight k' as a self-correcting factor. Whether chains are traced to longer lengths through one-year vacancies or are terminated there, the sheer number of *moves* found in a given year should be unaffected. This has been seen to be true in the recomputation of the sample set.

The most significant result of terminating chains at one-year vacancies is not in change of lengths but in change of type of endpoint. Of the weighted chains just discussed, excluding the one loop, 44 percent began with a move to an empty or split job. Of the set of shorter chains, naturally, a much larger percentage, 71 percent, begin thus. Similarly, only 3 percent of the original weighted sets of chains ended with a move out of a job left empty or merged, whereas 36 percent of the shorter chains end thus. One-year vacancies are not numerous enough to reduce the average length of chains drastically; if accepted as true empty states, they do become the dominant boundary events, and thus would force a reconceptualization of the dynamics that generate chains.

A.5. Biases in Samples from Diocesan Lists of Resignations (d' Samples)

A major problem creating biases in samples is that some departures from 1–1 jobs never appear in the official yearly lists of resignations published in Episcopal diocesan journals. That usually occurs only when the job or the incumbent is minor. A problem that occurs earlier in the procedure is the lack of coordination between the calendar period covered in a diocesan list and the period covered, by inference, in a national annual (see Section 12.1). As an illustration, consider not only the list of resignations but also the list of appointments published in the *Diocesan Journal of 1958* for Massachusetts. October 1, 1958 is the date of the latest event included, and a cluster of events in September is reported; one infers the journal must be in the hands of the printer soon after. Four of the seventeen appointments fall outside the twelve-month period ending October 1, 1958, but the earliest is July 1, 1957; it seems a scattering of appointments missed in the previous issue are belatedly covered in the next year's journal. In confirmation of this, five appointments in that twelve-month period (which appear in vacancy chains traced from that year) are not published until the succeeding (1959) journal. The picture for resignations is similar. The latest two are September 30, 1958, the earliest is June 30, 1957; altogether six of the twenty-seven resignations fall before the twelve-month period beginning October 1, 1957.

Each list of resignations or appointments covers mainly a twelve-month period, although with appreciable scatter. The difficulty is that it is not a period coordinated with the publication date of the national annual, which one can infer to be approximately in February. Hence the sampling weight d', calculated for vacancy chains, which are inferred by comparing national annuals, are not accurate, except in an average sense (see Appendix B for sampling weights).

The obvious way to see if any resignations are actually omitted from the official journal lists is to trace all departures by comparing successive issues of the journals—"before and after" inference. However, the omission of some resignations, whether at random or dependent upon the prestige of the man, is not in itself important. Since full vacancy chains are traced, most omitted resignations have a chance to appear indirectly if not directly; at worst, there would be bias in sampling weights. The crucial resignations are those of men retiring from jobs thereupon left empty, merged, or filled by a man from seminary; those fall in chains of length $j = 1$. Both they and the chains suffer from any possible bias against short chains that could result from tracing vacancy chains solely from resignations given in the official list. Distributions of chain lengths in samples traced (in annuals) from resignation lists (d' samples) are reported for 1958 and three earlier years in the Massachusetts diocese and for one in the New York diocese in Section 12.1. The percentage of chains of length $j = 1$ is neither uniformly nor suspiciously low.

A more direct comparison is helpful. The samples are checked to see if any chains of length $j = 1$ are missing from the d' sample for Massachusetts traced from the 1958 journal resignation list. The criterion is the D sample of chains in Massachusetts derived from comparing all incumbencies in the 1958 annual with the 1959 annual; allowance must be made for sampling variability. Twenty-five chains are traced from the resignation list and thirty-six from the exhaustive inventory. The overlap is twenty chains, which appear in both samples. (There are forty-two changes in Massachusetts incumbencies turned up by the exhaustive inventory for that pair of years.) Against this background, the overlap just in chains of length $j = 1$ must be assessed. The data are simple. There are no chains of length $j = 1$ common to both d' and D samples: five in D but not in d' and one in d' but not D. Clearly, there is a tendency to miss short chains when tracing from resignation lists.

The length distribution for chains from a d' sample in a diocese must be treated with caution; it is usually biased against very short chains. The same stricture applies to a lesser degree for D'' samples of vacancy chains traced from both resignation and appointment lists. Results for different dioceses from the same type of sample can be legitimately contrasted.

Appendix B
Sampling Weights for Chains

The single chains diagrammed in Chapter 3 illustrate types of moves and the range of ways in which they cumulate into vacancy chains of various lengths. To characterize a system as a whole, sample sets of chains must be drawn by well-defined procedures. Sampling weights are necessary to compensate for biases in drawing chains.

B.1 Four Populations

There are four basic kinds of population from which one can draw sets of vacancy chains. The first and most natural is a population of vacancy chains themselves. However, since vacancy chains are being introduced only with this study, obviously there cannot be lists of them in the data. The second type of population is of boundary events (beginning or ending events) in some definite period such as one year. The rest of the chains would have to be traced out. Unfortunately, complete lists combining the various types of boundary events cannot be found. For example, although necrologies can always be found, and sometimes lists of new jobs (usually not reliable or complete for a given year), finding coordinated lists of retirements and of moves into empty jobs is not always possible. Much less feasible is finding separate lists for moves into "pool" jobs or "limbo," since the distinction between them and 1–1 jobs is introduced together with the idea of vacancy chains.

The third type of population is a list of all moves of men in a year (all departures and all arrivals to jobs or other statuses). Some of the moves drawn, say a departure of a man from one pool job who goes to another pool job, will not be relevant to vacancy chains. Each other move drawn in the sample is used as the entry point to the vacancy chain containing it: the chain is traced out back to the beginning event and forward to the ending event. Such lists of all moves in a year can be found, but usually only for each diocese of a church separately (either in the national annual as for the Methodist church or in the yearly Episcopal diocesan journals only).

Initially the entry points for all sample sets of vacancy chains were drawn from such lists. Unfortunately it proved impracticable to trace out the vacancy chains within those lists of all moves. Moves in one year were often published only in a later or in an earlier year's list. Hence the tracing had to be done through comparison of successive years' static reports of who was where, as stated in Section 2.2. Since the static reports were not keyed to the same reporting dates as the moves, there were errors in calculating sampling weights. For this reason alone, the third type of population proved an undesirable choice.

The main difficulty with the third type of population is simpler. The lists of moves are incomplete; many men who were listed in different jobs in successive static reports in annuals and thus must have moved were never included in the lists of moves for those (or neighboring) years. A short chain containing only one resignation that happened to be omitted from the lists of resignations would have no chance of entering a sample set of chains; and there would be less extreme biases even for longer chains. Nonetheless, sample sets of chains from the third type of population can be drawn quickly and can be used for comparing different regions, and results for them are reported (the d' and D'' sets in Chapter 12).

The fourth type of population is not a list of events but of statuses. Coupled with it is a procedure for inferring events by comparing the statuses of a sample of jobs or men drawn in one year with their statuses in a neighboring year. Those events become the entries to a sample set of vacancy chains. The remainders of the vacancy chains are traced out using the same inference procedure. It is the most costly procedure for drawing chains, since only a small fraction of jobs or men change status between a given pair of years. However, estimates of the fractions of stable men and jobs are needed anyway. The main point is that, at least in the churches of this study, but probably in most organizations, static lists of incumbencies are much more reliable than lists of moves; it is better to draw as well as trace moves in vacancy chains by inference from the static lists.

B.2 Weighting

Sampling weights should be defined so that each chain, whatever the length, has an equal chance to contribute to the representation of vacancy chains. With the first two types of population no weights would be required. A simple random drawing would, by definition, give every vacancy chain the same chance to enter the sample, which is an unbiased representation of the total population of chains. The other two populations, the ones actually used, are not of vacancy chains but of individual moves or statuses. There is no way to draw the sample so as to give each chain an equal chance to enter. Instead each chain traced must be weighted by the reciprocal of the number of chances it turns out, after the fact, to have had to enter the sample. (The logic is analogous to the estimate of population variance from variance in a sample, in order to infer the reliability of the mean estimated from that very sample.) In Section B.3 there are detailed rules for how to count the number of chances in each sampling frame used. That number is called the weight integer.

The necessity of weighting is most obvious when the question is what percentage of all chains has a given length j. The raw numbers of chains observed of various lengths cannot be used, since the number of chances for a chain to enter a sample is highly correlated with the number of vacancy moves in a chain, with its length j. If a chain of length 7 has, say, 9 chances of entering the given type of sample, this counts as 0.111 chains of length 7. Clearly this is a consistent procedure: in the limit where not a sample but the whole population of moves is drawn, the chain of length 7 will have appeared nine times, but each time with weight 0.111, yielding a total weight of exactly one. Weights are also necessary in estimating other parameters for a population of chains. For example, the type of beginning event of a chain is correlated with its length; new jobs tend to start chains shorter than ones started by deaths.

Moves by vacancies are a construct; they are inferred from juxtaposing observed changes in status for jobs and men. When parameters are to be calculated on a population base of vacancy moves rather than chains, as in Appendix C, two weightings must be combined; the sample weight must be multiplied by the number of vacancy moves j in the chain. The results are not the same as, although usually close to, the "raw results" for unweighted chains.

B.3 Sampling Frames

Six specific sampling frames are defined. The first three are used in Chapters 4–10 and the other three in Chapter 12. The weight integer of a given chain is counted differently according to the frame in which it appears. A different symbol is assigned to each sampling frame and is used to identify the weight integer. The six frames fall into three groups according to how vacancy chains are found. In the k, k', and K frames, systematic random samples are drawn from national lists of clergy so that statuses in neighboring years can be compared. In the D frame, an exhaustive inventory is made of all changes between neighboring years in incumbencies in the jobs in a particular diocese. In the d' and D'' frames, vacancy chains are traced from lists of resignations or appointments or of both in a particular diocese; those are the only frames from the third type of population defined in Section B.2. Whatever the frame, the chain is traced out in the same way, by comparison of incumbencies in national annuals in neighboring years.

For each sampling frame in turn the procedures used are stated. Compound chains, which occur in all frames, are then treated in a separate paragraph. Table B.1 reports a condensed version of one sample set of vacancy chains. Various problems in the interpretation of sample weights are taken up in Section B.4. In Section B.7 a procedure is developed for estimating some parameters, which is independent of and serves as a check on the weighting procedures described in the following discussion.

B. Sampling Weights

Weight integer k

National samples of vacancy chains were obtained in three stages. A systematic random sample was drawn from the clergy index in the annual for year $x + 1$. Each of the men was traced in the preceding year x. If his job was unchanged, he was not in a chain. The stable entries in the sample were tabulated; first by ordination date and second by type of job, size of church, and location of diocese. Also tabulated were men who moved without entering or leaving a 1–1 job. All other entries were men who left or entered a 1–1 job between year x and year $x + 1$. By definition, such moves are in vacancy chains; those men are entry points to vacancy chains.

The weight integer k of a chain, the number of chances it has to enter a k sample, is easy to compute. Each new incumbency in a 1–1 job contributes unity, and so do most beginning events—retirement, entry to limbo, appointment to a pool job. Those beginning events are not moves into 1–1 jobs, and k may be greater than the chain length j. A chain may end after a resignation from a job which then reverts to empty status or is merged or otherwise terminated. That ending event contributes 1 to j but nothing to k, and k may also be less than j.

A vacancy chain is traced through a one-year period of limbo, for an Episcopal or a Presbyterian clergyman, if the job he is going to or the one he has left is vacant in the same year; the period is assumed to be an artifact of clerical procedure. Nonetheless, that move contributes 2 to the weight integer, since it would be located by tracing back a year from the man's status in either of two successive annuals. Tracing a chain through a one-year vacancy has no effect on the k count since it is moves of men not jobs that are the entry points to the chain.

Weight integer k'

Procedures for the k' weight are parallel to those for the k weight frame, except the men drawn in an index sample of year x are traced forward one year to their status in year $x + 1$. The weight integer k' for a chain, since it is the number of exposures of the chain to the sampling process, counts departures instead of arrivals. Each resignation from a 1–1 job in the chain contributes 1 to k', wherever the man then goes. The beginning step of a chain can be the filling of a new or empty job; this contributes 1 to j but nothing to k'. The last step of a chain can be the filling of a vacancy by a newly ordained priest, which contributes nothing to k'; but ending the chain by recruitment of a man from a pool or limbo status contributes 1 to k' since he will be in the index in year x. It follows that k' can be less than j; usually it is greater than j.

Weight integer K

There is a glaring weakness common to the k and k' frames; there are some chains that have no chance to enter samples drawn in the frame. When a newly ordained priest enters the system to fill a new or heretofore empty job, a chain of length $j = 1$ is created. That chain has no chance to enter any k' sample, since there is no man in the index of one year who when traced forward a year will define a move in the chain. The chain does have one chance to enter a k sample. Conversely, a chain of length $j = 1$ started by the death of an incumbent and ended by the job being left empty has no chance to enter any k sample but does have one chance to enter a k' sample. Any chain has some chance to enter one if not the other of the two sampling frames. The K frame is not a new way to draw samples but a procedure for combining k and k' samples with appropriate weighting.

The procedure is simple. Draw a sample of the clergy index in year $x + 1$ in the k frame, that is, traced backward to year x and then trace out all chains encountered. Each chain is given the usual weight, $1/k$. Then do the same but in the k' frame, drawing in year x and tracing forward. Each drawing is a systematic random sample, one man per column in the index, and the number of men per column is essentially constant so that the sampling ratios for the k and k' samples are the same. Enlarge the k sample of chains by including any chains that appeared in the k' sample but have no chance to appear in any k sample; do the converse for the set of chains traced out from the clergy sample in the k' frame. Throw the two enlarged samples together to form the K sample of chains. The K weight integer of a chain is just its k value if it came from the k set and its k' value if it was in fact drawn in the k' frame; the weight itself is as always the reciprocal of the weight integer. When the two enlarged samples of vacancy chains are thrown together so are the total sample of the clergy index in year x and that in year $x + 1$.

The k sample when enlarged by the chains in the k' sample to which it would have been blind is, itself, an unbiased sample of chains, and so too for the enlarged k' sample. The complete distribution of chain lengths is reported only for the K sample because the latter is twice as large and gives more stable results for the given years. Averages and variances of chain length are reported for the enlarged k and k' samples separately, however, in Appendix C and Chapter 4, since the sampling variability of those parameters can be assessed empirically then.

Weight integer D

Each pastoral charge in a diocese was compared for two successive years, $x, x + 1$, in the national annuals. When there was a change, the vacancy chain in which it lay was traced out in both directions from this change as the "entry event." Some of the other moves in the chain would usually be other changes in pastorates in that diocese between the same two successive years. Those additional moves do not contribute anything to the sampling weight. If all moves in the chain are between jobs in the given diocese and between the same two years, the weight integer D is 1; there is no sampling correction. If even one move is a change between jobs in another diocese, another 1 is added to D, and so on.

If even one move is a change between a different pair of years—say $x + 1$ to $x + 2$ or $x - 1$ to x—for a given diocese, another unit is added to D. Successive states of pastoral charges were compared to find entry events to chains. Therefore if a charge is vacant in x but filled in $x + 1$ (or vice versa) that counts as a move. Unless the chain begins in a transition to empty, that charge must have had an incumbent in $x - 1$ too, and the change from $x - 1$ to the vacancy in year x also counts as a move. In short, a single replacement in the vacancy chain, of Jones by Smith in Crossville, will add 2 to D, although only 1 to j, if Crossville is listed as vacant for a year in between in the annuals.

The weight integer D of a chain is the number of diocese year-pairs between which at least one entry or one departure from a 1–1 job of the chain takes place. The sample is all chains with events in a given diocese between a given pair of years.

Weight integer d′

Entry to the vacancy chain in the d' samples is from a yearly list of resignations from jobs in a diocese. The sampled set is all those vacancy chains that contain at least one resignation from a job in that diocese published in that year's list. Because publication dates, and so on, differ, the list in a diocesan journal does not refer exactly to departures inferred from a given pair of national annuals. Nor does the yearly list always refer exhaustively and only to events in a period of exactly twelve months. Those overlaps are small and tend to cancel out; they are ignored in counting d'. The weight integer of a chain, d', is the number of diocese year-pairs between which at least one resignation of the chain appears.

Like D, d' is affected by how many one-year interim vacancies appear in a chain. If there is no such vacancy in jobs in a given diocese included in the chain, all resignations will appear in the same year; events in that diocese in the chain can contribute only unity to d'. The yearly list does contain resignations from pool jobs in which the man then goes to a 1–1 job; if the latter is in a different diocese the resignation from a pool job will add 1 to the d' for the chain. In contrast, only moves to or from 1–1 jobs in the list of churches in a diocese can contribute to the D count. However deaths are not resignations and so cannot contribute to d', whereas they do contribute to D.

Weight integer D″

In addition to the list of resignations, as in d' samples, the list of appointments are used in D'' samples as entry points to chains. The two-sided basis is like that in D. It again proved impractical to trace the complete chains just through appointment and resignation lists. Recourse had to be made to comparison of entries in successive annuals. Hence the actual procedure used to count D'' was identical with that used for D, except that changes from or to pool jobs, and so on, that led to chains can contribute to the count.

Application to compound chains

For compound chains, the weights in each frame are calculated so as to avoid any bias. When a job is split it is possible to determine which is the major portion of the job (the seat of the original pastoral charge), and the main vacancy chain is traced through that. The other part of the job is treated as a new job, the beginning event of a subsidiary vacancy chain. In the final tabulation, there are no compound chains, only separate chains, each with its own length j and boundary events. However, the two chains are uncovered from the same entry event. (The arbitrary code numbers of chains are assigned by the entry point; thus the secondary chain of a compound chain has the same number with the letter "S" added.) Whether the entry event drawn in the sample is in the main chain or subsidiary chain, both will be traced out following the coding rules. Hence both will have the same weight integer, that is, the same total number of entry events in the compound chain. That is approximately the sum of the sampling weights the chains would have in the given sampling frame if they were truly independent. The raw, unweighted number of chains in a set is thus larger than the number of sample entries to moves in or out of 1–1 jobs, larger by the number of secondary chains.

Table B.1 reports a complete set of vacancy chains drawn in the k sampling frame. It includes several compound chains. Each vacancy chain is written on one line, reading from left to right. Each rectorship is identified by the number of communicants in the church written above the title of the diocese. The standard abbreviations in the annual for dioceses are used, for example, E.O. stands for Eastern Ohio; Be., for the Bethlehem diocese in Pennsylvania; and so on. Between neighboring jobs is stated the year of ordination of the man who left the job on the right to enter the job on the left (or a " ? " if the date is unknown). A "V" indicates a one year vacancy in the job to the left, before the new man enters. An asterisk denotes the man who was the sample entry to the chain (there are eighteen asterisks). A subsidiary chain has no asterisk, is written next below the main chain, and is signaled by the letter "S" attached to the code number. The chain

Table B.1 A set of Episcopal Vacancy Chains for 1913 → 1912. The seventh entry in each index column was drawn; there were 146 clergy of whom 18 moved in vacancy chains and thus appear below. Chain No. C is written out in detail in Figure 3.1. See text for the explicit shorthand rules. Calculations of length distributions for this set are given in Table B.2

Chain code	Beginning	Linked moves	Ending	j	k
A	Pool: city missionary L.A.	1878 * 84(2)→24(1) V 1890 L.A. 131(5) V 1890 Minn.	Merge: the 5 merged into 3 other churches	2	3
AS	Split job: (see chain A)	60 1910 L.A.	Pool: ass't, L.A.	1	3
B	Retired	1867 V Har. 53 V 1900 N.Y. 335 1893 P. 332 1911 Har. 165 Be. [832-2] V 1911 Be. 101(2)→64 L 1911 Be. *	Empty	6	10
BS	Split job: (see Chain B; two other small jobs added)	99(3) V Har. 132(2) 1902 W.N.Y. 1913	Ordained: Gen. Th. Sem.	2	10
C	Pool: sem. instr.	443 1905 Ky. 425 1900 S. Va. 189 1900 * S.C. 105 1903 L.A. 46 V? At.	Merge: with church of size 503 in Atlanta diocese	4	4
DS	New job	43 1889 E.O. 42→99(3) V 1890 L.A. 105 1903 L.A.	Limbo: npc, Colo.	3	4
D	Split job: demotion to smallest of 3 churches held	9 1899 L.A. * 64(3)→57(2) 1899 L.A.	Merge: (see Chain DS)	2	4

Chain code	Beginning	Linked moves	Ending	j	k
L	Limbo: npc, Pa.	1903 145 1910 / Pa. *	Pool: ass't, Pa.	1	2
M	Limbo: npc, Newark (living in NYC)	1895 [1200–1] 105 V 1910 1907 / Newark (N'k) * N'k.	Pool: ass't, N.Y.	2	3
N	Limbo: npc, Olympia (living in Idaho)	1889 60 1900 26 1912 / Ol. Me. *	Ordained: Gen. Th. Sem.	2	3
O	Limbo: npc, Pa.	1875 538 V 1891 500(2) 1896 357(5) 81 → 122(3) / Pa. Alb. Alb. 1901 Salinas / V 1908 36(5) V 1907 101(8) 97 V 1881 L 1890 L 58 / W. Colo. Okl. * N'k. Me.	Empty	8	11
OS	Split job: plus a small mission	39(2) 41(2) 1871 / Sal. Sal.	Merge: (see chain O)	2	11
P†	Split job: from church of size 232, N.J.	N.J. 1912 *	Ordained	1	1
Q	Limbo: npc, L.I.	1883 96 / * L.I.	Empty	1	1
R†	Empty	170 1911 / Alb. *	Ordained	1	1

B. Sampling Weights

Chain code	Beginning	Linked moves	Ending	j	k
E	*Limbo*: npc, Colo.	84 1894 1903 Colo. *	*Pool*: ass't, Colo.	1	2
F	*Pool*: chaplain, infirmary in Md.	213 101(2) 105 1876 V 1895 V 1907 * Md. Md. C.	*Merge*: with small compound pastorate, Chi.	3	3
G	*Limbo*: npc, Wash.	205(4) 34 1897 1910 * W. Or.	*Merge*: to archdeacon	2	2
H	*Limbo*: npc, R.I.	135 1897 1907 R.I. *	*Pool*: general mission, R.I.	1	2
I	*Pool*: general mission, W.Va.	119(2) 120 1894 V 1904 1912 W.Va. * Tex.	*Ordained*: Gen. Th. Sem.	2	3
J	*Split job*: two missions split off and combined	62(2) 27 V 1881 Ia. * Ia.	*Merge*: with church of size 326, Ia.	2	1
K	*Limbo*: in England	302 [910–1] 131(2) 1896 1898 1895 V 1907 C. C. * C.	*Limbo*: npc, Chi.	3	4

† Chains P and R could never have occurred in any k' sample, in which tracing is forward. They are added to the 1912 → 1913 k' sample before combining the k sample to form an overall K sample (see Section B.4).

364

length, j, and the inverse of its sampling weight, k, are stated in the last two columns; each can be confirmed by inspection of the row.

In a compound job the (total) number of communicants is followed in parentheses by the number of separate churches combined. A split or merger of churches during a replacement is indicated by an arrow between before and after figures. A merger into or a split from a seat church whose pastor remains the same is a simple terminal event. If the latter also moves, the result is a compound chain, which is split into a main chain containing the sample entry and a subsidiary chain. An assistantship is indicated by brackets around the number of communicants followed by a dash and the number of assistants in that church. The number of communicants is always for the first year of the new incumbency in the job.

An "L" in the chain denotes that the man was listed in limbo for one year between the job on the right and the job on the left. Only if there were a vacancy in either or both of those jobs in that year is the chain traced through the limbo, which is taken to be a clerical delay. Otherwise even one year in limbo is a terminal event; but the potential chain, say for chain G, has to be traced out to establish that there is no vacancy in that year in any job to which the man might go in the next year.

In the columns for terminal events, "npc" means the man is listed without a job in the "nonparochial clergy" section for that diocese.

B.4 *Weights and One-Year Vacancies*

When chains are traced through one-year vacancies or limbos, a chain can spread across the annuals of several years. The sampling weight integer for any frame is defined as the number of chances a chain has to appear in a sample drawn from the annual of any year, not of the specific year used for the given sample. If the latter definition were used, a chain spread across several years would have more weight in length distributions than a chain of the same length that happened to be fully traceable in just two successive annuals. Since longer chains are more likely to spread across several years, the distributions of chain lengths would be skewed upward. The weighting procedure used estimates not the distribution of chains observable in a specific pair of annuals but rather the distribution from a series of annuals centered on that pair.

That definition of weights is essential for a consistent allocation of vacancy moves to years. Consider two chains A and B in a set drawn for year $x + 1$ in the k sampling frame. Let each have $j = 7$ and $k = 9$. Let the whole of chain A run between years x and $x + 1$, but let only four of the moves by men out of the $k = 9$ for chain B take place between years x and $x + 1$. The weighted number of vacancy moves in each chain is the same, 7/9. If the sample of clergy in year $x + 1$ were enlarged to include

B. Sampling Weights

the whole index, chain A would appear nine times and B only four in the resulting inventory of entries to chains. The weighted number of vacancy moves in chain A from the inventory would be $(7/9)9 = 7$, as it should be. The weighted number of vacancy moves observed for chain B would be $(7/9)4$, which indeed is the expected number of moves by vacancies in chain B just between years x and $x + 1$. Only if complete inventories for clergy samples in several years around $x + 1$ were combined would chain B turn up nine times and thus the weighted number of moves for chain B be the full seven (the number of moves for chain A of course would not be changed). The weight integer is defined so that the weighted number of moves contributed by a chain to a complete inventory is only that fraction of the vacancy moves in it that are expected to occur between the year sampled and its neighbor.

The topic is a difficult and confusing one at first encounter. An additional, very simple example is in order, in which estimates of lengths of chains as such and of numbers of moves are both analyzed. Suppose only four vacancy chains have ever occurred in a system of jobs. Three are from an ordained new priest moving into a newly created job in three successive years, and each has $j = 1$ and in the k sampling frame has $k = 1$. Let the remaining chain run through the same three years. It begins with a priest moving into an empty job and continues through two other jobs, each of which is vacant for one year before the replacement comes in. This fourth chain has $j = 3$, it can be entered just once in the k frame for each of the three successive years but, by the counting rule, has $k = 3$. Suppose a k sample is drawn for one year which turns up both the moves actually observable. From one is traced a chain with $j = 1$ and $k = 1$, and from the other is traced the chain with $j = 3$ and $k = 3$.

The raw result is that two chains are found and, without weighting, the estimate would be that 50 percent of the chains are of length one and 50 percent are of length 3. In a sense this is valid; half the chains one can find by tracing from changes just between years x and $x + 1$ are indeed of length $j = 1$. In the more useful sense this is false. There are, in fact, four chains altogether and three of them are of length $j = 1$. The weighting procedure yields the correct estimate. The weighted number of chains is 4/3, the sum of $1/k$ for each chain; 3/4 of this total is in chains of length $j = 1$. Furthermore the weighted number of moves is the sum of j/k for each chain, that is 1/1 plus 3/3 or, altogether, 2, which is the number actually observed in the given year. Half of the weighted moves are in chains of length $j = 3$, as is the true situation either in a given year or in all three years taken together.

B.5 Errors and Reliability

In every sampling frame except the K frame there are some chains with no chance whatever to enter a sample set. It is possible, as shown earlier, to extend the k and k' samples so as to allow for overlooked chains. In the d' sampling frame, the same chains missed in the k samples will be overlooked, since deaths are not included in lists of resignations; at the same time, the chains missed in the k' samples will also be overlooked in d' since there are no resignations in these chains of length $j = 1$. There will be chains with no chance of entry even to samples drawn in the D'' frame, in which lists of both resignations and appointments are used as entry events.

In the D-weight frame, all changes in incumbencies in churches in a diocese between two successive years are traced. The short chains to which d' or D'' samples are blind will not be missed. A few chains are missed in which all 1–1 jobs are ones in the national administrative structure or are other special types, such as deanships or named chairs in seminaries, that are not included in the alphabetical lists of pastoral charges for dioceses published in each annual.

Vacancy chains with moves between 1958 and 1959 in the Massachusetts Episcopal diocese are reported twice in Chapter 12, once using the d' frame and once using the D frame. The concrete biases for the d' frame are serious, but chains can be located much more quickly. The length distributions and other parameter estimates for samples in the d' frame cannot be trusted in an absolute sense. However, there is no reason to think the bias varies systematically from diocese to diocese; and the d' results can be used to see the direction of change in chain parameters in going from one diocese to another.

A more general issue is the reliability of entries in the national annuals, leaving aside possible flaws in the sampling schemes. The internal consistency in national annuals is outstanding. There are extremely few errors in the indices and listings; omissions have occurred less than one time in a thousand in the course of sampling clergy lists and tracing out the associated vacancy chains. Sometimes tenures included in a diocesan journal do not appear in the annuals. In every case found, it occurred because the tenure was shorter than a year and was in some sense a stopgap measure that did not affect either the availability of the job to others or the availability of the man for a real appointment elsewhere. It is reasonable to treat the successive national annuals as the canonical statements of who is the incumbent where and when.

The biographical directories do not include all clergy and cannot be trusted by themselves for statements of incumbencies. The entries are submitted by the men themselves, not by some disinterested official. Men do not make up imaginary appointments, but they fairly often omit small or distasteful appointments or periods of unemployment and then stretch the neighboring incumbencies to cover the gap. The continuity and level of incumbencies in the earlier career is often an issue in the minds of possible

B. Sampling Weights

"employers," and, not surprisingly, potential "employees" shape their reported histories accordingly.

Statistical inference could be applied to estimate how closely national samples of vacancy chains, in k, k', and K frames, approximate results for the total populations in the given years. The actual sampling processes are quite intricate in structure, and it is not evident what explicit tests are appropriate, especially with regard to the length distribution. Sampling variability in the mean length of chains is assessed instead by comparing means for two or more independent samples drawn in the k and k' sample frames in various decades.

Formal reliability estimates are not necessary since the reader can explicitly check the sampling and coding of each set of chains from the annuals. Ambiguous situations turned up quite frequently in coding, perhaps for one move out of five. There is an internal logic in the tracing procedure which generates cross-checks, especially since several independent sources of data are available (see Appendix A). Even so, there is bound to be variability between coders and for the same coder at different times. Whoever did the original coding, the tabulation sheets for the total sample were checked by the author. Usually, some changes were made (which were of course perceived as correction of errors) but not enough to substantially affect the parameter estimates for the sample set. The biggest single source of possible error is for short chains; for example, deciding when a single move by, say, a new recruit into a marginal job such as an assistantship is a vacancy chain started by a new job and when it is just a move among pool statuses. The serious problems are not so much with the application of given coding rules as with the justification of the rules.

B.6 Estimates

Percentage distributions by length j of each set of (weighted) chains are always given. Table B.2 shows the computations needed for the set in Table B.1. Three independent parameters summarize the gist of the distribution:

Number: N_w

The sum of the reciprocal of the weight integer of each chain in a sample set is always smaller than the raw number of chains. The generic symbol for this sum is N_w. It is the number of chains attributed to the given index sample of clergy.

For the D sample, the weighted number of chains, N_D, is just the total number of chains that would be allocated to changes in that diocese between the years x and $x + 1$. It is a kind of smoothed average. Since chains typically ran across several dioceses and years a number of chains for a separate diocese and pair of years cannot be directly observed.

The main use for the weighted number of chains is for national samples, those using the K weight. If this number, N_K, is multiplied by the sampling ratio (about 50 for all the index samples), an estimate of the total number

Table B.2   Length Distributions Calculated for the Sample Set of Vacancy Chains in Table B.1

j	Raw number of chains	Sampling weight integers, k	$\sum (1/k)$	$j \sum (1/k)$
1	7	3, 2, 2, 2, 1, 1, 1	4.833	4.833
2	9	3, 10, 4, 2, 3, 1, 3, 3, 11	3.273	6.546
3	3	4, 3, 4	0.833	2.499
4	1	4	0.250	1.000
5				
6	1	10	0.100	0.600
7				
8	1	11	0.091	0.728
Totals	22[a]		$N_k = 9.380$	$M = 16.206$[b]

$$J_c = \frac{M}{N_k} = 1.73$$

$$\sum j^2 \left(\sum \frac{1}{k} \right) = 38.846 \qquad J_m = \frac{38.846}{M} = 2.40$$

[a] Four of these are secondary chains in compound chains. Of the total sample of 146 clergy in the 1913 index, 90 were stable in 1–1 jobs, 14 in pool jobs, 14 in limbo statuses, and 6 in retired status. There were 18 entries in vacancy chains, and another 4 men were making moves not from or to 1–1 jobs. The sampling ratio is the average number of entries in a column of the clergy index; here it is 43.

[b] The sum, over all chains, of the number of one-year vacancies times the sampling weight is 4.213. (The weighted number of one-year limbos for men in the chains, which each must abut a one-year vacancy, is less than one-tenth of this.)

of vacancy chains is obtained. That is the total number of chains, given the observed length distribution, which would be needed to include all those and just those moves between years x and $x + 1$ in the national church.

Number of moves: M

First the weight of each chain is multiplied by its length j, then they are summed. The result is the number of moves of vacancies into, or equivalently out of, 1–1 jobs that are attributable to the given sample. This number is called M, and it is the basis for estimates of mobility.

B. Sampling Weights

The number of moves by men into 1–1 jobs, M_{in}, is usually less than M, because some chains end with jobs left empty, abolished, or merged. If for each such chain its weight $1/K$ is subtracted from M, the result is M_{in}; that is, j is decreased by unity for each such chain in calculating moves of men into jobs. From the total sample of entries in the index a tabulated number of men stable in 1–1 jobs, N_s is obtained. Then the mobility percentage, that is, in-mobility, is

$$\text{in-mobility percent} = \left(\frac{M_{in}}{N_s + M_{in}}\right)100$$

The value of M for the sample set of chains in Table B.1 is given in Table B.2 as 16.206. The amount to be subtracted to obtain M_{in} can be calculated, by inspection of Table B.1, as 3.948. The in-mobility is 12 percent. By similar logic (out-mobility) the percentage of men holding 1–1 jobs in year x who leave them to go to other 1–1 jobs or other statuses, is

$$\text{out-mobility percent} = \left(\frac{M_{out}}{N_s + M_{out}}\right)100$$

There, to find M_{out}, M is decreased by the sampling weight of each chain that begins with a new, empty, or split job. From Tables B.1 and B.2, M_{out} is 12.182 and the out-mobility is 11.9 percent.

Mean length: J_c

If M is divided by the weighted number of chains, the mean length of chains in the set has been computed. This sample estimate is designated as J_c. If the sample is a national one, J_c is the estimate corresponding to the predicted value $j(t)$ defined in Chapter 2. Any two of the three parameters N_w, M, or J_c determine the third.

Mean contextual length: J_m

J_c is not a measure of what length chain on the average is predominant in mobility. If one believes mobility is limited by the number and length of vacancy chains, one important question is what fraction of the total number of moves M are contained in chains of each length. Those percentage distributions are given in Appendix C for each sample set of chains. If each percentage is multiplied by j (and divided by 100) and the products summed, the result is J_m, the mean length of chain in which the average move is found.

If all chains happened to be the same length, J_m would equal J_c. Therefore, the ratio J_m/J_c is a measure of the variability of the length distribution. J_m is always substantially larger than J_c. The numerous chains of length $j = 1$, for instance, have as much weight as long chains in determining J_c, but the

370

long chains have far more leverage in fixing J_m. The distribution of chain lengths is always highly skewed, and the usual measure of variability, the variance, σ^2, is not very useful. The sample estimate of the variance can be easily computed if desired by the following formula

$$s^2 = (J_m J_c - J_c^2) \frac{N_w}{N_w - 1}$$

B.7   Validity Checks: Estimates from Sample Entry Events

National mobility rates can be estimated from the set of moves by sample entries alone. That estimate is partly independent of the one from the total number of weighted moves M in the set of chains traced from the sample entries. The number of men stable in 1–1 jobs, N_s, is the same in the two cases. To find in-mobility the number of sample entries that give moves of men into 1–1 jobs (whether new, empty, or previously occupied) from anywhere are counted and divided by the sum of it and N_s. The out-mobility rate is calculated in parallel fashion.

The average length of vacancy chains, J_c, can also be directly estimated from the set of sample entries plus certain additional information. That estimate is somewhat biased, as discussed in Sections 4.1 and C.3 but it provides a useful check on the validity of the weighting procedures. The idea is simple. The sample entry events are assumed to be actually linked together as complete chains and then the average length in such a set is calculated.

Consider a set of n sample entries to vacancy chains for a k, k', or K sample. Each will define a move of a man into either a 1–1 job or some other status in year $x + 1$. Each will also define a move of a man out of a 1–1 job or some other status in year x.

$a =$ number of moves of a man into limbo, pool, retirement or death in year $x + 1$ (and hence necessarily a move *from* a 1–1 job in year x, or the sample entry would not have led to a vacancy chain).

$b =$ number of moves of a man in year $x + 1$ into a new or split 1–1 job or one previously empty.

$c =$ number of moves of a man into a 1–1 job in year $x + 1$ that was occupied previously (either in year x or $x - 1$).

$d =$ number of moves of a man in year $x + 1$ into a one-year period of limbo (followed by a move to a 1–1 job necessarily).

Let c', b', and a' be the parallel counts for moves out of statuses in year x. There a' counts moves out of seminary, and so on, rather than moves into death, and so on, and b' counts moves out of jobs thereupon merged, left empty, or terminated. Observe that $a + b + c + d = n = a' + b' + c' + d'$.

Clearly $a + b$ is the observed number of beginning events of vacancy

B. Sampling Weights

chains among the sample entry events ($a' + b'$ is the observed number of ending events). The observed number of moves into 1–1 jobs in $x + 1$ is $b + c$. By definition, j is the number of moves of the vacancy out of 1–1 jobs in the running of a chain. Thus $b + c$ corresponds to j except for the cases in which the last job in a chain is left empty or terminated, which has been treated as a formal "move" of the vacancy out of the 1–1 job into annihilation. These terminal formal "moves" correspond to the events counted by b'.

J_c is the average value of j, which is the sum of j over all chains divided by the number of chains. Hence a consistent estimate of J_c from the sample entries is obtained from a count of all new tenures divided by the number of beginning events:

$$J_c = \frac{b + c + b'}{a + b}$$

By parallel reasoning, an estimate of J_c can be obtained from sample entries when chains are counted by their endpoints:

$$J_c' = \frac{b' + c' + b}{a' + b'}$$

In Table B.1, the sample entry to each chain is designated by an asterisk. There are $n = 18$ entries, split up into

1913	1912
$a = 4$	$a' = 6$
$b = 4$	$b' = 4$
$c = 9$	$c' = 7$
$d = 1$	$d' = 1$

Thus
$$J_c = \frac{17}{8} = 2.1$$

$$J_c' = \frac{15}{10} = 1.5$$

These two estimates bracket the J_c estimate from the weighted chains,

$$J_c = 1.73$$

Earlier in this discussion a verbal description of the calculation of in-mobility rates from sample entries alone for samples of types k, K, and k' was given. Now formulas can be stated:

$$\text{in-mobility} = \frac{b + c}{b + c + N_s}$$

$$\text{out-mobility} = \frac{b' + c'}{b' + c' + N_s}$$

The values computed from Table B.1 are 12.6 and 10.9 percent, respectively. These are quite close to the estimates in Section B.6 derived from weighted chains, 12.0 and 11.9 percent, respectively.

Naturally it is impossible to compute J_m from the sample entries alone, for they give no idea of the shape of the distribution of chain lengths.

Finally, consider the parameter N_w, the weighted number of chains in a set. The sum $a' + b'$ and the sum $a + b$ are estimates of N_k, the number of chains.

Table B.3   Comparison of Parameter Estimates from
Weighted Chains with those from Sample Entries,
for the Sample Set in Table B.1

	Weighted chains	Sample entries	
J_c	1.7	J_c (beginnings)	2.1
		J_c (endings)	1.5
J_m	2.40	None	
In-mobility (%)	12.0		12.6
Out-mobility (%)	11.9		10.9
N_k	9.380	beginnings	8
		endings	10

Table B.3 reports side by side the estimate for each parameter from weighted chains and that from sample entries, for the set of chains in Table B.1. More than the sample entries have actually been used to estimate J_c and N_k. The allocation of moves between b and c requires a look ahead to the general nature of the next step in the vacancy chain. In vacancy chains, men and jobs play dual roles so that one cannot measure the vacancy chain lengths from a sample based on either men or jobs alone.

Appendix C
Estimates of Moves

Tracing and sampling procedures for vacancy chains have been defined and illustrated in Chapter 3 and Appendices A and B. The natural first question is how long are vacancy chains in the organizations studied? In Chapters 4 and 6 the answer is stated in terms of the genesis of chains: the percentages of beginning events which lead to chains of various lengths. Here the perspective is mobility. What percentages of all moves by vacancies occur in chains of various lengths?

"Length" of chain is defined as the number of vacancies in 1–1 jobs. If most moves occur in chains of length 1 there may be little to gain from examining chains. A chain of length 1 always occurs when a man's move into a job is not contingent on other men's moves; then movement is free and conforms to the assumption implicit in most analyses of mobility. There are some chains of length 1 which do reflect contingencies. For example, the replacement of a retiring incumbent by a new recruit defines a chain with $j = 1$. Conversely, when a man enters a newly created job from a job left empty there are no contingencies and yet the chain length $j = 2$. On the whole, however, the percentage of vacancy moves in chains of length more than 1 is a reasonable indicator of the potential advantage in dissecting mobility into vacancy chains. Another obvious measure is the mean length of vacancy chains considered as contexts for moves, J_m.

Over time, the chain lengths most important to mobility in a system may change. National samples have been drawn in successive decades in each of the three churches. Loops are included in all these tabulations, but a separate section examines their contribution to mobility. A loop has neither beginning nor ending event and must be generated by a different process from that proposed in Chapter 2.

A church does not consist entirely of men in 1–1 jobs. There is much mobility among pool and limbo statuses, as is reflected in the national samples. Complete tabulations of all sample entries in each church are presented in Section C.3 in the form of turnover tables. The great majority of moves do fall into vacancy chains. (Tables C.8 and C.11 specify the index samples drawn so that a reader may check all results from public data.)

C.1 Distributions of Moves by Chain Length in Three Churches over Five Decades

In the Episcopal church, the percentage of moves in chains of length 2 or more fluctuates from 56 to 82 percent over five decades, as one can see from

Table C.1. J_m, the mean length of chains when weighted by the number of weighted moves, fluctuates in parallel between 1.91 and 3.48. Vacancy chains are too long to be ignored there; mobility cannot be treated as if moves were independent of one another in the Episcopal church.

Table C.1 Percentage of Moves in Chains of Length j,
K Weight Samples in Five Decades, Episcopal Church

j	1912–1913	1922–1923	1933–1934	1943–1944	1954–1955
1	34.2	22.5	44.3	34.8	17.7
2	30.2	33.4	32.3	21.1	31.2
3	7.9	3.0	12.0	20.6	16.4
4	8.2	16.0	11.4	12.0	9.7
5	5.8	10.5		0	4.4
6	5.1	7.7		2.7	8.6
7	0	6.9		5.9	3.5
8	5.5			2.8	1.5
9	3.2				2.8
10					2.5
11					0
12					1.5
	$M^a = 31.642$	$M = 34.926$	$M = 21.651$	$M = 31.589$	$M = 64.573$
In-mobility (%)^b	12.8	16.2	9.2	13.1	15.4
Out-mobility (%)^c	11.7	15.0	7.2	15.8	13.7
Total weighted number of one-year vacancies^c	7.619	5.567	4.633	4.690	15.061
	$J_m = 2.82$	$J_m = 3.09$	$J_m = 1.91$	$J_m = 2.67$	$J_m = 3.48$

^{a} M represents the total number of weighted moves, here and in subsequent tables.

^{b} See Section B.6 for formulas and Table C.3 for the number of men stable.

^{c} These estimates are used in Sections 6.4 and 7.1.

All these figures are sample estimates, subject to sampling variability. The variability in J_m can be assessed from Table C.2, where its values are given for the separate k and k' samples of which the K sample is composed (see Appendix B). Vacancy chains definitely are shorter in the Depression years 1933–1934, but no other differences between decades can be asserted with confidence. There may be an overall trend toward longer chains obscured during the Depression and during World War II. At least 10 percent of the clergy moves into military chaplaincies in the war and the number of ordinations drops sharply. In Section 5.3, these two decades are examined in detail.

C. Estimates of Moves

The number of one-year vacancies in the sample chains (see Section 3.2) average about one-fifth the total number of moves. That is consistent with a typical delay of two to three months in replacing a man who leaves a 1–1 job.

Table C.2   Mean Chain Lengths, J_m, for k and k' Subsamples in K Samples of Table C.1

Sample from	1912–1913	1922–1923	1933–1934	1943–1944	1954–1955
					2.94[a]
k	2.40	2.99	1.85	2.18	4.68
k'[b]	3.28	3.21	1.94	3.14	3.00
k' (before enlargement)	3.61	3.52	2.13	same	3.09

[a] Two systematic random samples of clergy were drawn for 1955 and traced back; these two k samples are reported separately as additional evidence on variability.

[b] The k' subsample was corrected by including those short chains (all with $j = 1$, $k = 1$) in the k subsample for that year which could not have entered any k' subsample (see Section B.3). There were two such chains for each of the first three decades, none in 1943–1944, and one for each of the two k subsamples in 1954–1955. In no years did there appear in the k' subsample a chain that could not enter the k subsample, and no correction is needed.

The mobility rates in Table C.1 are calculated from M, the total weighted number of moves in the sample of chains, corrected for moves of vacancies which do not imply moves by men into or, respectively, out of 1–1 jobs. The men in the index sample who remained stable in 1–1 jobs appear in the denominator of the mobility rate. Each chain was traced from a man in the index sample who moved into or out of a 1–1 job (or both) between the two years. The direct count of the number in the index sample who move into 1–1 jobs can be used in place of M in the numerator of the in-mobility rate and, similarly, for out-mobility (see Section B.7: note that there is no way to estimate J_m from single moves). Those alternative estimates of mobility (together with the actual counts of stable and mobile men in the index samples) are reported in Table C.3. They are slightly biased because some moves have more chances than others of entering an index sample (see Section C.3) and because all moves in a year are treated as if they occurred at a fixed date. The mobility rates in Table C.3 should, however, closely approximate those in Table C.1 if the weighting scheme used there is valid. They do. There is no clear trend in the mobility rates, except for the obvious drop during the Depression, whichever set of estimates is viewed. In-mobility rates tend to exceed out-mobility rates, as one would expect in an organization that has grown steadily except during the war years, when there were few recruits and many men leaving 1–1 jobs for chaplaincies.

In the Methodist church, about 10 percent of moves by vacancies occur in chains longer than any shown for the Episcopal church. Naturally the mean length of chains is much larger, and in addition the percent of moves

Table C.3   Direct Estimates of Mobility from the Index Samples[a]
Used as Entry Points to the Chains in Table C.1

Years	1912–1913	1922–1923	1933–1934	1943–1944	1954–1955
In-mobility (%)	11.8	16.0	7.7	12.0	14.9
Out-mobility (%)	11.4	16.0	8.2	14.4	14.9
	$N_s{}^b=177$	$N_s=147$	$N_s=180$	$N_s=161$	$N_s=325^c$
Number of entries	35	34	26	35	74^c
	$(N=290)$	$(N=267)$	$(N=306)$	$(N=315)$	$(N=590)^c$
Sampling ratio[d]	20.2	23.0	20.7	20.7	13.3^c
Official size of clergy (second year)	5678	6024	6356	6344	7367

[a] A systematic random sample of one man from each column on an index page was drawn in each of two years, and the two are combined. See Table C.8 for further details on samples. See Section B.7 for mobility formulas used and Section C.3 for biases in the formulas.

[b] N_s represents the number of men stable in 1–1 jobs, here and in subsequent tables.

[c] Two k samples as well as one k' sample are combined for 1954–1955.

[d] Estimated total number of clergy in the church is the sampling ratio times the N. The average number of men in a column of the index was estimated from a random sample of ten columns in each of the two years. The overall average is almost certain to be within the range 41.65 ± 0.7 (95 percent confidence interval). That overall average is used in the text for each sample since the observed variation among decades is no more than sampling fluctuation.

in chains of length 1 is smaller. There is, again in the Methodist church, no clear evidence for a trend over time in the length of chains. The figures are given in Table C.4.

(Only k samples, in which index entries are traced backward to the preceding year, were drawn for the Methodist church. Table C.2 showed that substantial corrections were needed, usually in the k' samples for the Episcopal church but none at all in the k sample. The k' sample overlooks chains of one move by a new priest into a newly created job, whereas the k sample misses cases of death in jobs thereupon ended. Since both the Methodist and Episcopal clergy have grown in size in the twentieth century, one would expect k' samples to be equally bad and k samples equally good

C. Estimates of Moves

for both. The Methodist k samples can, in fact, miss none of the short chains because of a simple reportorial advance; men who die or otherwise leave the church are included in the next year index, marked by an asterisk.)

Vacancy chains would be considerably longer still in the Methodist church if they were traced through one-year vacancies as is the rule for the

Table C.4 Percentage of Moves in Chains of Length j,
k Weight Samples, Methodist Church

j	1922–1923	1936–1937
1	16.7	13.7
2	22.2	16.8
3	10.2	15.4
4	9.4	14.1
5	11.9	13.3
6	6.4	6.4
7	3.2	6.0
8	1.0	2.1
9	3.4	0
10	0.7	2.3
11	2.4	2.1
12	2.1	0
13	3.2	1.9
14	2.1	0
15	2.0	2.1
16	1.0	0
17	1.0	0
18	1.0	0
$\vdots$		
26		2.0
$\vdots$		
30		1.8
	$M = 92.937$	$M = 47.754$
In-mobility (%)	41.8	28.2
Out-mobility (%)	45.3	28.6
	$J_m = 5.00$	$J_m = 5.23$

Episcopal church. Moves are announced on a fixed date in a Methodist conference and there are not the chronic delays of several months in replacing men. As explained in Chapter 3, it is the cumulation of these delays that forces the misleading vacant entries found in Episcopal annuals.

Mobility rates drop sharply between the 1920s and the 1930s in the Methodist church, but even then they are much larger than the Episcopal rates. Direct estimates of mobility from index entries are shown in Table

C.5 (which is parallel to Table C.3). Those estimates confirm ones from weighted chains in Table C.4. The traditional ideology of the Methodist church is that the clergy are "travelling ministers," and ideology matches the facts here.

Table C.5   Direct Estimates of Methodist Mobility from the
Index Samples Used as Entry Points
to the Chains in Table C.4

	1922–1923	1936–1937
In-mobility (%)	44.3	27.0
Out-mobility (%)	45.6	29.0
	$N_s = 93$	$N_s = 103$
Number of entries	95	47
	$N = 304$	$N = 258$
Sampling ratio	76	76
Official size of clergy (second year)	21,984	18,928

Table C.6   Percentage of Moves in Chains of Length j,
k Weight Samples, Presbyterian Church

j	1922–1923	1959–1960
1	22.7	20.2
2	17.8	14.9
3	25.8	25.8
4	5.4	9.5
5	12.1	12.7
6	4.4	8.9
7	2.9	3.9
8	0	0
9	3.3	4.0
10	5.5	
	$M = 27.121$	$M = 22.325$
In-mobility (%)	22.2	16.9
Out-mobility (%)	21.5	17.7
	$(N = 7.693)$	$(N = 11.357)$
	$J_m = 3.50$	$J_m = 3.46$
	$N_s = 78$	$N_s = 96$

Two national samples, each a k sample, have been drawn for the Presbyterian church also. These are reported in Table C.6. The mean chain length —percentage of moves in short chains—and mobility rates are all similar to those for the Episcopal church in recent years. In spite of formal differences, these two churches are more akin than either is to the Methodist in salaries, educational requirements, and general tone. There is one significant difference; control of moves is even more fragmented in the Presbyterian than in the Episcopal church, since there are no central prestigious figures such as bishops to exert such influence as they can. In Table C.6 the weighted number of one-year vacancies is twice as big a fraction of the weighted moves as for the Episcopal church: the typical delay in replacing a man is six months rather than two to three months.

In the Presbyterian sample 182 and 199 entries were drawn in the index of the 1960 and 1923 annuals respectively. Of these 96 and 78 were stable in 1–1 jobs, and 27 and 30 led to vacancy chains, respectively. The direct estimate of in-mobility is 15.8 percent and 22.2 percent and of out-mobility, 17.2 percent and 21.5 percent, which agree with the estimates in Table C.6 from M for each year. The sampling ratio is the average number of men in an index column, namely 70, since the thirteenth and fourteenth man, respectively, in every column makes up the sample. The official total number of clergy is 12,216 in the 1960 annual.

C.2 Mobility in Loops

Some of the chains included in Tables C.1–C.6 have no beginning or ending events. Such chains are closed loops of moves; the result of the changes they describe is a permutation of the original incumbents among the same set of jobs. Moves in loops contribute to mobility, and loops are included with normal vacancy chains in calculating both mobility and distributions of moves by chain length. However, loops do not conform to the picture drawn of mobility in Chapters 1 and 2: the view of moves generating other moves as the vacancy created by a death jumps from job to job over time. The number of moves in loops must be reported separately. Their frequency can be used as an index of the range of applicability for vacancy chain models.

A loop of length 2 is a simple swap of jobs by a pair of men. Unlike a longer loop it can plausibly be regarded as a localized event. Longer loops are likely to require some centralized, that is, authoritative planning. A long loop can come about by chance if all replacements are made very quickly and one man has gone from a job to an appreciable period in limbo; even so, it does not conform to the vacancy chain model.

All loops found in the Episcopal church are of length 2. There are only three altogether in the samples for five decades reported in Table C.1; two in 1954–1955 and one in 1922–1923. When all samples are lumped together, the total weighted number of moves M is 184.381. Each loop has not only $j = 2$ but also $k = 2$; the three loops together contribute exactly 3 out of the 184 moves, or 1.6 percent. In all samples combined, the weighted number of moves in chains just of length 2 is 26.022, eight times the number from the loops alone. Loops contribute very little to mobility in the Episcopal church, although this small amount could be crucial for testing the adequacy of various models.

In the Methodist church, loops play a larger role. In the two samples of Table C.4, besides eight loops of length 2 there are two of length $j = 5$, one $j = 6$ and one $j = 3$. Each loop contributed one weighted move to the total, whatever its length, because the sampling weight equalled j. Five of the 92.937 weighted moves in the 1923 sample were in loops. Mobility was sharply lower in 1936–1937; there were 47.754 moves, but 7 of them were in loops. Overall, 8.6 percent of the weighted moves in the Methodist church were in loops. No loops were observed in the Presbyterian samples.

C.3 Total Turnover

The empirical scope for vacancy chains is limited by the fraction of men in the system who are not in 1–1 jobs. These men do change positions within the limbo and pool categories, and a complete picture of mobility entails estimates of these rates also. Vacancy chains cannot be defined. Rates can be estimated only from the moves by men drawn in the index samples.

There are too few men in pool status for any one sample to provide a reliable base for estimating mobility. The index samples for five decades in the Episcopal church are combined in Table C.7, which is set up as a turn-over table. Each man in an index sample is counted in the cell that lies in the row for his status in the earlier year x and lies in the column for his status the next year, $x + 1$. Five employment categories are distinguished: retired, limbo, pool jobs, all 1–1 jobs, and outside. Each cell on the diagonal of the turnover table is bisected; the number of men stable in particular jobs is above the line, and the number who changed jobs between years x and $x + 1$ but remained in the same employment category is below.

Moves by men, not the cognate moves by vacancies, are tabulated; it is a sample of moves rather than all the moves in a sample set of complete chains. The last column of Table C.7 corresponds to the vector $\mathbf{F}_{man}$ describing new vacancies in Chapter 2. In Table C.7 the single outside category of Chapter 2 has been differentiated into four categories; in Chapter 2, the single 1–1 job category of Table C.7 had been differentiated into several strata of 1–1 jobs.

The row for the "outside" status counts new clergy who have a status for the first time in year $x + 1$. Such men have no chance to enter a k' sample, which traces index entries in year x forward to year $x + 1$. Hence the observed counts must be doubled, as indicated in the Table. Similarly, entries in the outside column are doubled to allow for the blindness of the

C. Estimates of Moves

k sample to deaths. These are much more severe corrections than those described in Section B.3 for weighted chains. The logic is exactly parallel, but the criteria are more severe. A death has a chance to enter *chains* traced from a k sample unless the dead man is not replaced.

Table C.7 Annual Turnover from Combined Index Samples
for Five Decades[a] in Episcopal Church

Year x	Year $x + 1$					
	1–1 job	Pool	Limbo	Retired	Outside[c]	Total mobile
1–1 job	887[b] / 86	11	16	12	8 × 2	141
Pool	17	136 / 9	10	3	1 × 2	41
Limbo	10	12	163 / 1	0	1 × 2	25
Retired	0	0	0	152 / X	2 × 2	4
Outside[d]	17 × 2	6 × 2	2 × 2	X	X	50
Total mobile	147	44	31	15	24	261

[a] The sampling ratio is 4.2. For example, the estimated number of clergy who move from pool status in one year to a 1–1 job the next is 71.4 on the average. See Table C.8 for details on individual samples.

[b] Men who do not change positions are counted above the line in each diagonal cell; below the line are counted the men who change positions but stay in the same status category.

[c] Clergy in year x who die before the annual for each year $x + 1$ cannot appear in the five samples traced backward from the index in year $x + 1$ (k samples); and the combined entries from k' samples are multiplied by 2 in the outside column.

[d] In each cell the first number is the sum of the observed entries for the five index samples drawn in year $x + 1$ and traced back to year x (k sample). That number must be doubled, since the other five samples (k' samples, drawn from the index in year x and traced forward) are blind to new recruits.

With those corrections for recruitments and deaths, the sampling ratio for Table C.7 is 4.2. The compositions of the ten index samples combined are spelled out in Table C.8. The total number of clergy in year $x + 1$ in the samples is 1575, the sum of all entries in Table C.7 except those in the

Table C.8 Ten National Index Samples Combined in Table C.7[a]

	1912	1913	1922	1923	1933	1934	1943	1944	1954	1955	Total
k' sample		✓	✓		✓			✓		✓	
k sample	✓			✓		✓	✓		✓		
Order of entry of column[b]	28	7	5	11	21	5	6	10	16	11	
	$(N=144)$	$(N=146)$	$(N=132)$	$(N=135)$	$(N=152)$	$(N=154)$	$(N=156)$	$(N=159)$	$(N=192)$	$(N=198)$	1568^c
	$N_s=87$	$N_s=90$	$N_s=75$	$N_s=72$	$N_s=93$	$N_s=87$	$N_s=80$	$N_s=81$	$N_s=111$	$N_s=111$	887

[a] The total clergy in k' samples above, 776, almost exactly equals the total for the five k samples. The turnover table parallel to Table C.7 for just k' samples alone is close to that for the five k samples combined—well within sampling variability—except for the outside row and column. A combined turnover table was also tabulated for the four samples from the first two decades, and a table for the six later samples. There were no striking differences.

[b] Drawn as a systematic random sample of the rth entry in each column of the clergy index. There are forty-two entries in the average column (the layout and typography of the index pages does not change); the sampling ratio, then, is forty-two.

[c] If in Table C.7 the factors of 2 are dropped in the outside row and column, the sum of all entries (plus four deaths and one recruit who turn up by fluke in k and k' samples respectively) matches this total.

outside. The estimated average number of Episcopal clergy during these five decades is 4.2 times that, or 6772. The official total number of clergy is 5678 in the 1913 annual, and it rises irregularly to 7367 in the 1955 annual.

There cannot be appreciable error in the estimate of total size from a systematic random sample. Estimates of death and recruitment rates, however, are subject to normal sampling fluctuation, and their accuracy is an index of the representativeness of the samples. It is obvious from Table C.7 that both rates are small. Of the 1575 clergy in year $x + 1$ in the Table, 50 are new recruits from outside (most of them newly ordained, but some transferred in from other Anglican churches or reinstated after earlier depositions). The estimated recruitment rate is 3.17 percent. The estimated retirement rate is 24/1549, or 1.55 percent. The number of new clergy per year should be 210 and the number of severances, 101 on the average. The

Table C.9   Composition[a] and Mobility of Episcopal Clergy by Employment Status. Averages Over Five Decades calculated from Table C.7   (percent)

	1–1 jobs	Pool	Limbo	Retired	Total
Composition of clergy, average year $x + 1$	65.7	11.4	12.3	10.6	100 ($N = 1575$)
In-mobility rate	14.2	24.4	16.0	9.0	1575
Out-mobility rate	13.7	23.2	13.3	2.6	1549

[a] There are many published estimates over the years of the distribution of Episcopal clergy among types of jobs and employment categories. Most are based on fragmentary censuses and are unreliable. One of the best analyses is for 1928 near the middle of the five decades covered here. It is an official report based on a complete census by the Church Pension Fund, supplemented by special tabulations, for the 6207 clergy in 1927. It appears in Appendix XXII, Part II, Section A, pp. 482–509, *Journal of the General Convention*, 1928. It is difficult to allocate their figures between the pool and 1–1 job categories, but the percentage in the two categories combined is 80.4. The percentages in limbo and retired are 8.6 and 9.9 respectively.

official number of deacons ordained runs between 150 and 200, with sharp fluctuations, from the 1920s until the early 1950s, when it jumps to 300 and then 400 annually. As many as thirty clergy a year came into the Episcopal church, until recently, by transfer. Depositions from the ministry (usually at own request), ran between five to fifteen per year in the five decades, after subtracting reinstatements. The number of deaths varies between 85 and 150 over the period. The sample estimates from Table C.7 are quite accurate.

In a given year nearly three-quarters of all clergy who are not retired are in 1–1 jobs. The remainder are split almost equally on the average between pool and limbo. About 10 percent of each sample of Episcopal clergy are retired. Those figures, together with estimates of mobility rates by employment category, are calculated from Table C.7 and reported in Table C.9.

Table C.10   Annual Turnover,[a] Combined Index Samples
for Two Decades,[b] Methodist Church

			Year $x + 1$			
Year x	1–1 job	Pool	Limbo	Retired	Outside	Total mobile
1–1 job	196 / 91	3	9	10	7	120
Pool	4	63 / 7	4	0	1	16
Limbo	7	3	24 / 3	3	2	18
Retired	2	0	0	103 / X	7	9
Outside	9	1	3	X	X	13
Total mobile	113	14	19	13	17	176

[a] Men in the same job during the two years are counted above the line in each diagonal cell; below the line are men who changed to another position in the same status category.

[b] The sampling ratio is 38. For example, the estimated number of Methodist ministers who shift in a year from one pool to another is 266, on the average over these two decades. All the index samples are drawn in year $x + 1$ and traced back to year x, that is, k samples. Men who die or otherwise leave the church are included in the next year's index; so no correction for bias is needed in the column for outside. See Table C.11 for details on the samples.

Mobility rates are high into and out of the pool positions, which are flexible jobs such as chaplaincies, typically held for brief periods to broaden experience. As a result, only 62 percent of observed mobility into positions (147 out of 230 moves) is into 1–1 jobs although 74 percent of the active clergy are in them. Remember, many of the moves into pool, limbo, and retired statuses are from 1–1 jobs.

(In Section B.7 formulas for estimating mobility around 1–1 jobs from an index sample alone were developed. They have been applied in Section

C. Estimates of Moves

C.1 to check on the estimate from the weighted chains traced from the index sample. The groupings of moves used for these formulas and the ones for J_c give counts $(a, b, \ldots)$ that can be related to entries in a turnover table

Table C.11   Four Methodist Samples[a]

	1923	1923	1937	1937	Total
Conference group[b]	Spring	Fall	Spring	Fall	
Order of entry in column[c]	4	30 (from bottom)	6 (from bottom)	5	
	$(N = 128)$	$(N = 176)$	$(N = 105)$	$(N = 153)$	$(N = 562)$[d]
	$N_s = 41$	$N_s = 52$	$N_s = 56$	$N_s = 47$	$N_s = 196$

[a] All are k samples, traced back to the preceding year.

[b] Before it merged in 1940, the Methodist Episcopal church published its national *Minutes of the Annual Conferences* in two self-contained volumes, one for conferences that had the annual clerical meeting in the fall, and one for those with spring meetings. Separate tabulations have been made but no consistent differences appeared, nor is there any obvious geographical or other distinction between the two groups. All tables combine fall and spring.

[c] Drawn as a systematic random sample. There are seventy-six entries in the average column in both decades.

[d] This is also the sum of all entries in Table C.10.

Table C.12   Composition and Mobility of Methodist Clergy by Employment Status; Averages Over Two Decades Computed from Table C.10   (percent)

	1–1 jobs	Pool	Limbo	Retired	Total
Composition of clergy, average year $x + 1$	56.7	14.1	7.9	21.3	100 ($N = 545$)
In-mobility rate	36.6	18.2	44.2	11.2	545
Out-mobility rate	38.0	20.2	42.8	8.0	549

like Table C.7. The sum $b + c$ corresponds to the sum of mobile entries in the 1–1 job column; $b' + c'$ to the sum of moves in the 1–1 job row. The count for a in Section B.7 is the sum of mobile entries in the 1–1 job *row* in the pool, limbo, retired, and outside columns; the transpose sum is the count for a'. However, the formulas in Section B.7 are also used for a single k or k' sample in isolation, and no attempt was made to correct for overlooked moves as done in the outside row and column of Table C.7. It is not surprising that the direct mobility estimates for each decade in Table

C.3 tend to be slightly smaller than the estimates from weighted chains in Table C.1. The latter average out close to the mobility rates in Table C.9 for 1–1 jobs.)

The best assessment of the importance of 1–1 jobs in mobility comes from adding up all the mobile entries in the first row and column in Table C.7; those 202 moves are 77 percent of all moves, in or out or both, in the table. Each such move lies in a vacancy chain. Only 23 percent of all moves by Episcopal clergy do not lie in vacancy chains.

Three-quarters of active Methodist clergy also are in 1–1 jobs, but 20 rather than 10 percent are retired. Turnover and mobility estimates for the whole clergy are reported in Tables C.10–C.12 (parallel to the three tables for Episcopal clergy). Mobility into and out of jobs is very much higher in the Methodist case. The estimated recruitment rate for new ministers is small (13/545) as in the Episcopal church, but it is actually less than the rate for death and deposition. The net loss in clergy is estimated at 140 per year on the average, for a decline of 2100 over fourteen years, which agrees with the official figures in Table C.5.

The central question to ask on total turnover is how much takes place in vacancy chains. In the Methodist clergy of this era, 81 percent of all moves (142 of 176) lie in vacancy chains, either as terminal events or as moves between 1–1 jobs. Vacancy chains encompass the great majority of all moves in each church. Few of the chains are loops, and most mobility is connected intimately to recruitment and death. The average move falls in a vacancy chain of considerable length and was thus contingent on a number of other events, at first sight unrelated.

Notes

1. Logic of Opportunity

1. See, for example, G. L. Palmer et al., *The Reluctant Job Changer* (Phila.: University of Pennsylvania Press, 1962).

2. O. D. Duncan, "Methodological Issues in the Analysis of Social Mobility," in N. J. Smelser and S. M. Lipset, eds., *Social Structure and Mobility in Economic Development* (Chicago: Aldine, 1966).

3. J. S. Coleman, *Introduction to Mathematical Sociology* (New York: Free Press, 1964), Chapter 5.

4. See, for example, K. Svalastoga, *Prestige, Class, and Mobility* (London: Heinemann, 1959), Section 5.3; and R. V. Clements, *Managers: A Study of their Careers in Industry* (London: Allen & Unwin, 1958).

5. A basic analysis of types of theories, emphasizing general issues, can be found in K. Davis, *Human Society* (New York: Macmillan, 1948), especially pp. 167–169. One of the four main approaches he distinguishes, "views a society as a system of social positions"; but the view ends with some simple categories of people (classes, strata, and so on) and a few principles of recruitment of individuals to categories (ascription versus achievement, and so on).

6. See, for example, J. A. Davis, *Great Books and Small Groups* (New York: Free Press, 1961).

7. See P. F. Lazarsfeld and M. Rosenberg, eds., *The Language of Social Research* (New York: Free Press, 1955), especially the article by A. Barton; see also C. Coombs, *A Theory of Data* (New York: Wiley, 1964). A recent survey of measures of association is Leo Goodman and W. H. Kruskal, "Measures of Association for Cross Classifications," I, II, and III, *Journal of American Statistical Association*, 49:732–764 (1954); 54:123–163 (1959); 58:310–364 (1963). Some effects of marginal constraints on how association should be measured have been discussed in several articles published in the 1940s; see G. A. Barnard, "Significance Tests for 2×2 Tables," *Biometrika*, 34:123–132 (1947).

8. S. B. Chrimes, in *An Introduction to the Administrative History of Medieval England*, 2nd ed. (Oxford: Blackwell, 1959), shows the slow and complex generation of a stable structure of offices in a society. No one office or title was meaningful except in the context of the interlocking set of positions at that time. The process of formation of organizations is greatly speeded once prototypes exist to be copied, and the real nature of positions in an interlocking structure is then obscured.

9. Paul Tillich, *Systematic Theology*, vol. III (Chicago: University of Chicago, 1963), especially pp. 12–13.

10. S. F. Nadel, *The Theory of Social Structure* (London: Cohen & West, 1956).

11. P. M. Sorokin, *Social and Cultural Mobility* (New York: Free Press, 1959).

12. V. Pareto, *Treatise on General Sociology*, ed. A. Livingston (New York: Dover, 1963), paragraphs 2025–2058.

13. R. K. Kelsall, in *Higher Civil Servants in Britain* (London: Routledge and Kegan Paul, 1955), has carried through one of the few intensive studies of career

mobility within a well-defined organization of men and jobs. Explicit selection of young men for elite positions has been maintained there so far but only after two adjustments: extensive superficial changes in the direction of impartiality of selection and more explicit allowance for promotion to elite positions at later ages.

14. Chains of matchmaking were used in earlier work by the author: H. C. White, "Cause and Effect in Social Mobility Tables," *Behavioral Science*, 8:14–27 (1963). Many abstract formulations of matchmaking problems, such as the committee chairman problem, can be found in O. Ore, *The Theory of Graphs* (Providence: American Mathematical Society, 1962).

15. A recent survey of game theory is R. D. Luce and H. Raiffa, *Games and Decisions* (New York: Wiley, 1957).

16. Some discussions of the philosophy of science which bear on these arguments are H. Weyl, *Philosophy of Mathematics and Natural Science* (Princeton, N.J.: Princeton University, 1949), pt. II, chaps. 2 and 3; and T. Kuhn, *The Structure of Scientific Revolutions* (Chicago: University of Chicago Press, 1964).

17. Terms such as "institutional system" are common in sociological writing. See the definition of "institutional complex" in R. M. MacIver, *Society* (New York: Rinehart, 1937). An explication of what is intended here by institutional system can be found in H. C. White and C. White, *Canvases and Careers* (New York: Wiley, 1963), pp. 2–4.

18. T. Whisler, "Measuring Centralization of Control in Business Organizations," in W. W. Cooper et al., eds, *New Perspectives in Organizational Research* (New York: Wiley, 1964), chap. 18.

19. A recent review of this area is by W. Starbuck, "Organizational Growth and Development," in J. G. March, ed., *Handbook of Organizations* (New York: Rand McNally, 1965), chap. 11.

20. See W. Evans, "Indices of the Hierarchical Structure of Organizations," *Management Science*, 9:468–477 (1963).

21. See Whisler, "Measuring Centralization of Control in Business Organizations"; and D. Roberts, *Executive Compensation* (New York: Free Press, 1959). Salary schedules for civil servants are not rigid in practice either; see, for example, Subcommittee on Manpower Utilization, "Legislative Control of Federal Positions and Salaries," Report to the Committee on Post Office and Civil Service, U.S. House of Representatives, 85th Congress, 2nd Session (November, 1958).

22. The National Industrial Conference Board in *Studies in Personnel Policy* has sponsored a number of useful surveys of practices that are partly normative but partly reportorial; see nos. 157, 168, and 183.

23. One work which directly attacks the problem of the generation of prestige structures is R. Tuck, *An Economic Theory of Rank* (New York: Oxford University Press, 1954).

2. *Markov Models of Vacancy Chains*

1. Both a basic discussion and detailed application of stochastic models, including Bernoulli trials and Markov chains, can be found in W. Feller, *An Introduction to Probability Theory and Its Applications*, vol. I, 2nd ed. (New York: Wiley, 1957).

2. A useful mathematical reference is J. S. Kemeny and J. L. Snell, *Finite Markov Chains* (New York: Van Nostrand, 1960). Their chapter 3 deals with absorbing chains. Section 6.2 can be used to define an artificial, closed-system form of the model, which would be useful in the comparisons of Chapter 9 of this volume. Their sections 6.3–6.5 demonstrate the difficulties in adequately defining concrete strata and should be read in conjunction with Chapters 4 and 6 in this volume.

Ways in which the Markov chain may be imbedded in stochastic processes in continuous time, which Kemeny and Snell do not consider, are taken up in Section 7.7 here. The basic reference is R. Pyke, " Markov Renewal Processes with Finitely Many States," *Annals of Mathematical Statistics*, 32:1260 (1961).

3. Unless moves occurred only at evenly spaced dates, the Markov property would no longer be plausible. Coleman sketches some ways to infer an underlying Markov process from turnover data gathered at regular intervals in *Introduction to Mathematical Sociology*, chap. 5.

4. A basic reference on the theory of statistical inference for finite Markov chains is P. Billingsley, "Statistical Methods in Markov Chains," *Annals of Mathematical Statistics*, 32:12–40 (1961). In concluding, Billingsley speaks of the need for investigation of inference for absorbing Markov processes (p. 35). Leo Goodman applies the theory, much of it developed in a prior series of his technical articles, to panel data on voting in "Statistical Methods for Analyzing Processes of Change," *American Journal of Sociology*, 68:57–78 (1962); again the methods are not directly applicable to absorbing Markov chains.

5. In two of the three organizations studied, some vacancy chains run longer than one calendar year. To preserve the convention of separate cohorts, each such chain is assigned in its entirety to a single cohort; see Section B.4 for further discussion.

6. In Chapter 9 the vacancy model will be placed in the context of a whole array of related models in various literatures. In particular a number of specific models close to the "constant turnover" model will be cited, all of them used for sociological or demographic purposes. It was, however, inappropriate to single out any of the latter to play the role of straw man here. These models had purposes other than the sheer prediction of turnover and have dealt with systems in which 1–1 jobs may not predominate.

3. Tracing Vacancy Chains

1. The most extensive early survey of clergy is M. A. May and F. Shuttleworth, *The Education of American Ministers* (New York: Institute of Social and Religious Research, 1934). The appendices (vol. IV) contain rich data not only on training but also on many aspects of the parish ministry, salaries, turnover, time budgets, size distributions, and so on. Dr. R. P. Scherer of the National Council of Churches has recently completed extensive comparative studies of salaries, careers, and work loads of the clergy of white Protestant denominations in the United States. For his preliminary reports see National Council of Churches, *Information Service*, vol. XLII, no. 9 (1963); and vol. XLIII, no. 19 (1964). See also F. E. Johnson and J. E. Ackerman, *The Church as Employer* (New York: Harper, 1959).

2. Appendix A cites the principal publications consulted for each church.

3. For a more critical recent assessment from inside the church, see Special Committee to Study Theological Education in the Episcopal Church, *First Findings* (New York: Episcopal Church Foundation, 1967).

4. There are other alternative events in principle: (1) The same man, C for example, can be listed as holding both job b and job c in 1920. That double listing, of the same man in two independent 1–1 jobs, is occasionally found. In all the churches examined there is, however, an implicit rule against such double listing; in the alphabetical list of clergymen, only one job is ever listed. (2) Two occupants would be listed for the same job.

5. Typically, in the main Protestant churches in the 1900s the time between a man's leaving one job and entering another is much shorter than the delay in filling a vacancy. One could code any one-year period in limbo as a boundary event. However, a man may be listed in limbo for a year as an indirect result of delays in filling vacancies. The two problems tend to interact. Often, for example, a man is listed as unemployed in a year in which the job for which he will be listed in the next annual is also listed as vacant. In fact, the man had already taken over the job in the middle of the year. There are less than a fifth as many listings of one-year limbos for a man as of one-year vacancies for a job in the Episcopal church in most years and areas. Usually a limbo abuts a vacancy listing. Hence a one-year limbo is treated as a terminal event only if it does not abut a one-year vacancy either in the job the man leaves or in the job to which he goes after the one-year listing in limbo. This is the rule in both the Episcopal and Presbyterian churches. A listing in limbo for successive annuals always constitutes a boundary event for a chain.

6. If the duality between man and 1–1 job were to be maintained, a similar duality should be recognized between 1–1 jobs listed simply as empty for a year and jobs to which some temporary coverage was assigned, say, from an archdeacon or general missionary. The latter status of "piecemeal empty" would be analogous to men in pool jobs, and a single entry in an annual would define a boundary event. The former status would be analogous to limbo for men, and a rule of tracing chains through one-year vacancies would apply to that status only. It was not practicable to make this distinction, however, because reporting practices varied widely.

7. *Yearbook of American Churches*, National Council of Churches of Christ in the United States, published in New York annually.

4. Specifying a Stratified Model

1. There is one difference between sample sets of chains used in this chapter and those used in Appendix C: loops are omitted here. The exact numbers and length of loops in each sample are specified in Section C.2.

2. About two-thirds of the total sample are in 1–1 jobs each year. This fraction is consistent with the combined result in Table C.7—the ratio of the first column sum there to the total in year $x + 1$.

3. The figures in the first column of Table 4.8 could not be obtained from sample entries alone. A substantial fraction of chains start with new jobs or with moves into empty jobs, which cannot be tabulated directly from the moves observed for men in the samples from the clergy index. The fraction is larger for the small than

for the big jobs. Similarly chain terminations cannot be tabulated from moves by sample entries into jobs (which are combined with moves out of jobs in the first column of Table 4.7). The total weighted number of chains in Table 4.8 disagrees slightly with the total for the observed length distribution in Table 4.4. The tabulations for Table 4.8 were made in the exploratory phase of work before all the samples of chains were checked again and a few corrections made in terms of the final version of the coding and weighting rules. Table 4.8 excludes loops but includes subsidiary and K-correction chains.

4. The figure of 800 communicants as the level above which an assistant pastor should be obtained has been mentioned in several official reports on the supply of ministers in the Episcopal church. All assistants in cathedrals are considered to be in the middle stratum regardless of the explicit number of communicants for the cathedral.

5. Bishops, except those who are retired, are assigned to the top stratum—pastorates above 300 communicants—whether the bishops are ordinaries, coadjutors, suffragans or missionaries. Combined with bishops are deans of cathedrals, heads of departments of the national council, archdeacons, and heads of city missionary societies in major metropolises. Chaplains at official Episcopal secondary schools are assigned to the bottom stratum of small pastorates. All other 1–1 jobs, such as university chaplaincies when stably maintained, are assigned to the middle stratum of pastorates—100–299 communicants.

6. Because two k samples instead of one are combined with the k' sample for 1954–1955 to form the K sample there, the row sums in the data for that decade in Table 4.12 should be divided by $\frac{2}{3}$ before comparing them in absolute size with earlier row sums.

7. The estimated size of the bottom stratum is notably small in 1943–1944, and it is true that the q_{i3} are smaller there. In 1912–1913 the top stratum is estimated to be smallest in number of jobs, but the q_{i1} are not noticeably smaller than in other decades.

8. The numbers from the sample set of weighted chains can be checked against the numbers of moves observed in the clergy index samples, which can be calculated from Table 4.6 or Table 4.7. The latter are not quite comparable since they refer to men not vacancies; in spite of that and sampling variability, there should be and is rough agreement.

9. As a rough test, the row sum of weighted moves in a stratum in Table 4.12 can be compared with the number of sample jobs in the stratum that year, which can be computed from Table 4.14.

10. The vacancies received in one wave are in turn sent on during the next wave. Ultimately the total number of vacancies received in a year equals the total number of vacancies sent on by a stratum and each reflects the whole matrix of probabilities Q in interaction with the numbers of vacancy creations, $\mathbf{F}(t)$, as shown in equation (2.10).

11. Section 2.4 showed that for a given sample of chains, overall length predictions of the forward and reverse models necessarily match exactly.

12. A fair comparison of constancy of parameters in the vacancy and turnover models requires either a reformulation or an extension; one of each is presented in Section 5.2 on turnover predictions.

5. Tests over Five Decades

1. The reciprocal of the number of chains is a rough indicator of a minimum difference in percentages that is meaningful in a distribution of chains. That is, if there are only 20 chains in a sample, a percentage cannot be smaller than 5 and can be measured in units of 5. Weights complicate the picture, but it is reasonable to assess differences between percentages in terms of a minimum increment that is meaningful for observed percentages.

2. A. M. Mood, *Introduction to the Theory of Statistics* (New York: McGraw-Hill, 1950); and Chapter 2, n. 4, in this volume.

3. In Section 5.1 it was possible to test prediction based on a set of chains with observations on the same set because parameter estimates came from individual moves whereas observations were on chains as entities.

4. A move by a man from a job thereupon left "empty" is not common enough to be reported separately. However, such instances are distinctive in that only after two annuals have appeared, is it known whether a job left "empty" has been so all along. Moves to empty jobs as beginning events are unlike other moves. In some sense it could be argued that the "vacancy" that is both created and moved by a man's entering an empty job has existed for a long time. The reasoning behind the rejection of this argument is given in Section 3.2. The possibilities of predicting frequency of beginning event in advance also differ among other types of beginning event.

5. There are some changes in provincial boundaries over 1920–1950, but generally the Northeast includes provinces 1, 2, and United States Overseas (New England, New York, New Jersey, Puerto Rico, Canal Zone, Hawaii, Alaska); the South includes provinces 3, 4, and 7 (Pennsylvania, West Virginia, Kentucky, Missouri, Kansas, New Mexico and all states south of these); and the West consists of all other dioceses in the continental United States, that is, provinces 5, 6, and 8. The three regions are roughly equal in size, each having about 2500 clergy in 1955. The South tends to be Low Church; the Northeast has both High and Low Church together with rather stable patterns of mixed churchmanship within dioceses; and the West tends to be High Church. Provinces in the Northeast have been stable in size; they have changed from a deficit to a surplus of priests over parishes and missions, in large part because of growing numbers of nonparochial staff jobs and declining numbers of rural churches. The South includes both stable and growing provinces, in all of which clergy have remained fewer in number than parishes and missions. In the West, a deficit of clergy with respect to parishes and missions continues within the stable province, but a surplus has developed in the growing provinces. Average salaries at the midpoint of the era, reported by the Church Pension Fund in Appendix 8 of the *Journal of General Convention* in 1940, are highest in the Northeast, intermediate in the West, and lowest in the South, although there is considerable variation between individual dioceses largely because of different proportions of rural parishes.

6. Models for Three Organizations Compared

1. The number of "full members" is equated with the number of communicants used for the Episcopal case; in earlier years when the distinction is made, the

"nonresident" members of each Methodist congregation have been subtracted from the total membership given in the minutes. District superintendents as well as bishops and national department heads have been assigned ex officio to the big stratum. As in the Episcopal church, the size refers to a whole pastoral charge, often a combination of distinct small congregations. Assistants are rare in Methodist churches, but they are assigned to the medium or the small stratum using the same cutoff size, 800, as in Chapter 4.

2. For each year, histograms were plotted for parochial clergy from the clerical index sample using intervals of $250 on salary from $0 to $5,000 (only 0.6 percent in the earlier year and 2.9 percent in the later year fell in the residual interval of salaries above $5,000). The combined index samples used in Table 6.4 are classified by status in previous year in the first column of Table C.10 (which also contains 16 entries for men in nonparochial 1–1 jobs in year $x + 1$).

3. In the random sample of vacancy chains from 1959–1960 identified in Appendix C, there proved to be only 2.29 weighted moves (6 raw moves) by vacancies out of jobs in the small stratum. An additional sample was therefore drawn, by tracing forward to 1960 from the seventh entry in each column of the clerical index of the 1959 minutes. Estimates of probabilities in the first two strata were not substantially altered by the sample enlargement.

4. Compare Tables C.6 and C.1. Turn to subsection 3.2 for the rules in coding prolonged vacancies in jobs as transition to the empty state.

5. Compare the totals reported in the first row (or column) in Tables C.7 and C.10 with the corresponding total (weighted) numbers of vacancy creations, that is of chains, over all samples.

7. Vacancy Models and System Evolution

1. A convenient reference is Edward J. Cogan and Robert Z. Norman, *Handbook of Calculus, Difference, and Differential Equations* (Englewood Cliffs, New Jersey: Prentice-Hall, 1958). Nonlinear versions of the vacancy model are treated in the last section of chap. 11.

2. The logic is the same as in "ex post" forecasting in economics. See T. C. Koopmans, *Three Essays on the State of Economic Science* (New York: McGraw-Hill, 1957), pp. 201 and 204.

3. Interpretations of coupled differential equations in social science models can be found in H. Simon, *Models of Man* (New York: Wiley, 1958) especially the chapter on Homan's theory of small groups; and J. Kemeny and J. L. Snell, *Mathematical Models in the Social Sciences* (Boston: Ginn, 1962), chap. 3, where, again, the coupled equations are nonlinear.

4. See any basic text on mechanics; for example, J. C. Slater and N. H. Frank, *Mechanics* (New York: McGraw-Hill, 1947), chap. 2.

5. A basic discussion of units, in the context of physics, is P. W. Bridgman, *Dimensional Analysis* (New Haven, Conn.: Yale University Press, 1963).

6. See Cogan and Norman, *Handbook of Calculus*.

7. A thorough treatment will be found in any advanced text on applied calculus; for examples, C. R. Wylie, Jr., *Advanced Engineering Mathematics* (New York: McGraw-Hill, 1960), chap. 4.

8. A thorough analysis of the solution of polynomial equations, in particular cubic ones, and proofs of the rules and theorems used in this chapter, can be found in H. W. Turnbull, *Theory of Equations* (Edinburgh: Oliver and Boyd, 1946).

9. See Wylie, *Advanced Engineering Mathematics*.

10. The term "imbedding" comes from D. G. Kendall, "Stochastic Processes Occurring in the Theory of Queues and their Analysis by the Method of the Imbedded Markov Chain," *Annals of Mathematical Statistics*, 24:338–354 (1953).

11. Markov processes are used extensively in models of queuing. An excellent brief guide is D. R. Cox and W. L. Smith, *Queues* (London: Methuen, 1961).

12. See W. Feller, *An Introduction to Probability Theory and Its Applications*, vol. I, 2nd ed. (New York: Wiley, 1957), p. 428.

13. The basic Kolmogorov equations for Markov processes among discrete states are stated in sec. 17.9 of Feller, *ibid.*, vol. I. In vol. II, Feller presents a more general and practicable formulation in terms of Laplace transforms in sec. 14.7; and he shows how to work directly with probabilistic interpretations of the transforms in secs. 14.8 and 14.9; see also sec. 10.3.

14. See *ibid.*, vol. II, p. 470, prob. 12.

15. R. Pyke, "Markov Renewal Processes: Definitions and Preliminary Properties," *Annals of Mathematical Statistics*, 32:1231–1259 (1961). The relation to a semi-Markov process is specified on p. 1234.

16. See D. R. Cox, *Renewal Theory* (London: Methuen, 1962). The example on p. 29 treats "renewal" of men in an organization, although without reference to the idea of a chain of replacements. Inventory theory also can suggest models for arrivals and departures of men, especially as to the coupling between them; see P. M. Morse, *Queues, Inventories, Maintenance* (New York: Wiley, 1958), chap. 10.

17. See Y. Taga, "On the Limiting Distributions in Markov Renewal Processes with Finitely Many States," *Annals of the Institute of Statistical Mathematics*, 15: sec. 4 (1963).

18. The chain length problem can be translated into a variety of standard problems in Markov processes. Consider a single-server queue with Poisson input at rate λ and negative exponential service at rate μ. Identify the service process with terminal jumps by a vacancy, $\mu = pv$. Identify the arrival process with internal jumps by the vacancy, $\lambda = qv$. Then the length distribution of vacancy chains is the probability distribution of how many new items arrive during the servicing of a given item. The latter distribution is known to be

$$\frac{\lambda^{j-1}\mu}{(\lambda + \mu)^j}$$

which is easily seen to be equivalent to equations (7.72) and (2.3).

19. See Wylie, *Advanced Engineering Mathematics*, p. 300.

20. The result on length distributions could easily be extended to the generalized Poisson process, with v a scalar as in previous sections.

21. Delays as a reflection of interaction among individuals at service facilities is the usual focus of queue models. Normally there is no analogue to the set of job strata, but see Section 9.5.

22. See Chapter 8.

23. A clear introduction to the ideas and conventions for graphs is 0. Ore, *Graphs and their Uses* (New York: Random House, 1963).

24. There is a large literature on the combinatorics of graphs, with various kinds of restrictions on the number of lines, components, cycles, and so on. See, for example, T. Austin, R. Fagen, W. Penney, and J. Riordan, "The Number of Components in Random Linear Graphs," *Annals of Mathematical Statistics*, 30:747–754 (1959). Even when a formal solution is obtained, actual calculations of the numbers, from which a priori probabilities of graphs with defined properties would be calculated, are formidable. No provision is made for the probability of a line between two points depending on what subset each point is in, as would be required for a stratified model.

25. See Feller, *Introduction to Probability Theory*, vol. I.

26. See Chapter 9 and the fixed turnover model in Sections 2.6 and 2.7.

8. Mobility Models with Interaction

1. T. C. Koopmans, *Three Essays on the State of Economic Science* (New York: McGraw-Hill, 1957), preface.

2. *Ibid.*, p. 154.

3. An interesting empirical analysis, consonant at many points with the vacancy model, is T. H. Smith, *The Marketing of Used Automobiles* (Bureau of Business Research, Ohio State University, 1941).

4. *Ibid.*, chap. 7–10.

5. It is obvious from equation (8.4) that the approach to equilibrium is rapid. The actual solution for T as a function of time, where T has the value T_0 at time $t = 0$, is

$$T(t) = \frac{T_-(T_+ - T_0) + T_+(T_0 - T_-) \exp[-(T_+ - T_-)t]}{(T_+ - T_0) + (T_0 - T_-) \exp[-(T_+ - T_-)t]}$$

Here t is measured in units of $1/\alpha$. The speed of approach to T_- from T_0 is governed by the decay rate, $T_+ - T_-$, in both exponentials. Equation (8.6) shows this rate is at least $[(\beta/\alpha)N_0]^{1/2}$ even when $N_0 = J_0$ and β/α is small. If $\beta/\alpha = 0.01N_0$, so that the equilibrium model T_- is 90 percent of N_0, the decay rate is $0.1N_0$, in units of $1/\alpha$.

6. N. T. J. Bailey, *The Mathematical Theory of Epidemics* (London: Griffin, 1957). The model diagrammed in Figure 8.2 is from his sec. 4.3, p. 22.

7. A convenient introduction is J. Kemeny and J. Snell, *Mathematical Models in the Social Sciences* (Boston: Ginn, 1962), chap. 3. The predation model in Figure 8.3 corresponds to their eq. 3 (the first model; their second model is a simplified version of the Lanchester models taken up next).

8. L. Dolansky, "Present State of the Lanchester Theory of Combat," *Operations Research*, 12:344–359 (1964). Although there are numerous misprints in the article itself, there is an excellent bibliography. A recent systematic study of data is H. K. Weiss, "Combat Models and Historical Data: The U.S. Civil War," *Operations Research*, 14:759–791 (1966).

9. See Bailey, *Mathematical Theory of Epidemics*, chaps. 5, 6, and 8; for a stochastic version of the Lanchester model, see R. H. Brown, "Theory of Combat: The Probability of Winning," *Operations Research*, 11:418–426 (1963).

10. For some background on membership in committees and mobility among committees see, for example, the discussion of committees and their relation to careers in T. Burns and G. Stalker, *The Management of Innovation* (London: Tavistock, 1961).

11. The importance of committees (called councils) in shaping the direction of change in a complex organization, an evolving central government, is emphasized in S. B. Chrimes, *An Introduction to the Administrative History of Medieval England*, 2nd ed. (Blackwell: Oxford, 1952), which is relevant background for the whole paragraph.

12. Most of the empirical studies of overlap in membership of committees deal with interlocking directorates that link together different formal organizations at a top level. A small table of individual memberships by a sample of forty-two elite males in the boards of sixteen prestigious institutions in 1940 is given in E. D. Baltzell, *An American Business Aristocracy* (New York: Crowell-Collier, Macmillan, 1962), pp. 408–411. A mathematical tool for dealing with such data is the rectangular incidence matrix of zeros and ones; for definition and development, see H. J. Ryser, *Combinatorial Mathematics*, Carus Mathematical Monograph 14 (New York: Wiley, 1963), secs. 5.4, 5.5, chap. 6, and references. Data from 1935 on gross features of the interlocking of directorates among the 250 largest United States corporations is presented in a 1939 report of the National Resources Committee reprinted in R. Bendix and S. M. Lipset, *Class, Status, and Power* (New York: Free Press, 1953), chap. 11, table 3 (distribution of marginal totals for directorships among individuals), and table 4 (numbers of corporations that share one or more directors with j or more other corporations, $j = 1, 2, 3$).

There also is a large literature on overlap between cliques, coalitions, or other informal social groups; but those have no permanent identities.

13. Ryser, *Combinatorial Mathematics*, is an incisive survey of combinatorial problems.

14. To say that counts of possible incumbencies of men in sets of committees are difficult without considering mobility could be misleading. Two quite different forms of counting can be used: the number of allocations of a population of men among a set of committees, and the number of ways a man could be assigned to a committee. The former could be used to compute an a priori likelihood of a given type of distribution of men among committees at one time. The latter is more relevant as a basis for estimating instantaneous rate of change. Both could be applied either to total populations of men and of committees or to some subsets of available men and unfilled committees. The main difficulty, for either form of counting, is allowing for the restriction that a given man appears, at most, once on a given committee. The second form of counting, more appropriate to rates of change and thus to mobility models, is actually simpler. Indeed, a simple product $N \times V$ could be a reasonable approximation.

15. One possible approximation to the ex officio case would be positions in county government in Tudor England as described by V. K. Dibble, "The Organization of Traditional Authority," in J. G. March, ed., *Handbook of Organizations* (New York: Rand McNally, 1964), chap. 21.

16. A survey of possible mobility models for systems of groups, focused on the

size distribution of groups predicted in equilibrium, is H. C. White, "Chance Models of Systems of Casual Groups," *Sociometry*, 25:153–172 (1962).

17. See, for example, B. J. L. Berry and W. Garrison, "Alternate Explanations of Urban Rank-Size Relationships," in H. Mayer and C. Kohn, eds., *Readings in Urban Geography* (Chicago: University of Chicago Press, 1959). Rather similar models have been used to find size distributions from "mobility" processes in which the units are indistinguishable entities such as dollars moving among, say, business firms; see H. A. Simon and C. P. Bonini, "The Size Distribution of Business Firms," *American Economic Review*, 48:607 (1958).

18. Extensive references and discussion can be found in L. A. Goodman and W. A. Kruskal, "Measures of Association for Cross Classifications," pts. I and II, *Journal of the American Statistical Association*, 49:732–764 (1954); and 54:123–163 (1959). Section 11.5 here reports on an alternative approach to association measures that is relevant to assessing interaction in mobility of men among job strata.

9. Single-Flows Models of Mobility

1. A convenient reference to the abstract aspects of diffusion and fluid flow theories in physics is P. M. Morse and H. Feshbach, *Methods of Theoretical Physics* (New York: McGraw-Hill, 1952), Sections 2.3, 2.4, 7.4, 12.1, and 12.2. Chapter 6 is a lucid description of the effects of boundary conditions in dynamic models, and Section 6.2 shows how the determinate analogue of random walks can be a useful approximation to models for a continuous state space. In diffusion, unlike in fluid flow, one assumes a medium through which the fluid moves; and diffusion models are therefore more closely related to the matching processes discussed in Chapter 8 in this volume.

2. There is a clear account of higher order chains in Section 6.6 of J. Kemeny and J. L. Snell, *Finite Markov Chains* (New York: Van Nostrand, 1960).

3. See K. K. Kurihara, *Introduction to Keynesian Dynamics* (London: Allen and Unwin, 1956), p. 87.

4. See R. Dorfman, P. A. Samuelson, and R. M. Solow, *Linear Programming and Economic Analysis* (New York: McGraw-Hill, 1958), p. 231 n. The account of the Leontief system in their Chapters 9 and 10 is relied on throughout Section 9.1. It is especially convenient that they do not "net out" the diagonal terms (p. 205 n.). The closed Leontief system will not be mentioned until Section 9.3 in this volume.

5. *Ibid.*, sec. 10.2.

6. *Ibid.*, p. 215.

7. *Ibid.*, p. 239.

8. For example, each element in the whole matrix $(I - Q)^{-1}$ will be decreased if a single q_{ij} is decreased (*Ibid.*, p. 254) so that all components of the predicted vector of flows will be decreased. Perhaps the most useful aspect of the Leontief literature will prove to be the discussion of problems of aggregation (*Ibid.*, secs. 10.4 and 10.8): how to define "industries," and the errors involved in lumping industries together. The approach in Sections 4.2–4.4 here to choice of church strata is rather arbitrary and would prove inadequate with larger samples available for larger systems. See particularly D. Rosenblatt, "Aggregation in Matrix Models of

Resource Flows," I and II, in *American Statistician*, 19:36–39 (1965); and 21:32–37 (1967).

9. One might construe the Leontief system in new ways. For example, request for goods could become the dependent quantity, with production possibilities calling forth demand. In an economy running near capacity, new consumption orders in a week could be fixed by the additional production orders possible from the sum of new production facilities and facilities just freed by completion of existing orders. Each available facility would call forth an order from goods at an intermediate stage of processing or from direct new orders. Instead of being an aggregative model for the total production system at any time, in which demand is the limiting factor, a Leontief system could be construed as an aggregative model for the available part of production facilities, in which demand is seen as insatiable. Instead of one good being thought of as the combination of various amounts of other goods, its production could be viewed as a sequence of processing stages, one triggering off another; in the aggregative model, individual sequence structures for particular batches of goods of a general type would be averaged.

10. Quite independent of the concern with the age variable is the question of treating time as a continuous rather than as a discrete variable (see Section 7.7).

11. See N. Keyfitz and E. M. Murphy, *Comparative Demographic Calculations* (Chicago: Population Research and Training Center, 1964), Introduction, and references in the introduction.

12. See P. H. Karmel, *Population Studies*, 1:249–274 (1947); 2:240–273, 354–360 (1948). See also G. Stolnitz and N. Ryder, "Recent discussion of the net reproduction rate," in J. Spengler and O. D. Duncan, eds., *Demographic Analysis: Selected Readings* (New York: Free Press, 1956).

13. Formally, the vector $\mathbf{b}'$ can be inserted into the matrix Q as its initial column (which otherwise is all zeros); then equation (9.13) has only one term on the right, and Q is the total transformation operator called T by Keyfitz and Murphy, *Comparative Demographic Calculations*, p. 10. The birth rate vector $\mathbf{b}'$ does not deal with mobility of the existing population among age states. It is better to keep it separate so that Q retains the character of a transition probability matrix, as it does for the vacancy model and for social mobility models in the next section.

14. The form of Q is so simple that the eigenvalue theory of matrices is not needed; mere difference equations suffice. For balanced growth at rate r to be possible, r must satisfy a polynomial equation in which the coefficients are certain combinations of birth rates and transition rates.

15. In note 14, it would be purely fortuitous for $r = 1$ to be a root.

16. For an introduction to the von Neumann model, see J. Kemeny, J. Snell, and G. Thompson, *Introduction to Finite Mathematics* (Englewood Cliffs, N.J.: Prentice-Hall, 1957), secs. 7, 9, and 10; or see the relevant chapters in Dorfman et al., *Linear Programming*.

17. See J. Matras, "Social Mobility and Social Structure: Some Insights from the Linear Model," *American Sociological Review*, 32:613–614 (1967).

18. T. W. Anderson, "Probability Models for Analyzing Time Changes in Attitudes," in P. F. Lazarsfeld, ed., *Mathematical Thinking in the Social Sciences* (New York: Free Press, 1954). Anderson himself uses the term "flow model," p. 22. He emphasizes the use of statistical inference and thus the calculation of

variability. A large literature in these models has grown up. Much of James S. Coleman, *An Introduction to Mathematical Sociology* (New York: Free Press, 1963) works with variations on Anderson's models, formulated in continuous time; and it contains a comprehensive bibliography.

19. Anderson, *Mathematical Thinking*, pp. 36–39. The meaning of powers of the matrix interpreted for individuals is given on pp. 28–30.

20. *Ibid.*, pp. 49–51. Anderson could plausibly assume a connection between changes—suggested by his statistical tests of the matrix—and explicit outside events. Because political attitudes are unconstrained even the structure and rates of change can fluctuate rapidly. As Matras in "Social Mobility and Social Structure," points out, there is no difficulty in representing long-term turnover as a product of different matrices; but the number of transition parameters assumed increases so fast that there is little genuine predictive or explanatory power in such a representation. In Section 2.8 here long-term turnover is calculated as the product of distinct matrices, but all the matrices are explicit transformations of a fixed basic matrix Q.

21. Anderson considers such population distributions; see his "second interpretation" of the model for aggregates, *Mathematical Thinking*, p. 40.

22. Essentially the same approach to total moves is used in Chapter 7, where the vacancy model is formulated in continuous time.

23. This qualification corresponds to "netting out" the diagonal entries in a Leontief array reporting amounts of a commodity used up in producing a unit amount of that commodity for consumption.

24. The analogous equation for a continuous time model is a differential one, like equation (7.43) for $V(t)$ in the vacancy model.

25. Anderson, *Mathematical Thinking*, pp. 36–44.

26. *Ibid.*, pp. 54–59.

27. D. V. Glass, ed., *Social Mobility in Britain* (London: Routledge and Kegan Paul, 1954).

28. S. J. Prais, "Measuring Social Mobility," *Journal of the Royal Statistical Society*, A118:56–66 (1955); and "The Formal Theory of Social Mobility," *Population Studies*, 9:72–81 (1955).

29. The most comprehensive surveys are for Denmark and the United States. See K. Svalastoga, *Prestige, Class, and Mobility* (London: Heinemann, 1959), which contains an application of the Prais model in Section 5.4; and P. M. Blau and O. D. Duncan, *The American Occupational Structure* (New York: Wiley, 1967).

S. M. Lipset and R. Bendix compare and interpret the results of various national studies in *Social Mobility in Industrial Societies* (London: Heinemann, 1959). Exhaustive references to both the primary literature and the extensive secondary literature on measures and interpretation will be found there.

30. O. D. Duncan, "Methodological Issues in the Analysis of Social Mobility," in N. Smelsen and S. M. Lipset, eds., *Social Structure and Social Mobility in Economic Development* (Chicago: Aldine, 1966).

In Glass, *Social Mobility in Britain*, respondents report current occupation and father's last main occupation; not even the stage of career is held constant. However, Svalastoga, in *Prestige, Class, and Mobility*, reports both that and a cross-tabulation by own status at age 30 and father's status at age 30 (when many of the sons will be well into school age, "set" in aspirations); the two tables are remarkably similar.

31. There is some similarity between the idea of a national standard and Anderson's test of whether transition probabilities among compound categories equal the product of separate transition probabilities among each set of constituent categories; *Mathematical Thinking*, pp. 60–63.

32. Matras in "Social Mobility and Social Structure," makes the even simpler assumption that differential growth in categories can be represented by a diagonal matrix, equation 3.

33. H. C. White, "Cause and Effect in Social Mobility Tables," *Behavioral Science*, 8:14–27 (1963).

34. Leo Goodman has argued that the inheritance model gives an adequate account of the mobility tables for Britain and Denmark. See *American Journal of Sociology*, 70:564–585 (1965). For a counterargument, see H. C. White, "Stayers and Movers," *American Journal of Sociology*, in press.

35. White, "Stayers and Movers."

36. James S. Coleman, *Introduction to Mathematical Sociology* (New York: Macmillan, 1964), sec. 14.5.

37. A main theme in Coleman, *Introduction to Mathematical Sociology*, is that the structure of parameters in a Markov process will be simpler in a differential equation version than in a difference equation version. The truth of this theme depends on three powerful assumptions: the states form some kind of ordered array; in the ordered array, individual moves are confined to the neighbors of the initial state; and the interval between moves is much shorter than the interval used in the difference equations. When the method of imbedded Markov chains is used, the last assumption cannot be satisfied or, rather, is meaningless; the "time" integer in the difference equation simply records the sequential order of moves. The vacancy model given in Chapter 2 here is construed as an imbedded Markov chain model.

38. *Ibid.*, pp. 178–180.

39. I. Blumen, M. Kogan, and P. J. McCarthy, *The Industrial Mobility of Labor as a Probability Process* (Ithaca, New York: Cornell University, 1955).

40. White, "Stayers and Movers."

41. Blumen et al. also emphasize the need to use separate subpopulations (see their Section 7.3). They show that the mover-stayer model is not valid for an aggregate population if it consists of separate groups, perhaps not identifiable by obvious attributes like age and sex, each of which follows a Markov chain of its own. The vacancy model, however, requires that the population be treated as an interacting whole.

42. *Ibid.*, sec. 7.2.

43. *Ibid.*, p. 9.

44. *Ibid.*, p. 142.

45. W. J. Gordon and G. F. Newell, "Closed Queuing Systems," *Operations Research*, 15:254–265 (1967). On page 260, they show how the works of a series of other authors fit in as special cases.

46. W. J. Gordon and G. F. Newell, "Cyclic Queuing Systems," *Operations Research*, 15:266–277 (1967). Their model is a generalization of the well-known model for a single server with queue of finite capacity that turns away surplus customers, the arrival of customers being a Poisson process with fixed rate.

47. A natural mathematical framework for developing such an equivalence in the case of Markov chains is given in Kemeny and Snell, *Finite Markov Chains*, sec. 6.2.

48. Gordon and Newell, "Closed Queuing Systems," equations 11, 10, 12, 3, 4.

49. *Ibid.*, p. 263, and equations 20, 17, and 21.

50. Gordon and Newell, "Cyclic Queuing Systems," equations 1 and 2.

51. *Ibid.*, equations 6, 7.

52. *Ibid.*, equations 20, 21.

53. *Ibid.*, equation 33.

54. *Ibid.*, pp. 275–276.

55. In both papers by Gordon and Newell counts of states are made according to partitions of customers among stages (see p. 255 and p. 275, respectively), which correspond to assuming customers are indistinguishable and thus to the use of Bose-Einstein or Fermi-Dirac statistics. Markov chain models, however, correspond to use of Maxwell-Boltzmann statistics in counting system states. See W. Feller, *An Introduction to Probability Theory and Its Applications*, vol. I, 2nd ed. (New York: Wiley, 1957), p. 39.

56. D. Bartholomew, *Stochastic Models of Social Processes* (New York: Wiley, 1967).

57. *Ibid.*, p. 158.

58. G. Carlsson has formulated hypotheses, concerning the role of education as an intervening variable, within the framework of a model like Prais's in *Social Mobility and Class Structure* (Lund, Sweden: Gleerup, 1958), chap. 7. By far the most ambitious investigation is that of Duncan, reported in Blau and Duncan, *American Occupational Structure*. Partly because of his dissatisfaction with concepts like generation, Duncan denies the usefulness of mobility as a concept; see Section 10.7 in this volume.

59. Scepticism about the worth of Markov models either for men or for vacancies is expressed by D. D. McFarland in his recent judicious review, "Intragenerational Mobility as a Markov Process" (unpublished, December 20, 1968, Population Studies Center, University of Michigan).

60. Matras, "Social Mobility and Social Structure," contains references to his own series of articles on linear models of mobility.

61. Aside from the special case of demographic models, there seem to be few models of mobility for open systems that use Markov chains. One useful example, not actually applied to data, is found in J. Kemeny and J. Snell, *Mathematical Models in the Social Sciences* (Boston: Ginn, 1962), chap. 6. Dollars are the analogue to men (and therefore the distinguishability assumed in the statistics underlying Markov chains may not be appropriate). There is no analogue to jobs, only a set of categories labeled "cities." It is instructive to compare that dollar flow model with the vacancy chain model, since the duality is missing but transactions with the environment are treated explicitly. Kemeny and Snell treat the model as a normative one for deciding monetary policy, in particular, for designing a pattern of inputs (if any is possible) that will lead to a fixed distribution of currency that is considered ideal. They allow components of the constant input vector to be positive or negative. They require no sharp distinction to be drawn between inputs as causal events and outputs as dependent events. In the vacancy model, the distinction is essential if the concept of a chain of events is maintained, as discussed in detail in Section 7.2

in this volume. In short, there is no interaction between dollars in the Kemeny-Snell model, except indirectly through the imposition of policy goals, whereas the interaction among men in filling jobs is the crux of the vacancy model.

62. Matras, "Social Mobility and Social Structure."

63. See, for example, F. D. Harding and J. W. Merck, "Markov Chain Theory Applied to the Prediction of Retirement Rates," Technical Documentary Report PRL–TDR–64–14 (June, 1964), Office of Technical Services, U.S. Department of Commerce; and the reports cited therein. Markov process models for continuous time are used in an interesting unpublished paper on promotion in the United States Navy by D. P. Gaver, Jr.; and see Bartholomew, *Stochastic Models*.

10. Careers, Attributes, and Replacements

1. Since death and retirement depend intrinsically on age and seniority, it is awkward to fit them into any model where states of the Markov chain reflect only current job—whether the career models in Sections 9.3–9.4 or the vacancy chain model of Chapter 2. Once substrata for seniority of men are introduced in the vacancy chain model, as in Sections 10.2 and 10.6, it is easier to assess the impact of retirement policy and life-tables on careers of men according to the model.

2. The overall distribution of career lengths for a cohort is the product of C_χ and the vector g defining the proportions of the cohort which enter the system in various strata. If total careers, rather than segments in 1–1 jobs, are considered, entries are concentrated in the lowest stratum; so that component of C_χ is dominant.

3. In an unpublished manuscript, Scott Boorman makes some interesting suggestions: the distribution of career lengths for *jobs* in number of tenures can be predicted quite naturally in terms of the vacancy chain model, whereas career lengths of men can be predicted quite naturally in the bump chain model (see Section 10.3 here). The main point is that retirement rates for items may be built into the model more easily (see Section 7.3) in these two cases.

4. The topic of churchmanship within the Episcopal church is a complex one. The best way to gain perspective on how various groups within the clergy see the issues is to read the symposia that were published from time to time by the Church Congress, an avowedly nonpartisan, nonofficial organization for clerical discussion within the church. See especially *Honest Liberty in the Church* and *Problems of Faith and Worship* (New York: Macmillan, 1924 and 1926). The various outbursts of party strife are treated in W. W. Manross, *A History of the American Episcopal Church* (Milwaukee: Morehouse, 1935), chaps. 15–17.

5. One advantage of the use of seniority as an attribute of men (Sections 10.6 and 10.7) is its radical divorce from any conceivable attribute of jobs.

6. Neither the relative sizes of the two row totals nor the ratio of the two column totals in Table 10.7 can be regarded as fixed. There are enough men in any seniority category, in a given stratum, to answer all calls to vacancies in a given year.

7. The major work to date is reported in P. M. Blau and O. D. Duncan, *The American Occupational System* (New York: Wiley, 1967). Other applications and a clear introductory discussion will be found in O. D. Duncan, "Path Analysis: Sociological Examples," *American Journal of Sociology*, 72:1–16 (1966).

8. Path analysis was developed by Sewall Wright to trace the observable conse-

quences of genetic laws in measurements on populations. Duncan has revived it in an inverted form and applied it to the study of careers. H. M. Blalock's pioneer work on sequential interpretation of correlations (for example, see *Causal Inferences in Nonexperimental Research*, Chapel Hill: University of North Carolina, 1961) is subsumed, at least in those aspects germane to the study of careers, in Duncan's work. The inversion of path analysis they both do amounts to a special form for multivariate regression analysis, although statisticians have contributed little to this form. A lucid account is given by K. C. Land in "The Principles of Path Analysis," in E. F. Borgatta, ed., *Sociological Methodology* (San Francisco: Jossey-Bass, 1969).

9. Subpopulations of men can be distinguished by ascriptive attributes like sex and age in Markov chain models for men such as the models of Section 9.4. It remains true that the states of the chain itself cannot very well be differentiated on more than one dimension, and categorical discrimination on a given attribute only is feasible. However, in Duncan's method, subpopulations cannot be treated as independent since variation in a parameter of the regression equations with attributes such as age is assumed itself to have a simple linear form.

10. Limitations of data force Duncan to work with synthetic cohorts in many instances, which obscures any test for constancy in path coefficients over time.

11. R. W. Hodge examines the meaningfulness of careers using a variant of the Markov chain approach of J. Matras, "Social Mobility and Social Structure: Some Insights from the Linear Model," *American Sociological Review*, 32:611 (1967), applied to data for the United States as a whole. Hodge's conclusion resembles that from the vacancy models; "Neither the concept of *status inheritance* nor the notion of an orderly and consistent *career* seems applicable to more than a minor fraction of the population, unless, of course, one intends these concepts to apply only to data classified in extremely broad and necessarily coarse status categories." See R. W. Hodge, "Occupational Mobility as a Probability Process," *Demography*, 3:34 (1966). Hodge does not assume that transition probabilities remain fixed but instead focuses on whether the transition matrix for a long period is indeed simply a product of the observed matrices for the constituent intervals. Thus his approach is a statistical interpretation like Duncan's and may be consistent with vacancy chain models (see Sections 2.6 and 2.7 here). Hodge's results raise questions about Duncan's assumption that there are meaningful relations among a man's statuses at widely separated times.

12. Duncan's interpretation like Hodge's refers to a system that is, in effect, closed.

11. Interaction among Vacancies

1. For moves of men rather than of vacancies, the model in Section 9.5 of W. J. Gordon and G. F. Newell, "Cyclic Queuing Systems," *Operations Research*, 15:226–277 (1967), illustrates such a process. See also H. C. White, "Chance Models of Systems of Casual Groups," *Sociometry*, 25:153–172 (1962).

2. The multinomial distribution also can be derived by counting partitions, as shown in the account of Maxwell-Boltzmann statistics in W. Feller, *An Introduction to Probability Theory and Its Applications*, vol. I, 2nd ed. (New York: Wiley, 1950).

3. A convenient reference on information theory is C. E. Shannon and W. Weaver, *The Mathematical Theory of Communication* (Urbana: University of

Illinois, 1963). See derivation in Appendix 2 and the definitions of channel capacity, p. 7.

4. See the beginning of Section 11.3 here.

5. The Stirling approximation is discussed in Feller, *Introduction to Probability Theory*, p. 43. Corrections to Stirling's formula are negligible by comparison with the neglect of terms of the order of $(V/N)^2$ in the power series used for log $(N - V)$.

6. See W. G. Cochran, *Sampling Techniques* (New York: Wiley, 1953), pp. 17 and 69.

7. In the models for aggregates in Chapter 7, nonlinearity in V in the differential equations corresponds to interaction from overlap of randomly selected candidacies in the stochastic model for individuals. The general behavior of the system deduced from standard phase diagrams for the nonlinear equations is not unlike the linear solutions. See the chapter on Homans' theory of group interaction in H. Simon, *Models of Man* (New York: Wiley, 1957), for a lucid comparison of linear and nonlinear models using differential equations.

8. H. J. Ryser, *Combinatorial Mathematics*, Carey Mathematical Monograph 14 (New York: Wiley, 1963), sec. 2.4.

9. H. Minc, "An Inequality for Permanents of (0, 1)—Matrices," *Journal of Combinatorial Theory*, 2:321 (1967). Minc also quotes (his eq. 5) an upper bound that would be a better asymptotic estimate when nearly all men were candidates for nearly all jobs as in Section 11.1 here.

10. Section 11.3 is based on definitions and results in Ryser, *Combinatorial Mathematics*, chaps. 5, 7, and 8.

11. *Ibid.*, p. 48.

12. If not all vacancies can be filled at the same time from the given candidacies, the interaction measure could be reformulated either in terms of the number of the most complete allocations possible or, perhaps, in terms of the maximum fraction of vacancies that could be filled. Allocation of vacancies among candidates is isomorphic not only to finding an SDR but also to constructing a matching of a simple graph, also called a bipartite graph. The latter construction is often called the personnel assignment problem; there the problem is turned inside out since vacancies are analogous to men and candidates to positions. See C. Berge, *The Theory of Graphs and its Applications*, A. Doig, trans. (New York: Wiley, 1962). Finding the most complete allocation possible corresponds to finding the maximal matching. Berge discusses a number of approaches, such as the Hungarian method.

13. Ryser, *Combinatorial Mathematics*, secs. 8.2 and 8.3.

14. *Ibid.*, pp. 104 and 124.

15. A more realistic model could be developed in terms of random mappings, in which there is no restriction on the number of choices received by a node but only one choice is made by each. Each component in a random mapping is a cycle with a tree appended to each node. Rules would be required for selecting among the candidates for a node emptied in the course of a chain begun by a death. For an account of probability distributions for various lengths in a random mapping, see B. Harris, "Probability Distributions Related to Random Mappings," *Annals of Mathematical Statistics*, 31:1045–1062 (1960).

16. See J. Riordan, *An Introduction to Combinatorial Analysis* (New York: Wiley, 1958), equation 4.1 and table 4.2.

17. *Ibid.*, chap. 5. The allocation of *d* indistinguishable balls among *n** distinct boxes grouped in specified sets is a standard problem.

18. In the binomial model, part of *p* represents terminations of jobs, which are not considered in the permutation model in Section 11.4.

19. If complete cycles of preferred moves are regarded as being realized without the intervention of death to "open" the chain, the model becomes similar to the simultaneous assignment model discussed in Section 1.4. The interaction measure, *I*, developed in earlier sections could also be regarded as based on a model of mobility as centralized assignments of men to jobs.

20. J. H. Levine, "A Measure of Association for Intergenerational Status Mobility," unpublished manuscript, Department of Social Relations, Harvard University, December 1967; *idem.*, "Measurement in The Study of Intergenerational Status Mobility," Ph.D. thesis, Harvard University, March 1967.

21. C. F. Mosteller, "Association and Estimation in Contingency Tables," *Journal of the American Statistical Association*, 63:4 (1968).

22. Levine, in "A Measure of Association," introduces assumptions about the shape of a continuous bivariate frequency distribution underlying the observed table, pp. 116–126. Levine himself justifies the shift by assimilating measurement of association to measurement of change in differential calculus terms, implying logarithms of counts as the metric corresponding to simple additive interaction effects. But Mosteller, in "Association and Estimation," treats the use of continuous bivariate frequency distributions as a competitor to the use of multiplicative invariance, p. 10. G. Carlsson, in *Social Mobility and Class Structure* (Lund, Sweden: Gleerup 1959) has used a hypothesized bivariate normal distribution to estimate diagonal entries in mobility tables for Sweden with conclusions rather similar to many of Levine's, pp. 157–163.

23. L. A. Goodman, "On the Statistical Analysis of Mobility Tables," *American Journal of Sociology*, 70:564 (1965), and earlier papers cited therein.

24. Y. M. M. Bishop and S. E. Fienberg, "Incomplete Two-Dimensional Contingency Tables," *Biometrics*, 22:119 (1969).

25. H. C. White, "Cause and Effect in Social Mobility Tables," *Behavioral Science*, 7:14 (1963).

26. Mosteller, in "Association and Estimation," discusses at length the use of lower order marginals, in effect interactions, to predict entries in an *r*-way table on the hypothesis that higher order interactions can be ignored. See also J. H. Levine, "The Definition of Association," unpublished manuscript, Department of Social Relations, Harvard University, October, 1967.

27. Levine, "Measurement in the Study of Intergenerational Status Mobility," pp. 62–65.

28. Mosteller, "Association and Estimation," p. 16.

12. Location, Elites, and Tenure Networks

1. For one of the few systematic attempts to model social networks see C. Foster, A. Rapoport, and C. Orwant, "A Study of a Large Sociogram II. Elimination of Free Parameters," *Behavioral Science*, 6:279–291 (1961). They examine only the population of a high school. The pioneer work by E. Bott on the effects of network

structure in broader contexts, *Family and Social Network* (London: Tavistock, 1957) is assessed and compared with later studies by C. Turner in "Conjugal Roles and Social Networks," *Human Relations*, 20:121–130 (1967). There is a large but rather speculative literature on the role of network structure in the diffusion of ideas and innovation. An interesting case study with a good bibliography is J. Coleman, E. Katz, and H. Menzel, *Medical Innovation* (Indianapolis: Bobbs-Merrill, 1966).

2. Overlaps in neighborhoods can be inferred from nonzero transition probabilities. See W. Feller, *An Introduction to Probability Theory and Its Applications* (New York: Wiley, 1957), chap. 14.

3. M. Schwartz derived results for a number of models for trees with less than ten jobs. The distributions of vacancy chain lengths were single-peaked curves. The mathematical complexities are much like those encountered with stochastic models of the geographical spread of epidemics; see N. T. J. Bailey, *The Mathematical Theory of Epidemics* (London: Griffin, 1957), secs. 8.33 and 8.34.

4. In the early 1900s an additional diocese, Western Massachusetts, was carved out of the 1877 Diocese, but the results would be little changed by adding this small diocese in the later distribution. Also, the computation of D is slightly different in the earlier year because the diocesan list is arranged alphabetically by men, not parishes. This slight clerical change makes tracing chains much more laborious, since the general index is of men not jobs.

5. My impression from inspecting the data is that the longer chains in the West and South result in large part from their having little access to the new graduates of seminaries, largely concentrated in the Northeast and Far West.

6. A square lattice in two dimensions also can be used for the topology of marriage relations among descent lines in the case of classificatory bilateral cross-cousin marriage, and for much the same reasons; see H. C. White, *An Anatomy of Kinship* (Englewood Cliffs, N.J.: Prentice-Hall, 1963), chap. 1. Of course topology in the strict sense does not apply to discrete networks; see F. Lorrain, "Notes on Topological Spaces with Minimum Neighborhoods," *American Mathematical Monthly*, 76:616–627 (1969).

7. For a succinct account of Latin rectangles see H. J. Ryser, *Combinatorial Mathematics* (New York: Wiley, 1963), chap. 7.

8. J. P. Boyd, "The Algebra of Kinship," *Journal of Mathematical Psychology*, 6:139 (1969).

9. M. F. Friedell, "Organizations as Semilattices," *American Sociological Review*, 32:46–54 (1967). Another suggestive analogy may be found in M. Delbrück, "Knotting Problems in Biology," in R. Bellman, ed., *Symposium on Applied Mathematics No. 14* (Providence: American Mathematical Society, 1961). Another algebraic approach is to the problem of job-shop scheduling of batch production, treated in the literature on operations research and management science.

13. Use and Meaning of Vacancy Models

1. Professor F. Balderston of the University of California has suggested extending the classical assignment problem to include chains of moves. The system-wide costs of given events, such as creation of a new job or death of a particular job-

holder, could be calculated from vacancy models, given a matrix of benefits to the system from each potential pairing of man and job. Or, however unreal the vacancy models suggest the answer to be, searches can be carried out for the set of replacement chains which would minimize system costs in filling a given set of vacancies. A brief technical article describing the assignment problem in a broader formal context is A. J. Hoffman and H. M. Markowitz, "A Note on Shortest Path, Assignment and Transportation Problems," *Naval Research Logistics Quarterly*, 10:375–379 (1963). For a substantive discussion, see J. G. March and H. A. Simon, *Organizations* (New York: Wiley, 1958), pp. 23–25 and 158.

2. The system-wide implications of everyone's understanding the inevitability of replacement in every job are little studied. See B. Levenson, "Bureaucratic Succession," in A. Etzioni, ed., *Complex Organizations* (New York: Holt, Rinehart and Winston, 1962), pp. 362–375.

3. In the natural sciences there are a number of partial analogues to vacancy chain models. See, for example, W. Shockley, *Electrons and Holes in Semiconductors* (New York: Van Nostrand, 1950), especially preface and pp. 182–185.

4. F. S. Kristof, "Housing Policy Goals and the Turnover of Housing," *Journal of the American Institute of Planners* (August 1965), pp. 232–245.

5. C. W. Clifton, private communication, July, 1968. The report on sequences of moves induced by new construction is J. Lansing, C. W. Clifton, and J. Morgan, *New Homes and Poor People* (Ann Arbor: Survey Research Center, 1969). See also an unpublished manuscript by this author, "Multiplier Effects and Housing Policy," August 1969.

6. W. McPhee of the University of Colorado suggests computer simulations of various processes for matching men to opportunities of many kinds in an unpublished paper entitled "Opportunity Structures," no date.

7. The *New York Times* in the past few years has drawn explicit analogies to "musical chairs" for the movements of first violinists, football coaches, and so on. Chains of replacements are traced down to the frontier of newsworthiness when a high government official is replaced; for example, when Prescott Bush was replaced in the Senate by A. Ribicoff; in turn replaced as Secretary of Health, Education, and Welfare by A. Celebrezzi; in turn replaced as Mayor of Cleveland by Ralph Locher; in turn, no doubt, replaced as City Law Director of Cleveland by some person invisible to the *Times*; and so on.

8. In a few cases when control of moves by middle-level officials was nearly centralized in one man's hands this control seems to have been the key to total domination of the system, quite apart from control of police, ideological prominence, legitimacy, and so on. See, for example, I. Deutscher, *Stalin: A Political Biography* (New York: Oxford University Press, 1967). On a more pedestrian level, changes in committee assignments in the U.S. Congress within party seniority rules might repay analysis using vacancy models.

9. Differentiating pool and limbo is most suitable at the one extreme of an inbred organization, like a Japanese business firm or a clergy, or at the other extreme of a whole national society wherein immigration and emigration are of little importance.

10. J. A. Kahl, *The American Class Structure* (New York: Rinehart, 1959), pp. 254–256 and 259–262. See also Section 8.3 here on the Holt-David model.

11. For a critique of Kahl's estimates, see O. D. Duncan, "Methodological Issues in the Analysis of Social Mobility," in N. Smelser and S. M. Lipset, eds., *Social Structure and Social Mobility in Economic Development* (Chicago: Aldine, 1966).

12. For example, adapting them to a national economy would require that bump chains in unionized plants during layoffs would have to be considered. See the discussion in Sections 8.1–8.3.

13. See T. Whisler, "Measuring Centralization of Control in Business Organizations," in W. W. Cooper, H. Leavitt, and M. Shelly, eds., *New Perspectives in Organization Research* (New York: Wiley, 1964).

14. See, for example, H. Wilensky, "Work, Careers and Social Integration," *International Social Science Journal*, 12:3–20 (1960).

15. Almost all the chains were traced by research assistants. In the French case, F. Lorrain traced a number of chains from annuals for the nineteenth century. Chains in the United States government units were traced by J. Levine.

16. W. McWhinney and P. Ballonoff of the University of California (Los Angeles) are completing a study of mobility in the California region of the U.S. Forest Service in which figure some ideas related to vacancy chains.

17. R. K. Kelsall, *Higher Civil Servants in Britain* (London: Routledge and Kegan Paul, 1955). Of particular importance in this case is the clear-cut definition of distinct "entry ports" for recruits of different educational and social standing.

18. Coding the numerous assistantships in the Roman Catholic Church was the most difficult problem encountered. In earlier centuries, clergy in many churches, for example, the Church of England, were in oversupply, and quite different parameter values in the vacancy model can be anticipated.

19. One example of work on new typologies of bureaucracies is T. Burns and G. Stalker, *The Management of Innovation* (London: Tavistock, 1961), especially pt. II.

20. The difference in effects from fixed age and up-or-out retirement rules might be profitably examined in terms of vacancy models. For an extensive treatment of such issues see D. Bartholomew, *Stochastic Models of Social Processes* (New York: Wiley, 1967).

21. See Section 7.8; "line" jobs correspond to fixed-roster jobs.

22. Ideas on equivalence structures are spelled out in H. C. White, *An Anatomy of Kinship* (Englewood Cliffs, N.J.: Prentice-Hall, 1963). Clarification and more powerful development of these ideas can be found in J. P. Boyd, "The Algebra of Group Kinship," *The Journal of Mathematical Psychology*, 6:139–167 (1969). See also an unpublished manuscript by H. C. White, "Notes on Finding Models of Structural Equivalence," March 1969.

Name Index

Ackerman, J. E., 390
Adler, M. E., 132, 133, 135
Anderson, T. W., 223ff., 229, 234, 245, 399, 400, 401
Austin, T., 396

Bailey, N. T. J., 396, 407
Balderston, F., 407
Ballonof, P., 409
Baltzell, E. D., 397
Bartholomew, D. J., 242, 243, 244, 402, 409
Barton, A., 388
Bellman, R., 407
Bendix, R., 397, 400
Berge, C., 405
Berry, B. J. L., 398
Billingsley, P., 390
Bishop, Y. M. M., 296, 406
Blalock, H. M., 404
Blau, P. M., 400, 402, 403
Blumen, I., 231, 232, 234, 236, 245, 401
Bonini, C. P., 398
Boorman, S., 204, 403
Borgatta, E. F., 404
Bott, E., 406
Boyd, J. P., 315, 407, 409
Bridgman, P. W., 394
Brown, R. H., 396
Burgess, G., 335
Burns, T., 397, 409

Carlsson, G., 402, 406
Chrimes, S. B., 388, 397
Clements, R. V., 388
Clifton, C. W., 318, 408
Cochran, W. G., 405
Cogan, E. J., 394
Coleman, J. S., 3, 231, 388, 400, 401, 407
Coombs, C., 388
Cooper, W. W., 389, 409
Cox, D. R., 395

David, M., 200ff.
Davis, J. A., 388
Davis, K., 388
Delbrück, M., 407

Deutscher, I., 408
Dibble, V. K., 397
Doig, A., 405
Dolansky, L., 396
Dorfman, R., 398, 399
Downing, E. H., 335
Duncan, O. D., 3, 5, 6, 229, 281, 282, 295, 388, 399, 400, 402, 403, 404, 409
Dunlop, J. T., 203

Eastburn, M., 317, 318
Etzioni, A., 408
Evans, W., 389

Fagen, R., 396
Feller, W., 389, 395, 396, 402, 404, 405, 407
Feshbach, H., 398
Fienberg, S. E., 296, 406
Foster, C., 406
Frank, N. H., 394
Friedell, M. F., 315, 407

Garrison, W., 398
Gaver, D. P., 403
Glass, D. V., 228, 231, 400
Goodman, L. A., 296, 388, 390, 398, 401, 406
Gordon, W. J., 233, 234, 235, 239ff., 401, 402, 404

Harding, F. D., 403
Harmon, N. B., 347
Harris, B., 405
Hodge, R. W., 404
Hoffman, A. J., 408
Holt, C., 200ff.
Homans, G. C., 394, 405

Johnson, F. E., 390

Kahl, J. A., 319, 408, 409
Karmel, P. H., 399
Katz, E., 407
Kelsall, R. K., 320, 388, 409
Kemeny, J. S., 390, 394, 396, 398, 399, 402
Kendall, D. G., 395
Keyfitz, N., 399
Kogan, M., 401

411

Name Index

412

Subject Index

Equations are indexed according to their designations in text: E followed by equation number (chapter number is left of period). An (F) following a page number indicates a figure; a (T) indicates a table.

Subject Index

Subject Index

Limbo status, 8, 9, 54, 341ff., 346, 349, 391; for Episcopal and Methodist data, 189(T); models with limbo, 158ff., 188ff.; versus pool status, 54. *See also* Bumper chains; Coding rules; Pool status

Localism, 298ff. *See also* Dioceses; Strata

Loops, 12, 61, 141, 380–381; and centralization, 18, 312; and cycles, 292ff.; example, 69(F); and tenure networks, 312

Loose systems, 8, 10ff. *See also* Bumper chains

Marginals, distribution of, 295ff.

Markets, *see* Automobile markets; Housing markets; Labor markets

Markov chains: absorbing, 28, 390; assessments of, 122, 141; first-order, 28f.; first-order assumption, 186–187, 189, 244, 295, 390; and flow models, 147; higher order, 29, 33, 122, 228, 256f., 260ff.; imbedded, 28, 179ff., 390, 401; reversibility, 29–30. *See also* Absorption probabilities; Irreversibility; Time; Vacancy models

Markov property, 100, 187(T)

Markov renewal processes, 180, 183, 390, 395

Marriage, 1, 9, 327; preferential, 296; bilateral cross-cousin, 407

Matchmaking models, 193–194, 204ff., 209–211, 210(F), 295ff., 389; basic equation, E8.3; and committees, 213; stratified, 206

Matchmaking system, 8f., 12ff., 284; example of matchmaking chain, 13(F). *See also* Interaction among vacancies

Maxwell-Boltzmann statistics, 185, 402, 404

Mean length, vacancy chains, by beginning event, 111(T), 112f.; contextual, 370, 376(T); for Episcopal data, 73(T), 374ff.; equation for stratified model, E2.8; estimates, 370ff.; by starting stratum, 80f., 81(T), 101f. *See also* Length distribution

Measures, of stratification, 229

Mechanics, analogy with man-job flow model, 162ff.

Men: attributes of, 255ff.; classes of, 53; measures on, 60–61. *See also* Seniority

Mergers, of organizations, 18f.

Methodist church: history, 50; data sources for, 345, 347–348. *See also* under desired substantive heading

Ministers, *see* Clergies

Mobility: alternative systems of, 8ff.; approaches to, 2ff.; among committees, 211ff.; effects of, 5ff.; exchange, 246; intergenerational, 3, 228ff.; church data, 78ff., 105ff., 78(T), 79(T), 85(T), 136(T), 143, 189(T), 380f.; for continuous models, 151ff.; rates, defined, 27, 148f., 377; structural, 245–246. *See also* Arrival rates; Committees; Departure rates; In-mobility; Out-mobility; Rates of vacancy movement; Replacement

Models, *see* 323(T) or under desired heading

Motivation, and mobility, 6f., 15f., 49, 93, 242. *See also* Behavior

Movement, *see* Mobility; Rates of vacancy movement

Mover-stayer models, 231–232, 401

Moves, *see* Mobility; Rates of vacancy movement

Multinomial distribution, 227

Multiplier effect: absence of in Reynolds' model, 199; for attribute category models, E10.12; general discussion, 321; for Leontief models, 217ff.; for other single-flow models, 217, 225f.; for stratified vacancy models, E2.10, 34, 38–39. *See also* Contingencies

Musical chairs, *see* Matchmaking models; Matchmaking system

Negative exponential distribution, 181–182, 233, 244

Negotiation, *see* Bargaining

Networks, 406–407. *See also* Acquaintance network; Tenure; Topology

Odds ratio, *see* Cross product ratio

One-one job, *see* Jobs, classes of

Open queuing system, *see* Queuing

Opportunities, *see* Contingencies

Organizations and vacancy models, 17ff., 183ff., 211ff., 318ff.; comparison of churches, 141ff. *See also* Churches

Out-mobility, equations for, E2.17, E2.18, 370, 373; estimates for Episcopal data, 375(T), 377(T), 384(T); for Methodist data, 378(T), 379(T), 386(T); for Presbyterian data, 379(T), 380. *See also* Mobility

Pastorates, 77(T). *See also* Compound pastorates; Jobs, classes of

Path analysis, 282, 295, 403–404

416